CELEBRATING THE VISION

THE REFORMED PERSPECTIVE

OF DORDT COLLEGE

CELEBRATING THE VISION

THE REFORMED PERSPECTIVE OF DORDT COLLEGE

Edited by John H. Kok

Dordt College Press

Printed in the United States of America.

Dordt College Press   www.dordt.edu/dordt_press
498 Fourth Avenue NE
Sioux Center, Iowa 51250
United States of America
ISBN: 0-932914-56-X

The Library of Congress Cataloging-in-Publication Data
is on file with the Library of Congress, Washington, D.C.

Library of Congress Control Number: 2004095978

Cover photographs: April Boogerd
Cover design and layout: Sarah C. Franken

Table of Contents

Editor's Preface

This jubilee volume of collected essays celebrates Dordt College's first fifty years of service in the Kingdom of God. Dordt College exists to help students grow in wisdom and insight with an eye to a flourishing life in God's world. Our goal is to teach students to think critically and to judge wisely as they learn how God's creation works, how things fit together, and what their calling is. In that regard the mission of Dordt College is to develop and implement an understanding of the entire creation in the liberating light of Scripture. We desire to be an institution of Reformed, Christian learning for the benefit of both students and the broader community by providing serviceable insight that prepares students for knowledgeable, competent, and caring service in all aspects of contemporary life. This volume provides a window on the Reformed perspective that permeates Dordt's curriculum and campus.

The light of Scripture and sound insight from people like John Calvin and Abraham Kuyper have helped shape the perspective that guides the college: Because God is the creator and redeemer of all reality, Christians are called to obedience and reformation in every area of life. All of life is religious; who one is, what one does, and the decisions one makes are ultimately a response to God and his covenantal faithfulness. This volume seeks to give voice to the contributions of Dordt students, faculty, staff, and supporters who cherish God's faithfulness and whose own persistent diligence has helped make Dordt's vision manifest in word and deed.

Dordt's curricular commitment is to provide sound glimpses of multi-dimensional insight in which faith and learning as well as theory and practice are integral. As mentors for our students, we seek to model and nurture within them a life-long desire to please God in all things. This volume is one way to document what we are doing in this regard.

Many areas of life and their related academic disciplines are represented in this volume. The first two chapters of this book are actually policy statements by the college that define its educational task and the curricular framework within which we seek to work. The other chapters were written by present and retired faculty members from a broad variety of disciplines to illustrate in an accessible manner implications of Dordt's Reformed perspective for various programs and some of the disciplines that make up its curricular core. About half of the chapters were written specifically for this volume; the others, as indicated, were published first elsewhere.

I want to thank the many who initially submitted manuscripts and abstracts to this project. Even though the book contains more chapters than we first anticipated, we could not include them all. In that regard, I want to thank Dr. Hubert Krygsman, Professor of History, and Dr. Mary Dengler, Assistant Professor of English, for helping me make those kinds of decisions early on. A special word of thanks goes to Sara Gerritsma for her patience and precision in bringing a proper Chicago Manual of Style conformity to all of the chapters and endnotes. She spent considerable time checking references and tracking down all the information needed. Thanks are also due to copyeditor Lisa Stracks.

Over the years some faculty members and administrators have spent innumerable hours fine-tuning college documents like the *Educational Task* and the *Educational Framework* to get them just right. Although some might be tempted to dismiss these official statements as so-many-words-on-the-shelf, this volume bears witness to the fact that they are not dead letters. We praise God for the serviceable insight granted us and the community of scholars that we enjoy at Dordt College.

John H. Kok

The Educational Task of Dordt College

....

Preface

Under the supervision of the board of trustees, the Dordt College faculty has written and adopted a statement of purpose describing the implications of a Reformed confession of biblical faith on Christian higher education.

The first such statement, adopted in 1961, consisted of seventeen propositions designed to guide the development of the educational program. A more detailed statement was formulated in 1968 under the title *Scripturally-Oriented Higher Education*. Finally, between 1979 and 1996, *The Educational Task of Dordt College* was formulated and adopted. This document now serves as the biblically-based, confessional foundation for the entire academic enterprise at Dordt College.

All who are associated with Dordt College are pledged to prayerfully pursue the purposes outlined in this document as together we engage in the education of God's covenant people for faithful service in the Kingdom of Jesus Christ.

Carl E. Zylstra
President

Introduction

The Educational Task of Dordt College sets forth the principles that are to direct the institution in the performance of its educational task.

Dordt College owes its origin and continuing existence to a society of God's people, whose faith commitment demands obedient acknowledgment of biblical principles in education. Those who first showed interest in establishing a college in northwest Iowa stated the following in a report submitted in 1937 by Classis Ostfriesland (now Classis Northcentral Iowa) of the Christian Reformed Church:

> That Classis Ostfriesland invite Classis Pella, Minnesota, Orange City, and Sioux Center to join with us in working towards the organization, support and control of a Christian junior college in harmony with Reformed principles. The aim of such a junior college is to give young people an education that is Christian, not merely in the sense that devotional exercises are appended to the ordinary work of the college, but in the larger and deeper sense that all the class work, all the students' intellectual, emotional, and imaginative activities shall be permeated with the spirit and teaching of Christianity.

This biblical perspective has continued to determine the direction of Dordt College:

> In the training and development of the redeemed in Christ the Holy Scriptures are basic, since they are indispensable to the proper realization of the individual's capacities and the proper fulfilling of his responsibilities. All education must be scripturally oriented. *(Educational Task of Dordt College*—Adopted in 1961, Proposition #9)

> The covenant parent recognizes the school, formal education, as the second sphere vital to the fulfillment of his task. In agreement with his covenantal-kingdom philosophy, he demands an education for his child that is scripturally oriented. *(Scripturally-Oriented Higher Education,* 1968, p.26)

This religious commitment, which is historically known as the Reformed faith, must also be honored in the articulation of the principles and purposes of the college.

The college faculty has a particular responsibility for the formulation of a purpose statement. The members of the faculty have received special gifts and training which qualify them and make them responsible for defining as well as implementing the educational philosophy of the college. The faculty, working under the supervision of the board of trustees, must remain sensitive to the religious perspective of the supporting society. But the faculty must also lead the members of the society, by means of Christian scholarship, to a deepening understanding of the demands of that perspective. This document, written by the faculty of Dordt College, is an attempt to go beyond what was set forth in previous documents.

2

Chapter I. Basis

Fundamental to the faith of the constituents of Dordt College is their confession that the scriptures are the Word of God. As God's infallibly and authoritatively inspired revelation, the Bible reveals the way to salvation in Jesus Christ, requires life to be lived in obedience to the Lord, and provides the key to the understanding, interpretation, meaning, and purpose of life. Only the Bible can unlock the door to a true insight into the nature of created reality. Ultimately, all things must be judged in the light of its teachings. Hence, Dordt College confesses that the Bible provides the determinative and essential principles for a Christian educational philosophy.

The Bible reveals to us a sovereign God: all things are under his control. Nothing can exist apart from him, and everything finds its goal and purpose in his glory.[1]

In the beginning, the Bible tells us, God created all things by his sovereign will.[2] The Son of God, the Word incarnate, was central in this work of creation. The Apostle John affirms that Christ is the Son of God, the Word, without whom nothing was made;[3] Paul explains that the Son is the image of the invisible God through whom and by whom the entire cosmos was brought into existence.[4] In the same context, furthermore, Paul makes clear that God upholds and maintains the entire creation by his Son.[5] Therefore, the creation is an integrated totality, a cosmos in which each part is designed to function coherently and meaningfully.

The creation belongs to God[6] and is under his sovereign rule;[7] it is God's Kingdom.[8] God controls and orders the cosmos by his will; and it is only by obedience to his will that the creation can fulfill its purpose in the service of God.[9]

By the Word, that is the Son of God, a *diversity* is brought about within the creation. We acknowledge this when we confess that God "has created of nothing the heavens, the earth, and all creatures, when it seemed good unto him, giving unto every creature its being, shape, form, and several offices to serve its creator."[10] Each creature is accountable to the sovereign King and must obey the laws which God has established for it.

The Bible also tells us that God created men and women in his image, religious creatures, covenantally bound to their creator by the law which calls for loving obedience. The religious character of human kind is manifested through the heart, which is the integrating center of human existence.[11] With hearts open to the will of God, people were to serve the creator by fulfilling the mandate to subdue the earth.[12] That is, God placed men and women in office and called them to the task of working in His Kingdom.

However, by disobeying God, men and women violated their office and broke the bond of covenantal fellowship. They closed their hearts to the will of God and exchanged the true service of the creator for the idolatrous service of the creature.[13] After the fall, people began to treat the creation not as the Kingdom of God, but as an object of exploitation for their own glory. Having rejected the source of true fellowship and harmony, humanity abandoned itself and the creation to division and strife, misery and death.

God determined not to leave his creation in such a state, however. He came to us with his word of grace,[14] promising to reclaim what had been deformed and distorted by sin. He fulfilled this promise in the death and resurrection of Jesus Christ, the Word of God incarnate. Through faith in Christ, we are restored to covenantal fellowship with God and made to live again as his office-bearers in the kingdom.

We must clearly see that Christ redeemed not only humanity, but the cosmos as well.[15] Even though the effects of the fall continue to be present, Christ has broken the dominion of Satan, rescued the creation from the curse of sin and reigns as King over all.[16] From this position of power, he summons the members of the new humanity to work for the expression of His Kingdom everywhere. As agents of reconciliation, they are called to labor together as one body in fulfilling the original mandate according to the claims of Christ.

God continues to sustain all existence through his Word and to require obedience of all his creatures.[17] While the redeemed joyfully comply with the demands of the will of God, the unregenerate willfully oppose them. Thus, an antithesis arises between the reconciling work of Christ's body and the resistance of unbelief. Although significant insight into the created order can be gained by unbelievers, true meaning and coherence remain inaccessible without the light of the Bible, a heart committed to Christ, and the operation of the Holy Spirit.[18]

Therefore, biblically oriented learning is both a possibility and a necessity for the Christian community. Recognizing this, the constituents of Dordt College maintain an institution of Christian higher education.

Chapter II: Context

To understand the nature of education, we must see it against the background of God's mandate to subdue the earth.[19] God called humanity to the task of dressing and keeping the garden, that is, developing and conserving the created order. Moreover, as God's image-bearers, people are capable of fulfilling this mandate, because God, in calling people to his task, also equips them. Education, in its broadest sense, is an essential element in the development and exercise of that capability.

Humanity's ability to develop the creation depends on insight. Consequently, people must study, examine, and understand the world. Furthermore, the results of such study and investigation must be preserved by transmission from one generation to another. Education, therefore, is fundamental to humanity's task of developing and conserving the created order.

Education also relates to the performance of humanity's cultural task in another way, however. God instructed men and women to be fruitful and multiply. This inevitably involves not merely the begetting but also the training of children. Such training, too, reflects the call to develop and conserve, for children must be trained to acquire and exercise insight.

Education, then, is a constituent of life itself, and in its broadest scope refers to all human efforts to gain and transmit insight, whether at the forefront of science in universities and research centers or in the kindergarten class or on mother's lap. Seen thus, education pervades all of life. It is operative in every human relationship. In marriage, it manifests itself in the deepening of understanding between the two partners. In the home, the rearing of children is essentially an educational activity. In the church, we are instructed in the Scriptures. In all other spheres, too, such as commerce, industry, the arts and the media, there is development and conservation which requires growing insight.

In the course of history, as the human community engaged in increasingly complex cultural activity, a differentiation of tasks and offices took place. And, whereas at one time the authority of a father and that of a ruler were combined in one office, soon such authority came to be distinguished and localized in different offices, in the spheres of family and state. As civilization marched on, a multiplicity of tasks developed, requiring a variety of offices and responsibilities. The school is one of the results of such historical differentiation.

The school is the sphere in which education has become institutionalized, and has therefore been endowed with a characteristically educational task. Its responsibility is to focus on the process of gaining and transmitting insights. This task, however, is so great and so complex that further differentiation within institutionalized education became necessary. As a result, there are today elementary schools, high schools, colleges, and graduate schools.

The elementary school and the high school develop insight on a relatively uncomplicated and preparational level. Elementary and high school pupils learn to understand the fundamental character of the creation and of the tasks that will confront them as adults. On the college level the insight acquired is more abstract and scientific. There the understanding of reality is both broadened and deepened. On the graduate level the emphasis shifts to research, the further expansion of the limits of human knowledge, and advanced levels of professional training.

Within the Christian community, education plays an especially significant role today, for the Christian's task of understanding God's handiwork is complicated by the extensive deformation brought about by centuries of secularization. Christians are tempted to view God's laws and our response through the screen of distortions fabricated by unbelief. This situation makes the work of Christian education particularly difficult.

As an institution of higher learning, Dordt College addresses itself to the task of Christian education. It seeks to acquire and transmit genuine Christian insight, that is, to develop and implement an understanding of the entire creation in the liberating light of the Scriptures. Dordt College desires to be an institution of Christian learning for the benefit of both the attending student body and the entire Christian community, so that the Lord's Kingdom may come to greater expression.

Chapter III: Structure

The educational task of Dordt College is to be understood as a calling whereby the Lord summons committed and insightful men and women to educational service. When they hear and accept the calling to participate in the task of the college, they accept and occupy a variety of offices.[20] As office-bearers, board members are elected, professors, administrators, and support staff are appointed; and students voluntarily join in the work of the educational community. These office bearers, endowed with God-given competence and insight, are thus authorized to take part in the educational work of Dordt College.

Authorization to office entails responsibility.[21] The educational office-bearers at Dordt College are responsible to carry out their specific tasks in a spirit of loving service to their fellow office-bearers.[22]

Since God authorizes this educational task, it is important that a sense of office pervade all aspects of the college. To participate in the work of developing and transmitting insight is not merely an occupation or a means to gain financial security or self esteem, but a task to which God calls. To occupy a position at the college means to be placed in a God-ordained office requiring educational service in self-effacing love and obedience to the Lord. When office consciousness is lost, the essential meaning of this work is lost, though the connection to Dordt College may continue to be of personal interest, or prove materially rewarding. Dordt College, therefore, seeks to develop and foster an atmosphere in which the sense of calling and meaningful office consciousness can flourish.

Since the educational mission of Dordt College comprises a diversity of tasks, there is also a diversity of office. Historically, the educational activities of the college involve at least five distinct kinds of office.

Out of the community which accepted the challenge of college-level education, trusted persons were chosen to constitute a board. The board's specific task was to start and to oversee the college. They were and are mandated to provide leadership, especially to guide the religious direction of the college and to ensure its academic excellence.

Competent educators have been engaged to serve Christ in their specific tasks. As educators, these office-bearers have the primary responsibility for the development and transmission of insight. They constitute the faculty, who, through research and teaching, are called to carry out the central educational task of Dordt College.

The students also are called to share in the educational task. As office-bearers they are required to advance the educational enterprise by acquiring, contributing to, and serving as the agents for the transmission of insight from its theoretical beginnings to concrete applications.

The administrators and support staff participate in the educational task of the college as well. They are to construct and maintain the context within which the educational work of the college can grow and thrive.

A distinct office is occupied by the chief executive officer, the president of the college, whose special task is to oversee, guide, and direct the entire academic and administrative life of the institution. The president serves as liaison between board and constituency on the one hand, and faculty, students, administration, and support staff on the other.

These tasks compose the one, common educational calling which pervades every segment and activity of Dordt College. Yet, though these tasks are similar in that they all respond to the one, all-encompassing educational calling, each task is unique and functions properly only when the others are duly recognized and allowed free expression. It should be noted, however, that there is not an exclusive identity of office with person, and that a person can occupy more than one office.

To avoid incompetence and to promote responsible use of office, Dordt College aims to provide the kind of educational service which will deepen the insight of its office-bearers. Faculty, administrative, and staff development, therefore, must rank high on the institutional agenda. Board members, too, must continue to grow in insight if they are to function effectively. And students, as a result of their education at Dordt College, may be expected increasingly to exhibit a degree of maturity and wisdom. To ensure that the tasks of the various office-bearers are carried out responsibly and competently, the college community should maintain an effective program of evaluation on all levels.

Chapter IV: Authority

The specific callings, tasks, and offices are associated with specific kinds of authority. Such authority is not to be regarded as supreme. Only God is the Sovereign. All authority among human creatures has been given by God and is therefore always delegated and representative authority.[23]

The kinds of authority associated with the various kinds of educational office share with one another the requirement that they be exercised in servanthood.[24] Educational authority, therefore, is not to be used in order to dominate or exercise presumed rights. It must be exercised in order to serve, facilitate, and edify. The goal of authority is to permit and to encourage office-bearers to perform their tasks as fully and as effectively as possible in response to the will of the Lord.. At the same time, the various kinds of educational authority differ from one another in the extent to which those who exercise such authority are authorized to hold other office-bearers accountable. Some office-bearers are called to oversee the work of other office-bearers; their task, responsibility, and concomitant authority, therefore, are more extensive.

At all levels, authority must go hand in hand with responsibility. Every office-bearer has the responsibility to serve others, and to ensure their freedom to carry out their task and exercise their authority. A spirit of mutual responsibility and accountability to each other before God must exist, if authority is to be exercised in a biblical manner.[25]

Specifically, the board possesses the authority to make and implement decisions which affect the direction of the entire educational enterprise. Normally the board will entrust the actual day-to-day operation of the college to the other office-bearers. But wherever the board detects a departure from the stated goals of the college, there the board is authorized to act.

The faculty, through its officers, is authorized to exercise authority over the academic and curricular program. As educational office-bearers they must at the time of their appointment give evidence of possessing the requisite competence, insight, and expertise to make and implement curricular, academic, and institutional decisions. Such insight and competence constitute important grounds on which their authority is to rest.

Because they are not the primary initiators of the curricular program, students exercise a more limited, yet meaningful authority. Since by virtue of their task they are directly involved in the actual teaching and learning process, their judgments regarding elements of instruction should be taken seriously. The students must evaluate whether the promise to them by the board, president, and professors is actually being fulfilled. If, through working conscientiously, they find no maturation of personal and communal insight, they are called to express their dissatisfaction, and their voice must be heard. It must be observed, moreover, that the students are significant participants in a major segment of the supporting and facilitation side of Dordt College, namely, student life; in this area, too, their judgments should be given careful consideration by those whose task it is to oversee the work of the entire institution.

The authority of the administrators and the support staff is circumscribed by their special task of organizing and facilitating the educational process. Their expertise lies in the administering and carrying out of the academic, financial, operational, and public relations matters.

The office of president of the college is endowed with a broad range of authority. As liaison between board and staff, he speaks to the staff with the specific authority of the board; he speaks to the board with the specific authority of the staff. Moreover, since the president is called to the task of overseeing, guiding, and directing the entire college, it is his responsibility to ensure that the college functions effectively and efficiently. Thus he is authorized to exercise both academic and administrative authority. All office-bearers on the campus, in the performance of their various functions, are accountable to him. The president, in turn, is accountable to the board.

Authority on campus can be exercised effectively and responsibly only if the office-bearers carry out their tasks competently. Board members, as overseers of the college, must exhibit insight and wisdom as they are called to deal with the larger questions of direction. Office bearers endowed with educational authority at the curriculum and academic heart of the college must show themselves competent in their research and teaching. Student authority, as it develops through several years of maturation, is to be closely associated with evaluation of levels of understanding. The administrators and the support staff, too, must be competent to supply an enabling con-text for the educational process. The president, as leader of the entire institution, must have a special measure of experience and understanding.

The exercise of authority requires structured and open lines of commu-nication. Any person may examine or question procedure, policy decisions, or the college's effectiveness in developing and transmitting serviceable insight. Such questioning should not be regarded as failing to submit to authority or as attacking the legitimacy of authority, but necessary testing of the spirits of the college's activities. Such questioning should, however, be done in a communal spirit of love.

Dordt College recognizes that a distinction must be made between arriv-ing at a decision and implementing a decision. The decision-making process should involve not only the persons who have the authority to implement, but also those who are impacted by the decision. Thus the communal nature of the educational enterprise must constantly come to the fore. Conflicts and disputes are to be resolved not by the force of coercion, but in a spirit of love and mutual trust. Principles guiding the resolution of conflict must be the recognition of proper areas of authority, determined by the specific task of the office-bearers involved, and the willingness to exercise authority in servanthood and stewardship. Thus the exercise of authority may never be designed to advance one's personal viewpoint or advantage, but, rather must always be prompted by the desire to advance, unitedly, the educational purposes of Dordt College.

Chapter V: Content

The central educational task of Dordt College is to provide genuinely Christian insight on an advanced level. In our increasingly complex age, such insight is no luxury. To function effectively as a Christian in a technological and secular civilization requires deepening wisdom and understanding.

Members of the body of Christ need the ability to distinguish sharply, to think critically, and to judge wisely. In their daily lives they are continually confronted by the difficulties and problems of our age. National and international tensions enter their homes through the media; political and economic problems touch their everyday lives; and the power of technology and mass communications affects them all. In addition, Christians are surrounded by the subtle influences of the secular spirits of our century. Coping with these multi-dimensional problems requires an advanced level of insight. Furthermore, many vocations and occupations have been professionalized to the extent that broad knowledge and a wide range of skills frequently are prerequisites for one's career. Hence, as our civilization advances, more and more insight is needed, not only by leaders, but by all Christians as they seek to do the Lord's bidding in our complex culture.

This situation puts a particularly heavy responsibility on Dordt College and other Christian institutions of higher learning. Such institutions are faced with the need to meet increasingly varied demands. They can no longer be satisfied with the transmission of abstractions. They must provide the kind of insight that enables Christians to carry out their task effectively in a complicated world. Whereas the majority of North American educational institutions transmit little more than the kind of insight that contributes to secularization and foster individualism, it is the educational task of Dordt College to provide genuinely Christian, that is, truly serviceable insight. Such insight is not designed to enhance the service of one's self, but rather, seeks to equip the Christian community to respond obediently to the central Scriptural command, "Love God above all, and your neighbor as yourself."

Such serviceable insight is, in effect, a contemporary expression of the Scriptural references to wisdom and understanding. The Bible teaches that "the fear of the Lord is the beginning of wisdom, a good understanding have all they that do his commandments."[26] Also, "Look carefully, then, how you walk, not as unwise, but as wise, redeeming the time, because the days are evil. Therefore don't be foolish, but understand what the will of the Lord is."[27] And again: "Who is wise among you? Let him show by his good life his works in meekness of wisdom."[28]

The Scriptures, then, admonish us to seek wisdom and understanding so that we may be able to discern the will of the Lord and to redeem the times. Dordt College must take this injunction very seriously by seeking to provide and promote such wisdom and understanding. Dordt College must strive to transmit the kind of insight that will enable Christians to discern the will of the Lord for any situation and to develop the capacity to implement it. Serviceable insight, therefore, prepares for kingdom citizenship. And Dordt, as a Christian college, aims to train kingdom citizens aware of the demands of the cultural mandate, equipped to take their place and carry out their tasks within the community of believers, able to discern the spiritual direction of our civilization, and prepared to advance, in loving service, the claims of Christ over all areas of life.

The Christian insight that Dordt College seeks to impart is, therefore, not merely abstract and theoretical. While at its most fundamental level it reflects an understanding of the structure and workings of God's created order, insight includes other dimensions as well, such as the practical ability to carry out one's task in loving obedience and service. Moreover, built into Christian insight is the motivation and desire to function effectively as a kingdom citizen.

It is clear, therefore, that Dordt College is to provide multi-dimensional insight in which theory and practice, though formally distinguishable, are nevertheless closely integrated. The Dordt College graduate must have both a theoretical understanding of a situation and the practical ability and skill to be reformingly busy in response to God's call to service. For that reason, practice or skill is not to be separated from its imbeddedness in the wider structural context to be theoretically understood; nor is the theoretical understanding of God's creation to be divorced from the practical capacity to implement the will of the Lord in everyday situations.

It is evident that in our complex society a growing number of vocations require deepening insight of the kind that Dordt College seeks to provide. One goal of the college is to identify those occupational areas where serviceable insight is increasingly needed. In principle, no legitimate profession, occupation, vocation, or station in life can be precluded from Dordt's educational concern. Wherever insight is required, there Dordt College is called to supply it. The college must therefore continually examine the nature and scope of its offerings and programs. Decisions about programs, however, can no longer be made on the basis of traditional distinctions between professional and nonprofessional vocations. Rather, criteria such as the level of insight required—as well as financial, geographical, and other practical considerations—must play the deciding role. In this way, Dordt College, by remaining aware of the demands of the times, can carry out its educational task of providing leadership that is not only uniquely Christian, but also dynamic and relevant.

Chapter VI: Implementation

Central to the implementation of the educational task of Dordt College is the curriculum, the basic means for transmitting serviceable insight. The curriculum consists of an organized encyclopedia, that is, a range of fields of investigation. These fields do not constitute a random collection of disciplines and subjects; rather, they reflect a coherent creation order.

Within the encyclopedia those fields that focus on the structure of the created order constitute the backbone of educational activity at Dordt

College. Hence there is a strong stress on a core curriculum of various academic disciplines. The created structure is determinative for all of life's functionings. It provides the condition for all creaturely activity. Historical and cultural development, as well as vocational endeavors, take place within and always reflects an ordered creation. The energy question, for example, reflects physical, economic, and other dimensions of reality. To understand this question as a whole requires insight into the nature of the physical and economic aspects. Insight into all kinds of practical situations and problems, therefore, demands concomitant insight into various aspects of God's creation.

At Dordt College the dimensions of reality are examined in order to obtain an understanding of the underlying unity in diversity. Dordt College attempts to convey the perspective of an ordered creation continuously upheld by God's word of power,[29] the cosmos in which people are placed and called to carry out their task. Dordt College, therefore, stresses the indispensability of Biblical study and Christian philosophy to our understanding of the character and coherence of the created order.

Insight into the structure of the creation is to be integrally linked to an investigation of man's response to God's call to service. In their building of civilizations, God's image bearers have been guided by a variety of spirits. Dordt College, therefore, requires the student to engage in a broad study of history and of contemporary problems. The investigation of historical developments is designed to enable the student to recognize the various deformations effected by secular and humanistic spirits, as well as the wholesome result of God-obedient activity. Such an investigation equips students to discover and evaluate the character of their own civilization. In addition, Dordt College seeks to provide insight into a number of the most crucial problems of our age. As the world seems to be shrinking, more and more of the great questions of our time impinge on our lives and require our judgment. Contemporary examples of such problems are the energy question, the role of the media, and the impact of technology. Dordt College aims to implement a curriculum sufficiently flexible to address the problems as they arise. By requiring the study of history and contemporary problems, Dordt College, as a Calvinistic institution in the tradition of the Reformation, seeks to instill the ability to discern the spirits and to engage in genuinely reforming cultural activity.

Lastly, Dordt College seeks to provide insight into the nature and demands of the various vocational and professional tasks. Graduates of Dordt College must be equipped to carry out their tasks as kingdom citizens in the professions, careers, and occupations to which they have been called. As a result, majors and preprofessional programs form another essential component of the curriculum.

While the various disciplines and programs, together with historical and contemporary studies, constitute the core of the curriculum, Dordt College by no means neglects the various skills required by graduates as they continue in their calling. Emphasis is placed on analytic, communicative, artistic, and physical skills, as these are essential for effective Christian service. Other skills, too, as demanded by the nature of vocational tasks, are included in the curricular offerings. The teaching of such special skills forms an integral part of majors and preprofessional programs, and thus of the entire curriculum.

The components of the curriculum—namely, courses in academic disciplines, studies of history and contemporary problems, major and preprofessional programs, and skill courses—together constitute the basic ingredients required by the student to attain genuine Christian insight and wisdom. None of these facets may be isolated from any of the others. For this reason, Dordt College seeks to offer an integrated curriculum conducive to contextual learning.

Since, as stated in the preceding chapter, truly serviceable insight involves theoretical comprehension, practical ability, and proper motivation, the curriculum of Dordt College aims at coherence and interrelatedness. Education at Dordt College is not a concatenation of unrelated facts or isolated bits of information; nor does the curriculum consist of dissociated academic subjects and unconnected skill courses. Rather, the various areas of the curriculum, whether they involve academic disciplines, creative activity, or skills, are to be interrelated within the unifying framework of a Biblical perspective.

In order to implement such an integrated curriculum more effectively, Dordt College strongly encourages and promotes communal scholarship. Faculty members responsible for the various components of the curriculum are to become increasingly aware of each other's work. Dordt's faculty ought to develop into a team of teachers and scholars, competent professionals who are vitally concerned about their teaching effectiveness, their area of academic specialization, and their responsibility to contribute to the overall development of integrated serviceable insight.

While the curriculum, organized as an encyclopedia of fields of investigation, constitutes the central part of the educational task of Dordt College, the non-curricular aspects of the college also play an essential role in the implementation of that task. Both curricular and extracurricular activities have the same goal: the development and transmission of insight. It is clear that much extracurricular activity on campus relates to one or more of the fields of investigation formally treated in the curriculum. Conferences, clubs, special events, and guest lecturers, for example, normally deal with specific topics already considered in the disciplines. Dordt College, therefore, seeks to provide a wide range of extracurricular opportunities to develop and enhance serviceable insights.

Finally, inherent in all of Dordt's educational activity, whether curricular or extracurricular, is the goal of developing a desire to serviceable insight. To a large extent Dordt College will have failed if it graduated knowledgeable and skillful students who lack the desire to carry out their tasks in service and loving obedience. The college must therefore, cooperate closely with church and home to develop and foster genuine Christian attitudes by promoting Scripturally-oriented devotional and social activities. Such activities ought not to be considered mere additions to the academic task; rather, they should be integrated into the total pattern of curricular and extracurricular activity, all of which is designed to provide the student with serviceable insight, i.e., wisdom according to the mind of Christ.[30]

Chapter VII: Academic Freedom

The implementation of the educational task described in the preceding chapters includes an institutional commitment to the principle of academic freedom. A Reformed view of academic freedom rests in part on the biblical concept of sphere sovereignty.

Dordt College occupies a distinct societal sphere with its own God-given authority and responsibility.

The college desires to cooperate with other nonacademic institutions such as businesses, churches, or governments; but these institutions must not infringe on the academic integrity of the college.

Academic freedom must also be acknowledged and promoted within the institution. The college must simulate, not inhibit, genuine Christian scholarship and teaching. The faculty must be free to explore and investigate.

Such freedom, however, is not to be equated with enlightenment philosophy. Individual autonomy, the traditional idea of academic freedom, suggests that freedom knows no bounds. This view is not acceptable because all perceptions of academic freedom are, in fact, based on worldviews that set parameters for the academic enterprise. All scholarship and teaching is governed by an allegiance to prior commitments. The enlightenment view of academic freedom is grounded in assumptions about individual autonomy that exclude institutional and communal claims.

Unlike secular-religious views of academic freedom that do not acknowledge limitations and restrictions established by unexpressed assumptions, Dordt College boldly maintains that the academic freedom on its campus is restricted and bounded by the Word of God and a Reformed view of academic life as set forth in *The Educational Task of Dordt College.*

When appointments are made, all parties must clearly understand the nature and parameters of the statement of purpose, *The Educational Task of*

Dordt College, and agree to carry out their academic responsibilities within the framework articulated therein. At the same time they must agree that if, in the performance of their academic task, they find themselves departing from the stated goals and purposes of the college, they should be prepared for the reevaluation and possible termination of their appointment by the board of trustees.[31]

Explicit affirmation of *The Educational Task of Dordt College* and contractual obligations establishes a framework from which faculty are encouraged to engage in creative and innovative Christian scholarship. Faculty are free to explore and investigate—to "think new thoughts." Dordt faculty are busy exploring and developing our world by asking probing questions, formulating new insights, wrestling with new ideas, and freely dialoguing with differing perspectives.

Encouraging such scholarship motivates Dordt College both to actively promote an environment of trust and mutual responsibility and to discourage a climate of suspicion and judgmentalism. Academic freedom implies, therefore, a cooperation with one another and a growing understanding that disagreement does not necessarily imply error and need not lead to confrontation and division.

Dordt College confesses that the source of true freedom is Jesus Christ. Christ empowers us by His Spirit and directs us by His Word. He frees us to perform our academic task in a liberating way that enables us to respond obediently to His call.

Notes

1. Romans 11:36.

2. Revelation 4:11.

3. John 1:3.

4. Colossians 1:15–17; 1 Corinthians 8:6; Hebrews 1:2; Hebrews 11:3, 2 Peter 3:5.

5. Colossians 1:17.

6. Exodus 9:29; Exodus 19:5; Psalm 24:1; 1 Corinthians 10:26.

7. Psalm 103:19.

8. Psalm 22:28; Psalm 47; Psalm 103:19; Psalm 145:10–21; Obadiah 1:21; Zechariah 14:16–21.

9. Psalm 119:89–91.

10. Belgic Confession, Article 12.

11. Proverbs 23:7; Proverbs 4:23; Matthew 12:34, 35; Luke 6:45; Mark 7:18–23; 2 Corinthians 9:7.

12. Genesis 1:26, 28.

13. Romans 1:25.

14. Genesis 3:15.

15. John 1:29; John 3:16; Ephesians 1:9, 10; Philippians 2:9, 10; Colossians 1:19, 20; 1 John 2:2; Revelation 21:5.

16. Matthew 28:18.

17. See page 3.

18. See page 3.

19. See page 3.

20. Romans 12:6–8.

21. Psalm 8:6–8; Matthew 25:14, 15.

22. Romans 12:10; 1 Corinthians 12:4, 5.

23. Matthew 28:18; Romans 13:1; 1 Peter 3:22.

24. 2 Corinthians 4:5; Philippians 2:3, 4.

25. 1 Peter 4:10, 11.

26. Psalm 111:10.

27. Ephesians 5:15–17.

28. James 3:13.

29. Hebrews 1:3; 2 Peter 3:5.

30. 1 Corinthians 2:15–16.

31. See page 8.

The Educational Framework of Dordt College

....

Introduction

The *Educational Framework of Dordt College** sets forth a structure for the overall educational program at Dordt College. We begin with a section on the underlying educational principles of the college. This part contains a number of statements that spell out our confessional basis and religious affiliation and that delineate the main features of our educational task. What we say on these topics is not new; it summarizes what has been said elsewhere: in *Scripturally Oriented Higher Education, The Educational Task of Dordt College*, and *Renewing Our Vision*. We include these statements here to give an explicit context for the remainder of the document.

The second section contains some parameters for organizing the curriculum, both with respect to curricular content and curricular design. It describes in general terms what the curriculum should be and how it should be structured in order to fulfill the mission of the college.

Our treatment of the content of the curriculum, as well as of the curricular goals in the following section, is organized under four broad headings: *religious orientation, creational structure, creational development*, and *contemporary response*. These categories are meant to be comprehensive and inclusive, not the exclusive domain of particular disciplines. They sum up our curricular responsibility

---

* Adopted by the Dordt College Faculty Assembly on August 20, 1993.

before God, regardless of specialty. Each part of the curriculum should be infused with Christian perspective, should reveal how God has structured that field of investigation for the benefit of his creatures, should show how that area of creation has unfolded over time and how human beings have responded to God's law there, and should prepare students to fulfill their contemporary responsibilities relative to the insights it provides. Different courses may weight these things differently, but all four sides should be present in a balanced way in every student's program.

This fourfold classification provides a coherent curricular framework that is consistent with a Reformational Christian perspective. None of these dimensions can be considered in isolation from the rest, but each highlights an important feature of the curriculum and of life itself. In a sense, the first three may be viewed as culminating in the last: we respond in contemporary situations according to our religious orientation, the structure of the situation, and the possibilities for action that are available to us at the time. The conceptual schema we have adopted directs our attention to each of these points in turn, as well as on the need to respond.

In the last section we focus on curricular goals and student outcomes. These are the general abilities and characteristics we would like to see developed by the curriculum in all those who graduate from Dordt College. We have not tried to separate student outcomes from curricular input, since we see these as two sides of the same coin. Nevertheless, more specific curricular objectives for accomplishing the overall goals will need to be fleshed out for each program.

In formulating student outcomes, we have consciously incorporated what are usually called "skills" into the section dealing with creational structure. This was done for two reasons. First, we did not want to artificially separate skills from knowledge and commitment: all three are and should be woven together to provide students with the abilities and resources needed to engage our world Christianly. Each area of study must help students acquire and develop theoretical and intuitive insights (knowledge or understanding), cultivate those abilities necessary for appropriating and applying them (skills), and build personal responsibility and initiative (commitment). Secondly, these competencies are essential to the nature of learning. They are practiced abilities students should possess in order to be effectively engaged in the educational process and be prepared for the challenge of Christian discipleship in today's society.

The principles, parameters, and goals comprise the framework for the total curriculum and a context in which each individual program can take shape. The General Education Program, professional and pre-professional programs, majors, and minors should each articulate its own framework and relate it to that of the total curriculum. Once this is done, programs can be evaluated and redesigned, if necessary, to make them more productive participants in fulfilling the mission of the college.

I. Underlying Principles for Christian College Education

A. Confessional Basis and Tenets

1. *Scriptural Direction and Reformed Tradition*
The Bible is God's written Word. It reveals his will for creation and provides guidance for our lives. Our understanding of the implications of Scripture for the scope and meaning of our task as a Christian community stands within the Reformed tradition of John Calvin, Abraham Kuyper, and their followers.

2. *Creation*
Our entire world, in all its parts, aspects, and relations, is the revelatory creation of the triune God, Father, Son, and Holy Spirit. God orders and preserves the cosmos by His Word as an expression of covenantal love. All things are unified under God's rule and exist to give Him glory.

3. *Humanity*
Human beings were created to bear God's image. As such, they were given a mandate to cultivate creation, to develop its potential and take good care of it.

4. *Fall Into Sin*
Through humanity's willful disobedience to God, sin entered the world. Sin disrupted communion between God and humankind, spawned disharmony between people, set men and women in harmful opposition to the rest of creation, and brought about a curse on creation that resulted in hardship and death.

5. *Redemption and Restoration*
God sent His only son, Jesus Christ, the Word made flesh, to save us from sin and restore all things to Himself. Jesus' death and resurrection broke the dominion of the Evil One and inaugurated the renewal of creation. The divine campaign to regain full control over the world will be completed when the Lord returns to make everything right.

6. *The Kingdom of God and the Task of the Church*
As God's people, the church, we are called to be agents of reconciliation. Under the leading of the Holy Spirit and in communion with God and one another, we are to summon sinners to repentance and strive to advance God's rule in all areas of life. We seek to transform culture and bring shalom to a broken world.

7. *Christian Education*
Christian education is an integral part of the Christian community's contemporary responsibility before God. It assists each new generation of God's people to discern His will for their time and place. It prepares them to care for and unfold all of creation in praise to Him, and it helps them to fight against the works of the Devil.

8. *Christian College Education*
Christian college education develops insights, capabilities, and Christian perspective across a broad spectrum of areas and at an advanced level of theoretical reflection and practical competence so that God's people can become better equipped to serve Him as mature adults in all areas of life.

B. Educational Task of Dordt College

1. *Educational Mission of Dordt College*
Dordt College strives to develop and share serviceable insight into the meaning, structure, and development of the world God has created and graciously maintains.

2. *Serviceable Insight*
Education at Dordt College is not pursued for its own sake nor for its civilizing qualities nor for the strictly pragmatic purpose of vocational instruction, but to provide insight and develop talents that will sustain lifelong responsible service in God's Kingdom. The knowledge, competencies, and commitments gained through the educational process aim to prepare students to live thankful lives before the Lord; to serve others with integrity, in common everyday activities as well as in specific vocations; and to unfold and care for the creation.

3. *College Community*
Within the context of Dordt's administrative support staff and its constituency among God's people, the faculty and students of Dordt College form a community of scholars responsible for developing and sharing serviceable insight on all aspects of creation.

4. *Curriculum*
Dordt College accomplishes its educational task primarily via the curriculum, which is the formally structured set of interconnected learning activities and experiences designed to realize the mission and goals of the college. The curriculum thus constitutes the central focus of the college's organization and activities.

5. *Living Environment and Cocurricular Activities*
While remaining focused on its educational task, the college must treat its members as whole people. It should therefore maintain an environment that promotes responsible Christian living and supports scholarly investigation and practice. Cocurricular activities and organization of college life in general should facilitate and complement study of the curriculum, so that the college can better realize its mission.

II. Parameters of Curricular Organization

A. Curricular Content

1. *Religious Orientation*
The curriculum should be rooted in the Word of God and infused with a Reformational worldview to reflect the fact that all of creation is related to God as its Creator, Redeemer, and Lord.

2. *Creational Structure*
The curriculum should be organized into a balanced cohesive whole of complementary academic programs to faithfully reflect the diversity and coherence of reality. The curriculum should include the study of general areas of common concern to all people, and it should contain in-depth study of selected fields of specialization.

3. *Creational Development*
The curriculum should reflect and promote knowledge of the dynamic unfolding of creation, and it should highlight the various aspects of human responsibility and involvement in this process.

4. *Contemporary Response*
The curriculum should help students convert their insights and competencies into committed action. It should enable them to translate the results of theoretical investigation into faithful response to God and practical Christian service to their neighbor. Insofar as resources permit, the curriculum should contain a focused range of programs that explore the main areas of contemporary life, giving opportunities for study in those academic fields where genuine biblical insight has been developed and the Christian community's need and significant student interest have been demonstrated. The curriculum should be broad enough to address the pressing concerns of today's world, but narrow enough to be able to treat these issues with the sustained thoroughness required to develop genuinely serviceable insight on them from a Christian perspective.

B. Curricular Design

1. *Sequencing of Learning*
The curriculum should be organized vertically into a sequence of courses and learning activities that build upon previous learning experiences and that demonstrate sensitivity to and understanding of the various types and stages of maturation that normally take place during typical college-age years.

2. *Coordination of Learning*
Curricular programs should be organized horizontally to complement and interconnect with one another and to provide a well-rounded understanding of creation. The curriculum should arrange ways in which insights from

different fields of investigation can be integrated to provide comprehensive understanding of issues.

3. *Pedagogy for Effective Learning*
The curriculum should be organized to employ instructional styles and strategies that suit the subject matter being studied, that recognize different stages of late adolescent development and help students progress in their learning, that employ learning experiences to match the various ways students learn, that foster communal scholarship, that capitalize upon and broaden faculty members' strengths, that encourage student reflection and response, and that connect learning with real-life situations.

4. *Assessment of Learning*
Students' progress should be regularly assessed as part of the educational process in order to monitor their success and that of the various programs in meeting the goals of the college.

5. *Extension of Learning*
The curriculum should be organized to facilitate interaction with Dordt's constituency, other Christian organizations, and the surrounding community. The curriculum should reach out through appropriate study centers, workshops, practicums, internships, and other channels to develop and extend serviceable insight into the life of contemporary society.

III. Curricular Goals/Student Outcomes

A. Religious Orientation

1. *Biblical Basis*
Students should recognize the guiding role of the Bible in a life of Christian discipleship. They should be familiar with the main themes and teachings of the Bible, and they should be able to develop Scripturally based perspectives and strategies on contemporary issues.

2. *Reformed Faith and Worldview*
Students should have a good working understanding and appreciation of the Reformed Christian faith, both with regard to its roots in God's revelation and its elaboration in a distinctly Christian worldview. They should be able to discern, evaluate, and challenge the prevailing spirits and worldviews of our age in the light of God's Word and our Reformational perspective.

3. *Christian Lifestyle*
Students should know the nature and implications of living a life of Christian discipleship in today's world, and they should be committed to developing such a lifestyle and to transforming those features of our culture that oppose it.

B. Creational Structure

1. *Lawful Regularity of Creation*
Students should understand that all of creation has been structured in an orderly way by God and that He faithfully preserves it through His laws, thus making possible the systematic organization experienced in each field of investigation.

2. *Coherence of Creation*
Students should understand that all of creation is unified in Christ Jesus as its sovereign head and that nothing exists apart from Him or has a right to our ultimate allegiance. They should also learn to appreciate and properly distinguish the rich diversity within creation. They should recognize the interdependence of the various parts and aspects of creation, and they should be able to connect what they learn to their everyday experience and their future vocations.

3. *Place of Human Beings in Creation*
Students should recognize the central position human beings hold in creation as image bearers of God. They should learn to exhibit proper care and respect for everything God has created, acknowledging their responsibility to treat all creatures justly and with compassion; and they should know how to maintain a balanced, wholesome lifestyle.

4. *Disciplined Focus of Learning*
Students should be able to use the ideas, theories, and procedures from a variety of disciplines in order to conceptualize issues, solve problems, and provide service to others in daily life. They should be competent in one or more specialized fields of inquiry, and they should be acquainted with the main contours of other fields of study.

5. *Structural Conditions of Learning*
Students should develop the various abilities and understandings necessary for engaging in college level learning and for continuing to develop, share, and apply serviceable insights after graduation. They should be able to work professionally and cooperatively with others, taking responsibility for their work and striving to build community among people with diverse backgrounds, interests, and capabilities.

C. Creational Development

1. *Dynamic Character of Created Reality*
Students should appreciate the developmental nature of reality. They should understand in broad terms how our world has developed, and they should be equipped to cope with a rapidly changing world.

2. *The Cultural Mandate and Stewardship*

Students should recognize their calling to give form to culture as creative historical agents acting in obedience to God. They should comprehend and appreciate their God-given responsibility to unfold the potential of creation in stewardly ways, exhibiting care for and proper use of the things they employ, and showing concern for those creatures that suffer from the misery caused by human sin and error.

3. *Development of Culture and Civilization*

Students should understand and critically evaluate the formative processes and religious spirits by which our civilization and others have been shaped. They should understand how creation has developed historically and how human civilizations have helped to form today's world. Students should be familiar with the different ways in which major world cultures and civilizations have responded to the cultural mandate, and they should be aware of the interconnected global nature of contemporary life.

4. *Historical Development of Fields of Study*

Students should be able to identify and evaluate influential formative traditions operating in their particular disciplines and vocations and in common areas of life. They should be familiar with the resources available to them for developing new perspectives or plans of action consistent with a Christian worldview.

D. Contemporary Response

1. *Learning for Service*

Students should develop the insights, skills, and strategies needed to contribute entry-level expertise and work in their special vocations and the common tasks of adult life. They should realize that they are called to vocations and communal responsibilities by God Himself, and they should seek those areas of service that further his Kingdom.

2. *Gaining in Wisdom*

Students should exhibit increasing wisdom, rooted in a mature fear of the Lord, in their understanding of His world and their service to His Kingdom. They should be equipped for, and committed to, lifelong learning so that they can continue to develop and apply insight in faithful response to God.

3. *Commitment to Transforming Culture*

Students should be sensitive to the impact of sin and idolatry in their own lives, in human society, and in the world around them. They should show a desire to transform the world for the service of God's Kingdom and the good of all his creatures. They should seek Christian responses to the world's contemporary needs, and they should actively participate in their various communities, supporting with their time, money, and prayers those institutions and ventures that serve God's Kingdom and promote a Christian vision of life.

Authority in Christian Higher Education

John B. Hulst[*]

....

In order to understand the nature and proper exercise of authority in Christian higher education, we must begin with a consideration of the sovereignty of the social spheres. Sphere sovereignty and authority are closely related concepts. Henk Van Riessen makes this clear when he writes: "By 'sovereignty' he [Abraham Kuyper] understood an authority that includes the right, the duty, and the power to break and to avenge any resistance it encounters."[1]

The Sovereignty of the Social Spheres

When God brought forth the creation, he did so in orderly fashion. He gave to each part of the creation its own nature, and he subjected each and every part to his law so that the various parts of creation might serve him.

---

[*] This article was first published in *Pro Rege* in June 1973. At the time Dr. Hulst had B.D. and Th.M. degrees from Calvin Seminary, Grand Rapids, Michigan. Prior to coming to Dordt College, he served three congregations of the Christian Reformed Church. He started out at Dordt in 1968 as Campus Pastor and Instructor in Biblical Theology and in 1971 became Dean of Students. He served as President of the college from 1982 to 1996. He received his Th.D. in 1981 from the Iliff School of Theology in Denver, Colorado.

God also created humans. As part of God's creation, humans were also made subject to God's law for the creation. But, in distinction from the rest of creation, humans were made in the image of God and were mandated to serve God by developing and unfolding the potentialities of creation according to God's laws for the various parts of his handiwork. In this way, humankind—and the rest of creation through the activity of humankind—was to serve God and show forth his glory.

In fulfilling their task before God, humans were not to live and work in isolation. They were to do so in relationship with other humans as part of a human community. And, just as they structured every other part of creation (including humankind), the laws of God were to structure humankind's societal, community life. It must not be thought, however, that humankind's societal relationships and the laws governing them were to be vague and indefinite. They were relationships in which humans were to work in developing the creation order. Therefore, the structure that each relationship evidenced was to depend upon the work, the activity to be performed, within that particular community.

Initially the human community was undifferentiated, and many spheres, which we now recognize as such, were subsumed under the family. But in the course of history, as humans performed their task of developing and unfolding the creation, differentiation occurred. Different associations of society developed, according to the laws of God, and these associations became independent according to their respective natures and functions. Thus there is today a "wide variety of distinct, though related spheres which arise out of the complex life of mankind, each having its own task to perform, its own mandate entrusted to it by God."[2] These spheres are not only the result of humans' communal cultural activity, but within each of these spheres (societal relationships) we find a human community working with a certain aspect of the created order.

As already indicated, humankind was commissioned by God to work within the creation in service to God and for his glory. In doing so, humans were to obey God and his law. But humans disobeyed and fell into sin. They continued to live and work, and everything they did, in spite of their sinful nature, was done within and directed by the law-structures of the creation. But, instead of working developmentally within the creation to the glory of God, humankind "exchanged the truth of God for a lie, and worshiped and served the creature rather than the Creator, who is God blessed forever" (Romans 1:25 ASV). As a result, humankind—and all of the creation—was brought under the wrath and the condemnation of God.

But God sent his Son, by whom all things were created (John 1:3), to redeem his people and to restore his creation as that arena where his people could and would serve and glorify him. Through his redemptive work Jesus Christ, the last Adam, fulfilled the will of his Father. Therefore Paul writes:

> For it was the good pleasure of the Father that in him should all the fullness dwell; and through him to reconcile all things unto himself, having made peace through the blood of his cross; through him, I say whether things upon the earth, or things in the heavens. And you, being in time past alienated and enemies in your mind in your evil works, yet now hath he reconciled in the body of his flesh through death, to present you holy and without blemish and unreprovable before him. Colossians 1:19–22 (ASV)

As a reward for his redemptive work, Christ was appointed by the Father as Sovereign over all. Thus, prior to his ascension and coronation, Christ declared to his redeemed servants:

> All authority hath been given unto me in heaven and on earth. Go ye therefore, and make disciples of all the nations, baptizing them into the name of the Father and of the Son and of the Holy Spirit; teaching them to observe all things whatsoever I commanded you: and lo, I am with you always, even unto the end of the world. Matthew 28:18–20 (ASV)

Therefore, while the unredeemed continue to work in opposition to God, the redeemed are charged to work under and according to the will of their Sovereign, Jesus Christ. For we hear in these words of Christ a renewed mandate to the new humanity to work in his renewed creation according to his law and unto his glory. Which is to say that the charge given to humankind at creation has been republished to us by Christ through the Scriptures. Thus just as humankind, created in the image of God, was to work communally in the various spheres according to the law of God and for his glory, so we, recreated in the image of God, must work as members of his body in the various spheres according to the will of Christ and unto his praise (1 Peter 2:9).

Now that we have spoken of the various spheres, which developed in the course of history, we must ask the question: What is meant when we speak of the sovereignty of the social spheres? Van Riessen answers this question as follows: "Generally speaking, in our case sphere-sovereignty expresses the mutual *independence* of the social units or lasting relationships of society. And it expresses in particular the mutual independence of the authority inherent in units of a different nature."[3] Later Van Riessen makes two statements that appear as qualifiers of what he has said concerning the *"independence* of the social units"*: "Each *sphere of authority is limited by its own societal relationship*"[4] and *"Societal relationships properly stand in a coordinate relation to each other, not in a preferred or subordinate position."*[5]

It appears that there are at least three "laws" operative in the one principle of sphere-sovereignty.

First, there is the "law" of *independence*. Each social sphere has its own nature, its own laws according to which it must operate, and its own function that it is to perform. Thus each sphere has authority by virtue of the charge given it by Christ, to whom God has given all power and authority in heaven and on earth. In this sense each sphere has "sovereign rights within its own domain."

Second, there is the "law" of *limitation*. Because each sphere has "sovereign rights within its own domain," no sphere may seek to dominate or usurp another. To do so would be not only a violation of the independence of the spheres, but also a usurpation of the power and authority of Jesus Christ.

Third, and closely related to the others, there is the "law" of *coordination*. "The social relationships exist together on a basis of equality; the one is not subordinate to the authority and control of the other."[6] This is not to say that all spheres are of equal importance. According to the order established in creation, there is an obvious difference in value between the various spheres. But recognition of a difference in value does not imply a hierarchy of spheres with the lower receiving authority from the higher and being dominated by it. The authority of one sphere is not derived from the authority of another. All authority is from Christ, who alone is sovereign (Ephesians 1:21). Thus, instead of the lower being subordinate to the higher, all spheres are subordinate to Christ and exist in a coordinate relationship to one another within the totality of the created order.

If we take the preceding and apply it to the sphere of education, it becomes clear that we must acknowledge that in education there exist:

(1) The law of *independence*. To the extent that education has its own nature, laws, and function, it is independent from other spheres and may not be dominated by them either in whole or in part. It must be allowed the "freedom" or the "right" to exercise the God-given authority necessary unto the performance of its God-given task.

(2) The law of *limitation*. The very nature, laws, and function that give education its independence also limit the authority of the sphere of education. Just as it may not allow itself to be dominated by another sphere, so also it may not dominate or usurp the authority of another sphere.

(3) The law of *coordination*. Instead of submitting to a sphere of "greater value" or dominating a sphere of "lesser value," the sphere of education should seek to work in a coordinate relationship with other spheres. In this way all of the Kingdom spheres will be free to give harmonious and obedient response to the commands of the King.

The Biblical Concepts of Office and Authority

Up to this point we have spoken primarily about the authority of the various spheres as they stand in relationship to one another. Before we consider the exercise of authority within the sphere of education, we must inquire concerning the biblical concept of office.

A further comment should be made before proceeding. We recognize that, as both the redeemed and unredeemed function within the various life spheres, so also both the redeemed and the unredeemed are in office and exercise authority. The redeemed occupy their office and exercise authority obediently, while the unredeemed do so disobediently. However, for the sake of brevity and because our primary concern is with Christian higher education, we wish from this point on to concern ourselves primarily with office and authority within the redeemed community.

The *1972 Agenda for Synod of the Christian Reformed Church* contains a report entitled "Ecclesiastical Office and Ordination." Although it addresses itself almost solely to *ecclesiastical* office, it does make clear that if we come to Scripture seeking a ready-made definition of *office* we are going to be disappointed. "In fact, it may safely be said that the writers of the Old Testament had no word for office as we understand it."[7]

The report goes on to state: "As a general term for what we call *office* (namely, a certain type of the sense of precedence, ruling, being at the head) or *timee* (office in service within the church), the word *diakonia* (service) is commonly used by the writers of the New Testament."[8] What this report says about *diakonia* is, in a sense, quite true. However, it would appear from a further study of the Bible that *diakonia* is but one aspect of office. In a far broader sense the biblical concept of office seems to refer to how God uses humankind to administer the creation, or to humans' *stewardship* of their lives and those things that are placed under their control.

In 1 Corinthians 4:1 Paul speaks of himself and the other apostles as "ministers of Christ, and stewards of the mysteries of God." In Titus 1:7 he speaks the same way about bishops: "For the bishop must be blameless, as God's steward." Nor is the idea of stewardship limited to apostles and bishops. Peter applies this concept to every member of the body of Christ:

> According as each hath received a gift, ministering it among yourselves, as good stewards of the manifold grace of God: if any man speaketh, speaking as it were oracles of God; if any man ministereth, ministering as of the strength which God supplieth: that in all things God may be glorified through Jesus Christ, whose is the glory and the dominion for ever and ever. Amen. 1 Peter 4:10–11 (ASV)

This concept of office as stewardship finds its origin in the Genesis account of creation. The Bible states that God placed humankind over the creation to rule or administer the creation in obedience to the will and the law of the Creator (Genesis 1:28). The creation belongs to the Creator (Psalm 24:1, 2). But humankind, created in the image of God, is "to have dominion" over the creation (Psalm 8:3–9). Humans are to manage the creation on behalf of and as a representative of God. Humans are God's vice-regents. Humans are God's stewards.

The writer of the book of Hebrews picks up both the theme and the words of Psalm 2 in Hebrews 2:6–8. But, in doing so, he points out that humans failed in their office, in their task as stewards of God. Therefore, the writer of Hebrews turns away from humankind. To angels? No, he turns to Christ through whom the worlds were made (Hebrews 1:2). He turns to Christ, who, "when he had made purification of sins" (Hebrews 1:3), finished the *work* God had given him to do (John 14:4). He turns to Christ who, as a reward for his finished work was made to sit down "on the right hand of the Majesty on high" (Hebrews 1:3). He points to Christ, crowned with glory and honor, as the One to whom God has subjected the administration of the creation.

Thus, as God worked in the creation before the Fall through one man, Adam, so now he works in the restored creation through one man, Jesus Christ. Christ is the image of the invisible God (Colossians 1:15). It is the purpose of God, "unto a dispensation [stewardship] of the fullness of times, to sum up all things in Christ" (Ephesians 1:10). Christ is put into office. He is made the *Servant* of God. But, because he takes over where humankind has failed, Christ is made God's *Suffering* Servant. He is born into a humanity cut off from God and a world cursed by God. As God's Suffering Servant he humbles himself, "becoming obedient even unto death, yea, the death of the cross" (Philippians 2:8). By his death ("the blood of the cross") Christ makes peace and reconciles all things on earth and in heaven to the Father (Colossians 1:20). The curse is lifted and, through Christ, that which was cut off from God is restored to him again. And thus Christ finishes his work as Suffering Servant.

But Christ continues in his office. Having completed his task as Suffering Servant, Christ is made Servant in *glory* (Philippians 2:9–11). He is made King of kings (1 Timothy 6:15). He is given all authority in heaven and on earth (Matthew 28:18) in order that he may administer the affairs of the restored creation according to the will of the Father and unto his glory. And some day he will also complete this work. One day all things will be put under his feet. And then, as a faithful steward, Christ will render account of what he has done by presenting the perfected Kingdom to the Father, "that God may be all in all" (1 Corinthians 15:28).

Scripture further indicates that Christ administers the affairs of the restored creation through the agency of restored, redeemed humankind. God, in Christ, has foreknown and foreordained certain people "to be conformed to the image of his Son" (Romans 8:29). Being conformed to the image of Christ, redeemed humankind not only reflects the glory of God (2 Corinthians 3:18) but is also restored to office. Christ, to whom all authority has been given, assigns to the redeemed person a task. As God, before the Fall, assigned to humankind the task of administering the creation (Genesis 1:26–28), so Christ assigns to redeemed humankind the task of administering the affairs of the restored creation (Matthew 28:18–20). Redeemed humankind is to recognize that they hold this office in dependence upon Christ (John 15:5) and according to the will or under the law of Christ (1 Corinthians 9:21). In other words, the redeemed person occupies the office of "steward." He or she administers as a servant of Christ, and he or she serves as an administrator over the restored creation, the Kingdom of the Lord Jesus Christ.

We must be careful not to suppose that the redeemed, the people of God, can be divided into those who have an office and those who do not. All the redeemed are taken into that body of which Christ is the head (Romans 12:5). While there are indeed differences of gifts and abilities, all the redeemed share the same Spirit, the Spirit of Jesus Christ (1 Corinthians 12:4). As "partakers of his anointing," all Christians are in office.[9] All Christians have a place to fill and a task to perform. Individually and collectively, all the saved are called to administer the affairs of the restored creation in the name of and according to the law of Jesus Christ. It was in recognition of this truth that the Protestant Reformation proclaimed the universal office of believers.

As we have already noted, all *authority* was given to Christ in order that he might fill his office as God's Servant in glory. This means that Christ was "authorized" to do that which was necessary to rule and bring to completion the Kingdom according to the Father's will and unto his praise. He was given whatever "rights," whatever "powers," were needed to administer the affairs of the restored creation on behalf of the Father.

Now when Christ restores the redeemed to office, he gives to them the authority, rights, and powers necessary for the performance of their office or task. The biblical meaning of office is authoritative service. This authority does not come from humankind. "There is no authority but of God" (Romans 13:1). The origin of this authority is God in Christ, who gives it to those who work for him in his world. And, because this authority comes from Christ, it is to be exercised according to the will and the law of Christ. Trusting Christ and obeying the law of Christ, the redeemed have from Christ the authority necessary to fulfill their office as Christ's stewards. They are "authorized" by Christ to administer, in his Name, the affairs of his Kingdom, as that Kingdom comes to expression in its various spheres.

We have emphasized the *unity* and *equality* of the redeemed in Christ. All of the redeemed are in Christ; all are restored to office; all have received the authority to carry out their task. This does not mean, however, that all members of Christ's body are the same. There are also *diversity* and *inequality* within the body of Christ, which result in *particular offices*. Diversity and inequality do not destroy the unity of the body; they enrich the body and make clear the ways in which the members of the body are dependent upon one another.

Diversity within the body of Christ comes to initial expression in different abilities and qualifications, which are *gifts* of God's grace, to be used in his *service* (Romans 12:6–8, 1 Peter 4:10, 11). Thus, some are able to teach. Others are able to preach. Still others are able to rule, and so forth. This

31

diversity of abilities qualifies the members of the Christian community for a variety of tasks.

It must not be supposed, however, that ability or qualification is the sole basis for particular offices. There must be "recognition" or "acknowledgment" on the part of the Christian community that a person does possess a certain ability before that person can be regarded as occupying a particular office. This acknowledgment can occur in many ways. Some office bearers are appointed, some are elected, and some are simply recognized as such. In any case, as God gives differing abilities to the members of the body of Christ, so he appoints by leading the Christian community to "acknowledge" these abilities (Acts 6:1–7 serves as a good example). And by these twofold means (appointment and qualification, if you will), he places humans in particular offices.

The result is *inequality* within the body, the Christian community. By putting humans into particular offices, God establishes within the various spheres of the Kingdom the relationship of higher and lower. There are those who rule and those who are ruled. There are those who are responsible for and those who are accountable to others.

The various particular offices coincide with the various spheres within the restored creation, the Kingdom of God. In fact, it was through the exercise of particular offices that the different spheres were given form. This does not mean that the spheres within the Kingdom are the creations of humankind. They are based upon and reflections of the laws, ordinances of God. But they are given historical formation through the instrumentality of humans exercising a particular office.

Thus, while all the redeemed are in that universal office in terms of which they are to administer the affairs of the entire Kingdom of Jesus Christ, the various particular offices coincide with the various particular spheres of life. Each office has its own sphere within which it is to function—parents within the family, teachers within the school, elders within the church, rulers within the state, and so on. Each office has a task to perform, a task defined by the nature of the sphere within which it functions. And each office carries with it the authority necessary for the performance of its task, an authority limited to a particular sphere of operation. In other words, every particular office has its own specific task, law, responsibility, and authority defined by its particular sphere. But—and this is the burden of this paper—each office does receive *authority* from Christ necessary for the performance of its task.

Nor should we fail to recognize that a measure of diversification also takes place *within* the several life spheres. Again, this diversification is not a result of human planning. God carries out his design. But he realizes his will through the work of humans. And, as humans work within the various spheres, a process of specialization takes place. Eventually the point is reached where no one can administer all the affairs of one sphere. The result is that also *within* the various spheres various specialized offices emerge. Paul takes note of this process of development within the church. "And he gave some to be apostles; and some, prophets; and some, evangelists; and some pastors and teachers" (Ephesians 4:11, ASV). These specialized offices also carry their own specialized task, laws, responsibilities, and authority.

Office and Authority within the Sphere of Education
One of the spheres that has emerged as a result of the development of the creation order is the sphere of education. In the beginning humans performed their common task within the context of the family. But as that task became more complex, the offices of humans became specialized. Thus the office of teacher emerged alongside the office of parents, and the sphere of education alongside the sphere of the family. Further, within the sphere of education a process of specialization occurred, so that we find special offices charged with different aspects of the one educational task. Thus we find within the Kingdom today the sphere of education; within the sphere of education we find particular offices, such as board member, teacher, administrator, and so on.

To understand how the affairs of this sphere are ordered, we return to what was said before concerning the universal office of believers. All believers are in Christ and, as members of his body, occupy the office of stewards. Together they are to administer the affairs of the Kingdom of Christ. They have a communal task to perform relative to the entire Kingdom and within every sphere of the Kingdom, including the sphere of education. The task of the believing community in the sphere of education is to prepare the members of the community for the performance of their cultural responsibilities—their offices—by leading them, according to the Word of God, to a deeper understanding of the creation and its history.

The apostate community seeks to prepare its members for cultural life and activity apart from and in opposition to God. The redeemed community endeavors to prepare its members for cultural life and activity that will be pleasing to God and by means of which they can function as qualified citizens and office bearers in his Kingdom. This is the task that God has assigned to the redeemed community and has authorized them to perform in the sphere of education.

Now while it is true that all believers are qualified and authorized by God to fill the office of believer, not every believer is equally qualified to fill every particular office in every sphere within the Kingdom. As the tasks of humankind and the various social relationships that humans sustain become more and more complex, no one can administer the affairs of all the life spheres. In fact, no one can even administer all the affairs of one sphere. This is the case in all spheres, but especially in education.

Therefore, the Christian community must seek out and appoint those who can fulfill for them the responsibilities and tasks within the sphere of education. In doing so Christians must seriously consider at what point in history they stand. They cannot make decisions solely on the basis of what has been done in the past. They must carefully and prayerfully decide what tasks must be performed and what offices must be filled to carry out their educational responsibility before the Lord.

It would seem that today it is incumbent upon the Christian community at least to appoint people to the offices of teacher, board member, and administrator. Anything less would make it most difficult to carry on the work of education effectively. Further, though some may differ, we could define the offices mentioned as follows:

(1) The office of the *teacher* is to study, to understand, and, in harmony with the school's religious direction, to lead his or her students into a deeper understanding of the creation (or an aspect thereof) and its history.

(2) The office of a *board member* is to articulate the basic religious direction of the school; to see to the provision of the necessary facilities for carrying on the educational enterprise; and to select and make provision for those qualified for teaching and administering the affairs of the school.

(3) The office of the *administrator* is to supervise, to manage, and to direct the various aspects and affairs of the school, such as academic affairs, student life, finances, facilities, and so on, according to the policies established by the board.

How many kinds of appointments are to be made and what the precise nature of each office is not of great importance here. These matters must be decided according to principles applied to time and circumstance.

In order to illustrate the significance of office and authority within the sphere of education, we will concentrate on the office of *teacher* since the teacher is most directly involved in the fundamental task of the educational sphere.

It is important to understand, first of all, that those appointed to the office of teacher must be *qualified* to teach. Further, when recognition is given to those qualifications by means of an *appointment,* the person appointed must be regarded as occupying the particular office of teacher. And what if the teacher proves to lack certain qualifications for his or her office? This must concern the Christian community, because lack of qualification results in mismanagement of the office. But until the community, through the action of the board of trustees, removes such a person from office, he or she must be regarded as occupying that particular office, with all that that means.

It is important to acknowledge, secondly, that those occupying the office of teacher possess the authority necessary for the performance of their teaching task, such as presenting lectures, making assignments of books to be read and papers to be written, marking, and so on. Possessing authority, the teacher is placed over the student. This does not mean, however, that he or she holds authority over the student as an end in itself. The teacher has authority *in order that* he or she may prepare the student for the performance of his or her cultural responsibilities, by leading him or her to a deeper understanding of the creation and its history. In this sense the teacher is responsible for the student and the student is accountable to the teacher.

It must also be emphasized that the office and authority of the teacher do not ultimately depend upon the person and qualifications of the teacher. Authority is "localized" in the person of the teacher, but, at the same time, it must be distinguished from the person of the teacher. Van Riessen makes this clear when he writes:

> But to be effective, leadership ought to have power. Only if power is derived from a constitution can such leadership be called authority. The personal aspect is of course not irrelevant in the obedience to parents, the government, or a supervisor, but this obedience depends fundamentally upon the constitution by which authority is established as a delegation from the authority of Christ.
>
> Even if such constituted leadership is not effective due to a serious lack of personal power or wisdom, e.g., in a factory, other, and in that case informal leadership will emerge and take over. Such leadership and, in general, leadership without a constitution, will depend solely upon personal qualities. It has no real authority, although it may be of use.[10]

Van Riessen's reference to a "constitution" is very much to the point. We are talking about authority within a school, an *institution* within the Kingdom sphere of education. Fundamental to an educational institution is its constitution "by which authority is established as a delegation from the authority of Christ."[11]

It is important to recognize, thirdly, that teachers receive their office, including the qualifications and the authority they exercise, *from God.* The Lord endows them with authority.

The fact that they receive their office from God does not mean, however, that teachers may act as despots over their students. Quite the opposite is true. Teachers hold their office as *stewards,* and, therefore, they must carry out the various aspects of their office according to the *law* of God for their office. As stewards, teachers are *accountable* to God for what they do with their office. And as stewards, teachers must fulfill the *purpose* of God in the performance of their office and must seek to bring their students to the point where they can fulfill function and calling before the Lord.

This truth—that teachers received their office and authority from God through Christ—leaves teachers free to perform their tasks. At the same time it keeps them from *misusing* their office; for they are under the law of God, accountable to God, and bound to fulfill the will of God in their office. And what if a teacher does sinfully misuse his or her office? Again, as noted before, it would become the duty of the Christian community through those responsible to God for overseeing the office of teacher to correct the situation or remove the teacher from his or her office.

The fourth matter that must be emphasized is the necessity of making a clear *definition* of the task the teacher is to perform within the larger sphere of education. Such definition of task must make clear the extent and the limits of the authority that the teacher is to exercise.

Earlier we noted the importance of a clear understanding of the nature, laws, and functions of the various spheres within the Kingdom. We indicated that this understanding is necessary in order that the spheres may function in independence, in recognition of their limitations, and in coordination. For basically the same reason it is important to clearly define the office of the teacher. Especially in higher education, the teacher works in relationship to other bearers of a particular office—board members, administrators, teachers in the same and other departments. Thus the office of teacher must be defined in such a clear manner that the teacher may carry out his or her work freely, without dominating others, and yet in communal coordination.

Before bringing our consideration of authority to an end and acknowledging that our study has in no way been exhaustive, we must consider the place of the student in the sphere of education. Very often we hear people speak of "the office of a student," "student authority," and "student power." Is it legitimate to speak of student office, authority, or power?

No one would deny that Christian students are members of the body of Christ and, as such, share with other members of that body in the universal office of believers. It is clear from Scripture that all the redeemed are in Christ, are members of his body, and share in his anointing. Nor can anyone deny that students are essential to the sphere of education. Obviously, no school can exist without students anymore than a family can exist without children. But the student's membership in the body of Christ and his or her importance within the educational sphere do not speak to or resolve the matter of student office and authority.

The fact is, we find no biblical basis for speaking of the particular office of student, student authority, or student power. The *task* of the Christian community in the sphere of education is "to prepare the members of that community for the performance of their cultural responsibilities—their offices—by leading them to a deeper understanding of the creation and its history" (see earlier definition). How can a student hold a particular office in that sphere in which he or she is the very person who is being prepared for the performance of his or her cultural responsibilities, his or her own particular office? The one who holds a particular office in the sphere of education must have *qualifications* for leading others. How can a student be regarded as having qualifications for leading in that very sphere in which he or she is being led? The one who holds office in an educational institution must have an *appoint-*

ment to office. How can we speak of a student as being under appointment? The one holding a particular office in education is given *authority,* which places him over others. How can we speak of students as being in authority over others? It seems to us that we must answer these questions by acknowledging that the student *does not have office,* qualifications, appointment, and authority in the educational sphere or in an educational institution.[12]

This does not mean that students should not be allowed to engage in investigation of the creation order, or express themselves, or pass judgment upon their education and evaluate various aspects of the school of which they are a part. Students should not only be allowed, but also be encouraged to do such things. But it should be clearly understood that, while they are students, they do these things *under authority.* What we have said does not mean either that students may not be involved in discussion or making decisions concerning certain campus matters. Especially in higher education (on the college level) students may be allowed participation in discussion and decision-making. But they should be allowed to do so only to the extent determined by the institution, for, to the extent that they are involved in discussing and making decisions relative to campus life, they are under authority, and the authority they do exercise is *delegated* only for certain specific and predetermined purposes.

This may appear to be very authoritarian and designed to establish a structure in which a domineering board, administration, and faculty are capable of and encouraged to squelch all student incentive and motivation. Such indeed would be the case if we were describing a secular, cut-off-from- and opposed-to-God situation. If we were describing a secular institution, we probably would be forced to consider a concept of shared authority in order to seek a compromise whereby we could avoid domination by the college administration on the one hand and total revolution by the student body on the other hand. (In our opinion much of the discussion concerning student authority and student power has been in terms of problems and solutions taken over from the secular situation and perspective.) But we have been speaking of the *biblical* concept of office and authority and its expression in *Christian* higher education. We have been speaking of office and authority as they come from God and are exercised according to his will and for the benefit of the members of Christ's body. If we, as the redeemed of the Lord, live and work according to that biblical perspective, we will see the formation of a truly Christian academic *community* in which the administration and faculty need not be "troubled" by a rebellious student body and in which the student body need not feel "threatened" or "hindered" by an authoritarian administration and faculty. In such a community every member will know the meaning of living and working in humble obedience to the Lord.

Notes

1. Hendrik Van Riessen, *The Society of the Future* (Philadelphia: Presbyterian and Reformed, 1952), 70.

2. H. H. Meeter, *Calvinism* (Grand Rapids, MI: Zondervan, n.d.), 159.

3. Van Riessen, *Society of the Future*, 70.

4. Ibid., 71.

5. Ibid.

6. Ibid.

7. A. A. Hoekema et al., "Report 40: Ecclesiastical Office and Ordination," *1972 Agenda for Synod of the Christian Reformed Church* (Grand Rapids, MI: Board of Publications of the Christian Reformed Church, 1972), 299.

8. Ibid.

9. Publication Committee of the Christian Reformed Church, ed., "Heidelberg Catechism," in *Doctrinal Standards of the Christian Reformed Church* (Grand Rapids, MI: Publication Committee of the Christian Reformed Church, 1959), 27.

10. Van Riessen, *Society of the Future*, 79.

11. Ibid.

12. This article was written while serving, along with others, as a member of Dordt's Purposes Committee—the work of which eventually resulted in *The Educational Task of Dordt College* (first adopted in 1979). The position that "the student does not have office" was that of a majority of the committee working on this question, as well as of myself. The position found in *The Educational Task of Dordt College* is the result of further reflection and a more developed understanding of the educational community and the various offices that function within that community. *The Educational Task of Dordt College* does acknowledge the office of student (see pages 6 and 7 above).

A Writing Exercise in Identity:
Abraham Kuyper's *To Be Near Unto God*

James Calvin Schaap[*]

....

I'm not a fatalist or a determinist, and I don't hold much faith in those who argue that our identities are entirely prescribed by the DNA particles that make our fingerprints unique or determine the length of our toes. Even so, about some bits and pieces of who we are, I'm afraid it's true that we don't have much choice.

I am, for better or for worse, someone shaped by the work of a portly historical figure named Abraham Kuyper, a former Prime Minister of the

[*] Dr. Schaap is a Dordt graduate (1970), Professor of English (since 1976), and a well-known Christian writer. He has a M.A. from Arizona State University and a Ph.D. from the University of Wisconsin at Milwaukee. He has written devotional books for teens, like *Every Bit of Who I Am;* a history of the Christian Reformed Church in North America, *Our Family Album;* the World War II memoir of Diet Eman, a Dutch Resistance fighter, *Things We Couldn't Say;* collections of short stories like *The Privacy of Storm, Paternity, Thirty-Five and Counting,* and *Fifty-Five and Counting;* and the novels *Home Free, The Secrets of Barneveld Calvary, Romey's Place,* and *Touches the Sky.* This text is a slight revision of the introduction to his rewrite of Kuyper's *To Be Near Unto God* (Grand Rapids, MI: Eerdmans, 1997).

Netherlands, a noted clergyman and theologian, and a prolific journalist, about whom I know very little more than I've just related.

I've never studied Kuyper's theology, read his political treatises, or paged through much more than a chapter or two from his biography. What I know is he was and still is central to the ethos in which I was raised, an ethos I continue to work within, the precious baggage of a diminutive American immigrant subculture, the Dutch Reformed, a group of folks long ago forgotten by its contemporary European siblings and slowly now disappearing, as all ethnic subcultures do, within the stew constantly brewing in the American melting pot.

This man Kuyper is an intimate of mine, even though I never met him. Somewhere inside me he holds sway with much more authority than, say, President Teddy Roosevelt, who would have been his contemporary and was himself Dutch-American. Kuyper's mind—his ideas and vision—are a part of me that has always been there, even when I didn't know he was or they were.

All of which is not to say that Abraham Kuyper doesn't haunt me. He's not a bad memory or anything close to a nightmare image. He is very much a part of my ancestral heritage, a heritage I respect and appreciate, warts and all. I believe that something good of what I am I can attribute to Abraham Kuyper, and do so thankfully.

That I even know the man's name may well be a legacy of the quest for identity most North Americans mount at some time in their lives—Jewish, Irish Catholic, Russian Orthodox, Swedish Baptist, Norwegian Lutheran. My ethno-religious roots are deeply planted in nineteenth-century Dutch Calvinism, a legacy I didn't choose any more than I chose my parents or the place of my birth.

Rootedness suggests values, and my own immigrant great-grandparents stuck with old country traditions via an adherence defined and bolstered by faith. Some anthropologists, I'm sure, would likely assert that my ancestors' holding to the old ways was a means by which they could maintain an identity in the nineteenth-century ethnic polyglot that was America. Maybe that's true.

But I am convinced that part of the vision of things they held to, for whatever reason, was inscribed in their souls by this man, Abraham Kuyper; so he was part of what they passed along to me, even though, growing up, I never heard the man's name in my own family home. In that way, I was "Kuyperian," long before I knew of the man.

For me, therefore, getting to know Abraham Kuyper is an exercise in getting to know myself. If the greatest knowledge, as Socrates maintained, is knowledge of self, then gaining an understanding of what we've come from is no mean accomplishment. The Nobel Prize-winning Nebraska novelist Willa Cather maintained that every major theme a writer would or even could consider in his or her work grew from questions planted within the soul long before adulthood. If that's true, then for me, knowing something about Kuyper helps me visualize more clearly what I've been considering for nearly most of my life and two decades of writing—and why and even how.

What I'm suggesting by all of this is why I wrote a book titled *Near Unto God.* There's a history in my interest in Kuyper, and it's part of the story, part of that same Kuyper's legacy.

Several years ago, *The Banner,* the denominational magazine of the Christian Reformed Church in North America, asked several of its members to list books they love. Dr. Richard Mouw, President of Fuller Seminary in California, named *To Be Near Unto God* as his favorite nonfiction book, saying, "Kuyper is one of my heroes, and these meditations are a regular source of spiritual nourishment for me."

That recommendation sent me to our old oak bookcase, the one that holds what I have of my grandfather's library, as well as of that of his father-in-law, my great-grandfather. My grandfather was Rev. John C. Schaap, a preacher in the Christian Reformed Church; his wife, Nelle Hemkes Schaap, was the daughter of the Reverend Gerrit Klaas Hemkes, a professor a century ago at what became Calvin College and Seminary, Grand Rapids, Michigan.

From one of them—probably my grandfather—I inherited *To Be Near Unto God,* a volume of Kuyper's meditations growing close to a century old, in English translation by a Reverend John De Vries. It is an Eerdmans publication, 1918, the year both my father and mother were born.

The copy I own is tattered, a little brown book, small enough to fit in your hand, but thick as the Bible. It has many underlined and bracketed passages, and some of the pages look as if they've been folded back for quick and ready access. The binding is torn, but only a few pages are loose. It looks used, very much so.

However, even before I picked it out of the old books in our library, even before I read Mouw's recommendation, I knew something about that book. I knew it contained a more risky Abraham Kuyper than the crusading imminence my own immigrant tradition remembers him as. I remember hearing people say that the Kuyper of *To Be Near Unto God* was a highly "spiritual" Kuyper, someone whose religious enthusiasms made at least some of his twentieth-century disciples somewhat anxious, a man who was something of a mystic really, if you believed what he said and preached.

Let me stop here for a moment to explain something of the Kuyper legacy as I've come to know it, a legacy I actively pass along to my students, even today. Christianity bestows on its adherents a double identity: we are citizens of both this world *and* the next. That joint citizenship often creates an identity crisis, not to mention some confusion of purpose. We are, as recipients of grace, inheritors of a spiritual Kingdom, the world to come in eternity. "This world is not my home; I'm just a passin' through," claims the old hymn. Whenever eternal peace is compared with the turbulent listing of our lives on earth, placid heavenly waters seem especially inviting.

But as long as we live here on earth, we are citizens of this world—not simply heaven-gazers. To look only toward heaven means looking past the world God tells us, in John 3:16, he loved so breathtakingly much. Total investment in the life hereafter, some contemporary Kuyper followers might say, means shirking the responsibilities and joys of the world God lovingly sets us within.

What we live with is not so much a paradox as a pair of mutually exclusive demands on our time and interests. It's very simple for Christians to fall off the tightrope created by Christ's injunction about "in and not of": some fall toward what some believers still call "worldliness" on one side, while others fall into other-worldliness on the other. Balance is both difficult and demanding. Our job is to look to glory without overlooking His world. That's not easy.

What I've always believed about Kuyper is that he sensibly walked the line between our spiritual and earthly concerns. Even in his life, one can't miss the balance. He was *both* preacher and Prime Minister, *both* theologian and politician, *both* writer of meditations and social theorist. Those who knew his personal life better than I do may well call me a victim of his mythos, but the Kuyper who has given me a paradigm by which to see my own calling is a Kuyper who was, at once, both near unto God and near unto God's world.

In fact, I believe it was Kuyper's ability to balance the claims of a Christian's inherent double identity that, at least on this side of the Atlantic, made his name into an adjective I've used respectfully time and time again—Kuyperian—even though I had never read a word of his work. With that adjective, the institution where I teach often defines its mission, with equal doses of the respect and admiration we might give the word *Calvinistic.*

But I also knew that this little devotional book I pulled from the bookcase, *To Be Near Unto God,* would offer me an Abraham Kuyper who occasionally, well, embarrasses his followers, a Kuyper whose soliloquies tinker with a spirituality so akin to religious ecstasy that it brought furrows to the brows of the more stolid Dutch ancestral character. What made Kuyperians anxious about *To Be Near Unto God,* I knew, was the riskiness of Kuyper's spirituality. Quite simply stated, the book was potentially dangerous, not to his image but to his people, who might, on reading it, become so caught up in his quest for (what many came to call at the turn of the century) "spirituality," one's personal relationship to God, that they might renege on their commitment to the world. This Kuyper, I was told, was a bit scary.

So I had several reasons to read my grandfather's old John De Vries translation of Kuyper's devotional classic. First, Richard Mouw recommended it; I respect him. Second, that my own ancestors had read it faithfully was clear from its condition. The book would be a means by which I could know them, and myself, better. Third, some people considered the book, well, chancy; I've always liked controversial books. I started writing, in fact, after reading a novel by Frederic Manfred, a writer good Christian people out here in Siouxland said shouldn't be read.

And then there was this other reason: reading Kuyper was, after all, something of a duty for me. For years I'd called myself a Kuyperian, but never read a word the man wrote. I owed it to him. What's more, I owed it to myself. For that matter, I owed it to my students. It was simply time I got to know something, firsthand, about someone whose name and ideas I'd assumed somehow my own.

I started reading *To Be Near Unto God*, in English translation, with no thought of writing anything. I'd just finished writing a novel, and I thought my grandfather's book would make a good daily devotional. I started reading, knowing that what I was going to discover was something already vaguely within me. Call it self-discovery, sentimentality, or nostalgia. It was all of that.

I loved what I read. I found myself deeply engaged by a mind worth knowing well. I was impressed, not only with the range Kuyper must have had over both this life and the next, but also with the nature of the deep spirituality that drives the book. Our whole purpose here, the purpose of life, Kuyper would say, is, first and foremost, *To Be Near Unto God*.

I read six or seven meditations and decided to keep a journal. I've never had a particularly sticky mind; if I want to remember what I read, I take notes, either in the margins or in a notebook. So I started writing notes to myself, pulling what I thought was the essential Kuyper from sentences translated in a prose style probably perfectly preacher-ly at the turn of the century, but exhausting, even aggravating today. The Reverend John De Vries likely intended to make Kuyper sound like a turn-of-the-century learned Princeton divine. Reading that prose demanded, on its own, substantial pruning and cutting, even slashing, to get at the Kuyper within the stodgy style. Redoing sentences was something I had to do if I wanted to understand.

That process prompted me to think that it might be enjoyable to cut the meditations down to the heart of their strength. So I started editing some of the meditations as an exercise, a writer's aerobics in the early morning.

I'd done maybe a half dozen when I realized that Kuyper's meditations in *To Be Near Unto God* needed badly to be freed from prose as exaggerated as the wings on an old Chrysler. What I discovered, very quickly, is that what this man Kuyper has to say is simply too good to be petrified in a style that might be defined as "terminal."

That's how I came to write—or rewrite—*Near Unto God*. From beginning to end it was a wonderful experience.

What did I learn? A number of things. First, those who claim that inheritors of a Reformed or Calvinist worldview have no tradition of piety are, at best, uninformed. No one can read this book and come away believing such nonsense. Kuyper's spirituality is a witness, a century after the devotions were penned. I honestly wish that more people, more people in Kuyper's own tradition especially, would give the man a try. His meditations make almost anything in a Christian bookstore look paltry.

But I also learned that Kuyper's expression of spirituality is a world away from contemporary public demonstrations of piousness—for him, to be near unto God is something private, quiet, and deep, what he calls so often the "hidden walk." From the outside, and in the pew, the countenance Kuyper wants to create may very well appear cold. It may seem to lack drama or a heavy bass, but it isn't at all without animation. His soul is warm with the Spirit. Read him yourself. You'll see.

Some things that I learned by reading and rewriting didn't surprise me. Look at the way Kuyper uses science in, for instance, "Hearken unto Me." The man was not afraid of life, of technological change; his desire, seemingly, is to locate God Almighty in every inch of His creation. That, of course, is the way the mythos created him in my mind.

But I *was* surprised, I guess, to find him as tolerant as he is, exhorting his readers in several meditations to allow for individual differences in both coming to God and in expressing their individual faith (see "O God, my God," for example). If the caricature of the Dutch Reformed is something cut from glass, and not stained glass, then we see little of that here. He is rarely judgmental and never quick to dismiss. What impressed me about his toleration was his understanding of human nature. At one point, he reminds his readers how easy it is for us, for believers, to want to prescribe the means by which others should find the Lord because that way was so rich for us. What's almost shocking about Kuyper is his understanding of the human character.

For me at least, the greatest discovered joy in reading a nearly century-old book of meditations comes from Kuyper's vivid exposition of the attributes of God. Let me try to explain. Preaching, like writing meditations, becomes tinny and moralistic when the word *should* is too liberally sprinkled about. I believe an old rule of thumb for writing extends to preaching as well: "show, don't tell." Convincing writing always pictures, never points— always demonstrates, never demands. Kuyper describes God and His love so thoughtfully and so caringly that our response to what he says is not so much directed as it is discipled by the reality he pictures. Kuyper doesn't need to *tell* us how to be, because in so many of the meditations, he *shows* us, beautifully, by describing God with intimate respect and awe. I don't know of other writers who do that as well as Kuyper.

Read him for yourself. Trust me, there are much better reasons than nostalgia to read Kuyper's meditations, greater goals than a search for identity.

The best motivation for reading Kuyper's soul-stirring devotionals is simply this: *To Be Near Unto God.* The book may well be 100 years old, but aside from a few paragraphs about *thee* and *thou* and a reference to outdoor plumbing, very little needed to be cut. This book is, to me, a devotional classic.

And I know this about the man, too—Kuyper honored ordinary people. That's evident in the book. The De Vries translation may well have been wonderful for my grandfather, but a contemporary lay reader will find much of the strength made almost inaccessible by the stiff prose style. In my rewrite I tried to condense the essential Kuyper for the ordinary people he respected. This is partially conjecture and a good deal of wishful thinking, but something in me says that were Kuyper alive today, he'd approve of this abridgment.

Finally, a story I've waited too long to tell. Dr. Henrietta Ten Harmsel, emeritus professor of English at Calvin College, told me that when her father was dying, she used to read to him, daily, passages from Abraham Kuyper in the Dutch language. Her father, Anton Ten Harmsel, lived and died a long way from Amsterdam, the Netherlands. He immigrated from Holland and came to the same region of North America where I now live, Iowa, a place most notable for corn and beans and hogs—and back then, in Ten Harmsel's time, immigrant farmers. Here in Iowa he farmed in a number of places, a devoted Christian and avid reader, who with his wife raised their children and led an active life in the community's church and school.

Dr. Ten Harmsel read her father his daily dose of Kuyper. But one day the literature professor in her plotted what she believed to be a healthy and notable diversion. Instead of *To Be Near Unto God,* she pulled out a John Donne sermon, a sermon on Peter's denial, which contains the repeated refrain, "Has the cock crowed for you?" She read this famous homily from the very famous Anglican preacher and poet.

When she was through, her father nodded his head, barely raising it from the pillow, then looked up at his daughter and said, in the Dutch language, "*Net zowat zo goed als* Aberaham Kuyper," which is to say, "Almost as good as Abraham Kuyper."

There's something in that story, just as there is in my grandfather's tattered copy of *To Be Near Unto God,* that makes me believe these Kuyper meditations are worth keeping fresh for another century of God's people, no matter what their particular brand of ethnic baggage. In a way, identity was what I was looking for, but a wholly different identity was what I found.

The Coinage of a Dordt Degree

Calvin Jongsma[*]

···

Introduction

Families and friends, faculty and staff, but especially graduates: Today is a special day for you, a day of new beginnings. Your graduation is a sign of God's love, extended from generation to generation.

You are graduating today with an Associate of Arts degree, a Bachelor of Arts degree, a Bachelor of Science degree, or a Master of Education degree. That's what I'd like to talk about, not whether you really deserve these degrees but what these degrees certify and what makes their being conferred on you by Dordt College any different than if they came from DeVry University or Grinnell College or the University of Waterloo.

What is distinctive about a Dordt degree, and what can you do with it? You may be thinking that I am asking these questions a few years late. Maybe you and your parents did some "comparison shopping" among

[*] Dr. Jongsma is Professor of Mathematics at Dordt College and was Chair of the General Education Committee from 1992–2002. He joined the faculty in 1982, after completing his Ph.D. at the University of Toronto. This article was the 2001 Dordt College commencement address by Dr. Jongsma. It was also published in *Pro Rege* in September 2003.

colleges before you came here, but now that you're ready to leave, it's too late to do anything about the kind of education you have received. Well, yes; but maybe you could think of this as an opportunity to reflect on what you've done and examine the details of your warranty. You've purchased an education—though like all big acquisitions, you may be paying it off for a while—and now you're ready to try it out and see how it works. What can you realistically expect from it?

Foci of Collegiate Education: Three Strands

You just heard the words "arts" and "science" when I mentioned the different degrees being awarded. Do these terms indicate a two-culture rift between the sciences and the humanities? Yes. More than that, they hint at two different ways of thinking about higher education that came to be joined in an uneven synthesis. But these aren't the only strands; there is also a third trend in higher education that has generated its own tension. We'll look at each of these three viewpoints in turn.

The oldest way of thinking about education goes back to the Greeks and Romans. They thought an educated person should study the liberal arts: these were the subjects that made one truly free, that liberated one from, and elevated one above, the work-a-day world. Three of these arts are now classified as humanities: grammar, rhetoric, and logical argumentation. The other four arts were mathematical fields: number theory, geometry, music, and astronomy.

In the Middle Ages and the Renaissance, mathematics received the short end of the stick, and a liberal-arts education came to be associated primarily with the study of classical literature. By studying writings from a golden era, students would absorb classical ideals and would have their maturing characters shaped and nurtured to make them virtuous. A liberal-arts education was backward-looking; it attempted to take the best that past civilizations had to offer in order to prepare students for their civic respon-sibility. A Christianized version of this approach, which combined biblical faith with pagan wisdom, was adopted by Oxford University in the late Middle Ages and by Harvard College in the early modern period. A liberal-arts education focused on civilizing the whole person and aimed to produce Christian gentlemen, not teach facts about particular subjects or prepare people for careers. Teachers were mentors and generalists, not specialists trained in a certain field of study.

The collapse of the classical liberal-arts approach came in the nineteenth century with the rise of the research university in Germany. Eighteenth century Enlightenment thinkers had extended the Scientific Revolution of the seventeenth century, and the result was felt in the educational arena after the French Revolution. The enormous success of mathematized physical science in understanding the clockwork-like structure of the world led many to emulate its scientific method as the way to pursue all truth. This approach was widespread: it was not restricted to just physics or natural science. Literature moved away from poetic flights of fancy to embrace plain speech and the essay, and dictionaries and grammars were written to standardize proper usage of language. Business enterprises began to use scientific analyses of all aspects of the production process to decrease costs and increase profits. Morality became a matter of maximizing utility, determined by calculating the greatest good for the greatest number. The scientific approach to knowing ourselves and the world thus became authoritative, supplanting both Scriptural revelation and classical modes of thought and models of behavior. The scientific research ideal was adopted in American schools such as the University of Michigan and Johns Hopkins University during the last half of the nineteenth century. The purpose of these schools was to develop and transmit specialized knowledge. Education now focused on subject matter, not students, and it was forward-looking, incorporating the latest discoveries. Students and professors were jointly responsible to acquire the truth about a field, using rigorous methodology. Instructors were now trained as specialists, and their first responsibility was to their academic profession, not their students, who come and go.

Older liberal-arts institutions also caved in to this new pressure, even schools that concentrated primarily on undergraduate education. A traditional liberal-arts core was retained, but now students attended college mainly to major in particular fields of study. Schools began to include a mixture of classical courses and progressive specialized studies. Those who favored the liberal-arts approach criticized the new trend for leading to fragmented and overspecialized knowledge, but there was no holding back the tide. In fact, what had earlier been a fairly holistic liberal-arts curriculum now became another set of subjects for students to take. Literature, history, and philosophy became specialized fields of study alongside of mathematics, biology, and economics, each with its own method of inquiry. In this way, the old liberal-arts approach to education was incorporated into and co-opted by the new research model, even though the resulting synthesis came to be known as a liberal-arts approach because it favored developing a well-rounded education rather than specializing in one area. We'll call this synthesis the *liberal-arts-and-science approach* to distinguish it from the older approaches.

Academia also felt the impact of other societal developments. The third major trend in North American higher education, following the Industrial Revolution, promoted advanced vocational and professional training. At first, in the last half of the nineteenth century, separate land-grant institutions were established for pursuing agriculture and engineering. But a century later, these fields, along with other technical and vocational programs, entered mainstream post-secondary education. In the 1960s and '70s, in order to compete with technical schools and community colleges for a shrinking pool of post-war baby boomers, colleges and universities began to add vocational programs in areas like business, engineering, and social work. Prior to this period, the only full-fledged professional program had been the teacher education program; now such programs began to swell and attract students away from traditional majors.

Vocational programs thus presented a thorny challenge for academic institutions. These programs were needed to attract more students so as to keep colleges afloat, but they also threatened to change the character of the institution. Whatever the differences between the liberal-arts and scientific approaches to higher education, they agreed on the theoretical nature of education. Instruction kept daily life at arm's length, adopting a rather general and disinterested study of its subject matter without much concern for practicalities. But this approach was diametrically opposed to the thrust of vocational training, which focused on applied skills and techniques. So if a college was going to add vocational programs, how could it do so without damaging the essential nature of the enterprise?

That the place of vocational training remains a central polarizing issue today is clear from how *U.S. News* ranks colleges and universities. Undergraduate institutions are classified either as liberal-arts schools or general schools: not liberal arts in the original sense but according to a looser definition of the term. A liberal-arts course is now any course not intended for specific vocational training. A college is considered a liberal-arts institution if at least half of its graduates obtain degrees in nonvocational fields of study. In other words, a school has to be predominantly a liberal-arts-and-science school in order to call itself liberal arts.

Education at Dordt College:
Beyond Traditional Dilemmas and Toward a New Model

So how does Dordt fit into this story? When we try to capture who we are with a short phrase, we usually say, "We're a Christian liberal-arts college." By this statement we mean that Dordt offers a broad, well-rounded education, that we don't allow students to take too many specialized courses in a major, and that we are not narrowly concentrated on vocational studies. All of this is quite true, but using the term "liberal arts" in this way is a bit misleading and fails to recognize the history and central mission of the college. Even by current definitions, Dordt is not a liberal-arts institution and hasn't been for some time. Count up the numbers: roughly three-quarters of current graduates were in a professional or vocational program. Notwithstanding this fact, Dordt is also not a vocational school.

So just what is Dordt, then? What type of degrees does it confer? Let me sketch a few historical moments in Dordt's development before I try to answer these questions. Dordt began in the mid-1950s as a liberal-arts-and-science junior college for training teachers, patterning itself largely on

Calvin College. From the beginning, its founders wanted a school that stood in the tradition of Reformed Kuyperian thinking, which emphasized the Lordship of Christ over all of creation and the need for Christians to transform culture. However, not much independent thought was given at the time to the contours of the curriculum: it was accepted as a given.

As Dordt moved to become a four-year college in the early 1960s, it adopted a skeletal *Statement of Purpose,* which spelled out some basic principles to guide its development. A more expanded formulation called *Scripturally Oriented Higher Education* was written toward the end of that decade. The purpose of academic study was to prepare students for Kingdom citizenship in all spheres of life. Now higher education was described primarily in terms of transmitting scientific insight, using a broad notion of science that included any specialized area of thought. This description fit quite well with the traditional liberal-arts-and-science viewpoint.

In the late 1960s and early '70s, Dordt experienced major turmoil over the nature of its Reformed perspective and the future direction of the college. In resolving the crisis in the mid-1970s, the Dordt Board reaffirmed the basic outlook taken in *Scripturally Oriented Higher Education* but asked that the outlook be clarified and refined. This clarification resulted in the document *The Educational Task of Dordt College,* which was approved in 1979.

The *Educational Task* document did more than reformulate the earlier statement; it tackled the deeper issue of the character of a Dordt College education. Similar to what had happened elsewhere, a number of vocational programs had been added to Dordt's curriculum during the late 1960s and '70s, so the authors of the *Educational Task* felt that they needed to give a rationale for the range of subjects the college was beginning to offer. Rather than side with the liberal-arts-and-science approach or shift toward vocational training, *Educational Task* advocated taking a new approach grounded in the concept of biblical wisdom or serviceable insight. Students should experience their education in the biblical terms of hearing and doing the Word of the Lord, not in the Greek categories of learning abstract theories (thinking) and applying them to practical affairs (doing).

Knowledge, according to this biblical viewpoint, is not to be pursued for its own sake or in order to get a job but to be of service to the people of God in all aspects of their daily walk. Dordt College should develop and transmit insight, but insight that leads to wise and committed action by God's children as they fulfill their several callings. Serviceable insight is thus multidimensional. It includes practical insight, such as that provided in methods courses or engineering labs, but it also covers insights generated by biblical studies, historical analysis, poetry writing, theories of psychology, chemical research, mathematical modeling—anything that helps us understand our place in God's world and prepares us with the knowledge, skill, and motivation needed to do the will of the Lord. Serviceable insight should be the focus of career training, but it should also prepare students to take up family, church, civic, and cultural responsibilities.

The concept of serviceable insight was put forward as a way to transcend the age-old debates between liberal arts, scientific research, and vocational training. Both the theoretical emphasis of the liberal-arts-and-science approach and the narrow pragmatic emphasis of the vocational approach were rejected in favor of an approach that would balance theory and practice within a different context. But if serviceable insight was to become more than a slogan, it needed to permeate the curriculum. Serviceable insight ought to be the concern of each course, but should it also affect the overall structure of the curriculum? Should a Dordt education consist of specialized departmental majors and vocational programs alongside a core of distribution requirements to round out the curriculum? Or is there a way to organize the curriculum that would better translate the thrust of serviceable insight and achieve the desired result? These sorts of questions shaped the General Education Committee's agenda as it began its work in the early 1990s. The document *Educational Framework of Dordt College* attempted to develop a conceptual framework for the curriculum in line with the new approach.

As we debated curricular goals and student outcomes, we found it helpful to think in terms of four curricular coordinates: *religious orientation, creational structure, creational development,* and *contemporary response.* The final coordinate— contemporary response—connects most closely to the outcome sought by serviceable insight. We want to become responsive Kingdom citizens, to use our insights in the service of God, our neighbors, and the creation around us; we want to understand contemporary society and the environment in which we live. This goal in turn presupposes an understanding of who we are in the depths of our being (*religious orientation*), the nature of the reality we're dealing with (*creational structure*), and how things came to be the way they are now, both for good and ill (*creational development*). A curriculum that pays sufficient attention to these four coordinates, fleshed out in a number of curricular goals, should help faculty and students develop genuinely serviceable insight. In so doing, it would provide further substance to a Reformed Christian alternative in collegiate education.

We could have reacted to the different viewpoints on the nature of higher education in a more eclectic fashion, for Dordt shares features with all three approaches. We could have said that we would use liberal-arts courses to develop character and religious perspective; that majors would provide specialized theoretical knowledge about different aspects of creation; and that vocational programs could give career training for those who want it. However, this tack ignores the fundamental incompatibility of the three approaches in their views of knowledge and work, leaves the religious motives behind each trend unchallenged, and denies the integral character of reality and our experience of it. We cannot relegate Christian perspective to theology courses; religious orientation makes itself apparent in every field of study from mathematics to ethics. Nor can we ignore historical development while we study the physical interconnection of forces or learn about managing a business. Christian engineers and computer scientists need to know more than mathematical algorithms, scientific data, and design procedures; they need to demonstrate care for those they serve and be committed to stewardship and the appropriate use of technology. On the other hand, doctors need more than good people-skills and a pious demeanor; I want my surgeon to have a good grounding in anatomy and be skilled with the scalpel. As each part of the curriculum, then, must strive to produce full-orbed serviceable insight, each should focus in its own way on religious orientation, creational structure, creational development, and contemporary response.

In the last few years, Dordt has begun a thorough and systematic review of all majors and programs. The extra administrative work makes faculty grumble, but it also gives us an opportunity to reflect more deeply on what we do and how we might improve it. Program review and student assessment activities give us opportunities to analyze whether our courses and programs are organized to help students catch a Kingdom vision. The official categories adopted by the secular press may not recognize the kind of college we aim to be, but Dordt wants to be known as a serviceable insight institute.

Conclusion

You graduates may have come here two or four years ago to get a satisfying and well-paying job, but that's not what Dordt's about. You may have come here to get the background you need to do graduate research in a specialized area that you love studying, but that's not what Dordt's about, either. You may have come here to become a more well-rounded person or develop your personality through friendship and study, but that's still not what Dordt's about. Yes, we hope many of you enter a career that pays an adequate wage and that gives you personal fulfillment, and we hope that we've laid the groundwork for doing more intense specialized research, and we want you to develop friendships and explore the many facets of God's creation so that you stretch your range of interests and abilities and attitudes. But all of this is secondary. We want you first to seek the Kingdom of God and his righteousness, to do his will as you glorify him and serve your neighbors. We want you to stand up against evil and offer hope to a corrupt generation and a lost world. We want you to be Christ's hands and feet as you strive to reconcile all things to him.

Spending yourself in this way requires the currency of Dordt's education: multifaceted, biblically grounded insight embodied in service. You must know whose you are, you must be at home in God's world and able to

recognize forces of deformation, and you must know what time it is historically as you respond in love to the culture around you with the good news.

Graduates of Dordt College, it is our wish as faculty and staff, families
and friends, that God will richly bless you and give you joy in your work as
you leave here to join his people around the world in obedient service,
working in his Kingdom and for his sake. We give you our sincerest con-
gratulations!

Learning to Teach from within a Christian Perspective

John H. Kok[*]

···..

Christians are called to obey and honor God in every area of life, within the church and beyond, for our world (creation) belongs entirely to him, the Creator. In doing so, we are called to use our gifts and talents with discernment in his service, as knowledgeable, competent, caring disciples of Jesus Christ. For those with academic ability, this call demands ways and means of higher education that acknowledge the fear of the Lord as the beginning of wisdom and that equip students for lifelong learning and leadership in service to the King of kings. As students gain insight into the diversity within creation and culture; into the interrelatedness of creation and culture; into God, his laws, and his norms for the same; and into their own personal abilities and interests in responding obediently to God where he has placed them, they too

---

[*] Dr. Kok is Professor of Philosophy and Dean for the Humanities. He received his Ph.D. from the Free University in Amsterdam and has been teaching at Dordt College since 1983. This paper was presented at the IAPCHE conference at Hilltop University in Mikar, Nigeria, in 1999. It was also published in *Pro Rege* in June 2003.

will celebrate the purpose and potential of Christian higher education as so much more than an inside track to a respectable life of social and material success. To achieve these ends, Christians in higher education will need to work at learning to teach from within a Christian perspective.

In this article I consider a few of the many facets involved in Christian higher education. I will refer to the social and natural sciences along the way, but my comments apply in most cases to all of the disciplines. First, I sketch the place of theoretical pursuit, in the various sciences and academic disciplines, within the context or framework defined by a Christian perspective, a biblical worldview. Then I turn to a number of observations and suggestions related to teaching within a Christian perspective. The last section touches on just a few factors that play a role in learning to teach from within a Christian perspective. Much of what follows is not, as such, my own but belongs to me as a benefit of ongoing discussions about learning to teach from within a Christian perspective, discussions in which I've been privileged to participate for some twenty years at Dordt College.

The Context Cut by a Biblical Worldview

A worldview may well be defined as one's comprehensive framework of basic beliefs about things, but our talk (confessed beliefs or cognitive claims) is one thing, and our walk (operative beliefs) is another and even more important thing. A lived worldview defines one's basic convictions; it defines what one is ready to live and die for. We know and live within the context cut by this perspective. And for Christians, Scripture ultimately defines the contours and framework of that perspective. In the light of Scripture, Christians boldly claim that God, his law, and the cosmos can all be grasped to the extent that these things are made known to us in Scriptural and creational revelation.

However, there is knowledge and there is knowledge. Most mathematicians know what complete induction is and how it can be applied to prove various theorems. Most children know what mud is and how it can be applied to various and sundry surfaces. Not only is the knowledge in each case different—the first is knowledge of something one can see only with the mind's eye, while the second is knowledge of something most people, at least once in their lives, actually get in their eyes—but the *kind* of knowing is in each case different. A mathematician's mathematical knowledge is a theoretical kind of knowing, whereas a mathematician's knowing to avoid getting mud in her eye is an everyday kind of knowing.

People's knowledge of parents, siblings, relatives, and neighbors, as well as of those animals, plants, and physical things with which they have had contact, to mention just a few examples, is an everyday kind of knowing. This nonscientific kind of knowing is the concrete, ordinary knowledge that everyone has. It is foundational for all other kinds of knowing. Like all knowledge, everyday knowledge is not something had instantly or from the start. It always comes as the result of human activity: through experiencing, listening, trusting, watching, thinking, learning—through coming to know. Perceiving, recollecting, and expecting are important contributing factors to this process.

Coming to know in an everyday sense can occur in the context of knowledge communicated by others or through personal investigation and discovery. It is true, however, that the truths we receive from those we trust do establish the "home base" from which we proceed when initiating the investigation of some point or problem.

Scientific, theory-laden knowing differs from nonscientific knowing in that the human activity that precedes scientific knowing proceeds methodically and is not primarily directed to concrete things or specific relations but to a defined (limited) field or domain. It is important to note that no matter how prominent scientific knowing has become, it never stands alone but is continually undergirded and propelled by the nonscientific knowing that chronologically and logically precedes it. Time and place are givens and were givens in the beginning. Human knowing presupposes and builds on more than it will ever know completely.

Knowledge of oneself (one's needs and wants), of other people, of parents, of spouse and children, of what spouse and children may expect of us, and of what one takes to be important in life constitutes what we may call the factual or existential starting point for all scientific, theoretic activity. This point of departure that we leave unquestioned, at least for the moment, does not dissipate; it remains presumed when one turns to theoretical matters and scientific questions.

Science, then, is one way of coming to know. It presupposes, builds on, and is borne by many kinds of nonscientific knowing. Science and theoretical pursuit help us see what otherwise might be impossible to see; they help us articulate what could be said on no other basis. Scientific knowledge, however, is not necessarily a better kind of knowing. Those who think that it is tend to put their hope and trust in science or in abstract universal truths. But even then, that faith, as all faith, is a matter of the heart, commitment, and conviction, not of scientific proof.

Christians know, not scientifically but in that concrete everyday kind of way, whom they are to believe, and they are persuaded that only he—the King of kings and Lord of lords—has the key to life. However, knowing that truth does not mean that academic pursuits are out of bounds for Christians. Believing in God, they know that he demands obedience to his ordinances in all of life, including academics, from art history to zoology.

Likewise, science involves someone (a person moved by love for or rebellion against God) thinking methodically (that is, investigating and analyzing correctly or incorrectly; distinguishing that which is different or failing to do so; and keeping in mind or forgetting the context in which these differences occur) about similarities, differences, and relationships, at least some of which are normed, within some limited field of investigation. When someone successfully analyzes a thing—distinguishes among its parts in its contexts—the result will be knowledge about that something, whatever it be. Whereas when one thinks poorly, the result will not be knowledge but error. In this process, what the person knows already remains foundational, particularly what she knows in her heart (or thinks she knows) to be the case. Scientific or theoretical thinking and knowledge are different from, but not better than, nonscientific knowledge, upon which they are built. In addition, whether or not our thinking results in knowledge or error, we can say that the things we are thinking about were either knowable or unknowable before we thought about them. There are, after all, some things about which we can know nothing—at least not on this side of the grave.

When we take "belief" in the active sense of "believing," it may be understood in its most basic and important sense as the acceptance of God's Word-revelation or of whatever else one takes to have the last word in life. In other words, faith or belief is not always Christian; usually it is the opposite. This opposition—of belief and unbelief—is of course very important, and Christian thinking can only gain by doing full justice to it. I would claim that as long as this belief has not been undermined by certain influences, every human being believes something, indeed, *believes in* something or someone. Believing, taken in that last sense—giving one's heart to someone or something—comes with being human. In other words, there are thousands of believers, and even more unbelievers; but there are no healthy, mature human beings who are *non*believers.

To take God at his word, or to reject that word, is ultimately what believing is all about. This believing is not simply cognitive, but it does comprise an element of knowing or erring. This knowing that comes with believing in someone or something is never a scientific, theoretical kind of knowing, at least certainly not in the first place. It is a nonscientific kind of knowing that lays the foundation, that defines the home base and the context within which we live and move and have our being before the face of God.

Academics may study these matters, realizing, of course, that they will at most gain only some limited insight into these things. Theoretical reflection can also ponder the place and task of heartfelt believing and the resultant beliefs. But you don't need an expert to tell you what "heart" refers to: your innermost being, your gut, the deepest center of your existence, what gets transformed when one no longer conforms to the patterns of this world, the wellspring of your thoughts, feelings, and actions. And, as even Marxists and capitalists are well aware, what lives in your heart is going to make a difference in what you say and do and don't do. Basic beliefs that are not just confessed but also operative will influence everything you do.

Knowledge of fundamental realities, commonly received through the nurture of parents and schooling, delineates the horizon of a person's life. So too, the *basic realities* of creation, sin, wrath and grace, and re-creation, once grasped and understood by the Bible-believer as major issues, exhibit an all-inclusive character. Concepts of these realities do so as well. These nonscientific, *circumscriptive concepts* help to define the framework within which the Christian lives and moves and understands his being. What we are talking about here, in other words, is *worldview*.

Worldview, of course, is more than a collection of concepts that rests on a gradually widening horizon, on repeatedly meeting other people, on expanding the extent of one's sense perception. Worldview is the vision that one gets from home or from the public square, the vision that one has assimilated for oneself with difficulty or has grown up with, so much so that one almost takes it for granted. It is not a scientific or theoretic conception but a view, a sense— of God, the world, life, human nature, one's neighbor, oneself—that has become second nature, as obvious as the nose on one's face and as ready at hand as an instinctual reaction. And, of course, it marks one for life (or death).

The vision that I am calling "worldview" as well as the beliefs and circumscriptive concepts it includes are all nonscientific in character. They are also prescientific, not only in the sense of being prior to (and not dissipating during) theoretic investigation, but also in the sense of determining the basic contours of the presupposed foundation from which the theoretician proceeds and to which she returns. What one finds through scientific, theoretic, possibly highly abstract research fits in there eventually.

A Christian (theoretic, discipline-focused) conception, then, not only will contain thoughts concerning the nature and the task of basic beliefs, but must also completely agree or comport well with what we know to be the case in the light of Scripture. In other words, a Christian's disciplined conception ought to be Scriptural or, if one prefers, in line with Scripture.

Therefore, what one considers tenable and reliable ultimately depends on the lived worldview or perspective that defines one's basic convictions that mark the meaning coherence, the frame of reference, of everyday living. "Perspective" here does not mean, first of all, *what* one, standing in a particular historic tradition and situation, sees, accepts, expects, and understands but rather *that which predisposes* one to see what one sees, to understand what one understands, to choose what one chooses. One's perspective is that which discloses one's situation and that which directs one and makes one take sides in a situation. One stands within a perspective as within a light beam; that perspective illuminates one's existence, one's situation, and one's world and thus enables one's sense of everyday orientation. As one matures, the framework that this perspective provides becomes intuitively immediate, second-nature if you will—something that we have learned over the course of time and that now, so often, "goes without saying."

We have come to know the difference between a house and home; we know when a storm is brewing; we know how revolting sour milk tastes. The meaning of these things as well as our understanding of them lies interwoven in a rich fabric of reference to still other things. For example, one probably cannot understand what a nail is without knowing what a hammer is. The things we experience every day stand in internal relation to each other—an experience of things rooted in our sense of authority, respect, and allegiance; in the regularities and expectations operative in our life; in our past; and in our vision for the morrow. But they are also rooted in how we came to know these things. Our responsibility is to teach all of these: the what and the how and the why.

Teaching . . . from within a Christian Perspective

Teaching our students requires that we *lead* them into ("intro-duction") places and ways unknown or less known to them when they begin; that we *guide* them through what more often than not seems initially to be a maze of theories, concepts, facts, and procedures; and that we do this all the while with an eye to *enabling* them to walk these paths confidently on their own—in community—in the future.[1]

Along the way a number of things need to be tended to. I will mention two: the need for what Dordt College calls "curricular coordinates" and the importance of exposing the nature of methodic analysis and theory formation.

Curricular Coordinates

An institution of Christian higher education that holds academic excellence and biblical faith dear will want to equip its graduates to deal insightfully with issues, theories, and problems; with past alternatives and new movements and initiatives in one's field; and with a depth and breadth of well-versed understanding that is also informed by, and in line with, Scripture. To that end, a planned course of studies—a curriculum defined by principle—is crucial. The curricula will obviously differ per discipline, yet given the common confession that our world belongs to God, it will allow similarities to persist. Whether one teaches physics or theology, the institution's "shared coordinates" will be evident. At Dordt College, for example, we try to make transparent in each of the disciplines the shared coordinates of "religious orientation," "creational structure," "creational development," and "contemporary response."[2] These should also be evident in the general education program, such that we are wont to say the following of all our graduates:

• They will recognize that everyone, in whatever area of life, career, or occupation, holds dearly to someone or something, to some power or presence, and that whether that allegiance be to fame, fortune, flag, family, money, might, mutiny, the King of kings, the dialectic of history, or whatever has the last word in one's life, it manifests itself in one's everyday as well as academic sense of place, purpose, prognosis, and posterity. But more important, when it comes to *what has the last word* in their lives, graduates will "recognize the guiding role of the Bible in a life of Christian discipleship. They should be familiar with the main themes and teachings of the Bible,"[3] understand the practice as well as the confessions of the Christian faith and a biblical worldview, and evidence a commitment to living a life of Christian discipleship.

• They will realize that almost everyone is familiar with and counts on an abundance of regularities in life, nature, and society and that many academic disciplines study these recurrent themes and patterns, for most acknowledge that at least some things hang together and few deny the order and structure that are present in their world. Of course, not everyone agrees that norms are adequately grounded in consensus or the common weal or that laws of nature are purely emergent or simply constructs of the mind: concerning the *regularities* of and *criteria* for the world as it turns, graduates will have an eye for and appreciate creation in all its diversity and interrelatedness as brought into being by God the Father, as preserved by the power of his Spirit, and as called to an obedience exemplified in his love for the world in Jesus Christ. They will be "competent in one or more specialized fields of inquiry"[4] and be open and able to integrate ideas, theories, and procedures from a variety of disciplines.

• Most people readily acknowledge that change happens, that things unfold and become more or less complex or diverse, but to what end? Some people deny that there is an end. Graduates, assessing and dealing with the *reality of change,* will stand ready to articulate their hope for the future and will understand how today's world has unfolded historically. They will "critically evaluate the formative processes and religious spirits"[5] that have shaped diverse cultures as well as present conundrums, will appreciate both "their God-given responsibility to unfold the potential of creation in stewardly ways" as well as the "interconnected global nature of contemporary life,"[6] and will be able to analyze influences formative today with an eye to contributing to healing and integrity within their particular discipline or vocation as well as in more common areas of life.

• Every person responds to the time, place, and calling that defines and yet lies open before him or her. No one can avoid the question, "What should we do now?" However, given the times and *contemporary challenges* facing them, graduates of a Christian college should learn "to exhibit proper care and respect for everything God created";[7] "be sensitive to the impact of sin and idolatry in their own lives, in…society, and in the world";[8] stand equipped "to discern, evaluate, and [when necessary] challenge the prevailing spirits of our age in the light of God's Word"[9] and informed by a biblical perspective on things; and be able "to maintain a balanced, wholesome lifestyle,"[10] while continuing to develop, share, and apply fruitful insights in diverse communities long after graduation.

A well-situated curriculum, as well as its delivery, involves so much more than covering the material. Course content usually changes with time and often differs with the instructor. What should remain the same is that those who leave the classroom continue to be equipped to tell the difference between what is true, correct, or just accurate. Not everything people grasp and hold for certain is *true*—often it does not promote Christ's lordship of the world (rather than the devil's) and often it does not please Christ. Some of the cognitive claims that are false in that regard can nonetheless be *correct*—the knowledge gained is correct if and when the relative states of affairs that are known are kept relative, limited, and in their proper place in relation to the rest of the world. However, even those whose theories are incorrect can ascertain or highlight things that are *accurate,* for their knowing, too, can agree with the structural laws (which need to be more-or-less correctly articulated by one's community in the light of the truth) concerning a particular feature or function of a knowable object.

The reality of religious roots, of ordered fields of learning, and of change and constancy over time, underscored with an eye to a sound contemporary response that is in line with Scripture, should constitute the framework for both a general education program and departmental majors. When that framework happens, graduates committed to Christ and his Kingdom will be readied for lifelong learning and servant leadership under his banner of truth and grace.

The Limits and Logic of Doing Science

There is not a social scientist who lacks the fabric of everyday knowing; none come or go without a worldview. Having a comprehensive framework of basic beliefs about things simply comes with being (a mature, healthy) human. However, science and theory, as we know these, do have peculiar ways of looking at things and relationships. The theoretical perspective is by definition a limited one, focusing on just one or two facets of the fullness of reality. When we put on the spectacles of methodic, scientific, disciplined analysis, a frame of reference different from that of nonscientific, everyday experience is introduced. Every science abstracts from the full fabric of everyday experience, from the coherence of meaning that is a part of everyone's life, bracketing out various properties and relations in order to focus on one aspect or dimension of things. The result is a reality different from everyday reality. Obviously, this difference does not mean that one should downplay or disregard science, for what it can uncover is awesome. But we shouldn't forget what is more important—therapists do get divorced and cancer shows up in doctors too.

Priorities and the answer to the question "What is real?" depend on the framework within which the phenomena are viewed. In most cases, what we aim to study scientifically is a complex of factors, some of which are more or less independent of, or logically distinct from, each other. For example, in the case of phenology, climate is one thing and the migration of birds is another; in phonetics, the position of the tongue with respect to the oral cavity is one thing and the sounds produced another; in sociology, the suicide rate is one thing and the degree of social integration another. Distinguishing what is different within its limited field of investigation, science seeks to grasp universal, enduring, or resolute relations that are obtained within the field. In scientific analysis, many things are left out of the picture for the moment. Many internal relations are either ignored or externalized, coaxed to speak for themselves through a process of theoretical distillation, statistical analysis, or experimentation in the laboratory, all other conditions remaining the same. The sum of the parts of the scientific experience, which aims at a coherent, communicable theory, is thus no longer identical to or congruent with the whole as it presents itself in the original (pre-scientific, everyday) experience of individuality and communality, of similarities and differences, of diversity, regularity, and change. It is *more* in that it can deepen our understanding or enhance our ability to describe something; at the same time it is *less* in that it is the compilation of a limited number of dimensions and not the whole, where it is seldom the case that only one or two things change and everything else remains the same.

For example, one significant ingredient in the natural sciences' peculiar way of looking at things is that it usually assumes the principle of uniformity. In doing so, it presupposes coherence in accordance with a universal law, namely, that like causes have like effects. In other words, adopting this principle predisposes one to look at phenomena from the point of view of causality. And, of course, when one says that every object has a cause, one is indicating what one really means by an "object." Things that do not fit or cannot be made to fit into a causal nexus are then usually dismissed as scientifically insignificant or, given the dictates of methodological naturalism, ruled out of order and are all too often forgotten.

I am not suggesting that we may not avail ourselves of scientific abstraction. My point is rather that we must remain aware of (and repeatedly show our students) what this artificial way of dealing with reality implies. All of the sciences can be said, in their way, to be mapping created or encultured reality. What their "maps" look like will be similar in some ways, for they are all human artifacts on the one hand and records of an investigation of the same earthly creation on the other. But they will also be different, in part because different disciplines focus on different aspects or fields within that same earthly creation, in part because some cartographers consider their map or their aspect of reality to be the only important one, and in part because some cartographers will confuse the reality of their map with the reality it attempts to map.

Modern technology, for example, as it imposes the "uniformity of nature" onto society in a concerted effort to meet real and perceived needs, all too often fails to critically engage these kinds of foundational questions. For example, while all theoretical statements of causal/correlative "necessity" ("If x, then y") *can* usually be translated into technological imperatives ("Do x in order to bring y about"), fewer than ought question the validity of such a translation. When "the average" or the majority begins to define the "norm" for Christians, we have lost sight of God's standard.

Likewise, social scientists who do their work well will not only be aware of and follow the methodological rules that hold for their science in general, but also inquire into the presuppositions and conditions that underlie their discipline and its methods. A good social scientist will inquire into what the methods used in her discipline presuppose with regard to the reality being investigated (that is, into their implicit ontology and veiled value system). Students may be taught first about scientific practice, but they will never know their discipline well until they understand what their methodic analysis is actually uncovering and what it also leaves out of the picture.

Learning to Teach

Learning to teach has many dimensions. Knowing one's stuff as well as one's students is absolutely crucial: mastering the former and being open to the latter. You don't have to be your students' buddy, but do try to connect with them, poll them, talk to them. Ask them about themselves and about their aspirations. As a teacher you are responsible for knowing and communicating your material well, but as a teacher you are there, ultimately, not for yourself but for them, to facilitate their learning and their learning how to learn. You should work with them, pray for them, make time for them outside of the classroom, have them over to your home. This kind of intimacy is sometimes hard to make time for, but it is a great encouragement and inspiration for those given to your care.

Another important way to connect with and engage one's students is to share with them one's vision and sense of vocation. Don't hesitate to share with your students what inspires and excites you, also and even primarily within your field of expertise. One thing that I have found particularly helpful in this regard is to share the journey I've taken along the *thetical-critical* pathway, trying to make plain to them what I stand for, my position positively articulated, as well as my attempts to listen to, evaluate, and learn from what others have to say. This method, which I describe a bit below, has kept me, I like to think, from becoming self-satisfied or complacent and yet has given me a sense of theoretical place and home, such that I have something to profess as professor.

Rather than cursing the darkness, I think Christians should seek with the power and insight of the Holy Spirit to light a candle. In other words, rather than defining one's position in terms of what one rejects, Christians should proceed *thetically*. (According to the *Oxford English Dictionary*, *thetical* means "Of the nature of or involving direct or positive statement; laid down or stated positively or absolutely."[11]) That is to say, Christians should approach the problems and questions they are confronted with from their own positively stated point of view. Christians should be uneasy, for example, about describing the methodological route of the social sciences as one that rides the line between positivism (i.e., we can know, quantify, and scientifically control all natural phenomena) and skepticism (i.e., we can know little or nothing with certainty). People who acknowledge that God is both sovereign and personal should not be satisfied with a standpoint described in terms of a conceptual mean somewhere in between the extremes of pantheism and deism. The first priority should be to work out a basic conception of man, society, and public justice in line with Scripture that affirms and articulates as clearly and succinctly as possible one's perspective on the matter in question. In other words, one should proceed boldly, articulating, clarifying, and honing the coherence of the comprehensive framework of basic beliefs that Christians hold dear.

This thetical procedure—dealing with situations and questions new and old from one's own (communal, Christian) point of view—presupposes an increasingly specific and consciously delineated basic conception such that one can say in confidence, "Here I stand." However, in confidently living out a biblically informed and religiously grounded framework, Christians should definitely avoid the temptation to pontificate: "This is the way I see it and, therefore, that's the way it is." Brazen oracular pronouncements help no one. A related disease is what some call "ethnocentrism": thinking that there is nothing more to the world than that which lies within one's own purview, with its well-entrenched beliefs, attitudes, standards, methods, and procedures. No, in addition to proceeding thetically, Christians also need to work critically.

That social scientists must analyze and evaluate the claims, data, theories, and theses that come their way is to state the obvious. So what I would have you consider is that for Christians to do a good job of proceeding critically in this first sense, they need to be nurtured in this attitude as Christians long before they become social scientists, lest they analyze and evaluate only some things and not others. Critical thinking is sorely needed within the broader Christian community. Even those committed to Christian day schools need to do a better job of leading, guiding, and enabling the next generation to get to know, question, analyze, size up, and re-evaluate with an eye to determining both the insights and shortcomings of

(a) the ethos that shapes the culture in which God calls us to live as his people; (b) what others, for example, what non-Christians, are actually saying and have said; (c) what those dearly beloved within the Christian tradition have said; and (d) what we ourselves communally or individually have held to date to be the case. Discernment is needed in our everyday experience as well as in our scientific work. If we don't know how to examine and test the spirits that seek to impact our lives from day to day, how will we ever be able to examine and test the spirits that permeate the more abstract realms of our existence?

Data, theories, and theses all arise within a context, usually as answers to questions. None of these are neutral; all come with "strings" attached. No one can even ask a question without making some assumptions. Any question takes for granted many things that remain, at least for the moment, unquestioned. In fact, when listening to other people's questions as well as to their answers, one must remember to have at least *some sense* of the unstated and unquestioned *presuppositions* that lie at the basis of those questions—some knowledge of what, for them, goes without saying. Our task is not to remove all such presuppositions but to listen for, test, and evaluate them (critically) in the course of our inquiries.

Some Christians I know have a hard time developing an anticipatory and open attitude toward everyday living and learning, let alone toward a life of scholarship. However, the advantages are obvious: we come to understand what is "other" than us but also to better understand ourselves. The reliability of one's experience and learning in the light of Scripture will nurture an orientation toward new experiences and challenges, helping us to acknowledge the possibility of learning from what is different and alien. Doing so will help us even more to grasp an understanding of what it means to be finite historical beings who are on the way, who must assume responsibility for our decisions and choices, and who also must always be ready to give account of the hope that lives within us, even while we methodically go about the work of doing social science. So, when possible, in your discipline, leave no stone unturned and model for your students the patience and persistence that turning over stones demands. And as they mature, involve them in the discussion of authentic questions—the ones you don't have clear or definitive answers on either—all the while making evident which are the nonnegotiables in your book and why.

How one responds to God and his promise-command to his earthly creatures affects everything one thinks and says and does. Values are not added but are part and parcel of being creatures. Obedience in these things requires a wisdom that is defined and informed by Scripture, self-critique, and lived conviction.

Only Scripture can help us keep creaturely diversity and relationships in proper perspective. Without his word, we wonder and wander in a world without God. In its light we must work together at distinguishing differences in their historical, cultural, social, economic, political, and ultimately religious context. We have to realize that science as prosthesis, a scoping device, making what is small large and bringing what is far away near, always gives a warp to reality. Because of this effect of science, scientists and theoreticians should, along the way, concern themselves with the foundations and history of their discipline. If you have not taken time to learn about these things, what will it take to have your students do so? A critical Christian scientist not only makes use of the optical apparatus that the discipline places at her disposal, but should also inspect the apparatus itself. She knows when to use it to enhance her vision, but she also knows when to lay it aside. What the academic pursuit sees must in turn always be evaluated in terms of the perspective of the whole.

This approach implies that Christian teachers and students must together seriously consider the claims bandied about, both pro and con, with an eye to a self-critical evaluation that is rooted in a positively articulated and biblically informed thetical stance. When that happens, the fruits of faithful teaching and learning will follow.

Notes

1. John Van Dyk, *The Craft of Christian Teaching* (Sioux Center, IA: Dordt College Press, 2000).

2. Dordt College, "The Educational Framework of Dordt College" (an institutional document, adopted by the Dordt College Faculty Assembly on 20 August 1993). See pages 17–24 in this volume.

3. Ibid., section III, A1, page 22.

4. Ibid., III, B4, page 23.

5. Ibid., III, C3, page 24.

6. Ibid., III, C2, page 24.

7. Ibid., III, B3, page 23.

8. Ibid., III, D3, page 24.

9. Ibid., III, A2, page 22.

10. Ibid., III, B3, page 23.

11. Oxford English Dictionary, s.v. "thetical."

Calling, Task, and Culture:
General Education 300

John C. Vander Stelt[*]

···..··

In 1988 Dordt College added a general-education course requirement for all juniors and seniors, a course known as General Education 300 (GEN 300): Calling, Task, and Culture.[1] The debates within the administration, in the curriculum committee, at several faculty meetings, and around coffee tables centered on a number of underlying principles concerning the nature of Christian higher education in general and Dordt College in particular. All of this debate was intimately connected with Dordt's ongoing search for an identity as a *bona fide* and Scripturally directed *Reformational* academic institution.

Participants in these dialogues (faculty members and administrative leaders) raised critical questions about the viability of Western classical *liberal arts* education. At the same time, we tried to avert the danger of turning the college into a kind of *vocational* school with a certain biblicistic bent.[2] We searched for a religiously integral, Scripturally dynamic, academically authentic, and culturally relevant way of educating young men and women. "How can we help

---

[*] Dr. Vander Stelt is Professor of Theology and Philosophy Emeritus. He taught at Dordt College from 1968 to 1999. His Th.D. is from the Free University in Amsterdam.

them," we asked, "deepen their awareness of the incredible privilege of living as God's children in our fascinating, yet deeply disturbed world in which God's Son lived as 'the way and the truth and the life' (John 14:6)?"

The larger context for this interest was Dordt's assumed, though not explicitly expressed, commitment to the tripod of proclaiming, articulating, and implementing the Gospel of God's Kingdom. What Christians confess in their faith life must come to concrete expression in all their daily activities. For Christians, moving from hearing the Good News to applying it in their daily lives and work is a demanding and often delicate endeavor. This difficulty is especially apparent in our highly differentiated and complex modern world. Not only elementary and secondary education, but also college and often even graduate education are now necessities for most people who desire to use their talents in some public and meaningful way. Higher education is no longer restricted to a privileged few.

Christian higher education is exciting, but it can at times also be daunting.[3] It calls for viewing all of created reality in light of the new hope and life that radiates from the open tomb. It requires exploring various areas of interest in order to discover there something of the nature and contours of God's revelation and to learn what our response to that revelation should be as his covenantal developers and caretakers. Christian colleges have often limited God's all-encompassing revelation to primarily his redemptive revelation in Jesus Christ. When no, or improper, recognition is given to God's creational revelation in what churches preach and academies teach, society and culture suffer the harmful consequences of such neglect.

An inadequate academic *articulation* of God's creational and redemptive revelation, *proclaimed* in Christian faith communities called "churches,"[4] adversely affects how the Christian community *implements* God's Kingdom mandates in their daily responsibilities. In light of this three-pronged duty to respond to God's revelation, I will first indicate something of the historical background of GEN 300, then take a closer look at the specific intent and content of GEN 300 by reflecting on the three terms in the carefully chosen title for this course, and finally conclude with some observations about the fundamental and all-pervasive Scriptural theme of Jubilee in GEN 300 and at Dordt College as a Christian academic community.

Historical Background

In the 1960s, five two-hour "Bible" courses and two history courses were required of all students, but no course in philosophy. In the 1970s, History 100, Philosophy 201, and Theology 201 were adopted as core courses. In the early 1980s, the History, Philosophy, and Theology departments were asked to determine the content of the last, or fourteenth, core course. Gradually, the notion developed of a course that did not belong to any of these three departments and yet included some important features of all of them.

Given, first, Dordt's mission to provide Scripturally directed serviceable insight into created reality and, second, the need for fundamental renewal in all areas of life, I selected in 1982 from nine possible titles "Calling, Task, and Culture" as the most appropriate one for this core course.[5] By its very nature, this upper-level course assumes some basic insights and skills students have already learned in their thirteen other core courses, as well as in their field of concentration and electives. Furthermore, focused on fundamental, "religious"[6] renewal in all of life, this course assumes at least a modicum of knowledge about certain critically important historical, philosophical, and theological features of living in God's presence at all times, in all places, and in everything one does.

A proper understanding of our place in culture as servants of the Lord calls for keen *historical* awareness of the dominant and often subtle powers operative in the culture where one lives and works. Do these powerful forces manifest or defy God's will for all his creatures? What explains past and present reform movements in, for example, farming, labor, business, politics, industry, entertainment, health care, family, faith life, and education? And what accounts for their demises or failures? What about the need for those who belong to the Way (Acts 9:2) to huddle together, not only on the first day of the week but also, and especially, during the other six days of the week, for the explicit purpose of developing a communal strategy to be followed in the spiritual/religious conflict in every zone of culture?[7]

With respect to some of the *philosophical* aspects of GEN 300, what are the religiously simple yet culturally complex issues associated with the relation between calling and task, the fabric of a society, the tenor of a culture, the nature of revolution, and the role of utopias? As for the *theological* features of the course, subjects that need further reflection, in a cross-disciplinary and cross-career manner, are such matters as the relation between heart commitment and faith life, the meaning of Kingdom and church, the role of idolatry and ideology, the importance of confessional huddling, the need for prophetic witness, and the reality of persecution and martyrdom.

Calling

The intent and content of GEN 300 are reflected in its title. Each of its three terms is important, as are their combination and sequence. The first term, *calling,* is not used here in the limited sense of occupying a special position (e.g., deacon, elder, pastor, preacher, evangelist, youth leader, liturgist, church secretary) in some organized church or other faith community. Nor is it used in the more general sense of holding some job in a Christian school, hospital, agency of mercy, counseling center, prison ministry, or "Christian" book and music publishing company. Rather, calling refers to what makes all humans (Christian and non-Christian) do what God created them to do. It points to what he intends them to be as his representatives in all of their daily activities. It has to do with what he expects them to be and how he wants them to reflect him in the totality of their lives in a full-bodied way. Calling explains why, in everything they do, all humans act as inherently *religious* beings who cannot escape God's will for created reality. A correct understanding of calling implies viewing it within the covenantal context of the fundamental and all-encompassing correlation between God's revelation and human religion as responsiveness to that revelation.

The secret of this correlation between revelation and religion is God's covenant with created reality, in particular, with humanity. According to the structure of this covenant, God reveals his will in and to what he has made, and to that holy will all his creatures have to respond, each according to its own kind. Only in the case of human creatures is this response always religious in nature, that is, ultimately one of obedience or disobedience, gratitude or defiance, acknowledgment or disregard. In short, God's revelation is the condition for religion; it is not a product of religion or a result of human projection. Revelation is the ground for religion, and religion is the essence of human response to this always-impinging revelation.[8]

Although certain distinctions can be made within revelation, the different forms and periods of revelation may not be separated from each other. God's revelation in creation, incarnation, and inscripturation[9] form an integrated whole, for they all, albeit in different ways, manifest God's undivided will for life. Ignoring any part of this revelation does injustice to the importance of the other parts. To recognize this integrated character of revelation is crucial to seeing the integrated nature also of religion. Religion is not some optional, private affair that can be restricted to only a part of life and kept separate from the rest of life. According to Scripture, religion is not something sacred and related to what is only supranatural, in contrast to what is secular and merely autonomous or natural. Religion is not confined to the vertical dimension of life, isolated from the horizontal relationships humans have with each other and with nonhuman creatures. This dualistic medieval, modern, and contemporary myth has blinded Western Christianity to the biblical notion that "life *is* religion."[10] This religious dichotomy has fractured Western thinking and given rise to numerous misleading dilemmas in our society and culture. Above all, the dichotomy has created many vexing problems to think about, teach, and study in an integrally Christian way, and it presses educators to devise an academic community with a (more) wholesome curriculum and pedagogy.[11]

To limit religion only to organized or unorganized private faith life violates the unique correlation between revelation and religion and, thus, skews the rest of life. Covenant keeping and covenant breaking are both equally matters of the heart. At this center of our existence as humans, we reveal who we really are through what we do in our daily activities, including our jobs and careers, in relation to our Creator. As humans, we are naked in that we are unable to escape the Maker's laws for life. When this human heart is closed to God, we become deaf to his voice, blind to his will, insensitive to his care, and indifferent to his grace. When, however, this heart is open and directed to him, we become eager to hear his call, receive and radiate his love in whatever we do, discover his will, and know more about his world for the benefit of all his creatures.

Task

Living within the freedom of this all-encompassing revelation/religion correlation epitomizes what it means to live in the core of one's embodied existence according to God's will. Such living provides authentic freedom, whereas refusing to live this way results in a loss of genuine freedom because such a refusal is covenant breaking. Understanding God's call requires a clear understanding of what the term *task* means within the larger context of our human calling and our "culture." Other words that can be used for task in this connection are place, position, station, authority, responsibility, charge, obligation, assignment, duty, role, or office. All these terms imply some form of authorization, knowledge of specific disciplines, criteria for assessment, and a sense of relationship among all our tasks.

We live in an intricately structured world. Out of deference to God, the Creator/Redeemer, our calling is to represent him in what we do in and with his creation. To truly acknowledge this Creator is as broad as life and constitutes the essence of religion as total response to his revelation. The fundamental correlation between revelation and religion, described above, is reflected in the correlation between our calling and task(s). Our calling to serve him finds expression in the diversity of our human tasks. This Scripturally directed anthropology, or view of what it means to be human, is basic to Dordt's entire core program, especially GEN 300. Just as God's full revelation is always creature-directed and just as our total human life, or religion, is always God-directed, so our calling is from God and our tasks are always concrete responses to him.

This insight stimulates a covenant-sensitive awareness of the two-way relationship between calling and task. To perform a particular task presupposes being in a position or office to assume and carry out a specific responsibility. Through a rich diversity of duties, each of which is somehow associated with an office, God authorizes humans in concrete, practical ways to care for his human and nonhuman creatures.[12] In each task, God makes us responsible for his world, including animals, plants, and things, and holds us somehow accountable to him for doing—and therein displaying—his sovereign will.

Our ultimate calling is always to be finely attuned to God's all-embracing will for life. This central calling is manifested in the great array of human tasks or responsibilities. The relation between this calling and the tasks can, metaphorically speaking, be compared to that of the hub and spokes of a wheel, the one main shaft and many blades of a windmill, or a high fireworks rocket that, after exploding, releases its glowing contents that, umbrella-like, cascade downward in many streams of brilliant colors that illumine the sky above and earth below. If any of these spokes, blades, or rays of color are missing, the wheel will not turn, the windmill will not pump water, and the fireworks will not be a success.

The point of these three analogies is to indicate that God's will is differentiated in a great array of general imperatives for humans, such as to be social, fair, just, clear, sensitive, loyal, trustworthy, economical, and inventive.[13] All these basic commands are further specified in different ways at different times and places. Shaped by local traditions and customs, these norms, laws, rules, or values are put into practice by men and women, young and old, in all their personal and public relationships with each other and with the world of animals, plants, and physical things like water, air, soil, and oil.

All fundamental tasks are given to humanity as a whole. Not all of these tasks can be or need to be carried out by all people in all places and at all times. Many of them, however, have to be performed by all human beings at one time or other. Often, we have to assume various responsibilities at the same time. In those cases, we are faced with what could be called the principle of simultaneity of norm-realization. This principle is both crucial and practical if one wishes to avoid a lopsided way of living. For example, someone who is a parent may also be, at the same time, a spouse, a citizen, a member of a faith community, an employee, and a friend. Though the number of hats to wear will differ from person to person, from place to place, and from one period in life to another, we have no choice about having to wear diverse hats concurrently.

Each task requires that a person is authorized to perform the duties implied in it. Authorization is an essential feature of any office one holds because this authorization determines the rights and responsibilities one has to carry out one's office. No matter what kind of task someone has been assigned, each office associated with a task has two basic features: a direct or indirect *responsibility for* other human and nonhuman creatures and a direct *accountability to* God, the ultimate Authorizer.[14]

In this connection, it is extremely important to recognize that the task Jesus was assigned and lovingly performed to the bitter end was a truly incomparable and unique one. As the name Christ Jesus (Anointed Savior) indicates, he was in an office and accomplished a task no other creature would or could have done. He revealed in his birth, life, death, resurrection, and ascension the depth of God's faithfulness to his law(s) for created reality. He did not abolish God's central law of love, but fulfilled it. In his name and for his sake, the Spirit enables those engrafted into him, as the

Tree of Life, to respond to God's call to show, in dependence upon him, their great joy for the Lord in how they carry out his mandate (cf. Matthew 28:21–22) in all their daily tasks and to testify in some small but significant way to the power and contours of God's royal reign in the midst of our broken and suffering world.

Students are usually aware of this fascinating diversity of tasks in life. The many options at their disposal about what to become and do are at times bewildering to them. How do their preferences for what they want to study and the areas in which they hope someday to make a difference for good affect their interaction with students having different preferences and future responsibilities? Because their opportunities for service are innumerable and the complexities in our culture often daunting, the need for huddling together for a semester in a Christian academic setting is crucial and the benefits are invaluable.

To get some handle on issues that often seem simple but are actually intricate and personally sensitive, it is necessary to make some comments on a larger framework within which to place these issues. Assumed in the comments above about revelation, religion, and the unique relation between them and the idea that *life is religion* is a certain awareness of what it means to talk about God's will for created reality. In this context, God's will and law are used in the same sense. We know the former through the latter. In light of Scriptural revelation, "law" can be used in three different ways: a creational (or structural) sense, a religious (or directional) sense, and a positive (or cultural) sense.[15]

Creational laws refer to God's will manifested in the intricate structure and rich diversity of created reality. They indicate why physical things, plants, animals, and humans are what they are: unique kinds of creatures with a distinct development *within*[16] each of the four different realms. To discover what these things are or how they function and interrelate with one another is the goal of any bona fide curriculum. This creational law also determines who humans really are and why they function as they do, no matter when and where they live. In distinction from all other *earthly* creatures, humans respond to God as Creator in a peculiarly heart-centered and responsible way. Religion is for them not an option, but a condition of being. This is the reason why humans who refuse to acknowledge God as Creator replace him with some substitute taken from within creation and elevated to the ultimate source of meaning.

To humans created in this unique way, God gave his central religious law to love him and to love their neighbors as themselves. This love command presupposes two things: first, *that,* as creatures, they respond to God as their Creator; and, second, *how,* as religious creatures, they must respond to him in love.[17] That someone is a judge, social worker, journalist, pastor, farmer, healer, parent, soldier, or whatever is one thing; how, in the sense of in what spirit one performs the tasks associated with these roles, is something else. The latter concerns the religious *direction,* not creational *structure,* of life. It has to do with the way people image God in what they do, comparable to the way children in their everyday behavior reflect their parents. This *how* of living can also be appropriately called our "spirituality." It indicates what kind of children of our heavenly Father we are.

In addition to the many *structural* laws and the one *religious* law, there is also a third kind of law, namely, *positive* law. Whereas the former are God-given and unchangeable, the latter is human-made and changeable. It refers to all sorts of rules, regulations, formulations, stipulations, customs, traditions, constitutions, creeds, insights, ordinances, and so forth that humans have made in their everyday responses to the two kinds of God-willed and unalterable laws. As humans formulate in different times and in different places their understanding of God's laws, they positivize, i.e., express what they perceive to be, God's will. *Positive* laws, in other words, embody how humans believe life should be lived, society structured, history directed, and culture shaped. They reveal what people believe their calling to be, tasks to consist of, and culture to be all about—fundamental topics dealt with in GEN 300.

Our whole-bodied activities evidence what really motivates us as humans and what determines the direction of our all-permeating and all-encompassing spirituality. Is our spiritual direction ultimately one of obedience or disobedience to God's life-creating and life-maintaining will? Is it one of gratitude for or contempt of the Lord's life-restoring grace? Do we genuinely serve other human as well as nonhuman creatures, or do we abuse them because of blindness resulting from intolerable self-centeredness and spiritual myopia?[18] This difference between two opposing directions in life is a conflict that embraces all of life, a conflict that at its heart is a spiritual antithesis.[19] This clash between *shalom* and distortion, order and chaos, peace and war is not inherent to the many unchangeable creational commands and the one central religious commandment God gave, but is, since the Fall, present in all the positive laws we make as humans. These are the issues students wrestle with in GEN 300.

As humans, we have the important and exciting responsibility of discovering God's will not only in a confessional or faith sense but also in a total and concrete manner in all daily activities. This mandate to discover God's will holds true also for our life in the academy. For example, what is God's (structural and religious) will within the context of a history class, a chemistry laboratory, the career counseling center, a political studies seminar, the art studio, a bio-engineering course, or a social-work internship? In all these academic situations, we are faced with an unavoidable and difficult problem. While we acknowledge the givenness of all God's unalterable laws for life, as humans we never fully know these God-willed "words" apart from our human positive laws! With the hands of our sin-tainted responses to

God's revelation, we try to understand what God requires of us (in our political life, business practices, marriage and family life, environmental habits, recreational activities, industrial priorities, and so on). As creatures who are still-sinning Christians, we not only see in part but also remain blind in part. These two limiting conditions should keep us from confessional hubris, false certainty, and unwarranted speculation.

Four erroneous options are possible in all of life, including the academy, especially in a course like GEN 300.[20] First, when we talk about God's abiding structural laws and religious law without sufficient awareness of the effect of human positive laws on our knowledge of these two kinds of God-given laws, we may contribute to some form of mythical thinking, platonic speculation, and, even worse, a mystical escape from our daily human responsibilities. Second, when we think about God's love command and our positive responses to it without acknowledging the givenness of God's creational laws, we encourage some form of individualistic pietism and privatized faith. Such a faith does not significantly affect how we perform our differentiated tasks and will not have a wholesome impact on the overall shape and direction of culture. Third, to ignore God's love commandment and focus only on God's creational revelation and human responses to it creates a vacuum into which secular[21] and revolutionary forms of Western humanism[22] can enter and dominate public domains of a society and culture.[23] Fourth, to concentrate on positive laws as though they are all that exist and to reject any God-ordained creational and religious laws not only reduces Christian discipleship to a private and personal affair but also opens the floodgates to pragmatism with its relativistic contingency thinking, a pragmatism now prevalent in North American culture and in much of Western culture's postmodern thinking.[24]

What has already been discussed above in a detailed and systematic fashion can briefly be revisited in terms of the practical question of the nature and interrelationships of revelation, experience, and normativity.[25] In my teaching of GEN 300 for nearly a decade, this question arose somehow in every idea developed, lecture given, topic discussed, journal written, book read, seminar held, and paper evaluated. This central practical issue compels participants in this course to put their heads together and share their insights. In this huddling, mentors and students learn to call the plays that are needed in the game of life. Who does what? What are the options? What is the overall and specific game plan? How can we move together and block the opponent in a strategically effective way?

Culture

To know what the game of life is all about presupposes some understanding of what is meant by the term *culture*. Against the background of what was said above about the first two terms in the title of GEN 300, culture refers first to the way people, over a certain period of time and in a certain place, have disclosed the possibilities latent in human and nonhuman creatures and second to the ways these people have preserved the results of these disclosures through customs and traditions that reflect a particular diversity of interests, level of expertise, range of priorities, and shape of societal structure.[26] Culture indicates the ambiance in which people experience their place and task(s) in everyday life. It is something that can cause them to face daunting challenges when, because of choice or necessity, they leave their own culture and learn to live in a different culture.[27]

Because we as Christians are not saved by the works of our own hands, we must clearly distinguish our tasks, and our culture as their product or result, from our salvation. According to Scripture, salvation is never a reward for tasks performed. Being a gift in and through Christ, in whom all things are centered and cohere,[28] salvation is received, not achieved, by us. We are redeemed despite, not because of, any of our successes, including our toil, pain, tears, and struggles, in all our tasks performed in response to God's mandate (Genesis 1:28–29) and to the risen Lord's deepened renewal of it (Matthew 28:20–21).

Not recognizing their central calling does not mean that people are absolved from having to respond to it. On the contrary! However, their response will be in the form of an abuse of their God-given calling, which, in refracted manner, comes to expression in an amazing diversity of human tasks and is embodied in any given culture. Non-Christians are not taskless. Ironically, they realize all too well, albeit often in a distorted fashion, the importance of their tasks and roles in society, culture, and the world at large.

Despite the faithlessness of humanity, God remains faithful to his Word for created reality. To acknowledge this truth at all times in our (academic) thinking about our place in the world is truly a formidable task. Having their social, economic, political, and other habits influenced by the tenor of their cultural customs and traditions, how can mentors and students in a course like GEN 300 begin to sense and address the challenges of disobedient cultures, to develop a lifestyle more in line with living in the constant presence of the God of love, and to become more keenly aware of the beckoning voice of the liberating and protecting Shepherd? In a course focused on all sorts of preeminently practical and personal issues, it is tempting to lose oneself in these issues rather than placing them sufficiently within the larger and deeper context of culture's conflicting powers and spirits. How can we teach and learn, in this last core course, who God *really* is and who we *really* are and are supposed to be within the context of our world, privately and publicly,[29] locally and globally?

Being faithful to his Word(s) and his promises, God calls us to be faithful in our response—not successful, but self-effacing; not self-centered, but visionary; not blind, but lovers of the God of life; not creators of gods of death, but peacemakers in the Name of the God of life—in short, to be in the world, not of it. Because of humanity's rebellion against God's revealed will, spiritual forces of order and disorder are locked in a fundamental conflict with each other and vie for dominance in society and culture. This struggle between heeding God's call and ignoring it becomes evident in the way we humans perform our daily tasks.

In this connection, Christians desperately need the support of the Holy Spirit to enable and guide them in everything they do in the totality and down-to-earthness of their daily tasks. Filled with the Spirit and grounded in the Risen Lord, Christians not only endure opposition, mockery, hardship, persecution, suffering, and death,[30] but also, above and through it all, experience great joy, incredible resilience, and wonderful surprises.[31] With a view to this individual and communal "spiritual" conflict, the Christian community pleads with the Spirit to help it properly discern the spirits of the age and recognize the dangers of dead traditions, deceptive powers, misleading dilemmas, deadly ideologies, and distorted priorities.

All of this, in turn, calls for a careful yet prophetic and prayerful form of historical strategizing about what to do and how to proceed, not just as individuals but also as a total Christian community whose desire it is to follow Christ in all daily activities. What spiritual forces are operative in history, determine the fabric of society, and dictate the priorities of a culture? Especially in a course like GEN 300, it is tempting to major in mostly minor personal issues and ignore larger cultural questions. For example, what is the essence and what are the practical effects of certain major revolutions in our history and culture? Not to deal with these and other larger challenges in our society and culture is not only shortsighted but also detrimental to meaningfully articulating and concretely implementing service to our Lord.

Jubilee

If there is one secret to what should motivate Christ's followers to live as God's children in all their daily activities, it is their irrepressible desire to restore what is broken, heal what is diseased, bring hope where there is despair, and press for justice in the face of injustice. This kind of gratitude is clearly expressed by Hannah in the Old Testament (1 Samuel 2:1–10) and echoed by Mary in the New Testament (Luke 1:46–56), and it is powerfully summarized by Isaiah at the time of Israel's captivity in Babylon (Isaiah 61:1–2) and by Jesus Christ himself at the very beginning of his public ministry in the ignoble town of Nazareth (Luke 4:18–19). There is hope for the poor, freedom for the prisoner, sight for the blind, and release for the oppressed! Why? All because of "the year of the Lord's favor."

Genuine covenant living is at its core life-enhancing. Key to this liberty is the coming of God's royal reign, his Kingdom rule.[32] Jubilee is not an old-fashioned and outdated principle, but a preeminently relevant and astonishingly wonderful reality promised in the Old Testament and incarnated in the New Testament. It indicates what our redeeming Creator requires of us in what we think about created reality and do in it. It is not what some students in GEN 300 told me on several different occasions, "an antiquated idea no longer relevant" (or, in pragmatistic terminology, "useful" or "practical") in our modern society and world. According to both the Old[33] and New Testament,[34] at the core of Jubilee is God's unchanging covenant love for his human and nonhuman creatures.

At the center of this Creator's love for his marvelous handiwork lies the celebration, every fiftieth year, of the Day of Atonement, i.e., the removal of the evil humans committed by not living within the liberty-guaranteeing boundaries of his laws. The intent of Jubilee is liberation and restoration not just of enslaved people, but also, indirectly, of animals, plants, and things. In Jubilee's celebration of divine expiation of human sin and liberation for service, God signifies that he is good and that sin's bondage need not be permanent. Jubilee celebrates the right-of-redemption in the day-to-day affairs of God's people.

This liberation and restoration are not merely private or personal events related to our soul as a spiritual reality isolated from the rest of everyday life. On the contrary, they are by their very nature public in the sense of being structured into the fabric of society. The intent of Jubilee is to cultivate a lifestyle of both emancipation and restoration. Freedom without restoration or some kind of new socioeconomic order in society is an empty dream, a cheap form of grace. God's law-affirming love calls forgiven sinners to release debts and liberate (male and female) slaves. This love provides a new lease on life for all the oppressed and opens new doors to a more meaningful future—not in a world up there and after death, but in this world of their daily existence.[35]

Refusing to live according to this Jubilee mandate (see Jeremiah 32:7) resulted in Israel's seventy years of slavery in Babylon. In an attempt to avoid a similarly devastating personal and collective experience, most Jews after this captivity resorted to (Pharisaic) legalism in their strict sabbath observance and caused considerable trouble for Israel's faithful remnant, especially, in the fullness of time, for Christ Jesus.

This "Anointed Savior" did not do away with the Jubilee character of the covenant but made it a reality, at least in principle. In his incomparable work, he positivized God's will, in a uniquely personified way, for the redemption of his sheep who hear the voice as this Great Shepherd calling them to follow him in all their daily responsibilities and activities. The social, economic, political, and all other public facets of life are not separable from the Gospel, but they are integral to it. Jubilee is not an addendum to the Gospel, but essential to it; not an option, but an obligation for all

Christians as "followers of the Way." Just as Israel of old, by heeding the Jubilee-principle, was intended to be(come) the envy of the nations of the world, so Christians today by celebrating the reality of Jubilee in Christ are called to arouse the nations of the world to jealousy for the gracious God of the universe.[36]

Just as land functioned in ancient Israel, so skills and resources in medicine, education, labor, farming, parenting, finances, business, engineering, and so forth function in our culture and world, first, to enable other people to live as God's liberated and restored office-bearers and, second, to allow nonhuman creatures to benefit from his goodness. To help the poor and disadvantaged by merely giving them alms is not sufficient. Instead, they must also be enabled to become (more) self-reliant and therein reclaim their human dignity. Such enablement usually calls for structural changes in society. It is at this third step that Christians, also in North America, encounter numerous economic, social, political, and racial obstacles because of deeply vested interests in society.

GEN 300 has always tried to face these challenges head-on.[37] In this bold endeavor, there is no room for triumphalism. Also in this course, all we can do is open our ears anew to hear God's call to serve him in all our daily tasks and provide "marginal resistance" to the dominant spirits of our age not in line with his Spirit.[38] Our challenge is not to be successful but to be faithful to the Risen One who has placed our feet on the path of Jubilee.[39]

Notes

1. By 1979, thirteen General Education courses were approved, but no agreement was reached concerning the fourteenth course. In 1980/1981, D. Vander Kooi taught "Issues and Problems" as a one-year experiment. In 1982, I proposed a course entitled "Calling, Task, and Culture." In 1984/1985, the administration asked me to develop another proposal. It was narrowly approved in November 1985, as something to be taught on a three-semester, *trial* basis, starting the spring semester of 1986. Under the name "General Education 300," this was approved as a *required* course for all upper-level students in May 1988.

2. Teaching and learning focused almost exclusively on becoming teachers, secretaries, athletes, musicians, counselors, doctors, pastors, business persons, bankers, and so on, and quite often this was done in a biblicistic and simplistic manner, i.e., without sufficiently taking into account the relevance and complexity of God's creational revelation.

3. Not just for administration, faculty, and students, but also for supporting community and campus support staff.

4. In the case of non-Christian Jewish, Islam, Buddhist, Mormon, and Humanist circles, the faith traditions are centered in, respectively, synagogues, mosques, temples, stake houses, and reflection centers.

5. Other titles I considered for the course: "Reformation, Revolution, and Culture," "Anatomy of Renewal," "Man in Culture," "Structure and Practice of Reformation," "Christian Discipleship in Today's World," "Calling and Renewal of Life," "Christian Perspective on Vocation," and "Calling of Kingdom Citizens." "Calling, Task, and Culture" is a translation of the first chapter of K. J. Popma (professor of Reformational

philosophy at the University of Groningen, philologist, theological commentator, and novelist), "Roeping, taak en cultuur" in *Eerst de Jood maar ook de Griek* (Franeker: T. Wever, 1950), 13–23.

6. Used in the broad and deep sense that life *is* religion, not in the restricted sense of religion as a private *part of* life and *apart from* it.

7. These "huddles" often become organizations designed to discern and carry out God's will: for example, Center for Public Justice (CPJ), Christian Labor Association of Canada (CLAC), Canadian Christian Business Federation (CCBF), Christian Schools International (CSI), Christian Farmers Association (CFA), Justice for All (JFA), Prison Ministry Fellowship, International Association for the Promotion of Christian Higher Education (IAPCHE), and Council of Christian Colleges and Universities (CCCU).

8. A clear example of God's revelation and a proper human response to it is recorded in 1 Samuel 3:10: "Speak, [Lord], for your servant is listening." It is God's prerogative to speak, reveal, or make known to humans, and it is our human calling to listen, i.e., to respond, with the disposition of a servant.

9. Also, "cosmos," "logos," and "biblos." See especially John 1 and Colossians 1.

10. A phrase coined by H. Evan Runner (1916–2002), professor of Reformational philosophy at Calvin College in Grand Rapids, MI, and spiritual founder of the Institute for Christian Studies (ICS) in Toronto, ON, in 1967.

11. Because of an insufficiently integral Christian teaching at both the Academy of Geneva (established by J. Calvin in 1559) and the University of Leiden (founded by Dutch Calvinists in 1575), a theology student at the former and *first* doctoral theology graduate at the latter was, irony of ironies, J. Arminius (1560–1609).

12. See Article 52 of "Our World Belongs to God: A Contemporary Testimony" of the Christian Reformed Church in North America about our "Response to God's calling to care for the creation and each other." "Our World Belongs to God," in *Psalter Hymnal,* ed. Emily R. Brink (Grand Rapids, MI: CRC Publications, 1987), 1035.

13. For an attempt to describe in systematic fashion these and other divine imperatives, see the reformational philosophy developed in the tradition of Calvin (1509–1564), G. Groen van Prinsterer (1801–1876), A. Kuyper (1837–1920), H. Dooyeweerd (1894–1975), D. H. Th. Vollenhoven (1892–1978), and many other Christian thinkers throughout the world, especially, since 1967, at the Institute for Christian Studies in Toronto, ON, Canada. See, regarding the Institute, http://www.icscanada.edu, and regarding Dooyeweerd, http://www.redeemer.on.can/dooyeweerd-centre.

14. Because of space restrictions, it is not possible to elaborate on certain complex anthropological issues involved in this life-encompassing (not just ecclesiastically limited) idea of "office." For details, see Peter Schouls, *Insight, Authority and Power: A Biblical Appraisal,* AACS Christian Perspectives Series 1971 (Toronto: Wedge Publishing Foundation, 1972); Bradshaw Frey, William Ingram, Thomas McWhertor, and William D. Romanowski, *At Work and Play: Biblical Insight for Daily Obedience* (Jordan Station, ON: Paideia Press, 1986); John A. Bernbaum and Simon M. Steer, *Why Work? Careers and Employment in Biblical Perspective,* Christian College Coalition Study Guides, ed. John A. Bernbaum (Grand Rapids, MI: Baker/Washington, DC: Christian College Coalition, 1986); and Lee Hardy, *The Fabric of This World: Inquiries into Calling, Career, Choice, and the Design of Human Work* (Grand Rapids, MI: Eerdmans, 1990).

15. For details, see works by D. H. Th. Vollenhoven (1892–1978), professor of philosophy at the Free University in Amsterdam from 1926–1963. He and his colleague and brother-in-law, H. Dooyeweerd, professor of jurisprudence at the same university, de-

veloped what has come to be known as Calvinistic, neo-Kuyperian, Reformational, or Christian philosophy. Vollenhoven has suggested that these three senses of law can be associated with (respectively) creational, incarnational, and inscripturated revelation, and with God as Father, Son, and Holy Spirit. See Vollenhoven, "The Unity of Life," (commemoration lecture for the Utrecht chapter of the S.S.R., held on October 13, 1955, draft translation from the Dutch "Levens-eenheid" by J. H. Kok, 1997, Dordt College).

16. *Not between* these qualitatively different realms, as advocated in evolution*ism*.

17. The relation between God's Word and human response is clearly expressed in *Woord* and *antwoord* (Dutch) and *Wort* and *Antwort* (German).

18. See Romans 7:7–25 regarding the struggle between doing what one *wants* to do and what one *actually* does and the resultant cry for redemption from the misery of such a conflict. Calvin indicated that life is not either white or black, but it is gray. The crucial question is whether it is more white than black or more black than white. Cf. *Institutes*, II,ii,27 and IV,xv,12.

19. Christians are (supposed to be) thetical, positive, known for what they are *for*; those who reject God's will are (actually) antithetical, negative, known for what they resist.

20. The meaning of this paragraph may require more than one reading.

21. Used in the sense of rejecting not just any organized faith, but anything related to any faith or commitment.

22. One thinks in this connection of such eighteenth-century radical French revolutionaries as Voltaire (1694–1778) and J. J. Rousseau (1712–1788), of North American humanists like B. Franklin (1706–1790) and T. Jefferson (1743–1826), and of numerous famous nineteenth- and twentieth-century Western thinkers in natural, social, economic, political, theological, psychological, aesthetic, and pedagogical sciences.

23. See Luke 11:25–26: "When [the evil spirit] arrives, it finds the house swept clean and put in order. Then it goes and takes seven other spirits more wicked than itself, and they go in and live there. And the final condition of that man is worse than the first."

24. Inasmuch as postmodernism is a negative reaction to myopic and arrogant Enlightenment religion and ideology, it is commendable, without implying that it is less idolatrous; it is, in a sense, actually more hostile to God's revelation.

25. For example, What is the relation between God's revelation and human experience of it in different places and at different times? How do we learn what is structurally (non)normative and religiously good or evil? To stress biblical revelation and some form of normativity without doing justice to both creational revelation and human experience fosters biblicism and a privatized faith. To focus on our experience and normativity without acknowledging divine revelation promotes liberalism and humanism. To emphasize normativity without recognizing the importance of experience and revelation encourages certain forms of Platonism and gnosticism.

26. "Culture" is derived from the Latin *colere*, to till, and *cultura*, cultivation or care. It indicates improvement, development, and refinement and denotes the results of beliefs, habits, skills, instruments, priorities, and institutions of a given people in a given period.

27. Concomitant with the development of GEN 300 was the growing interest during the latter half of the 1980s in off-campus and international education programs.

28. See Colossians 1:15–23; and Ephesians 1:3–14 and 2:1–22.

29. The private–public distinction has its origin in the religion of radical Western humanism. It presents the Christian community with the formidable challenge to reject it and to replace it with a more just form of democracy! For details, see Center for Public Justice, under the

directorship of James W. Skillen, former professor of political theory at Dordt College, regarding a drastically different view of "private," "public," "faith-based community organizations," and so on. See James W. Skillen, *Recharging the American Experiment: Principled Pluralism for Genuine Civic Community* (Grand Rapids, MI: Baker, 1994).

30. See Psalms 1, 2, 73; and 2 Peter 2:8.

31. See Romans 8; 1 Corinthians 15:55–58; and Revelation 5.

32. When my colleague in the art department, J. Van Wyk, asked me what terms would best describe the views and work of John B. Hulst, Dordt's second president, I responded, "covenant and Kingdom." For Van Wyk's artistic depiction of these two terms, see the back cover of this volume or the glass display case in the foyer of the B. J. Haan Auditorium.

33. See Leviticus 25, esp. 15–17; Isaiah 58–61; Ezekiel 16:49–52; Amos 6:4–7 and 8:4–6; and Proverbs 10:3 and 30:8–9.

34. See Luke 1:52–53 and 19:1–10; 2 Corinthians 8:9; and James 5:1–9.

35. The need for and nature of the Jubilee principle must be seen in connection with the concrete forms of structural evil that had crept into Israel's society. Living a semi-nomadic life at first, Israel emphasized tribal cohesion, blood solidarity, role of land, and obligation to help one another. Most of the people lived in villages of about four to six hundred persons. Many of these villagers were poor. It was not uncommon to have to pledge one's cloak in payment for debts incurred, to remind employers to pay wages on the same day the work was done, to seize children as slaves, or to sell a pair of shoes to keep a creditor at bay. Prominent in Israel's history were its dehumanizing experiences for nearly half a millennium in Egypt, for many decades under disobedient kings in the North and South before Israel and Judah went into captivity, and for seventy years in Babylonian captivity.

36. In his inaugural address as Senior Member in philosophy at the Institute for Christian Studies in Toronto, ON, on November 21, 2003, Lambert Zuidervaart, a 1969 graduate of Dordt College, focused on "societal" (not "natural" and "moral") evil. For details, see his "Earth's Lament: Suffering, Hope, and Wisdom," unpublished document available at http://www.icscanada.edu.

37. For details about Dordt's entire General Education program, see Hubert R. Krygsman, "The Soul of the Curriculum: A Framework for Integral Christian Education," (paper given at a conference on Christian Higher Education held at Baylor University in Waco, TX, on March 25–27, 2004), and published (as an eight-page insert) in *Contact,* Newsletter of the International Association for the Promotion of Christian Higher Education (IAPCHE), May 2004. Regarding availability of this paper, see http://www.iapche.org.

38. See also *Marginal Resistance: Essays Dedicated to John C. Vander Stelt,* ed. John H. Kok (Sioux Center, IA: Dordt Press, 2001), v, ix–xiii; especially David Van Heemst's essay, "A Conversation with John C. Vander Stelt," 89–108, especially 100.

39. I am indebted to my Dordt colleagues Hubert Krygsman and Charles Veenstra for their helpful comments about the content of this article and to Kim (Van Soelen) Van Es, a former student in GEN 300, for her editorial assistance.

Common Grace or the Antithesis?
Toward a Consistent Understanding of Kuyper's "Sphere Sovereignty"

Timothy I. McConnel[*]

....

Introduction

When Abraham Kuyper presented his seminal speech on "Sphere Sovereignty"[1] at the founding of the Free University of Amsterdam, he used his key phrase in two different ways. The first usage of "sphere sovereignty" referred to the different spheres or areas of life, which are free to develop within their own bounds, following their own God-given laws. These spheres, such as the family, education, the state, and the church, were derived from the structure of human life in the creational order. The second usage, later in the speech, referred to the freedom for different philosophies or "life-principles" to develop across the whole "sphere" of thought. This usage was based on the conflict Kuyper perceived between the different ideological groups within society. Was Kuyper confused and inconsistent in this presentation? Was

---

[*] Dr. McConnel was Assistant Professor of Theology at Dordt from 2001 to 2004. His M.Div. is from Columbia Biblical Seminary and his Ph.D. from Marquette University. This essay was first published in *Pro Rege* in September 2002.

his approach contradictory at the core? Or did this twofold development of his theme, admittedly in very different senses, reveal an underlying unity in his thought that spanned his lengthy, illustrious career?

In his excellent study on Abraham Kuyper, entitled *Creating a Christian Worldview: Abraham Kuyper's Lectures on Calvinism,* Peter S. Heslam argues the following:

> It should be pointed out here that this secondary meaning of the concept of sphere-sovereignty was incompatible with the first. . . . The contention of this book is that the same confusion amounted to two usages, one creational and the other socio-ideological; that the two were irreconcilable with each other; and that this double us-age is likely to have served as a stimulus to the development of *verzuiling* in Dutch society.[2]

Heslam claims to be following Herman Dooyeweerd's critique of this prob-lem in Kuyper.[3] William Edgar, in his review of Heslam's work, seems to agree, and if anything states it more strongly when he summarizes Heslam's thinking:

> Heslam's point is that there was confusion in Kuyper's writings between at least two notions of the spheres, one from the Creation, the other an organic social or ideo-logical grouping. Though contradictory, the double usage is the key to the later development of *verzuiling* in Dutch society.[4]

However, as James D. Bratt points out in his introductory remarks to Kuyper's essay "Sphere Sovereignty," there seems to be a studied ambiguity in the Dutch term itself, pointing to its application in both senses, as Kuyper did within the essay.[5] The two usages do not function as an exact parallel, as the first refers to God's creation and the second to the working-out of human sinfulness and redemption in society, as Heslam and Edgar note. Neverthe-less, it is the contention of this paper that the two usages do not display a confusion in Kuyper's thought but an application of his tension between common grace and the antithesis, which thus demonstrates his ability to hold them in balance—something many of his followers have had trouble doing. Sphere sovereignty as a notion is distinct from common grace and the an-tithesis, but Kuyper's twofold exposition of it in his speech in 1880 is consistent with his later developments of these themes. As each are explained in turn below, it will become clear that the two usages are neither confused nor contradictory, but consistently fit together in Kuyper's thought.

Sphere Sovereignty

The notion of sphere sovereignty was developed early by Kuyper as the justification for his political and educational endeavors. The definitive statement of his view was given in the speech he delivered at the founding of the Free University of Amsterdam, on October 20, 1880. It was pub-lished at the same time as *Souvereiniteit in Eigen Kring.* The title translated literally is "Sovereignty in Its Own Circle." As mentioned above, Bratt suggests that the very title points to an ambiguity in Kuyper's thought and use of the term. On the one hand, the first usage of the term "circle" refers to the different spheres of human life, such as art, education, the family, the church, the state, and so on. Kuyper viewed each of these as answering directly to God as a result of creation. In this view, the differences between the spheres are ontological in nature, and each sphere displays development due to God's "common grace." On the other hand, the second usage of the term is that the various "circles" refer to those who hold differing world-views. This second approach would divide each sphere of human life into two or more partitions. Each worldview "circle" then, according to Kuyper, must be given the freedom to work out its own principles in every area of life. In this second usage, the differences are ethical and epistemological and express the working-out of the antithesis. The first usage generally dominated Kuyper's thought regarding sphere sovereignty, but the latter usage is also clearly there, as will be shown below.

Kuyper located the origin of sphere sovereignty in the sovereignty of God, who established each of the various spheres of life:

> This perfect Sovereignty of the *sinless* Messiah at the same time directly denies and challenges all absolute Sovereignty among *sinful* men on earth, and does so by dividing life into *separate spheres,* each with its own sovereignty.
>   . . . Just as we speak of a "moral world," a "scientific world," a "business world," the "world of art," so we can more properly speak of a "sphere" of morality, of the family, of social life, each with its own *domain.* And because each comprises its own domain, each has its own Sovereign within its bounds.[6]

Kuyper saw a multitude of divinely established, intermeshing spheres as comprising the complexity of human life. The State had a special function of protecting individuals and of defining the relationships among the various other spheres, but its role was to acknowledge the authority of other spheres, not to confer authority upon them.[7] In Kuyper's view, the only safeguard for freedom was to submit to the sovereignty of God in every area. This submission would prevent the State from claiming supreme sovereignty, which is its sinful tendency. For Kuyper, the totalitarian state was the natural working-out of the principles of the "Revolution." The followers of the "Revolution" were those who rejected revelation and replaced it with the autonomy of human thought, as typified for Kuyper by the French Revolution. This opposing principle saw the highest sovereignty as embodied in the supreme State, the final authority for all other spheres of life.

The last section of his speech, in which he focused on sphere sovereignty "As a Reformed Principle," developed the second usage of Kuyper's notion. In it he argued for the necessity of a university founded on Reformed principles that would be able to develop freely those principles. He based this argument on the subjective character of knowledge and argued, as in his later writings on the antithesis, that the Christian principle affects every area of scholarship:

> I readily grant that if our *natural sciences* strictly limited themselves to weighing and measuring, the wedge of principle would not be at the door. But who would do that? What natural scientist operates without a hypothesis? Does not everyone who practices science as a *man* and not as a *measuring stick* view things through a subjective lens and always fill in the unseen part of the circle according to subjective opinion?[8]

The inevitable "subjective opinion" to which Kuyper refers he would later call the conflict in "world-views." Thus, he argued that in scholarship there must be freedom for each group or circle to work out its own principle. Kuyper goes on to claim to following:

> Rather, considering that something begins from principle and that a distinct entity takes rise from a distinct principle, we shall maintain a distinct sovereignty for our own principle and for that of our opponents across the whole sphere of thought. That is to say, as from their principle and by a method appropriate to it they erect a house of knowledge that glitters but does not entice us, so we too form our principle and by its corresponding method will let our own trunk shoot up whose branches, leaves, and blossom are nourished with its own sap.[9]

Note that while Kuyper was arguing for the right of Calvinists to establish their own educational institution on the basis of sphere sovereignty, he was also safeguarding the right of his opponents to do the same. In effect, in his development of the second usage of sphere sovereignty, Kuyper argued for a pluralism without succumbing to a notion of ethical or epistemological relativism.

As he came near to the end of this seminal speech, Kuyper sounded the cry for action in terms that recalled his emphasis on the antithesis, but especially sounded the note so dear to his Calvinist heritage, that of the sovereignty of Christ:

> How could it be otherwise? Man in his antithesis as fallen *sinner* or self-developing *natural creature* returns again as the " subject that thinks" or " the object that prompts thought" in every department, in every discipline, and with every investigator. Oh, no single piece of our mental world is to be hermetically sealed off from the rest, and there is not a square inch in the whole domain of our human existence over which Christ, who is Sovereign over *all,* does not cry: "Mine!"[10]

These words were a call for the Christian to social and academic engagement, not withdrawal from the world. This call recognizes the sovereignty of Christ over every area of human endeavor, reflecting Kuyper's first usage of sphere sovereignty, but it also indicates the need to subject oneself to Christ in these cultural endeavors, which, in the "antithesis as fallen sinner," necessitates his second usage. It also underscores the fact that Kuyper was seeking both to confirm and to build on the Reformed heritage, to extend it in the face of the circumstances of the modern world.[11]

The Antithesis

The term *antithesis* had been popularized in nineteenth-century philosophy by Hegel's use of it. Kuyper took over the term, but gave it his own specific meaning. He also developed his notion of the antithesis in terms of a Christian worldview, as opposed to a non-Christian worldview.[12]

The classic exposition of Kuyper's notion of the antithesis occurs in his *Principles of Sacred Theology* (volume two of the *Encyclopaedie der Heilige Godgeleerdheid*).[13] He outlines the application of the antithesis to worldviews in *Calvinism*.[14]

Kuyper began developing his notion of the antithesis in the second part of the *Principles of Sacred Theology*, entitled "The Organism of Science," specifically in his discussion of "Science Impaired by Sin."[15] Here he identified a number of ways in which sin interferes with the pursuit of any science, resulting in falsehood, mistakes, and self-deceit. "The chiefest harm," he writes,

> is the ruin, worked by sin, in those data, which were at our command, for obtaining the knowledge of God, and thus for forming the conception of the whole. Without the sense of God in the heart no one shall ever attain unto a knowledge of God, and without love, or, if you please, a holy sympathy for God, that knowledge shall never be rich in content. Every effort to prove the existence of God by so-called evidence must fail and has failed. By this we do not mean that the knowledge of God must be mystic; for as soon as this knowledge of God is to be scientifically unfolded, it must be reproduced from our thinking consciousness. But as our science in no single instance can take one forward step, except a bridge is built between the subject and the object, it cannot do so here. If thus in our sense of self there is no sense of the existence of God, and if in our spiritual existence there is no bond which draws us to God, and causes us in love to go out unto him, all science is here impossible.[16]

This quote contains the basic thrust of Kuyper's notion of the antithesis. He distinguished between those who can and those who cannot obtain a true knowledge of God. There must be a spiritual bond with God in order to have knowledge of God, and not everyone has this bond. His argument also reveals his own attitude toward a traditional apologetic based on proofs for the existence of God. Kuyper simply states that they fail and, furthermore, implies that the one who lacks any sense of God will simply reject such proofs.

Kuyper went on to connect this failure in the knowledge of God with failure in the knowledge of the cosmos as a whole. He argued that in order to answer basic questions about the cosmos as a whole, such as its origin and end, "in your consciousness you must step out from the cosmos, and you must have a starting-point . . . in the *non*-cosmos; and this is altogether impossible as long as sin confines you with your consciousness to the cosmos."[17] Kuyper found the starting point he needed in God's revelation.

What did a starting point mean for the attainment of truth? In his section on "Truth," Kuyper introduces the terms *antithesis* and *worldview* into his argument. Here he distinguishes between mere observation in the "domain of pure matter" and the "domain of the real spiritual sciences," the latter of which he thought had shown very little agreement or unity in results. He explains this fact in the following way:

> Because here the subjective factor becomes preponderant; and this subjective factor is dependent upon the antithesis between falsehood and truth; so that both the insight into the facts and the structure which one builds upon this insight must differ, and at length become, first contrary and then contradictory.
>
> The fatality of the antithesis between falsehood and truth consists in this, that every man from his point of view claims the truth for himself, and applies the epithet of "untrue" to everything that opposes this.[18]

According to Kuyper this conflict explains the development of opposing schools of thought:

> If this concerns a mere point of detail, it has no further results; but if this antithesis assumes a more universal and radical character, school will form itself against school, system against system, world-view against world-view, and two entirely different and mutually exclusive representations of the object, each in organic relation, will come at length to dominate whole series of subjects. From both sides it is said: "Truth is with us, and falsehood is with you." And the notion that science can settle this dispute is of course entirely vain, for we speak of two all-embracing representations of the object, both of which have been obtained as the result of very serious scientific study.[19]

Note that Kuyper here connects the "antithesis" between truth and falsehood with a difference in "world-views." He recognizes the inevitability of a subjective factor in knowledge and thus even the desirability of dealing with that factor; yet he also insists that in a fallen world, sin prevents the possibility of a general agreement, due to that subjective factor.

Kuyper spells out both the basis and the results of the antithesis in the area of knowledge through his analysis of "The Twofold Development of Science." Beginning with the notion that there are "Two Kinds of People," he argues that the unity of the human consciousness is broken by the fact of regeneration. He concludes the following:

> We speak none too emphatically, therefore, when we speak of two kinds of people. Both are human, but one is inwardly different from the other, and consequently feels a different content rising from his consciousness; thus they face the cosmos from different points of view, and are impelled by different impulses. And the fact that there are two kinds of *people* occasions of necessity the fact of two kinds of human *life* and *consciousness* of life, and of two kinds of *science;* for which reason the idea of the *unity of science,* taken in its absolute sense, implies the denial of the fact of palingenesis,[20] and therefore from principle leads to the rejection of the Christian religion.[21]

For Kuyper, to deny this distinction in fact proves it, as the denial involves the rejection of the Christian religion, a rejection that is the operating principle of unregenerate humanity!

The "Two Kinds of Science" thus results directly from the two kinds of people. Kuyper clearly states that he does not mean that there are two different "representations of the cosmos" that are equally valid. Ultimately, only one can be true, and thus the other must be false. He explains the difference in this way:

> But however much they may be doing the same thing formally, their activities run in opposite directions, because they have different starting-points; and because of the difference in their nature they apply themselves differently to this work, and view things in a different way. Because they themselves are differently constituted, they see a corresponding difference in the constitution of all things. They are not at work, therefore, on different parts of the same house, but each builds a house of his own.[22]

Kuyper goes on to say that, while the builders of each house can recognize the "scientific character" of the other's efforts, they are bound by their own principles to reject the other's work as false.

However, Kuyper immediately mitigates this stark contrast by giving several reasons why this division has often not been apparent. First, he distinguishes between the "natural" and the "spiritual"[23] sciences. The beginnings of the former consist of observation and the operations of weighing, measuring, and counting:

> The entire domain of the more primary observation, which limits itself to weights, measures and numbers, is common to both. The entire empiric investigation of the things that are perceptible to our sense (simple or reinforced) has nothing to do with the radical difference which separates the two groups. By this we do not mean, that the natural sciences as such and in their entirety, fall outside of this difference, but only that in these sciences the difference which separate the two groups exerts no influence on the *beginnings* of the investigation.[24]

Thus Kuyper claims a large "common realm" that both kinds of science share, in the area of empirical observation. Regeneration does not give new sense organs or change the ones that all people share in common. He recognizes a common realm in the "spiritual sciences" as well, using examples from history and the study of language.[25] In general, Kuyper recognizes a more "objective" area of study in all sciences, in which the fact of *palingenesis* plays no discernible role.

Kuyper also sees logic as part of the common realm of the two kinds of science. He argues that the "formal process" of thought has not been attacked by sin and thus is shared by both kinds of people. While the starting point—and therefore the conclusions—are radically different, the reasoning process remains the same. Thus, each side can understand and follow the demonstration of the other. As Kuyper puts it,

> . . . the accuracy of one another's demonstrations can be critically examined and verified, in so far at least as the result strictly depends upon the deduction made. By keeping a sharp watch upon each other, mutual service is rendered in the discovery of logical faults in each other's demonstrations, and thus in a formal way each will continually watch over the other.[26]

He concludes that in spite of the inevitability and irreconcilability of the divergence between the two kinds of science, nevertheless there is some common task to almost every form of science, and that both sides are able to give a clear account of their starting point.

Another reason for continued agreement between the two kinds of science, according to Kuyper, is the fact that palingenesis is a slow process that begins with repentance and conversion and continues to develop over a person's lifetime. The fact and effects of sin remain with the regenerate so that they continue to experience a false "unity" with the unregenerate in any number of areas in science.[27] However, Kuyper expected the separation of the two kinds of science to continue and to become more pronounced as the various sciences progressed. The previous unity had been only apparent. He argues the point in these terms:

> Neither the tardiness, however, of the establishment of this bifurcation of science, nor the futile effort of Conservatism to prolong its existence, can resist the continuous separation of these two kinds of science. The all-decisive question here is whether there are two points of departure. If this is *not* the case, then unity must be maintained by means of the stronger mastering the weaker; but if there *are* two points of departure, then the claim of two kinds of science in the indicated sense remains indisputably valid, entirely apart from the question whether both will succeed in developing themselves for any good result within a given time. This twofold point of departure is certainly given by palingenesis.[28]

Kuyper pointed to the universities at Brussels, Louvain, Amsterdam (his own institution), and Freiburg as the places where an attempt was being made to develop science on a consistently Christian basis.

At this point in his argument Kuyper emphasizes the subjective aspect of knowledge. In this regard, he writes the following:

> In the abstract every one concedes that the subjective assimilation of the truth concerning the object cannot be the same with all, because the investigating individuals are not as alike as drops of water, but as unlike as blades of grass and leaves on a tree. That a science should be free from the influence of the subjective factor is inconceivable, hence with the unlikeness of the individuals the influence of this factor must appear.[29]

Inasmuch as regeneration affects human consciousness at its deepest level, and in every aspect, Kuyper regards it as the fundamental dividing point for human consciousness and, hence, for science.

Kuyper admits that as soon as the two kinds of science developed separate results, they would no longer acknowledge the other side as being science, but rather as being "science falsely so called." He puts it this way:

> So far, on the other hand, as the antithesis between our human personality, as it manifests itself in sinful nature and is changed by palingenesis, governs the investigation and demonstration, we stand exclusively opposed to one another, and one must call *falsehood* what the other calls *truth*.[30]

The existence of two kinds of science does not mean, therefore, that the different sides recognize each other as valid. They may have a "formal" appreciation for the other science, but can only accept as true what is in accord with their own premises. Kuyper also explains that neither side has unity in its own development, due to the subjective factor. Rather, both kinds have experienced the development of numerous schools of thought in the various sciences. However, he does not consider this development to be necessarily negative, as this is the process by which science advances.

Kuyper's conclusion on the impact of the antithesis on knowledge is that Christian and naturalistic science not only operate with different theologies, but develop different *sciences*.

> The proposition, that in virtue of the fact of palingenesis a science develops itself by the side of the *naturalistic*, which, though formally allied to it, is differently disposed, and therefore different in its conclusions, and stands over against it as *Christian* science, must not be understood in a specifically theological, but in an absolutely *universal* sense. The difference between the two is not merely apparent in theological science, but in *all* the sciences, in so far as the fact of palingenesis governs the *whole* subject in *all* investigations, and hence also, the result of all these investigations as far as their data are not absolutely material.[31]

Naturalistic science and Christian science each claim to be true whereas the other is false; they are formally similar, but operate on different premises and hence reach different conclusions. The divergence between the two is not limited to theology but extends to every area of human knowledge, inasmuch as the knowing subject is either regenerate or unregenerate.

Kuyper's division between Christian and naturalistic science is consistent with his second usage of "sphere sovereignty." Both types of science demand the freedom to be developed from their own controlling principles and should be allowed to do so.

Worldviews as an Expression of the Antithesis

Kuyper went on to develop his notion of sphere sovereignty and antithesis further into a Christian worldview. He did so especially in his initial Stone Foundation Lecture, delivered at Princeton Theological Seminary in 1898, where he urged that Calvinism be understood as a whole "life-system" that included politics, science, and art, as well as theology.[32]

Early in the first lecture, Kuyper alludes to his Anti-Revolutionary background by raising the specter of Modernism in its fullest sense, not restricting it to the theological realm as he had earlier in his career.[33] Now he links it directly to the French Revolution:

> But, in deadly opposition to this Christian element, against the very Christian name, and against its salutiferous influence in every sphere of life, the storm of Modernism has now arisen with violent intensity.
> In 1789 the turning point was reached.[34]

Thus Kuyper points to the ideology of the Revolution as being directed against Christianity. He goes on to say, "There is no doubt then that Christianity is imperiled by great and serious dangers. Two *life-systems* are wrestling with one another, in mortal combat."[35]

In a footnote, Kuyper explains his use of the term *life systems* thus:

> As Dr. James Orr . . . observes, the German technical term *Weltanschauung* has no precise equivalent in English. He therefore used the literal translation *view of the world*, notwithstanding this phrase in English is limited by associations, which connect it predominatingly with *physical* nature. For this reason the more explicit phrase: *Life and world view* seems to be more preferable. My American friends, however, told me that the shorter phrase: *life system*, on the other side of the ocean, is often used in the same sense.[36]

At that time, the English term *worldview* had not yet come into general acceptance. Kuyper clearly intended his use of the term *life system* to include the broadest view of reality, which undergirds all other beliefs and actions. He expresses himself in this way:

> From the first, therefore, I have always said to myself,—"If the battle is to be fought with honor and with a hope of victory, then *principle* must be arrayed against *principle;* then it must be felt that in Modernism the vast energy of an all-embracing *life-system* assails us, then also it must be understood that we have to take our stand in a life-system of equally comprehensive and far-reaching power. And this powerful life-system is not to be invented nor formulated by ourselves, but is to be taken and applied as it presents itself in history. When thus taken, I found and confessed, and I still hold, that this manifestation of the Christian principle is given us in *Calvinism.*"[37]

While Kuyper's opening mentions just two worldviews as being in conflict, the later parts of the chapter refer to numerous other worldviews: Romanism and Lutheranism as other Christian worldviews; Islamism and paganism as other non-Christian worldviews. Kuyper views Calvinism as the purest manifestation of the Christian principle and also considered Modernism to be the chief threat to Christianity in Europe and America. Although recognizing a greater complexity to the world, Kuyper epitomizes the contemporary antithesis as a battle between the systems of Modernism and Calvinism.[38]

Kuyper considers one's understanding of three key relationships as essential for a general system of life. These include "(1) our relation *to God,* (2) our relation *to man,* and (3) our relation to *the world.*"[39] After discussing the various ways in which these relationships have been developed in different worldviews, Kuyper concludes that Calvinism offers a distinct view on each of these points:

> Thus it is shown that Calvinism has a sharply-defined starting-point of its own for the three fundamental relations of all human existence: viz., our relation to *God,* to *man* and to the *world.* For our relation *to God:* an immediate fellowship of man with the Eternal, independently of priest or church. For the relation of man *to man:* the recognition in each person of human worth, which is his by virtue of his creation after the Divine likeness, and therefore of the equality of all men before God and his

> magistrate. And for our relation *to the world:* the recognition that in the whole world the curse is restrained by grace, that the life of the world is to be honored in its independence, and that we must, in every domain, discover the treasures and develop the potencies hidden by God in nature and in human life.[40]

This last relationship points us to the next aspect of Kuyper's thought, that of the doctrine of common grace, as well as back to his notion of sphere sovereignty.

In his last Stone Lecture, dealing with "Calvinism and the Future," Kuyper gave this charge to his Princeton audience:

> With such a coherent world and life-view, firmly resting on its principle and self-consistent in its splendid structure, Modernism now confronts Christianity; and against this deadly danger, ye, Christians, cannot successfully defend your sanctuary, but by placing, in opposition to all this, *a life- and world-view of your own, founded as firmly on the base of your own principle, wrought out with the same clearness and glittering in an equally logical consistency.*[41]

Thus Kuyper sought to respond to the challenge of Modernism by using modern means, namely the development of a consistent, self-conscious worldview based on the traditional Christian beliefs of orthodox Calvinism. His development of a "worldview" analysis had by this time replaced Kuyper's earlier second usage of the notion of "sphere sovereignty," while maintaining the same distinction between opposing systems of thought across the various spheres of human life.

Common Grace

Kuyper's notion of common grace underlay his positive, world-engaging approach to Calvinism in the Stone Lectures. He developed this notion over a period of years, 1895 to 1901, in his weekly columns in *De Heraut* (*The Herald*). These were later collected and published in three volumes as *De Gemeene Gratie* (*Common Grace*).[42] In his chapter on "The Forms of Grace," Kuyper distinguishes two basic forms: special grace, which is saving grace, and common grace, which is extended to all aspects of life. He writes,

> For that reason we must distinguish two dimensions in this manifestation of grace: 1. a *saving* grace, which in the end abolishes sin and completely undoes its consequences; and 2. a *temporal restraining* grace, which holds back and blocks the effect of sin. The former, that is saving grace, is in the nature of the case *special* and restricted to God's elect. The second, *common* grace, is extended to the whole of our human life.[43]

For Kuyper the doctrine of common grace expresses God's gracious dealing with this fallen world in two different aspects. First, sin is restrained and the effects of sin tempered. In this sense, common grace serves a necessary, albeit negative role. God's grace holds back human rebellion and, furthermore, alleviates to a large extent the destructive results of that rebellion. This grace allows, secondly, for the possibility of human development of culture and society. All good gifts, whether employed by believers or unbelievers, are seen to come from God and to result in the glory of God. As a result, believers can enter into cooperation with unbelievers in the various cultural tasks, e.g., science and politics. As Kuyper states, "The fundamental creation ordinance given before the fall, that humans would achieve dominion over all of nature thanks to 'common grace,' is still realized *after* the fall."[44] Kuyper sees God as working through common grace to restrain the effects of sin and thereby to develop the creation through human cultural development.

For Kuyper, special grace presupposes common grace and could not function without it. While he sees a major purpose of common grace being that of preparation for the special grace given to God's elect, he definitely does not confine the purpose or operation of common grace to salvation. Rather, he puts both special grace and common grace into a doxological context, namely that all things are done to the glory of God. He goes so far as to subsume common grace under special grace in the following way:

> In that sense, then we must acknowledge that common grace is only an emanation of special grace and that all its fruit flows into special grace—provided it is understood that special grace is by no means exhausted in the salvation of the elect but has its ultimate end only in the Son's glorification of the Father's love, and so in the aggrandizement of the perfections of our God.[45]

Kuyper does not see either special grace or common grace as operating on its own, but rather as being intertwined in accomplishing God's purposes. To express this relationship, he compares them to two branches of one tree. Both branches of grace are rooted in Christ:

> Does not the apostle write to the church of Colosse that the self-same Christ is simultaneously two things: the root of the life of creation as well as the root of the life of the new creation? First we read that Christ is "the first-born of all creation, for in him all things were created, in heaven and on earth," so that he is "before all things and in him all things hold together." It could hardly be stated more plainly and clearly that Christ is the root of creation and therefore of common grace, for it is common grace that prevents things from sinking into nothingness. (Does not the text say that all things *hold together* in him?) But we immediately note in the second place that the same Christ is "the *Head of the Body* and the first-born from the dead," hence also the root of the life of the new creation or of special grace. The two things are even stated in parallel terms: he is the root of common grace, for he is *the first-born of all creation,* and simultaneously the root of special grace, for he is *the first-born from the dead.* There is thus no doubt that common grace and special grace come most intimately connected from their origin, and this connection lies in Christ.[46]

By focusing on Christ, rather than merely on one's own salvation, the believer is relieved of the tension of relating common grace to special grace in an unbalanced way. Kuyper sees this sort of imbalance as tending toward the Anabaptist error that sharply distinguishes between the spiritual realm and the world all around. Instead, creation and redemption both belong to Christ, and redemption is of the whole world, not just human souls. He concludes his chapter on the "Two Forms of Grace" by claiming the following:

> For that reason Scripture continually points out that the *Savior* of the world is also the *Creator* of the world, indeed that he could become its Savior only *because* he already was its *Creator.* Of course, it was not the *Son of man,* not the *incarnate Word,* who created the world. All that was human in the Mediator was itself created, creaturely as it is creaturely in us. Still, Scripture repeatedly points out that he, the first-born of the dead, is also the first-born of creation, that the Word Incarnate nevertheless always was and remained the same eternal Word who was with God and was God, of whom it is written that without that Word nothing was made that is made. Christ then is connected with *nature* because he is its Creator, and at the same time connected to *grace* because, as Re-creator, he manifested the riches of grace in the midst of that nature.[47]

In this way Kuyper roots both common grace and special grace in Christ: common grace in Christ as Creator, special grace in Christ as Redeemer. In every aspect Christ is to be seen as Lord and Sovereign over all.

In fact, Kuyper views the doctrine of common grace as an implication of the Reformed doctrine of the sovereignty of God. As he expresses it in his foreword to *Common Grace,*

> . . . the doctrine of common grace proceeds directly from the Sovereignty of the Lord which is ever the root conviction of all Reformed thinking. If God is sovereign, then his Lordship *must* remain over *all* life and cannot be closed up within church walls or Christian circles. The extra-Christian world has not been given over to satan or to fallen humanity or to chance. God's Sovereignty is great and all-ruling also in unbaptized realms, and therefore neither Christ's work in the world nor that of God's child can be pulled back out of life. If his God works in the world, then there he must put his hand to the plow so that there too the Name of the Lord is glorified.[48]

A major part of Kuyper's agenda in writing the lengthy series of articles on common grace for *De Heraut* was to call the Reformed community in the Netherlands to action. He completed the series as he was about to become prime minister of the Netherlands in 1900, and it was published in book form during the latter part of his term. The doctrine of common grace provided the theological justification and the spiritual motivation for Christians to be actively involved in every aspect of their culture, including politics, science, and the arts. Common grace also provided an understanding of history, from paradise to the Second Coming, as the working-out of God's sovereign plan for humanity, in cultural and scientific development as much as in spiritual and ecclesiastical growth. All people, believers and unbelievers alike, serve God through the developments of human history.

Conclusion

Sphere sovereignty provided Kuyper with a conceptual tool for Christian action in society in its various aspects. God had created all things, and Christians were called to develop each "sphere" in accordance to its own God-given ordering and potential. Kuyper himself contributed significantly in a number of different spheres during his career. As an educator, he founded and taught at the Free University of Amsterdam. As a politician, he started the first modern political party in the Netherlands, the Anti-Revolutionary Party, and served in parliament, including four years as prime minister of the Netherlands. He spent several decades as a journalist, editing a daily paper. As a pastor, he opposed liberalism in the church of his day and was one of the leaders of an eventual split from the established church. In theology, he contributed the works surveyed above, as well as a lengthy commentary on the Heidelberg Catechism and three volumes of collected columns on the work of the Holy Spirit.

Abraham Kuyper's most enduring legacy has been in the realm of theology, particularly in his attempt to take account of both common grace and the antithesis. The former provided a basis for unity and cooperation in the cultural task, while the latter maintained a sharp distinction and even cleavage. Kuyper held this tension in balance consistently throughout his career, as can be seen in his 1880 speech on "Sphere Sovereignty." While Kuyper had not yet worked out the doctrines of common grace and the antithesis at that point, their presence is felt.

Common grace, according to Kuyper, was the basis of human achievements in the different spheres of life. Progress can and has been made in each of the spheres as creation has been developed through human history. While it has clearly been tainted by sin, the progress has been real and will rebound to the glory of God. Kuyper's first usage of "Sphere Sovereignty," the different societal spheres, and common grace were both firmly rooted by Kuyper in creation, and both were seen as expressions of the sovereignty of God. To repeat his claim from *Common Grace,* "If God is sovereign then his Lordship *must* remain over *all* life and thinking."[49] This statement clearly echoes his theme from "Sphere Sovereignty": "Oh, no single piece of our mental world is to be hermetically sealed off from the rest, and there is not a square inch in the whole domain of our human existence over which Christ, who is Sovereign over *all*, does not cry: 'Mine'!"[50]

On the other hand, the antithesis demanded a separate development by the regenerate and unregenerate in every area. In "Sphere Sovereignty" Kuyper also argued in his second usage of the term that there must be freedom for developing scholarship in every area from the Reformed principle, in contrast to the opposing principles of his "opponents." By the time of the Stone Lectures, he had developed this analysis into a call for developing a consistent and well-thought-out Christian worldview to oppose Modernism. Kuyper never denied the accomplishments of the unregenerate, but he always saw the need for the regenerate to build consistently on their own principles.

For Kuyper, to have abandoned either of the usages of "Sphere Sovereignty" in his inaugural speech would have been to deny either the goodness of God's creation and providence or the pervasive effects of sin on humanity. This Kuyper was unwilling to do, and we would do well to emulate his example as we engage our own culture in our day.

Notes

1. Abraham Kuyper, *Souvereiniteit in Eigen Kring: Rede ter inwijdin van de Vrije Universiteit, de 20sten October 1880 gehouden, in het Koor der Nieuwe Kerk te Amsterdam* (Amsterdam: J. H. Kruyt, 1880). This work was republished in W. F. de Gaay Fortman, ed., *Architectonische Critiek: Fragmenten uit de Sociaal-Politieke Geschriften van Dr. A. Kuyper* (Amsterdam: H. J. Paris, 1956). A slightly abridged translation by George Kamp appears as "Sphere Sovereignty" in *Abraham Kuyper: A Centennial Reader*, ed. James D. Bratt (Grand Rapids, MI: Eerdmans, 1998).

2. Peter S. Heslam, *Creating a Christian Worldview: Abraham Kuyper's Lectures on Calvinism* (Grand Rapids, MI: Eerdmans, 1998), 160. *Verzuiling*, or "pillarization," was a practice during the earlier part of the twentieth century in the Netherlands of the ideological grouping of society, including Catholics, Calvinists, socialists, and so on. Each group developed on its own institutions, such as schools, newspapers, and labor unions. This is one approach to coexistence within a pluralistic society.

3. Ibid., 160.

4. William Edgar, "Review of Creating a Christian Worldview: Abraham Kuyper's Lectures on Calvinism by Peter S. Heslam," *Westminster Theological Journal* 60 (1998): 356.

5. Introduction to "Sphere Sovereignty," in *Abraham Kuyper: A Centennial Reader*, trans. George Kamp, ed. James D. Bratt (Grand Rapids, MI: Eerdmans, 1998), 461–62. Bratt suggests applying Heidegger's twofold division of "Being and Time" to Kuyper's two usages.

6. Kuyper, "Sphere Sovereignty," in Bratt, ed., *Abraham Kuyper: A Centennial Reader*, 467.

7. In the immediate application of sphere sovereignty to his historical situation, Kuyper was justifying the founding of a "Free University"; that is, one that was free from state control. Funding to go along with the freedom to establish independent educational institutions has just recently been granted in the Netherlands, which was one of Kuyper's early political goals. Thus, the sphere of education and scholarship was fundamentally independent of the state in Kuyper's view, and it could not legitimately be made to serve state purposes of an ideological nature.

8. Kuyper, "Sphere Sovereignty," in Bratt, ed., *Abraham Kuyper: A Centennial Reader*, 487–88.

9. Ibid., 484–85.

10. Ibid., 488.

11. Gordon Spykman argues that the notion of sphere sovereignty finds its beginnings in Calvin, who left it as an undeveloped idea, and has been extended by subsequent Reformed theologians, including Kuyper and Bavinck, but also their successors, including H. Dooyeweerd. Spykman wrote, "What was left to later Calvinists was to take the germinal principle of sphere-sovereignty in Calvin, delineate it more clearly with respect to church and state, and then to extend it to the other spheres in society as one by one they came to the fore in more clearly differentiated ways: commerce, for example, arising from modern capitalism; labor unions, emerging from the Industrial Revolution; modern universities, resulting largely from the scientific explosion." Gordon J. Spykman, "Sphere Sovereignty in Calvin and the Calvinist Tradition," in *Exploring the Heritage of John Calvin: Essays in Honor of John Bratt*, ed. David E. Holwerda (Grand Rapids, MI:

Baker, 1976), 194. Spykman does a good job of addressing the historical development of the first usage of Kuyper's thought regarding sphere sovereignty, but does not deal with the second.

12. The Dutch term *wereldbeschouwing* (*weltanschauung* in German) has no exact English equivalent, though the term worldview has become common since Kuyper's day. Early translators often used the cumbersome "life-and-world-view" or "life-system" when they did not want to bring over the Dutch or German term into popular discussion. The notion of the contrast between the Christian view and the non-Christian view has a long pedigree in theology, dating at least as far back as Augustine's massive study on the *City of God*.

13. Abraham Kuyper, *Encyclopaedie der Heilige Godgeleerdheid*, 3 vols. (Amsterdam: J. A. Wormser, 1894). Volume 1, Part 1, and Volume 2 were translated by J. Hendrik de Vries as *Principles of Sacred Theology* (Grand Rapids, MI: Baker, 1980 [1898]).

14. Abraham Kuyper, *Calvinism: Six Stone Foundation Lectures* [1898] (Grand Rapids, MI: Eerdmans, 1931).

15. This is the first part of Volume 2 in Kuyper, *Encyclopaedie der Heilige Godgeleerdheid*. Kuyper used "science" (*wetenschap*) broadly, as the equivalent to the German *wissenschaft*. For an examination of Kuyper's use of the image of "organism," see K. Veling, "Kuypers Visie op de Wetenschap als Organisme: Kanttekeningen bij een Metafoor," in *Bezield Verband* (Kampen: Van den Berg, 1984).

16. Kuyper, *Principles of Sacred Theology*, 112–13.

17. Ibid., 113. This argument would seem to be applied to the materialistic scientific positivists who were beginning to gain influence in the late nineteenth century.

18. Ibid., 117.

19. Ibid., 117–18.

20. Note that Kuyper often transliterated the Greek term παλιγγενέσια (Dutch, *palingenesie*; English, *palingenesis*) rather than using the Dutch term *wedergeboorte* (English, regeneration). This practice will be followed in the paper, since Kuyper's notion is somewhat different from the common evangelical usage that restricts regeneration to what Kuyper calls conversion.

21. Kuyper, *Principles of Sacred Theology*, 154. A significant aspect of Kuyper's thought is revealed in this section. He argued that the subject of scientific endeavor is, properly speaking, the general human consciousness, not particular individual scientists. Thus the idea that there is an antithesis between the regenerate and the unregenerate consciousness takes on a greater significance than that of individuals, but sharpens the cleavage within humanity as a whole. This approach to the problem reveals the degree to which Kuyper was influenced by nineteenth-century idealistic thought.

22. Ibid., 155.

23. The Dutch *geestelijk* (like the German *geistig*) has no English equivalent; it can refer to either spiritual, mental, or intellectual, corresponding to the noun form *geest* (German *geist*), which can mean spirit, mind, or intellect. The ambiguity in use can be intentional, making a translation difficult.

24. Kuyper, *Principles of Sacred Theology*, 157.

25. Ibid., 159.

26. Ibid., 160.

27. Kuyper also noted another, historical cause for the apparent unity of the two kinds of science, in that both kinds of science for several centuries operated under an outer con-

formity to special revelation, although the unregenerate never assimilated its point of view.

28. Kuyper, *Principles of Sacred Theology*, 167–68.

29. Ibid., 169. Kuyper went on to make reference again to the "universal human consciousness" as being the "subject" of science. "For this reason science in its absolute sense is the property of no single individual. The universal human consciousness in its richest unfoldings is and ever will be the subject of science, and individuals in their circle and age can never be anything but sharers of a small division of science in a given form and seen in a given light." Ibid., 169.

30. Ibid., 177.

31. Ibid., 181.

32. Abraham Kuyper, *Calvinism: Six Stone Foundation Lectures* (Grand Rapids, MI: Eerdmans, 1931). This edition is more readily available than the original 1898 one published in Amsterdam. While Kuyper himself did not translate his Dutch original into English, he played an active role in editing the English translation before its publication. It is his only work that was originally published in English, although later it was published in Dutch. The six lectures are entitled: "Calvinism a Life-System," "Calvinism and Religion," "Calvinism and Politics," "Calvinism and Science," "Calvinism and Art," and "Calvinism and the Future." A recent work that gives an extensive background on Kuyper by a thorough, historically grounded exposition of his Stone Lectures is Heslam, *Creating a Christian Worldview: Abraham Kuyper's Lectures on Calvinism*.

33. See Abraham Kuyper, "A Fata Morgana," *Methodist Review* 88 (1906): 185–208, 355–78. A more recent translation appears in Bratt, *Abraham Kuyper: A Centennial Reader*, 87–124, as "Modernism: A Fata Morgana in the Christian Domain." The original was published as *Het Modernisme, een Fata Morgana op Christelijk Gebied* (Amsterdam: H. de Hoogh, 1871), from a lecture delivered on April 14, 1871, in Amsterdam.

34. Kuyper, *Calvinism: Six Lectures*, 10.

35. Ibid., 11.

36. Ibid., 11, footnote 1. See James Orr, *The Christian View of God and the World as Centering in the Incarnation, Being the Kerr Lectures for 1890–91* (Grand Rapids, MI: Eerdmans, 1948 [1897]), 3. Peter Heslam writes of Kuyper, "Despite the existence of certain elements of this concept [i.e., worldview] in his earlier work, it was not until the Stone Lectures that he employed it in a deliberate and specific way, defining it in terms of weltanschauung and using it to give shape to his entire body of thought." Heslam, *Creating a Christian Worldview*, 92. Heslam goes on to attribute this change to Kuyper's encounter with James Orr's Kerr Lectures, *The Christian View of God and the World*. Heslam concludes, "The only significant difference between Orr's intention and that of Kuyper in presenting Calvinism as an independent and coherent worldview resistant to modernism, was that Orr pleaded the merits of a Christian worldview while Kuyper pleaded a specifically Calvinistic one—albeit Calvinistic in the broadest possible sense." Heslam, *Creating a Christian Worldview*, 95.

37. Kuyper, *Calvinism: Six Lectures*, 11–12.

38. At this point Kuyper did not follow the lead of Orr, who gave his taxonomy of worldviews in note B to Lecture I, *Christian View*, 367–70. There Orr gave one classification as 1) Phenomenalistic and Agnostic; 2) Atomistic and Materialistic; 3) Pantheistic; and 4) Theistic. He gave a second classification as 1) Scientific; 2) Philosophical; and 3) Religious. He admitted that the different types influence each other, so that in practice there are none free from outside influences. However, Orr's primary interest, like Kuyper's,

was in the religious worldview, especially that of Christianity in opposition to modern worldviews.

39. Orr, *Christian View*, 19.

40. Ibid., 31.

41. Kuyper, *Calvinism: Six Lectures*, 189–90.

42. Abraham Kuyper, *De Gemeene Gratie*, 3 vols. (Amsterdam: Höveker and Wormser, 1902, 1903, 1904). Significant selections from *De Gemeene Gratie* are included in Bratt, *Abraham Kuyper: A Centennial Reader*. See Introduction to "Common Grace" in Bratt, *Abraham Kuyper: A Centennial Reader*, 165–66, for background. Kuyper's doctrine of common grace has generated a great deal of controversy, including a denominational split in the 1920s, when Herman Hoeksema and others who denied the doctrine left the Christian Reformed Church to start the Protestant Reformed Church. For the debates over common grace, see Cornelius Van Til, *Common Grace and the Gospel* (Phillipsburg, NJ: Presbyterian and Reformed, 1972; this includes the text of his 1947 *Common Grace*); S. J. Ridderbos, *Rondom het Gemene-Gratie-Probleem* (Kampen: Kok, 1949); William Masselink, *General Revelation and Common Grace* (Grand Rapids, MI: Eerdmans, 1953); and Jochem Douma, *Algemene Genade* (Goes: Oosterbaan en Le Cointre, 1966).

43. Bratt, *Abraham Kuyper: A Centennial Reader*, 168. The selections from *De Gemeene Gratie* are translated by John Vriend.

44. Ibid., 179.

45. Ibid., 170–71.

46. Ibid., 186–87. This is from his chapter on "The Contact of Sphere and Sphere." Here the "spheres" seem to be referring to the "spheres" of grace, i.e., special and common.

47. Ibid., 173.

48. Ibid., 166.

49. Ibid.

50. Ibid., 488.

William Tyndale
and the Power of Words

Robert J. De Smith[*]

....

This essay began in a strange way. While teaching the last act of Shake-speare's *Richard III*, I brought my class to Richard's memorable line, which he exclaims twice, "A horse, a horse! My kingdom for a horse!"[1] In this brief scene—it is only twelve lines long and Richard's second cry ends it—Richard's despair, spiritual as well as physical, is emphasized by an allusion to Psalm 33, which came to me almost unconsciously in class. I quoted the Authorized (King James) Version of verses 16 and 17:

> There is no king saved by the multitude of an host;
> A mighty man is not delivered by his much strength.
> An horse is a vain thing for safety;
> Neither shall he [the horse] deliver any by his great strength.[2]

Inasmuch as the allusion sticks, it comments on Richard, linking his experi-ence to the Old Testament ethic that Israel, God's people, must rely on him,

---

[*] Dr. De Smith is Professor of English and chair of the department. He came to Dordt in 1988. He received his M.A. and Ph.D. from the University of Wisconsin at Madison. This article was first presented at the 10th Annual Northern Plains Conference on Earlier British Literature held April 2002 at Concordia College in Moorhead, Minnesota.

not on their armies, horses, power, or schemes. Other verses in the Psalm are readily applicable to Richard as well: for instance, verse 10 says, "The Lord bringeth the counsel of the heathen to nought: he maketh the devices of the people of none effect" (Richard is nothing if not full of this kind of "counsel"). On the other hand, verses 18–19 (AV) declare,

> Behold, the eye of the Lord is upon them that fear him,
> upon them that hope in his mercy;
> To deliver their soul from death.

Before Richard's final battle, we have seen him reject the fear of the Lord and his mercy, and this passage seems to lay out for him the consequences—soul death. Furthermore, in the eerie pageant of Act 5.3 in which a series of ghosts visits both Richard and Henry (Richmond), the two ways of the Psalm, the way of righteousness (vss. 1–5) and the way of unrighteousness—of faithfulness and of vanity—are contrasted.[3]

Cute, you may say, or intriguing, but just where does such a reading of this part *Richard III* come from? What habits of the mind, and of reading, foster it? Does it make sense to read Shakespeare in this way? Believe it or not, these were questions on the faces and tongues of my students as well: despite their tradition and their biblical training, they prefer not to mix the sacred and the secular unless absolutely necessary. Well, the short answer— one I'd like my students to hear—is that such readings come, at least in part, from the Protestant Reformation.

One way to describe the Reformation is to say that it was precipitated by, and facilitated, new ways of reading. One of the defining moments of the Reformation, Luther's recovery of the doctrine of justification by faith, was a reading moment. He writes that after struggling "with an extremely disturbed conscience"[4] to reconcile himself to Paul's words in Romans 1:17,

> At last, by the mercy of God, meditating day and night, I gave heed to the context of the words, namely, "In it the righteousness of God is revealed, as it is written, "He who through faith is righteous shall live." There I began to understand that the righteousness of God is that by which the righteous lives by a gift of God, namely by faith.[5]

The picture Luther gives us is of his reading, studying, and meditating himself into a discovery (though Luther would say that this insight, like faith itself, was a gift), and he particularly emphasizes reading contextually, paying attention to the whole and not just a part of his text.[6]

In addition, crucial to the Reformation was the recovery of biblical texts, Greek and Hebrew, which allowed readers to get behind the Latin of the Vulgate, and the dissemination of those texts in vernacular translations to a reading public. Here is William Tyndale, the first translator into English of the New Testament and a good portion of the Old from its original languages,[7] explaining in his "Preface" to the Pentateuch the motive of his life's work: "I had perceived by experience, how that it was impossible to establish the lay-people in any truth, except the scripture were plainly laid before their eyes in their mother tongue."[8]

Furthermore, as Tyndale's experience suggests, the Reformers aimed not just to have the words and doctrines of Scripture available to every believer but also to have those words apply to every facet of life. Of Tyndale, C. S. Lewis writes,

> He utterly denies the medieval distinction between *religion* and secular life. "God's literal sense is spiritual." Wiping shoes, washing dishes, nay, our humblest natural functions (he uses all these examples) are all equally "good works," and the ascetic life wins "no higher room in heaven" than "a whore of the stews if she repent."[9]

For many Reformers, this meant not only reading Scripture in new ways— essentially looking for contemporary and personal application—but applying the very words of Scripture to one's heart. Tyndale writes in his Prologue to *Genesis,* "As thou readest, therefore, think that every syllable pertaineth to thine own self."[10] It is this habit of reading that gives us, a century later, John Bunyan, for whom the words of Scripture "seize" or "fall on" his soul.[11] It is this same habit which Thomas Hardy later parodies when his character Tess comes upon a man who spends his Sundays painting pious graffiti in red:

> [He] began painting large square letters on the middle board of the three composing the stile, placing a comma after each word, as if to give pause while that word was driven well home to the reader's heart—
> THY, DAMNATION, SLUMBERERTH, NOT. 2 PET.ii.3.[12]

Critique aside, during the early Reformation in England, people were arrested and burned for their commitment to a book and its powerful words. One striking example is that of James Bainham, who after arrest and torture (at Sir Thomas More's home in Chelsea!) abjured, but later repented. Foxe writes that after his release, he

> was never quiet in conscience until he had uttered his fall to all his acquaintance and asked God and all the world forgiveness before the congregation in a warehouse in Bow Lane. The next Sunday after he came to St Austen's with the New Testament in his hand in English and *The Obedience of a Christian Man* in his bosom, and stood up in his pew, declaring openly with tears that he had denied God.[13]

This act, as Bainham understood, meant rearrest and certain martyrdom. The year was 1531, so the New Testament was Tyndale's. The other book he carried was also by Tyndale, published in 1528, though there is a double sense in which, symbolized by Tyndale's work on Christian living, what Bainham carried in his "bosom" was proper obedience to the gospel.[14] Books and words were taken to heart; they symbolized the doctrines they contain; they were identified with the beliefs they foster.

Having mentioned William Tyndale a number of times, I have tipped my hand, but this is what I wonder: whether Tyndale, who freshly brought the words of the Bible in the vernacular to England, did not have a role in creating new ways of using words and books—new ways of reading—that affect English readers not only of Scripture but of other texts as well. Or if at least his life and writings do not exhibit and foster these new habits. So my goal is to explore Tyndale and the power of words, looking first at some of his own words, then at the words of his Bible translations, and finally at his instructions for reading.[15]

To get to know Tyndale better, and to get a sense of the power of his own words, we must turn to Foxe's *Acts and Monuments*. Certainly, like the writer of *Acts* he was imitating, Foxe shaped his materials toward his end of witnessing to the spread of the gospel; nonetheless, he offers much accurate, eyewitness[16] information on his subjects. Tyndale[17] grew up in Gloucestershire, attended Oxford (and perhaps Cambridge), where he learned Greek and probably developed, or at least exercised, his evangelical tendencies: Foxe says he "read privily to certain students and fellows of Magdalen College some parcel of divinity; instructing them in the knowledge and truth of the Scriptures."[18] He was ordained a priest and served as a tutor in the household of Sir John Walsh in the early 1520s. In that household, he translated Erasmus's *Enchiridion,* probably began his project of translating Scripture, and, according to Foxe, caused some stir in the neighborhood on account of his anticlerical and reforming utterances.

Foxe relates a well-known incident that occurred at the Walshes' dinner table:

> Not long after, Master Tyndale happened to be in the company of a certain divine, recounted for a learned man, and, in communing and disputing with him, he drove him to that issue, that the said great doctor burst out into these blasphemous words, "We were better to be without God's laws than the Pope's." Master Tyndale, hearing this, full of godly zeal, and not bearing that blasphemous saying, replied, "I defy the pope, and all his laws;" and added that if God spared him life, ere many years he would cause a boy that driveth the plough to know more of the Scripture than he did.[19]

Tyndale's first statement here sounds Lutheran; his second, Erasmian (both figures are mentioned in Foxe's account[20]), suggesting a tension (if that is what it is) that seems to have motivated Tyndale throughout his career. With Erasmus, Tyndale was a humanist scholar—the best English-speaking scholar of Greek and Hebrew in his day—who linked his work with reform. With Luther, who was an important source for Tyndale's translations and prefaces,[21] Tyndale stood against the church and for the doctrine of justification by faith.

With something like Erasmian optimism, Tyndale says he sought service in the household of Tunstall, the Bishop of London, a man Erasmus had commended in his writings and who was an accomplished Greek scholar. But Tyndale was disappointed. A year in London convinced Tyndale "not only that there was no room in my lord of London's palace to translate the new Testament, but also that there was no place to do it in all England."[22] Tyndale left England, probably in April 1524, and never returned. There is time to tell his story only in briefest form. After an abortive attempt to publish his New Testament in Cologne, he did complete it in Worms, in 1526. Between that time and his arrest in 1535, he mastered Hebrew, perhaps in Wittenberg, eventually settling in Antwerp where he published the Pentateuch, *Jonah,* and a revised New Testament, as well as a few doctrinal and polemical works, notably his *Obedience of a Christian Man* in 1528.

Two other words of Tyndale's fill out his story. The first is a Latin letter, not discovered until the nineteenth century, which he wrote from prison to his keepers. Here is Duffield's translation:

> I believe, most illustrious sir, that you are not unaware of what has been decided concerning me. I therefore beg your lordship, and that by the Lord Jesus, that if I am to stay here through the winter, you will ask the officer to be good enough to send me from my goods which he has, a warmer cap. I suffer greatly from cold in the head, and have a perpetual catarrh, which is made worse in this cell. A warmer coat too, for the one I have is very thin, and also a piece of cloth to patch up my leggings. My overcoat is worn out, and so are my shirts. He has a woolen shirt of mine, if he will be good enough to send it. Also he has my leggings of thicker material to go on top, and my warmer night caps. I am making request to be allowed a lamp in the evening, for it is tedious sitting alone in the dark. But most of all I earnestly entreat and implore you to ask the officer to allow me my Hebrew Bible, Hebrew Grammar and Hebrew Dictionary so that I may spend my time in those studies. And in return may you be granted your greatest desire, so long as it is consistent with the salvation of your soul. But if, before the winter is over, any other decision has been made about me, I shall be patient, abiding the will of God to the glory of the grace of my Lord Jesus Christ, whose Spirit, I pray, may ever direct your heart. Amen.   W. Tindalus[23]

One is struck first of all by the humanity of this letter: Tyndale, who had been in prison for four months by this time,[24] is cold, wishes to do some sewing, wears a night cap, would like some light as the days shorten toward winter. But he also exhibits his single-hearted devotion, as a scholar, translator, and believer, to his work. We wonder, though, whether there is a humble boldness in Tyndale's request for Hebrew materials: wasn't he jailed for his translations? Perhaps, as a zek remarks in Solzhenitsyn's *One Day:* "The great thing about a penal camp is that you had a . . . lot of freedom"—you can get away with things in prison that you cannot outside.[25]

It is not difficult to see how a tradition grew that Tyndale translated a number of the Old Testament books while in prison, though this is unlikely.[26] Nor is it difficult to believe Foxe's account of Tyndale's imprisonment (recognizing Foxe did not know of this letter). Foxe writes, "Such was the power of his doctrine, and the sincerity of his life, that during the time of his imprisonment (which endured a year and a half), he converted, it is said, his keeper, the keeper's daughter, and others of his household."[27] Foxe evokes the model of St. Paul, who converted his jailor (Acts 16), and Tyndale's letter does as well, when he declares his patience in suffering and even asks for a coat and reading materials, as Paul did (2 Timothy 4:13). While this is a complex issue, perhaps Tyndale's movement from evoking the models of Luther and Erasmus to that of Paul summarizes his development as a Protestant believer, a reader of Scripture, and a person. And if I may be allowed a cheap shot, this movement suggests that Greenblatt has missed a great deal in his chapter on Tyndale in his landmark book *Renaissance Self-Fashioning.*

If you know anything about Tyndale, you know his dying words, words immortalized in a woodcut that appeared in the 1563 edition of Foxe's *Acts and Monuments.* "Lord, open the king of England's eyes," he cried just before being strangled and burned.[28] The irony of these lines, of course, is that Henry VIII was already well on his way to bringing about his break with Rome, and within a year of Tyndale's execution he had authorized the publication of the first complete English Bible, a folio edition compiled by John Rogers. This Bible was based on Coverdale's edition, which used Tyndale as far as his translations went: Coverdale finished translating the Old Testament, notably the Psalms. Roger's version was called "Matthew's Bible" for its pseudonymic translator, "Thomas Matthew" (a name with a nice apostolic ring to it!). And so while Tyndale's translations were in fact authorized, his name and contribution were hidden (the King's eyes were not opened to Tyndale).

Something must be said of Tyndale's translations themselves, of the power of his English words. Among Tyndale enthusiasts there is a mantra, "No Tyndale, no Shakespeare," which is meant to mark Tyndale's remarkable contribution to the English language. Tyndale's accomplishment was that he translated the New Testament and part of the Old directly from its original languages. He wrote that "the Greek tongue agreeth more with the English than with the Latin. And the properties of the Hebrew tongue agreeth a thousand times more with the English,"[29] and it is hard to decide whether he was a better scholar or wordsmith. His translations are with few exceptions accurate, direct, and clear. They are rarely quirky or awkward (though he calls the angels who appear to the shepherds in Luke 2 "heavenly soldiers" and tells us Pharaoh's "jolly captains" were drowned in the Red Sea). A brief example from the beginning of the Gospel of John (from Tyndale's revised New Testament) will illustrate how familiar—even how modern—Tyndale sounds:

> In the beginning was the word, and the word was with God: and the word was God. The same was in the beginning with God. All things were made by it, and without it, was made nothing, that was made. In it was life, and the life was the light of men, and the light shineth in the darkness, but the darkness comprehended it not. John 1:1–5[30]

It is estimated that nine-tenths of his readings are taken over by the Authorized Version. Indeed, Daniell shows a number of instances where the Authorized Version is less accurate and less clear than Tyndale, and Bruce points out that more often than not later revisions of the AV returned to Tyndale rather than departing further from his translations.[31]

Tyndale coined a number of words, like *scapegoat, mercy-seat,* and *passover,* as well as *Jehovah* as the English equivalent for the covenant name of God, and he used many more words in contexts that established their use in the language since, words like *swaddled* and *manger* in Luke, and *Mammon,* which he chose not to translate. More important are the hundreds of English phrases (or collocations) he contributed. Here's a short list: "And God said, let there be light"; "Am I my brother's keeper?"; "a law unto themselves"; "signs of the times"; "Ask and it shall be given unto you; seek and ye shall find, knock. . . ."; "Let not your hearts be troubled."[32] Daniell explains that Tyndale, working to translate the Hebrew possessive, "greatly extended" the use in English of Hebraisms like "the birds of the air, the fish of the sea."[33] The loose, coordinate style Tyndale uses in his narratives influenced the English plain style as well. Here is an example from Matthew 9:

> And as Jesus departed thence, two blind men followed him crying and saying: O thou son of David, have mercy on us. And when he was come to house, the blind came to him. And Jesus said unto them: Believe ye that I am able to do this? And they said unto him: yea Lord. Then touched he their eyes . . . and their eyes were opened. . . . And Jesus charged them. . . .[34]

To his first readers, Tyndale's Pentateuch was probably most striking, in large part because the recovery of Hebrew texts and the ability of Europeans to read them provided striking new insights into the biblical narrative and message. Tyndale's *Genesis* stories, for example, are vivid, even colloquial. For instance, when Eve tells the serpent (who is "subtler than all the beasts of the field") that God has told them they will die if they eat from the forbidden tree, he replies "tush ye shall not die"; a bit later "the woman saw that it was a good tree to eat of and lusty unto the eyes and a pleasant tree for to make wise."[35] Daniell explains that the *Genesis* stories "which would have been in part familiar . . . from references in sermons, from stained-glass windows, and sometimes from the mystery plays of the guilds, could now be read in full, in a way which made the text speak."[36]

Here is a good place to interject something I have wanted to say: David Daniell carefully and copiously illustrates that when Tyndale speaks in his own voice, in his prologues and prefaces, as well as in his other works, his language is steeped in Scripture. Daniell says of Tyndale's *Obedience,* "he builds his sentences, paragraphs and pages out of the bricks of Scripture. Every phrase comes from a mind steeped in both Testaments."[37] This is perhaps the natural consequence of translating, but it is also for Tyndale intentional.[38] Especially, it expresses his goal of making Scripture the basis of one's thought and language so that it is a part of everything one does and says. In short, it is this habit of breathing in and exhaling Scripture that a Protestant reader following Tyndale's example would bring to any reading.

Of course, some of Tyndale's translations were controversial, sparking his well-known and long-winded (on one side) printed debate with More.

As Daniell aptly points out, the controversy "can be boiled down to his objection to Tyndale's translation of six words."[39] Where the Vulgate suggests *priest,* Tyndale has *senior* (which he later revises to *elder*); for *church, congregation; charity* becomes for Tyndale *love,* and *grace* becomes *favour; confess* and *do penance* become *knowledge* (acknowledge) and *repent* respectively. Here is a chart representing these word choices:

Vulgate	Greek	More's word	Tyndale's word
maiores/ presbyterii	presbyter (πρεσβυτεροσ)	priest	senior (later, elder)
ecclesiam	ekklesia (εκκλησια)	church	congregation
diligeo	agape (αγαπη)	charity	Love
charitas	charis (χαρισ)	grace	favour
paenitentia	metanoeo (μετανοεω)	do penance	repent
confessio	homologeo (ομολογεω)	confess	knowledge

The Protestant doctrine of Tyndale's choices is clear. *Charity,* for instance, suggests giving that seeks to earn a reward, whereas *love* implies acting out of thankfulness. More understood that Tyndale's words were a direct threat to the church's authority, that they sought to overturn the established church's use of the Vulgate to interpret the faith. Were Tyndale's translations distorted? Most modern scholars of the New Testament would verify that his choices were based on a good understanding of Greek. What we see in Tyndale's use of these powerful words is two things: first, an acknowledgement that individual words matter, that they can be used as doctrinal missiles that get into one's heart and explode with new insight and meaning. Second, for Tyndale the head and heart must, and can, converge so that a new translation, based on the best available manuscripts, is not just neutral but bears the weight of new convictions.

There is a dilemma hiding here, I think, one that I find everywhere in Tyndale (don't worry, I'm not arguing for Greenblatt's fractured Tyndale!); it's a dilemma between the accessibility—or even the perspicuity—of Scripture and the need to be led to see it rightly. It is a dilemma between speaking and letting Scripture speak. Is *repent* a clear, heart-opening word for the Greek *metanoia* or a skewed, rhetorically motivated choice? To direct this dilemma at Tyndale's life's work, what happens when you dedicate your life to translating the Scripture into something clear and readable, motivated by the belief that all anyone need do is get the clear, perspicuous words of the gospel into his or her hand and it will open both head and heart—and then, instead of seeing your country explode in gospel words and ways, you find that your books are being burned! How could this happen?[40]

We can get a sense of Tyndale's reaction when we compare the opening of his introduction to the Cologne fragment of his New Testament—the 1525 edition that was aborted when its printing was discovered—with a later revision of that introduction published separately as *A Pathway into Holy Scripture* (1530). The original Prologue begins directly: "I have here translated, brethren and sisters, most dear and tender beloved in Christ, the New Testament, for your spiritual edifying, consolation, and solace."[41] Here it is, he says, plain and simple. Five years later, he replaces those lines with these:

> I do marvel greatly, dearly beloved in Christ, that ever any man should repugn or speak against the scripture to be had in every language, and that of every man. For I thought that no man had been so blind to ask why light should be shewed to them that walk in darkness. . . .[42]

The Scriptures are plain, they are light in darkness, and that is Tyndale's first principle of reading. One should read the plain, literal sense of Scripture, avoiding allegory except as a help to the weak.[43] He writes, "Thou shalt understand therefore that the scripture hath but one sense which is the literal sense. And that literal sense is the root and ground of all, and the anchor that never faileth whereunto if thou cleave thou canst never err or go out of the way."[44]

But resistance to Tyndale's project, which for him was resistance to the gospel itself, led Tyndale to elucidate at least two other principles for reading Scripture.[45] The first is to read having been armed with what he calls in *A Pathway into the Holy Scripture* "the first principles of our profession."[46] In other words, you have to know what to look for. Tyndale regularly identifies these as the (Lutheran) distinction between law and gospel, or rather as a process of law giving way to gospel in the stories of Scripture as well as in the story of all of Scripture. He often calls these "the keys which so open all the scripture unto thee, that no creature can lock thee out."[47] Here is Tyndale on Romans:

> The sum and whole cause of the writings of this epistle, is, to prove that a man is justified by faith only: which proposition whoso denieth, to him is not only this epistle and all that Paul writeth, but also the whole scripture so locked up, that he shall never understand it to his soul's health.[48]

The Scriptures are key to faith, but knowing that only faith justifies (which Scripture teaches) is the key to understanding Scripture. This is epistemologically complicated, but perhaps the more coherent if we remember that Tyndale begins to write only a few years after Luther nails his 95 Theses to a door in Wittenberg. These are utterly new insights, and they change everything.

This is what Tyndale means, I think, when he tells his readers, "Read God's word diligently and with a good heart, and it shall teach thee all things."[49] If this way of reading sounds circular, Tyndale also emphasizes a process by which one engages with a book. Tyndale emphasizes making available the whole of scripture in the vernacular not only because Scripture interprets Scripture (a good Reformation principle) but also because one needs to read the Bible, and individual books, in their entirety. This is what Tyndale calls "the process, order, and meaning of the text."[50] Repeatedly in his prefaces to books of the Bible, Tyndale rehearses the narrative or development of a book, its argument (Tyndale's "process"), in a particular way, that is, to illustrate how readers ought to follow the development of the text *in their own hearts.* Tyndale's habit is to use the imperative, as in his "Prologue to Genesis":

> As thou readest, therefore, think that every syllable pertaineth to thine own self, and suck out the pith of the scripture, and arm thyself against all assaults. First note with strong faith the power of God, in creating all of nought; then mark the grievous fall of Adam, and of us all in him, through the light regarding of the commandment of God.[51]

For Tyndale, reading is experiencing and responding, particularly responding to the entire story of the Scriptures—which is his reader's story. This is particularly clear in the final paragraph of his "Prologue to the Romans":

> Now go to reader, and according to the order of Paul's writing, even so do thou. First behold thyself diligently in the law of God, and see there thy just damnation. Secondarily turn thine eyes to Christ, and see there the exceeding mercy of thy most kind and loving father. Thirdly remember that Christ made not this atonement that thou shouldest anger God again: neither died he for thy sins, that thou shouldest return (as a swine) unto thine old puddle again: but that thou shouldest be a new creature and live a new life after the will of God and not of the flesh. And be diligent lest through thine own negligence and unthankfulness thou lose this favour and mercy again. Farewell. W.T.[52]

This paragraph is a fair summary of the teaching of Paul's letter. But is it also an assertion that the letter, as Scripture, is not dead but alive: it does something to us and enjoins us to do something as we read. The power of these words is to tell us who we are, and even more, to tell us who to be. In Tyndale's terms, they are gospel, interaction, even a covenant or agreement. In this spirit, he calls the book of Jonah "an obligation between God and thy soul, as an earnest-penny given thee of God, that he will help thee in time of need, if thou turn to him."[53] Tyndale enjoins his readers to be active, participating in the action of the text and applying the text to their hearts.

I wish I had time to apply these principles of reading to the text with which I began, Shakespeare's *Richard III* (or maybe I calculated my time in such a way so that I would not need to do the dirty work of application! Or maybe I need to write another paper, with this one as prolegomena). But for now, let's say this: Protestant readers, nursed by reformers like Tyndale, and growing up attuned to the power of gospel words, would have come to whatever they read in these ways: they would have come looking for the plain, literal meaning; they would have come with their minds soaked in Scripture, probably responding in their minds, if not with their tongues, using the words of Scripture. Further, they would have come looking for the truth as they understood it—that is, for affirmation of the Protestant beliefs they had taken to heart, like justification by grace and the story pattern that leads from sin (or law) through salvation (or grace) to service (or works). And they would come with the habit of engaging their hearts in what they read.

Notes

1. William Shakespeare, *Richard III*, in David Bevington, ed., *The Complete Works of Shakespeare*, updated 4th ed. (New York: HarperCollins, 1996), 5.4.7 and 5.4.12.

2. Authorized Version (AV), revised in 1881. *The Holy Bible*, Authorized King James Version (Cleveland: World Publishing, n.d.). For comparison, here is Coverdale's version from a copy of the first (1549) edition of *The Book of Common Prayer*, which I found online:

> There is no king that can be saved by the multitude of an hoste:
> neyther is anye myghtye man delyvered by muche strength.
> A horse is counted but a vayne thyng to save a man:
> neither shall he deliver any man by hys great strength.

The Book of Common Prayer—1549, *The Book of Common Prayer Homepage*, Anglican Resource Collection, 28 February 2001. http://justus.anglican.org/resources/bcp/index.html (accessed 20 March 2002).

3. To add two more examples, the play's politics may be caught up in the psalm's "Blessed is the nation whose God is the Lord" (Psalm 33:12a), and its view of providence may be glanced at in verses 13–15:

> The Lord looketh from heaven;
> He beholdeth all the sons of men.
> From the place of his habitation
> he looketh upon all the inhabitants of the earth.
> He fashioneth their hearts alike;
> He considereth all their works.   Psalm 33.

4. John Dillenberger, ed. and introd., *Martin Luther: Selections from His Writings*, The Anchor Library of Religion (Garden City, NY: Doubleday 1961), 11.

5. Ibid.

6. The persistence of this model of both reading and experiencing can be seen by considering John Bunyan, who, though writing more than a century later, consciously connects with Luther. In his spiritual autobiography, *Grace Abounding*, Bunyan writes,

> And now me thought I began to look into the Bible with new eyes, and read as I never did before; and especially the Epistles of the Apostle S. Paul were sweet and pleasant to me; and indeed, I was then never out of the Bible, either by reading or meditation, still crying out to God that I might know the truth and the way to Heaven and Glory.

John Bunyan, *Grace Abounding to the Chief of Sinners* (1666), ed. Roger Sharrock (Oxford: Clarendon Press, 1962), 19.

7. Tyndale published his New Testament in 1526, revising it in 1534. He published the Pentateuch in 1530 (revising Genesis in 1534) and Jonah in 1531. Probably he translated the historical books of the Old Testament through 2 Chronicles and, if we can believe Edward Hall's *Chronicle*, Ezra and Nehemiah as well, though these books were not published in Tyndale's lifetime. See David Daniell, *William Tyndale: A Biography* (New Haven: Yale University Press, 1994), 333–34, who quotes Hall; in his edition of Tyndale's Old Testament, Daniell publishes all the books mentioned here (David Daniell, ed., *Tyndale's*

Old Testament. Being the Pentateuch of 1530, Joshua through 2 Chronicles of 1537 and Jonah (New Haven: Yale University Press, 1993). Miles Coverdale completed translating the Old Testament (notably the Psalms), publishing the first complete English Bible in 1535. It incorporated a Tyndale's version work, slightly revised, whenever possible. This version is the basis of "Matthew's Bible," the first licensed English Bible, a folio published in 1537 by one "Thomas Matthew," a fictional name with New Testament overtones, which glossed over the contribution of the martyred Tyndale as well as the name of its compiler, John Rogers.

8. G. E. Duffield, ed. and introd., *The Work of William Tyndale* (Philadelphia: Fortress Press, 1965), 32.

9. C. S. Lewis, *English Literature in the Sixteenth Century Excluding Drama,* The Oxford History of English Literature (Oxford: Clarendon Press, 1954), 190–91.

10. Duffield, *The Work of William Tyndale,* 38.

11. See Brainerd P. Stranahan, "Bunyan's Special Talent: Biblical Texts as 'Events' in *Grace Abounding* and *The Pilgrim's Progress,*" ELR 11.3 (Autumn 1981): 333; and Stephen Greenblatt, *Renaissance Self-Fashioning from More to Shakespeare* (Chicago: University of Chicago Press, 1980), 98.

12. Thomas Hardy, *Tess of the D'Urbervilles* (1891), ed. David Skilton, with an introduction by A. Alvarez (New York: Penguin Books, 1978), 128.

13. G. A. Williamson, ed., *Foxe's Book of Martyrs* (Boston: Little, Brown, and Co., 1965), 96.

14. It is the same sense that Tyndale has in mind when he presents his revised New Testament (in 1534) to his readers in this way: "Here thou hast (most dear reader) the new testament or covenant made with us of God in Christ's blood." David Daniell, ed. *Tyndale's New Testament* (1534), Modern-spelling edition (New Haven, CT: Yale University Press, 1989), 3.

15. It is true that Tyndale might seem infertile ground for learning how to read Shakespeare. After all, this is his take on the English history Shakespeare takes up in his plays: Tyndale says that their "fathers" failed to listen to Wycliffe, preferring "holy hypocrisy" to repentance. He adds,

> But what followed? They slew their true and right king [Richard II], and set up three wrong kings a row, under which all the noble blood was slain up, and half the commons thereto, what in France, and what with their own sword, in fighting among themselves for the crown; and the cities and towns decayed, and the land brought half into a wilderness, in respect of that it was before.

Duffield, *The Work of William Tyndale,* 94.

16. For such a source behind Foxe's account of Tyndale, in the person of George Webb, see Daniell, *William Tyndale: A Biography,* 61–62.

17. For biographical information on Tyndale, I rely on Daniell, *William Tyndale: A Biography,* passim.

18. Williamson, *Foxe's Book of Martyrs,* 119.

19. Ibid., 121.

20. "Master Tyndale sitting at the same table [i.e., Walsh's], did use many times to enter communication, and talk of learned men, as of Luther and of Erasmus; also of divers other controversies and questions upon the Scripture." Williamson, *Foxe's Book of Martyrs,* 119.

21. When Tyndale's first attempt to publish his New Testament was discovered in Cologne, it was thwarted as "the Lutheran New Testament, translated into the English language" (quoted in Daniell, *William Tyndale: A Biography,* 109). One of Daniell's themes is to dis-

entangle Tyndale from Luther, recognizing Tyndale's indebtedness to the German reformer but also asserting his independence. See 113–15 for an example.

22. Duffield, *The Work of William Tyndale*, 34.

23. Duffield, *The Work of William Tyndale*, 401.

24. Daniell dates the letter to September, 1535. Daniell, *William Tyndale: A Biography*, 379. Tyndale had been arrested in May. He was condemned as a heretic in August of the next year and executed in early October, perhaps on the 6th (381–82).

25. Alexander I. Solzhenitsyn, *One Day in the Life of Ivan Denisovich* (1962), trans. Max Hayward and Ronald Hingley (Toronto: Windstone-Bantam Books, 1981), 177.

26. Daniell, *William Tyndale: A Biography*, 380.

27. Williamson, *Foxe's Book of Martyrs*, 130–31.

28. Daniell describes how the execution would have taken place. Daniell, *William Tyndale: A Biography*, 383.

29. William Tyndale, *The Obedience of the Christian Man* (1528), ed. and introd. David Daniell (New York: Penguin Books, 2000), 19.

30. Daniell, *Tyndale's New Testament*, 133. The AV (in my edition) is identical up until "made by it," where it substitutes "him"; the AV goes on "and without *him* was *not any thing made* that was made" (italics highlight changes from Tyndale). AV has "him" for "it" in the next clause ("In him was life"); it eliminates the article before darkness, and substitutes "and" for Tyndale's "but." Here for comparison is the New International Version, a late-twentieth-century translation:

> In the beginning was the Word, and the Word was with God, and the Word was God. He was with God in the beginning. Through him all things were made; without him nothing was made that has been made. In him was life, and that life was the light of men. The light shines in the darkness, but the darkness has not understood it.

31. Daniell, *Tyndale's New Testament*, 133; F. F. Bruce, *History of the English Bible*, 3rd ed. (New York: Oxford University Press, 1978), 44.

32. See Daniell, *Tyndale's New Testament*, ix–x, for another list.

33. Daniell, *William Tyndale: A Biography*, 3.

34. Daniell, *Tyndale's New Testament*, 32; see his *William Tyndale: A Biography* for another example.

35. Quoted in Daniell, *Tyndale's New Testament*, 286.

36. Ibid., 287.

37. Daniell, *William Tyndale: A Biography*, 226.

38. Daniell suggests regarding the Scriptural phrases in Tyndale's *The Wicked Mammon*, "It is likely that in writing it Tyndale had in mind that for some readers these pages could have been a first encounter with New Testament words in English, and a first exposition of the New Testament doctrine of faith before works. Accumulation of New Testament reference and quotation has a confirming effect." Daniell, *William Tyndale: A Biography*, 160. See also note 45 below.

39. Daniell, *William Tyndale: A Biography*, xx.

40. Daniell says Tyndale "never recovered" from the shock of having his New Testament burned and suggests that it produced a "sharp . . . alteration" in him. Daniell, *William Tyndale: A Biography*, 189.

41. Duffield, *The Work of William Tyndale*, 3, note 1.

115

42. Ibid., 3. As further illustration, in 1525 the sentence leading up to Tyndale's "so blind to ask," which is in both versions, is this: "The causes that moved me to translate, I thought better that other should imagine, than that I should rehearse them. Moreover I supposed it superfluous; for who is so blind. . . ." Ibid., 3, note 1. By 1530 such arguments are not superfluous. Indeed, in his introduction to his *Obedience,* published in 1528, Tyndale offers an extended defense of the Scriptures in English. Tyndale, *The Obedience of the Christian Man,* 15–25.

43. In his "Prologue to Jonah," for instance, Tyndale has this to say about reading Jonah's time in the whale's belly as an allegory of Christ's death and resurrection:

> And that Jonas was three days and three nights in the belly of his fish, we cannot thereby prove unto the Jews and infidels, or unto any man, that Christ must therefore die, and be buried, and rise again: but we use the ensample and likeness to strength the faith of the weak. For he that believeth the one cannot doubt the other.

Duffield, *The Work of William Tyndale,* 93. See also Tyndale's discussion of allegory in is Prologue to Leviticus. Ibid., 63.

44. Tyndale, *The Obedience of the Christian Man,* 156.

45. C. S. Lewis illuminatingly explains in his own summary of Tyndale's doctrine that one need not worry about which works of Tyndale one references:

> Tyndale's message is always the same and a single abstract would serve for nearly all his books. This repetition is intentional. . . . He never envisioned the modern critic sitting down to his Works in three volumes: he is like a man sending messages in war, and sending the same message often because it is a chance if any one runner will get through.

Lewis, *English Literature in the Sixteenth Century Excluding Drama,* 182. I will take the same miscellaneous approach to Tyndale's writings. See also note 38 above.

46. Duffield, *The Work of William Tyndale,* 24.

47. "Prologue to Jonah"; Duffield, *The Work of William Tyndale,* 100; see also 23.

48. Daniell, *Tyndale's New Testament,* 223.

49. "Prologue to Numbers"; Duffield, *The Work of William Tyndale,* 78.

50. "Preface to the Pentateuch"; Duffield, *The Work of William Tyndale,* 32. Tyndale uses numerous versions of this formula. In his "Pathway" he begins a summary by referring to the "order and practice of every thing afore rehearsed." Duffield, *The Work of William Tyndale,* 13. In his *Obedience* he argues the "lay people" need the Scripture in their language so they can "see by the order of the text" whether an interpreter tells the truth or "juggleth." Tyndale, *The Obedience of the Christian Man,* 16. A bit later he declares that "by the principles of the faith and by the plain scriptures and by the circumstances of the text should we judge all men's exposition and all men's doctrine." Tyndale, *The Obedience of the Christian Man,* 22. And on the last page of his introduction to that work he invites his readers to judge his uses of Scripture "by the circumstance and process of them." Tyndale, *The Obedience of the Christian Man,* 30.

51. Duffield, *The Work of William Tyndale,* 38.

52. Daniell, *Tyndale's New Testament,* 224.

53. Duffield, *The Work of William Tyndale,* 89.

Phonics, Whole Language, and Biblical Hermeneutics

Pamela E. Adams[*]

. . . .

During the last few years, the issue of how reading should be taught in our nation's schools has been a controversial one. Many of us have seen segments on television dealing with the "reading wars," have read articles in national magazines where prominent writers take a stand for or against whole language, or have heard phonics vs. whole language heatedly debated on the radio by reading professionals, parents, and politicians. Christians, who are people of the book, are rightly concerned with literacy and have therefore also entered the debate.

Support from conservative Christians for teaching phonics comes as no surprise because several Christian organizations and publishers have supported the teaching of phonics for a number of years. Phyllis Schlafly started writing about this issue long before whole language became a popular reading

---

[*] Dr. Adams is the Director of Graduate Education and Professor of Education. After nine years in grade school education and since coming to Dordt College in 1988 she completed the Ph.D. at the University of Iowa.

approach. In the September 1985 issue of *The Phyllis Schlafly Report*, Schlafly criticized the look-say (whole word) method as being associated with progressive education while phonics was lauded as being associated with traditional educational methods.[1] Schlafly clearly favors phonics because she believes it is a more effective way to teach reading, but she also rejects other methods, such as the look-say (whole word) method, using contextual cues, and guessing at words, because she associates them with liberal philosophical trends. Similarly, Christian publishers such as A Beka and Bob Jones Press have long supported a phonics approach to reading. In a pamphlet published by A Beka, James Chapman, professor at Pensacola Christian University, indicates why:

> Individual words may not be important to "progressive" educators . . . but *the emphasis upon individual words has always been of paramount importance to Christian educators, who believe in the verbal inspiration of the Scriptures and in quality education.* Orthodox Christians believe that God gave every word of Scripture, not just the thoughts.
>
> Christians therefore who are training young people to respond to Jesus' command to "live by every word that proceedeth out of the mouth of God" should reject a system of reading that trains students to guess at words and to be content with approximate meanings.[2]

Here Chapman goes one step further than Schlafly by linking the issue to biblical hermeneutics. Chapman worries that whole language strategies that put less stress on word-level accuracy will affect biblical interpretation and ultimately undermine biblical authority.

The central issue I will explore in this paper is the tie between teaching reading and biblical hermeneutics. If Christian teachers are indeed concerned about biblical literacy, I believe they will select reading methodologies that are consistent with their view of the Bible. For example, if a teacher takes a literalist view of biblical interpretation, then methodologies that have a word-level focus and include intensive phonics, attention to accurate oral reading, and literal comprehension will be appropriate. On the other hand, if a teacher embraces a nonliteralist hermeneutic, then whole language methodologies that focus on global meaning, context, multiple interpretations and pay less attention to oral reading accuracy will be appropriate. This paper will look to see if there is indeed a consistency between belief and practice for Christian teachers of reading.

Phonics and Whole Language: Terminology, Research, and Practice

Before taking up their relationship to hermeneutics, we need to describe intensive phonics and whole language and briefly explore their differences.

Phonics refers to the letter-sound clues one uses to read or pronounce a word. This process is often called decoding. To become a fluent reader, one must be able to automatically and effortlessly recognize letters, spelling patterns, and whole words. Eye movement studies on beginning readers show that they look at and process practically every letter in a word.[3] Most teachers would agree that teaching phonics is very important for beginning readers because they first need to overcome the hurdle of understanding the alphabetic nature of our language.[4] As children mature they are more able to successfully use context, picture, and syntactic cues, and with increased exposure to print, they can develop a vast store of automatically recognized words. More mature readers are also better able to use known words to decode unknown words, for example using the word *rain* to figure out the new word *train*.[5] Adherents to the phonics school of thought believe that children go through stages in their reading development and that, for beginning readers, attention needs to be placed on letters and sounds.[6]

The teacher who adopts an intensive phonics approach typically uses textbooks and closely follows the lesson plans outlined in the teacher's guide. Various phonics skills are taught to the whole class or in small groups with the students writing words on worksheets or small chalkboards under the close supervision of the teacher. If the teacher is creative, he or she will use songs, rhymes, and games to make the practice enjoyable. Skill knowledge is assessed by means of worksheets, and reteaching is often done in small groups for those needing the help. The books used for reading are chosen to fit the average reading level of the class and are most often basal readers, anthologies published specifically for teaching reading. When the children read, it is usually done orally, and accurate oral reading is the goal. When children don't know a word, they are encouraged to sound it out. The teacher then follows up the oral reading with a time to discuss the story. This discussion often takes the form of the teacher asking questions from the teacher's manual, many of which focus on literal details found in the story.

The controversy is not so much about whether beginning readers should be taught phonics, but how the phonics should be taught and how much time should be spent on its teaching. In an intensive phonics program, children are usually taught the letters and sounds before attempting any connected reading. There is also a tendency to teach these letters and sounds in a prescribed sequence. Often children memorize rules such as "when two vowels go walking, the first one does the talking"; do numerous work sheets; and read short pieces that help them to practice the skills taught. One potential problem with this approach is that children are often taught more than they really need to know. The tie between the sounds of letters and their actual pronunciation in words is approximate and there are many exceptions to "phonics rules." Many phonics programs, if followed rigorously, can cause a teacher to miss a teachable moment and to spend too much time on this part of the curriculum, taking time away from the enjoyment of good books.

In contrast, the whole language approach tries to ease children into reading by making use of what children already know. The whole language approach to reading regards the decoding aspect as just one part of this process. According to Frank Smith, reading is a psycholinguistic guessing game in which the reader relies on prior knowledge, the natural redundancy of language, and visual and graphophonic cues.[7] The controversy revolves around whether readers can indeed use all these cues when they are just beginning to read. With whole language, rather than starting with letters and sounds, children are given simple, predictable texts. They are taught to use context cues and picture cues and to guess at words using minimal letter cues. Once children understand and enjoy what reading is about, phonetic elements are introduced when the need for them arises. Rather than starting with the parts, the whole language approach starts with the whole. For example, a kindergarten teacher might print the words to the familiar rhyming poem "Ten Little Monkeys Jumping on the Bed" on a large piece of chart paper. First the teacher reads this rhyming, predictable, and repetitive poem to the class. Children are encouraged to join in when they can. Soon the whole class has the poem memorized. At this point the teacher might concentrate on certain words or letter sounds. Finally the poem is read again. The teacher then will tie in what was learned with reading the text so that the students will see how the knowledge of letters and words will help them in reading.

In a classroom where the teacher is a whole language advocate, instruction in reading typically involves reading self-selected trade books rather than textbooks. Children can be seen reading silently by themselves or orally with partners. The teacher circulates and has informal conferences with the children. During the conferences the teacher might ask the students about the types of books they like and if the books they are reading are good for them. In addition, the children may be asked to read a page or two, and the teacher will take note of what skills the children need help with. Since the emphasis is on meaning rather than words, the teacher ignores most miscues if the children are getting meaning from the text. When giving help to a child who doesn't know a word, the teacher encourages the child to "think it out" rather than "sound it out." The child is encouraged to use context, background knowledge, syntax, and other clues along with visual and phonic cues. When children discuss books, they often do this in student-led groups. Students are encouraged to personally interact with the book and relate it to their own life experiences. When written responses are asked for, they are more often in the form of journal responses than in answering teacher-generated questions. Skills are taught but on a needs basis. For example, the teacher in this class may notice that Kinsley, Jesse, and Luke need help with r-controlled vowels while Micah and Joshua need help with using context cues. The teacher will call temporary groups to work with these children.

One potential danger of this approach is that the teacher may overlook teaching important skills because the teaching is driven by the particular texts read. Evidence also suggests that some children need multiple opportunities to learn a new skill and that decontextualized exercises can give these children the practice they need. While there is much conflicting research about the values of the two ways of teaching reading, some evidence supports a whole language approach in kindergarten with a move to a more directive phonics approach—not necessarily an intensive phonics approach—in first grade.[8]

The differences between the two classrooms include: (1) lack of both teacher directed instruction and a set time line or sequence for teaching skills in the whole language class, (2) a more careful monitoring of skills in the phonics intensive classroom, (3) less emphasis on accurate oral reading in the whole language classroom, and (4) greater attention to phonics during skill lessons and oral reading with the phonics intensive program. I believe these differences are not simply driven by what the teacher thinks works; rather, these differences are consistent with the differing reading philosophies.

Historical Overview

One should also remember that ways of teaching reading have varied over the decades. Biblical literacy was the driving force behind the establishment of schools in the United States during the colonial period. Over the decades the key issues driving education have shifted with the times. To some degree the pendulum swings in educational methodologies reflect the social and political concerns of the era.

During colonial times, phonics was the method emphasized. Reading was taught with a hornbook and a limited number of texts. This emphasis extended into the nineteenth century with our schools still including Bible reading, prayer, and the direct teaching of morals. The *McGuffey Eclectic Readers* included biblical stories that did not leave any question about what was right or wrong.[9] For some teachers, this period of time is golden and the pedagogy of the time has become sanctified. Because phonics drills, memorization, and teacher-directed discussions were common in the past, some educators believe they are superior methods. However, these methodologies reflect both the uses of literacy during this period of time and materials available. Because few texts were written for children, texts were read and reread to the point of memorization. Often colonial families would gather around the stove at night to listen to one family member read aloud. Oral reading fluency and accuracy were highly regarded in this milieu. Comprehension was not taught in schools but assumed because the materials used were so well known.[10] Using the argument that phonics must have worked because people back then knew how to read while children today struggle does not take into account the evidence that children today are learning how to read and read very well in the primary grades.[11] During colonial times, a person was considered to be literate if she or he could simply sign their name; at other times the proof involved the oral reading of a well-known text.[12] Today the demands are much greater.[13] The popular belief that children can't read actually applies more to children in the middle grades and up. It is at the higher levels of reading that children fail. They have difficulties with critical thinking skills such as making inferences or drawing conclusions but not with decoding.[14]

The use of the *McGuffey Eclectic Readers* continued into the twentieth century, with a change in methodology becoming apparent after the First World War. The move away from the highly structured approach of phonics was consistent with the progressive educational philosophies of the day.[15] Colonel Francis Parker believed that drudgery and drill should be replaced with freedom. He saw the "word method" as being natural and in keeping with this new emphasis on making learning fun.[16]

Readers of this article who learned to read with Dick, Jane, Spot, and Puff probably had less phonics instruction than the typical child today. In the 1950s and well into the '60s, the look-say (whole word) method was popular. However, the whole word method should not be confused with whole language. The whole word method emphasizes the development of a large stock of sight words. With the whole word method, the teacher introduces a few new words with each story. With each successive story, these words are reviewed and new words added. The stories, famous for their unnatural language, were carefully constructed to build on each other. These texts are often referred to as vocabulary-controlled texts. The following is the entire text of the story "Look" taken from the New Basic Reader titled *The New We Look and See,* originally published in 1951:

LOOK

Look, look.
Oh, oh, oh.
Oh, oh.
Oh, look.[17]

Younger readers of this article probably were taught to read with phonics. During the 1960s, '70s, and '80s the pendulum swung away from the whole word method. The launching of Sputnik and the supposed superiority of Russian schools made for a climate of dissatisfaction with current methodologies. *Why Johnny Can't Read,* written by Rudolph Flesch and published in 1955, was a popularly read and influential attack on the whole word method.[18] While Flesch targeted the whole word method rather than whole language, the polemical nature of the language parallels some of the modern day debate between phonics and whole language.

Biblical Hermeneutics and Reading Pedagogy

The debate between phonics and whole language also emerged in Christian schools in North America, where it took on special significance because of the centrality of the Bible, God's written word, in these schools. In some Christian schools, decisions about reading pedagogy have been closely related to beliefs about how the Bible should be read and interpreted. Other Christian schools, however, appear not to have given adequate consideration to the connections between these issues.

The phonics-intensive classroom is more typical of what occurs in Christian schools, especially those with fundamentalist leanings. Studies of fundamentalist Christian schools indicate that a transmission model of learning is often used and that much attention is given to individual words and to accurate oral reading.[19] Peshkin and others have tied this to fundamentalists' literal view of Scripture, as does James Chapman.[20] If one believes that each and every word of the Bible is the literal Word of God, then it is not surprising that one would teach reading in such a manner. Fundamentalist schools also appreciate a transmission model of education over a child-centered one because of their belief in the sinfulness of their students. Traditional teaching strategies more closely match this view of the learner. Child-centered pedagogies, which assume the innate goodness of the child, are viewed as ineffective as well as being rooted in a humanistic view of the learner and the learning process.

While differences in hermeneutics can make for some differences in pedagogy, I would not expect an extreme reader-centered approach, where the reader's interpretation replaces the author's intention, to be acceptable to Christian teachers.[21] As Leland Ryken puts it, "[t]he very fact that God revealed the most important truth that we can imagine in written and literary form commits Christians to a belief in the ability of language to communicate truth."[22] Still, more subtle differences would be expected. If one holds to a literal view of hermeneutics then a word-based approach to teaching reading with a heavy dose of phonics seems consistent. Accurate oral reading and literal comprehension would also be important to the literalist. However, a teacher who takes a nonliteral approach for Bible reading would emphasize the global meaning of literary texts and give less attention to individual words and accurate oral reading. This teacher would also be more accepting of variations in interpretation. Following are summaries of four studies that look at these issues.

Old Order Amish

In *Amish Literacy: What and How It Means,* Andrea Fishman investigated how the beliefs of an Old Order Amish community relate to how reading is taught and how texts are read.[23] The very fabric of this Amish community is built on a belief that there are absolutes and that the ordinary person can know them. A belief that meaning resides in the text is part and parcel of their worldview. The Bible is memorized and recited, but never discussed or taught. One simply accepts what it says. This follows over to their use of lay ministers. The Amish believe the Bible is an open book to all and special training is not necessary to understand it. In their schools the approach to other texts is the same. Teachers present rather than explain material and the questions asked check the literal level of comprehension. Memorization and accurate oral reading are encouraged. For these Amish, teaching strategies match views of how the Bible should be read.[24]

Fundamentalists

Mark Thogmartin's "The prevalence of phonics instruction in fundamentalist Christian schools" is a study of fundamentalism and reading pedagogy.[25] Thogmartin wondered why fundamentalist schools are so pro-phonics and set out to find out what fundamentalist Christian educators believe about reading instruction and what reasons they have for holding these beliefs. What is particularly interesting about this study is that Thogmartin tries to look into the theological and philosophical underpinnings of the educators' beliefs about reading. All twenty of his research informants believe phonics is the correct way to teach reading. The responses they gave during interviews fit the following categories:

(1) Phonics works so why try anything else.

(2) Phonics is a traditional method used during our nation's beginnings.

(3) Whole language is associated with humanism, secularism, and New Age religions.

(4) Whole language teaching lacks structure; children learn better when they are disciplined and under the guidance of adults.

(5) The only available reading materials with a Christian perspective are intensive phonic programs. [A Beka and Bob Jones are the most popular.]

(6) The status quo is hard to change and change is not worth the effort.

Thogmartin's research calls into question whether teachers do work from a theoretical framework. The people in his study seem to be accepting of phonics for more superficial reasons. Thogmartin expected whole language to be unacceptable to these teachers because of whole language's belief that the reader brings meaning to print rather than meaning residing in the text.[26]

Fundamentalists and Charismatics

Another relevant ethnographic study, *Keeping Them Out of the Hands of Satan: Evangelical Schooling in America,* compares Covenant School, which has a charismatic orientation, with Lakehaven Baptist Academy, which is fundamentalistic.[27] Lakehaven Baptist Academy is concerned with doctrinal issues and sees itself in a war against modernism, while Covenant School emphasizes the experiential aspect of religion and is far less concerned with doctrine. While both schools are evangelical, their educational philosophies are quite different. Lakehaven is more doctrinally rigid and concentrates on factual learning, while Covenant is much more child-centered and less authoritarian. The author, Susan D. Rose, credits the differing outlooks to their differing views of the pervasiveness of human depravity as well as their social class. The working class, fundamentalist academy relies on supervision and rules to keep their children away from the evils of the world. The charismatic movement, of which Covenant School is a part, is a modern and largely middle-class variant of Pentecostalism. Covenant School's openness to discussion and emphasis on personal interaction reflects its theology and social class. While socioeconomic class was a factor in this study, there is a consistency between worldview and pedagogy in both schools.[28]

Reformed Christians

This study, conducted by the author, was done with teachers who teach in schools associated with Christian School International (CSI) and who, for the most part, attend churches in the Reformed tradition. The intent of this study was to ascertain the teachers' beliefs about literary interpretation, beginning reading, and oral reading and to determine whether they saw a tie between their view of Scripture and the way they taught reading. In order to see if there was a consistency, I tried to get a sense of what the teachers' view of Scripture was. Questions about how one reads the Bible tried to measure if the teachers took a literal or nonliteral view of biblical hermeneutics. Results from the survey data and interviews gave no evidence to support a view that the teachers were literalists. They believe the Bible is infallible in matters of faith and practice but are unsure of their abilities to correctly interpret Scripture and acknowledge that the various genres in the Bible should be interpreted in different ways.[29]

On the average, the CSI teachers in this study take neither a text-based nor a reader-based view of literary interpretation. CSI teachers believe that the text does convey meaning and they demand textual support from their students during literature discussions. However, they tend to stay away from teacher-directed strategies because they don't want to stifle their students' willingness to participate. In terms of where meaning resides in texts, the teachers acknowledge the role of both the text and the reader in the act of interpretation. In general the CSI teachers in this study take a view of beginning reading that tends toward a word-level emphasis. Direct and systematic teaching of phonics appears to be common in CSI schools. However, this attention to words is related to the effectiveness of phonics rather than a literal hermeneutic. For oral reading, the CSI teachers tended to be more concerned with meaning than with accuracy.[30]

The relationship between Bible beliefs and reading pedagogy was expressed in varying ways by the CSI teachers in my study. The ties teachers made were not with hermeneutics, but were expressed in terms of being "conservative" or "liberal" and "open-" or "close-minded." While not seeing the relationship in terms of hermeneutics, the teachers did make a connection between reading pedagogy and their worldview. However, a few teachers did not see how their view of the Bible affected how they taught phonics and other reading skills.[31]

A Reformed Christian Response

A Reformed view of pedagogy assumes that a teacher's philosophy of education influences practice. For me, this means that I reject the extreme whole language position that leads to an individualistic reading of a text. Christians should value community and the insights of others. While we should always be searching for fresh insights, we should also value what tradition tells us. An extreme whole language view of the reading process can also give children the impression that everything is relative and that for every issue there are multiple "right" answers. While not wanting to restrain student interpretations, I believe a teacher would want to ask a student for some textual evidence to support their interpretations. As Reformed Christians, we also need to acknowledge the effect of sin on all we do, including interpreting texts. Hard-heartedness can block our understanding of texts and make us see things from a self-centered perspective.

The other extreme, the one often taken by fundamentalists, is also one I reject. For these teachers the interpretation of a text is plain and this is the one the teacher expects the students to replay in oral recitations and on exams. I don't think this view is correct because it fails to acknowledge the very humanness of the reading process. I believe each person does bring his or her own experiences to a piece of writing and as humans our vision is always limited. These ideas are obvious to anyone who read a novel while they were a teenager, then read it again as an adult. Life experiences do change how we see things. Teaching with an objectivistic understanding of truth leaves little room for personal response and for discussion. Students are given the impression that a disinterested examination of the facts or words will allow us to arrive at the truth. Robert Lundin, professor of English at Wheaton College, says that evangelical Christians are especially susceptible to this inclination toward purely objective interpretations.[32] Contrary to this objectivistic assumption, I believe we need to acknowledge that we read through our worldview lenses.

While we disagree with the whole language romantic view of the learner, as Reformed Christians we would also want to disagree with the fundamentalist views. While we need to acknowledge how sin distorts everything we do, our belief in the covenant should cause us to disagree with the more literalist and authoritarian style of fundamentalists' pedagogy. God's covenant of grace is historical, so that the textual story of that covenant is always related to context. And in the light of that covenant of grace, we should see our students as redeemed creatures who can have significant insights that are worth listening to.

Reformed Christians need to be wary of both extremes. A balanced approach is more in keeping with a Reformed view of the child as well as hermeneutics. Bosma and Blok explain:

> Neither extreme addresses the scope of the complex nature of reading or the nature of the learner. The top-down model can lead to the mistaken ideas that with enough

time and exposure to good books and without direct instruction, all children will learn to read. The bottom-up model manipulates both the child and the text by placing the learner in a passive role and feeding the data bite by bite in minute linguistic pieces. The bottom-up model has its basis in behavioristic psychology which fails to account for the rational and creative nature of the child.[33]

A Reformed view of pedagogy should reject both the behaviorist and humanist view of the child. While each child is an image-bearer of God, each is unique in many ways, including how they learn to read and write. Some learn well auditorially, others learn well visually, and still others need the reinforcement of multiple cues. All teachers need to be aware of the diversity of learning strengths and weaknesses and to present lessons that try to meet the diverse needs of learners. Each child needs to be respected as a seeker of meaning and never taught in a manner that belittles the child. Instead, our reading pedagogy should be one that is both open to multiple interpretations and aware of the existence of objective truth.

Too often in education what seems to work in the short term becomes the popular method. Educational trends don't arise out of a vacuum, but reflect the worldviews of the originators. In turn, Christian educators need to consider more than what works or what is popular: they need to consider whether their methods are consistent with their professed view of the world and the learner. Just the fact that a certain program has research supporting its utility is not reason enough to use it. If the method treats the learner in a way that is not consistent with our view of children made in the image of God, then we should reject it. The goal of our reading pedagogy should be to create children who enjoy reading and who read with discernment, whether the text is a novel, newspaper, or that most special text of all, the Bible.

Notes

1. Phyllis Schlafly, "Phonics—The Key to Reading," *The Phyllis Schlafly Report* September (Alton, IL: The Eagle Trust Fund, 1985).

2. James A. Chapman, *Why Not Teach Intensive Phonics?* (Pensacola, FL: A Beka Book Publications, 1987), 13–14.

3. Marilyn J. Adams, *Beginning to Read: Thinking and Learning about Print* (Cambridge, MA: MIT Press, 1990).

4. Connie Juel, "Beginning Reading," in *Handbook of Reading Research: Vol. II*, ed. Rebecca Barr et al. (White Plains, NY: Longman, 1991), 759–87.

5. M. Moustafa, "Recoding in Whole Language Reading Instruction," *Language Arts* 70 (1993): 483–87.

6. A. Biemiller, "The Development of the Use of Graphic and Contextual Information as Children Learn to Read," *Reading Research Quarterly* 6 (1970): 75–96.

7. Frank Smith, *Understanding Reading—A Psycholinguistic Analysis of Reading and Learning to Read* (Hillsdale, NJ: Lawrence Erlbaum Associates, 1988).

8. S. Stahl and P. Miller, "Whole Language and Language Experience Approaches for Beginning Reading," *Review of Educational Research* 59 (1989): 87–116.

9. C. V. Alongi, "Phonics Battle in Perspective," *The School Administrator* 14 (1984): 16–19; Tim F. LaHaye, *The Battle for the Mind* (Old Tappan, NJ: Fleming H. Revell, 1984); and John H. Westerhoff, *McGuffey and His Readers—Piety, Morality, and Education in Nineteenth-Century America* (Nashville: Abingdon Press, 1978).

10. E. Jennifer Monaghan, "Literacy Instruction and Gender in Colonial New England," in *Reading in America: Literature and Social History*, ed. Cathy Davidson (Baltimore: The Johns Hopkins University Press, 1989), 53–80.

11. Regie Routman, *Literacy at the Crossroads: Critical Talk about Reading, Writing, and Other Teaching Dilemmas* (Portsmouth, NH: Heineman, 1996).

12. Monaghan, "Literacy Instruction," 53–80.

13. Michael F. Graves, Connie Juel, and Bonnie B. Graves, *Teaching Reading in the 21st Century* (Boston: Allyn and Bacon, 1998).

14. Routman, *Literacy at the Crossroads*.

15. Alongi, "Phonics Battle in Perspective," 16–19.

16. Herbert M. Kliebard, *The Struggle for the American Curriculum: 1893–1958* (New York: Routledge, 1985).

17. W. Gray, A. S. Artley, and M. H. Arbuthnot, "Look," in *Fun with Dick and Jane* (New York: HarperCollins Publishers, 1991), 3–6.

18. Alongi, "Phonics Battle in Perspective," 16–19; and Bette Bosma and Kathryn Blok, *A Christian Perspective on the Teaching of Reading* (Grand Rapids, MI: A Calvin College Monograph, 1992).

19. Nancy T. Ammerman, *Bible Believers: Fundamentalists in the Modern World* (New Brunswick, NJ: Rutgers University Press, 1987); Alan Peshkin, *God's Choice: The Total World of a Fundamentalist School* (Chicago: University of Chicago Press, 1986); and Susan D. Rose, *Keeping Them Out of the Hands of Satan: Evangelical Schooling in America* (New York: Routledge, 1988).

20. Peshkin, *God's Choice;* and Chapman, *Why Not Teach Intensive Phonics?*

21. Leland Ryken, *Windows to the World: Literature in Christian Perspective* (Grand Rapids, MI: Zondervan, 1985).

22. Leland Ryken, "Afterword," in *Contemporary Literary Theory: A Christian Appraisal*, ed. Clarence Walhout and Leland Ryken (Grand Rapids, MI: Eerdmans, 1991), 299.

23. Andrea Fishman, *Amish Literacy: What and How It Means* (Portsmouth, NH: Heinemann, 1988).

24. Ibid.

25. Mark Thogmartin, "The Prevalence of Phonics Instruction in Fundamentalist Christian Schools," *Journal of Research on Christian Education* 3 (1994): 103–32.

26. Ibid.

27. Rose, *Keeping Them Out of the Hands of Satan.*

28. Ibid.

29. Pamela E. Adams, "Biblical Hermeneutics and the Teaching of Reading" (doctoral dissertation, University of Iowa, 1995).

30. Ibid.

31. Ibid.

32. Robert Lundin, "Our Hermeneutical Inheritance," in *The Responsibility of Hermeneutics*, by R. Lundin, A. C. Thiselton, and C. Walhout (Grand Rapids, MI: Eerdmans, 1985), 1–29.

33. Bosma and Blok, *A Christian Perspective on the Teaching of Reading*, 23–24.

The Dangerous Safety of Fiction

David Schelhaas[*]

....

For the past three semesters, I have taught André Brink's *A Dry White Season* (1980), always with positive responses from my students. The last time, I invited a black South African, the principal of a school, to speak to my class. Talking to him before class, I discovered that he had a story very much like that of Gordon Nbubene in the novel. His son had been arrested and killed; the body had disappeared and then turned up in a distant police station. There had been hearings and inquests, but no answers and no justice. He told his story in my class, and at the end of the hour, one of my students came up to me and said, "Mr. Schelhaas, what can we do about this? We've got to do something." Clearly, the personal narrative of my guest speaker had spoken to her and other students with far more urgency than the novel had. This was more than a tragic story. This was real life, and it demanded action.

---

[*] Mr. Schelhaas is a Dordt graduate and Assistant Professor of English (since 1988). He is the author of *Angling in the English Stream* (Dordt College Press, 2004) and hosts a weekly broadcast on KDCR, "What's the Good Word?" This essay was first published in *English Journal* (February 1994). Copyright 1994 by the National Council of Teachers of English. Reprinted with permission.

This incident and others like it have raised questions in my mind. If one of my goals is to educate students for responsible action in a world overwhelmed with injustice, must I abandon my thirty-year belief in the affective power of fiction and become a sort of academic Oprah, inviting people with dramatic and important tales to speak in my classroom? Have I been naïve to hope that Sydney was correct in his assertion that fiction's purpose is "not only to make Cyrus [Xenophon's just prince], but to bestow a Cyrus on the world to make many Cyruses, if they will learn aright why and how that maker made him"?[1]

I believed that if my students cared about the fictional characters they encountered, if the lives and predicaments of Hester and Huck and Fiver and Frodo mattered to them, then they would carry back good things from the fictional world to their own worlds. After all, as Walter Wangerin has noted, stories are

> Always more than information that some poor kid must labor to understand. A story is a world . . . both radiant and real—a world into which the child is invited and she enters. And it is the telling of the tale that causes the world to be. The telling encourages the child to believe its being. The telling calls her into it so that she more than knows; she actually experiences.[2]

Is it possible, I asked myself, that literary fiction has lost its power to affect this generation? Is it possible that we educators have severely damaged literature by turning it into just another school subject, cramming it into textbooks that look like every other textbook, putting long lists of questions at the end of each story or play in the book, and then assigning it as homework? Kathleen Norris, in *Dakota: A Spiritual Geography,* talks of *The Grapes of Wrath* as part of "that remote entity called 'American literature' that has little relation to [students'] lives."[3] Norris is not being scornful of American literature here (she is arguing for the study of Lois Hudson's Dakota novel *The Bones of Plenty* in North Dakota schools rather than *The Grapes of Wrath*[4]), but rather acknowledging the fact that literature has become institutionalized. For most high-school and college students, a required literature class is just another subject to "take."

For teachers, meanwhile, literature has often become a kind of safe haven, a place of retreat from the messiness of life. We have lived so many years with our fictional characters that we care more for them than the flesh-and-blood characters sitting in our classrooms, forgetting that these fictional creations consist only of squiggly symbols printed on a page.

I have two concerns, then, about the use of fictional narrative in the English classroom: First, that fiction no longer has—or perhaps never had—the power I had attributed to it throughout my teaching career; and second, that literature teachers often prefer the distance and safety of fiction over the less manageable real lives of their students.

While I was a senior in college, my mother was dying of cancer seven hundred miles away. One day my seventeenth-century-poetry professor wept as he read from Donne's Holy Sonnets, and I thought to myself, "What do you know about grief, old man?"

Now, thirty years later, I have become that old man.

Every year in a course called "Methods of Teaching English," I read to my students selected passages from the letters of Maureen Wendall to Joyce Carol Oates found in the novel *them*. My students are never as moved by these letters as I think they should be, but I continue to read them the letters because I need to hear them. In one of her letters, Maureen, who had been Oates's students at an earlier time, describes the delight Oates took in reading aloud a certain passage from *Madame Bovary*. She says,

> you never talked like that to us; that was because you believed the book was more important than your students were. . . . Why did you think that book about Madame Bovary was so important? All those books? Why did you tell us they were more important than life? They are not more important than my life.[5]

Maureen is sitting in a library writing her letter to Oates. She continues,

> All around me are shelves with books on them and none of those books are worth anything, I know that now, not the books by Jane Austen I used to love or the book about Madame Bovary you liked so much. Those things didn't happen and won't happen. In my life something happened. . . .[6]

Set in Detroit during the turbulent sixties, *them* is a novel about the life of Maureen Wendall and her family.[7] Joyce Carol Oates informs us in her author's note that she responded to the letters of the real Maureen, who was her student at the University of Detroit, and that she eventually became aware of Maureen's life story and "her life as the possibility for a story."[8] And now, as I read these passages from *them,* misty-eyed, perhaps one of my students wonders, "How can he shed tears over a character in a book? My life is in the pits and I can't get out. Shed a tear for me." What shall I say, I, who don't have Oates's gift to make of a life a story?

Surely I am not the only literature teacher haunted by Maureen's accusing question: Why do we love our books and those fictional characters in them more than we love our students? Well, first of all, while students often drop into our classes for a year and then disappear, we have been living with these fictional characters for years. They have become good friends. Furthermore, these characters are an open book; we know everything there is to know about them. Our students, on the other hand, are often inscrutable. Besides, we may argue, we are literature teachers—not counselors or psychiatrists but literature teachers. Our job is to teach literature, not blunder about in the sweaty, anxious world of adolescence. I am a father as well as a teacher, and I remember thinking as I saw some of my colleagues—especially during the late sixties and seventies—using psycho-dramas and other methods to get students to expose their deepest emotions, "Hey, when my kid comes to your class, just teach him to write, teach him the literature. His mother and I will take care of his values and his emotional development."

But that is too simple. For literature must surely engage the emotions as well as the mind, and that caring for the characters mentioned above must surely result in some personal reflection and self-examination. The terribly difficult and important question facing us literature teachers is, "How deeply must we involve ourselves in the personal lives of our students?" As we answer that question, some of us must realize that sometimes we prefer fiction to the lives of our students because it is safe—at least once removed from the actual. When a young woman in my composition class describes being date-raped, I want to back off. "You ought to talk to a counselor about this," I write on the bottom of her paper, as if she hadn't thought of that herself. I want to run from involvement in the messiness of real life, flee to the safety of, say, an Oates story about rape.

In addition, there are all those students who keep their personal stories locked up but who nevertheless are crying out for attention. I think of some of my former students who were "much farther out than [I] thought/And not waving but drowning."[9] Mark sits smiling next to the cherry orchard, a blathering idiot, his brain fried with drugs. Kristi and Dave and Carl killed themselves before they reached the age of twenty. TJ languishes in jail—he's there for life because he killed his baby in an alcoholic rage. They all spent hours in my classroom, and sometimes in my mind's ear I hear their faint whispers: "My life was real, more important than Emily Webb's or David Copperfield's. Why did you think that book was so important?"

But don't you see, I want to say to them, don't you see that when I was talking about the book, I was really talking about your life and my life and all of us human beings? That's the beauty and power of art. It gives shape to real life. Form. I still believe that. Then I hear Maureen Wendall again:

> What is form? Why is it better than the way life happens, by itself? I hate all that, all those lies, so many words in all those books. What I like to read in the library is newspapers. . . . The old man is reading a newspaper, so is the man with the runny nose. Like me they want to find out what's going on, what is real. They don't have time in their lives for made up things.[10]

Perhaps I can convince Maureen that news of people we don't know is no more real to us than fiction. If I take a poem like Frost's "Out, Out . . ." and compare it to a news item about the accidental death of a child, it's no contest. The poem speaks with much more affective power than the news story. On the other hand, if that child who died accidentally is the younger brother of Charlie who sits in the second seat of the third row, then suddenly the poem pales in comparison.

Or perhaps I can convince her that often fiction is not really "made up things" but a re-rendering of real things. I might even show her the novel *them* and convince her. But what of all those other students we meet, whose lives are not contained in novels and for whom both Huck Finn and Holden Caulfield seem equally remote? That's a question for which no definitive answer exists, but I believe Maureen points us toward *one* answer.

I know she is right when she says that we literature teachers often prefer our fictional friends over real students; we prefer the safety and neatness of fiction over the involvement and messiness of daily living. And I know there is a danger in that safety, a danger that the power of the literature to affect the lives of students will be diminished by our indifference to their lives.

To counteract that danger, I must get to know my students, reading and studying them as diligently as I do my literature text. Perhaps one way to do that is to allow students to respond to the literature they read—in journals, personal essays, think-alouds, author's chairs—and then spend more time examining the personal responses that they make to that literature. I must also select literature that intersects at some point with their lives. Louise Rosenblatt tells of Native American boys and girls living on a reservation who were required to read Restoration comedies, an apt example of an absurd mismatch between students and literature.[11]

And finally, I must not flee from involvement in their lives. If all we do with the fiction is commiserate briefly with our students about the difficulty of Sophie's choice or the pain of Sonny's blues, make a moralistic statement of some kind and then move on to tomorrow's assignment, the stories will not have much impact on their lives. As Robert Coles says, "We worry about wrongs, think about injustices, read what Tolstoi or Ruskin . . . has to say. . . . Then, all of a sudden, the issue is not whether we agree with what we have heard and read and studied. . . . The issue is us, and what we have become."[12] Joyce Carol Oates responded to the letter of her student Maureen by entering her life. That act may have more truly revealed who she was than one of her stories does, especially if as Jonathan Kozol says, "Truth is something that occurs when actions take place; not when phrases are contrived."[13] So I must enter their lives. But how? Surely many will want me to stay out of their lives, and I must respect that. And quite likely some will have problems too large for me to handle. Still I must be available, willing to listen, willing to act on their behalf. I cannot lead them to that point where idea demands action and then sneak away.

But having acknowledged the vital importance of involvement in my students' lives, I will continue to teach lots of fiction, for I believe that Maureen Wendall is wrong when she attacks the notion that literature gives form to life. Sometimes we need the shaping effect of literature to make sense out of the news and the seemingly random events of our lives. Literature illuminates life, and though it may not make us better people as I have sometimes hoped, it can enable us to understand who and where in the world we are. Even without the added benefit of a guest lecturer who has "been there," *A Dry White Season* will not let involved readers go until they have struggled with their own blind acceptance of injustice and asked themselves if they would be willing to forego friends, family, and lifestyle for the sake of doing justice.[14]

I will continue to teach fiction because it has a power that most other kinds of information cannot approach, a power to draw readers into a world and experience vicariously what they otherwise might only know. Perhaps that is why Robert Coles, Pulitzer-Prize-winning author of the five-volume sociological study *Children of Crisis,* uses great literature as his textbook when he teaches courses in the medical school, law school, and business school at Harvard.[15]

I will continue to teach fiction because, like the narrator in Joan Didion's *Book of Common Prayer,* an anthropologist who lost her faith in her own method, I do not believe that "observable behavior defines anthropos."[16] I believe that good fiction acknowledges that every human being is a mystery, not something to be classified or categorized. And because fiction recognizes the essential mystery of being human, it speaks to us in ways that other information cannot.

I will continue to teach fiction, but I will work terribly hard to de-school my teaching of literature. Fiction can instruct only when it delights. If students read only so they can pass a quiz on the next two chapters in tomorrow's class, the power of the novel has been diminished. If they must laboriously fill in blanks on a *Huck Finn* study guide, they will miss the trip down the Mississippi, and if they miss the raft trip with Huck and Jim, they will probably also miss the significance of Huck's decision to tear up the note and go to hell.[17]

But what do I do with my concern that fiction is not as immediate or real as a personal narrative might be? Well, I might teach more personal narratives, narratives written by both students and professional writers. Personal memoirs. I am convinced they sometimes have a power and impact that is different from fiction—stronger, more earthy, more real and immediate, and often more upsetting. It is worthy to note, I think, that *Harpers* magazine, which has for years included a short story as one of its regular monthly features, has recently begun to also include a memoir in each issue.

I realize, however, that it is not only fiction that can become institutionalized. I know of few personal narratives with more power than the *Diary of Anne Frank.* Yet by treating it as simply another schoolbook for students to read and be tested on, a teacher can destroy the tremendous affective power of the narrative. Recently I saw this happen with a slightly different kind of text, the Anne Frank Museum in Amsterdam. As I walked through the museum, I observed swarms of school children racing about filling in blanks on a workbook assignment, concerned only with getting the correct answers written down. The narrative power of the museum had been mitigated by a stupid assignment.

I began this essay by asking rather facetiously whether I should turn my classroom into some sort of daytime talk show. Of course I know that the last thing most of my students need is more exposure to the often bizarre exhibitionism of the "real life" characters who parade across the stages of Oprah, Donahue, and Povich. But I do believe that the imaginative truth contained in fiction can be accentuated when it is combined with the factual truths of real life. Certainly not every novel or story needs to be augmented by a real-life documentation. But occasionally it can be effective. *Brave New World* might take on a new meaning if I bring in an expert to talk about virtual reality. Tim O'Brien's "How to Tell a True War Story" might speak with even more authority if I bring in a Vietnam veteran. Students might view Jack London's "The Law of Life" in a new way if they visit a retirement home after they read it.[18]

Bard College president Leon Botstein suggested in a recent speech that science replace the humanities as the center of the school curriculum. Teacher-writer Asta Bowen suggests that a society build around television, as ours is, should not expect its schools to teach literature effectively. Statements like these make one ask again, why and how we are teaching literature in our schools. These are good questions to ask and keep asking. For me the answer has changed over the years. I am not nearly as interested in *belles-lettres,* in literature as art, as I used to be. I am more concerned that literature be *literae humaniores,* humane letters, that it touch the lives of my students, educate their hearts, reveal truths of the human spirit, and goad them into responsible action in the world so that Sydney's words may yet prove true, and a Cyrus may make many Cyruses.[19]

Notes

1. Sir Phillip Sydney, *An Apology for Poetry,* ed. Geoffrey Shepherd (London: Nelson, 1965), 101.

2. Walter Wangerin, *The Manger Is Empty* (San Francisco: Harper, 1989), 30.

3. Kathleen Norris, *Dakota: A Spiritual Geography* (New York: Ticknor, 1993), 5.

4. See Lois Hudson, *The Bones of Plenty* (Boston: Little, 1962).

5. Joyce Carol Oates, *them* (New York: Vanguard Publishing, 1969), 312.

6. Ibid., 313.

7. Ibid.

8. Ibid., 11.

9. Stevie Smith, "Not Waving But Drowning," in *An Introduction to Literature,* ed. Sylvan Barnet, Morton Burman, and William Burto (New York: Harper, 1993), 488.

10. Oates, *them,* 318.

11. Louise Rosenblatt, *Literature as Exploration,* 4th ed. (New York: MAL, 1983), 57.

12. Robert Coles, quoted in Jonathan Kozol, *The Night Is Dark and I Am Far from Home* (New York: Bantam, 1975), 81.

13. Kozol, *The Night Is Dark*, 182.

14. André Brink, *A Dry White Season* (New York: Morrow, 1980).

15. Phillip Yancy, "The Crayon Man," in *Christianity Today* (6 February 1987): 14–20.

16. Joan Didion, *A Book of Common Prayer* (New York: Simon, 1997), 12.

17. Mark Twain, *The Adventures of Huckleberry Finn* (New York: Amsco School Publications, 1972).

18. See Aldous Huxley, *Brave New World* (New York: Harper, 1958); Tim O'Brien, "How to Tell a True War Story," in *The Things They Carried* (Boston: Houghton, 1990), 73–91; and Jack London, "The Law of Life," in *To Build a Fire, and Other Stories*, ed. Donald Pizer (New York: Bantam, 1986).

19. Sydney, *An Apology for Poetry*, 101.

Playing with Fire:
Toward a Biblical Approach to Theatre Performance

Simon du Toit*

Then King Nebuchadnezzar leaped to his feet in amazement and asked his advisors, "Weren't there three men that we tied up and threw into the fire?" They replied, "Certainly, O King." He said, "Look! I see four men walking around in the fire, unbound and unharmed, and the fourth looks like a son of the gods." Daniel 3:24, 25

Introduction

Viewed from a Christian perspective, theatre is an art form that uniquely offers Christian artists the opportunity to embrace the communities they serve.

Theatre is the most collaborative of the arts, bringing acting, music, painting, sculpture, literature, dance, and even video and computer technology all together into a single theatrical production. These many and various gifts of God are, at their best, unified in search of an event to be shared with an audience, a moment of transparency in which all present are brought to a discovery of truths about themselves they might otherwise not have examined.

---

* Mr. du Toit is Professor of Theatre Arts at Dordt College. He has studied at the London Academy of Music and Art and completed the M.F.A. at York University. This article was first published in *Pro Rege* in June 2001.

Of course, the power of the theatre to awaken our deepest thoughts and feelings makes it a much-contested cultural instrument. At various times in history the church, understood in its most catholic sense, has on the one hand appropriated and developed the theatre as a powerful tool of evangelism and instruction, and on the other hand condemned and rejected the theatre as an instrument of wickedness wrought by Satan's own hand. The suspicion with which theatre has been viewed remains a part of Reformed Christian culture. Dordt College students ask every year, how can Christians perform sin? Parents ask, why did you choose to produce this play? To master theatre's great power offers a challenge to theatre artists to rise beyond their own limits in search of great artistry. To become a great artist requires great passion and discipline: to give oneself entirely to the work and to play with a spirit of burning desire. In playing with fire, do we risk getting burned? Certainly. Hence the double meaning of this essay's title.

Much good work has been done in recent years to develop a Christian aesthetic theory grounded in the biblical tradition. More work, however, must be done to bring Christian aesthetic thought to bear specifically on theatre theory and praxis. This paper seeks to offer some preliminary ideas for discussion in the hope that we can move toward a comprehensive biblical approach to theatre performance.

A theoretical understanding of the theatre and its relation to a Christian worldview must begin by defining what theatre is and by placing it in its proper context. Theatre is traditionally understood to be an art form, and discussion of it most often proceeds from a given view of aesthetics. That purely aesthetic view of theatre has devolved in our consumer culture into commodification: the theatre is understood to be the experience of being entertained, preferably without also being challenged. However, theatre historically emerged from religious ritual, and it has continued to function as a method of investigating and describing a culture's worldview. Theatre has an inescapably religious aspect: not only in the confessional stances of those who practice it, not only in the degree to which it specifically acknowledges or is obedient to God's norms, but also in its structure and purpose. Theatre is an instrument whose very function and product is cultural examination and formation.

"The actor," says Mark Fortier in his *Theory/Theatre: an Introduction*, "is a thinking body performing blooded thought."[1] A theatrical performance is an event that unfolds in time, whose outcome must have a quality of contingency. Theatre that sacrifices contingency to reach for a more comforting certainty risks losing its theatricality and moving closer to the function of the school, church, or political party. Theatre achieves its fullest meaning not in a literary or plastic form, but in a living performance event that engages actor and audience equally in a moment-to-moment process. Its subject matter is the particulars of human history, on every level from that of individual ex-

perience through global and cosmic events. Particular theatrical styles emerge
from particular periods and cultures; what was important to actors and audiences in Shakespeare's day is very different from what is important to us
today. I hope to show in greater detail how performance style posits models
for human identity. Let us therefore begin with an approach to a biblical
model for human identity, and then survey how two historical approaches
to performance style have offered models for human identity. We can then
move from the principle that performance expresses worldview by means
of artistic form toward a biblical model for theatre performance.

The Gift and the Calling

Recent developments in Reformed Christian thought have underlined
the importance of a narrative view of the Bible and have labored to respond
to the challenges of postmodern cultural criticism. One of the fruits of this
labor that fits well with an integration of biblical principles and theatrical
process is *Truth Is Stranger Than It Used to Be* by Richard Middleton and
Brian Walsh. The heart of their project is to respond to recent charges from
postmodern critics that Christians have historically been responsible for
much bloody, oppressive, racist, and totalizing behavior. While they do not
deny the responsibility of Christians for a great deal of sin in history, they
also seek to show how the good news of the gospel, properly viewed, is the
best possible response to that sinful behavior. They stress the importance
of humans as the bearers of the image of God, not so that the people of
God as elect may claim a higher status over all others, but rather so that by
taking the role of servants God's people can be instruments of his shalom,
embracing others' pain, and working as agents of healing and reconciliation.

What ties together this entire spiral trajectory from Genesis to Revelation is the consistent biblical insight that humans are, from the beginning,
throughout history, and at the end of the age, both *gifted* by God with a
royal-priestly status and dignity (implying access to the divine presence and
genuine agency and power in the world) and *called* by God to actively
represent his rule as Creator and Redeemer by the manner in which they
use their power.[2]

To be sure, God's people have often strayed from that calling and mis-
used their power. If we are to tell the whole story of the House of Israel, no
doubt parts of the story will be very painful to hear. It seems, though, that
the hallmark of a biblical worldview is precisely the telling of painful stories.
Middleton and Walsh cite Walter Brueggeman:

> "Where pain is not embraced, critical uneasiness about every crushing orthodoxy is
> banished. It is certain that, where there is the legitimation of structure without the
> voice of pain embraced, there will be oppression without compassion." In postmod-
> ern terms such legitimation of structure without embracing the voice of pain is what
> totalization is all about. And it is indeed a deadly temptation to Western culture and

> Christianity in particular. . . . A covenantal creation order is dialogic in character, not the monologue of the order-giver to the subjects of order.[3]

The Reformed tradition is decisive for the theatre in its view of history. Rather than holding to a Platonic view of culture, which devalues the particulars of creation in favor of a transcendent divine form, Reformed thinkers have consistently emphasized the biblical focus on those very particulars, seeing in them the contours of covenant history. The theatre, by allowing us to truthfully examine those particulars, can serve as an agent of reconciliation. We signify the new creation when we recognize our sinfulness, our need to forgive and be forgiven, and our need to be transformed in our lives.

The biblical narrative includes a role for the people of God. God's people are called to hear the groans of the creation and respond obediently in service. Using specifically theatrical language, Middleton and Walsh further characterize the biblical narrative as an unfinished, open-ended drama, given to God's people as an incomplete text for our own future performances. In their words, "The extant text would function as a nonnegotiable given,"[4] but there is room for a variety of obedient responses. Even our relationship with the "script" is suggested here:

> It is important that our performance not simply repeat verbatim earlier passages from the biblical script. . . . Apart from the fact that repeating past acts of the drama means the abdication of our calling to contribute to the narrative resolution in the present, unthinking repetition of the script runs the risk of perpetuating precisely the sort of oppression and violence that we are called to counter by our enactment of God's redemptive purposes in our own time.[5]

If we heed that call to be performers of God's script in the here and now, looking outward at our world, we cannot escape confronting contemporary Western consumer culture with all its attendant ills. Middleton and Walsh trace the positivist roots of modernism to the rationalist philosophy of René Descartes and respond to it:

> It is, therefore, not trite to respond to Descartes' famous dictum *cogito ergo sum* (I think, therefore I am) with a more biblical *sum amatus ergo sum* (I am loved, therefore I am). The former results in a spirituality and ethos of self-created heroism and aggressive realism. The latter engenders a spirituality of thankful stewardship and fundamental kinship with all of creation.[6]

Confronting the modernist model for human identity is important because it helps us to be in the world while being a bit less of it. However, it is important also for the theatre because, as we shall see later, modernism has given us the currently dominant model for theatre performance. In contrast to the modernist model of human identity, Middleton and Walsh offer a biblical view of the self as a precious gift that comes with a calling:

> Contrary to the ideal of the autonomous dragon slayer, the self as gift implies that we neither construct ourselves nor effect our redemption by overcoming evil. . . . Instead

of passively mirroring the oppressive formations of the culture around us, we have the high calling of mirroring God's love in and to the culture in which we live.[7]

This view of our biblical calling to cultural engagement is helpful for the theatre because it gives us human creatures the gift of an identity as God's children and a calling to serve God by living out his love bearing the suffering of others, in the particulars of human history. It underlines our role-playing human nature, places us historically in the biblical narrative, calls us to live relationally, and obliges us always to be seeking God's will for our lives in the immediacy of the present moment. A biblical approach to theatre will speak the truth about the past and seek to celebrate God's gifts to us.

Theatre Performance in History

Character in performance either permits or fails to permit us as audience members to imaginatively engage with the play's events. Traditionally, that engagement has been described as the "willing suspension of disbelief." As audience members, our conscious minds may become sympathetically engaged by the symbolic event to such a degree that we are more aware of the "there and then" than we are of the "here and now." Our sense of time is altered, our physiology reacts sympathetically to actions within the event, and we may have strong emotional experiences or intellectual discoveries. Complete engagement will affect every aspect of our behavior. Engagement implies full presence before the symbolic event, without either absorption into it or mere sensory titillation. Such engagement requires that the event must resonate with our perceptions of our own experience, seeming "truthful," but it must also take us beyond our own experience so that we find our knowledge of ourselves and our world broadened and deepened.

Because it involves this engagement, character performance is related to its cultural context; conventions of character, broadly speaking, should reflect the worldview of a given culture, time, and place. If people in a given time and place were able to be engaged by a character in performance, then it is likely that the form of that character in some way reflects their view of themselves. Conversely, in understanding the use of character made by a given dramatist, we can also better understand the time and place in which he or she was writing. Postmodern and feminist criticism, for instance, have altered our cultural understanding of both theatrical and personal character to such an extent that some scholars, such as Elinor Fuchs in her book *The Death of Character,* have declared the modernist ideal of the autonomous subject to be dead.[8] Whether or not one accepts the notion that character is dead, it is clear that contemporary theatrical conventions of character are increasingly reflecting a fragmented, ambiguous, and multifaceted understanding of human identity.

In contrast to today's postmodern character conventions, theatrical realism was at the cutting edge of the theatre late in the nineteenth century. The works of Ibsen, Strindberg, and Chekhov have come to epitomize realism in the West. Of his Hedda Gabler, Ibsen has written the following: "What I principally wanted to do was to depict human beings, human emotions and human destinies, upon a groundwork of certain of the social conditions and principles of the present day."[9] Realism's diagnostic pretensions are clear in the above quote, and its aspiration to a scientific method clarifies its connection to the modernism of its day. Theatrical realism is first and foremost the drama of the hero; character produces action. As such it embodies modernist ideals of rational independence and self-conscious self-determination.

While modernist ideals have their roots in the Enlightenment, Romantic thinkers deepened the power of the modernist idea of the self by adding to it an awareness of inner depths, wrapped in mystery. Such values were particularly strong in the German theatre of the early nineteenth century, in the circle that included Schiller, Schlegel, and Schleiermacher. As the latter wrote, "As often as I turn my gaze inward upon my inmost self, I am at once within the domain of eternity. I behold the spirit's action, which no world can change, and no time can destroy, but which creates both world and time."[10]

The territory of the inmost self eventually became the territory of Freud's scientific inquiry and was renamed the subconscious. Human behavior in Freud is understood to be driven by forces from the subconscious that, if left undiagnosed or unexamined, remain mysterious to the conscious subject. Even though neither man studied the work of the other, the uncanny parallels between Freudian psychology and Stanislavski's Method have been documented by Timothy Wiles and others. Both paradigms demand that the subject uncover and release the emotion attached to powerful past events. Actors using the Method have often been encouraged to examine their family lives and significant friendships for material that parallels the circumstances of the character they are playing. Both focus on the physical and sensory details surrounding those past events. Method actors have been known to carry emotionally significant objects in their pockets or to wear kerchiefs soaked in their mother's perfume, using these sensory data as a stimulus to their performances that remains unknown to either the audience or their fellow actors. Both Freud and the Method predict that the living out of past events will produce a result in the present; and the diagnostic and therapeutic methods of both are designed to control that result toward some desired end.

As presented in the realist style of staging, the characters of the play exist in an air of mystery, by which we in the audience are invited to be enchanted. The realistic theatre's relationship with its audience is defined by the notion of the Fourth Wall, as Fuchs and others have recognized: "Walter Benjamin sees in the orchestra pit the physical emblem of this relationship, calling it 'the abyss which separates the players from the audience as it does the dead from the living.'"[11] The characters are lit, and we are not; they seem not to acknowledge us. This air of mystery permits the audience to project themselves into the characters, which become the exclusive vehicle of the drama. Stanislavski stressed the importance of the actor's engagement with the character as a real presence. Wiles writes, "His own circumstances and emotions which vary his performance from day to day, be seen as an integral aspect of the work of art: 'an actor cannot be merely someone, somewhere, at some time or other. He must be I, here, today.'"[12]

Yet from the actor's own point of view, working from her own subconscious material and submitting her conscious self to it as she is, the character remains mysterious, changeable, alive and in some ways absent. In Method acting, the character always knows more than the actor. The play's text takes at best second place to character, as Wiles points out: "Stanislavski's concern with the play's 'subtext' suggests that unspoken feelings and pregnant pauses contain more of the content of dramatic art than does the text, which he treats as a subterfuge and pretext for emotions."[13] Both actor and audience, then, remain in thrall to the presence of the mysterious other, the character, into whom each projects her own experience. This experience confirms the modernists' intuition of their own place at the center of the universe; as Nietzsche said, "Character is the fatal flaw of the 'death leap into the bourgeois drama.'"[14]

In this model of the self as performer, the actor aims to efface herself entirely, casting a spell over the entire audience, and projecting her ego into the character's. Method actors are taught to discuss their roles in the first person, as if they truly have become the character. Although the modernist audience member may not belong in that particular universe, the very act of projecting is comforting to him. Thus the modernist theatre makes far too much use of the gift character of the self, confirming it by its process in the powerful "presence" of the actor and the projected experience of the audience, while ignoring the calling to image and reflect the presence and suffering of the other. This is what gives Method actors their oracular, self-conscious quality; they are taught that they are somehow in touch with a mysterious higher truth that lies within them. Understood from a biblical stance, they are taught to make an idol of character in performance.

Bertolt Brecht abhorred the casting of spells that the bourgeois theatre of his day represented to him. As his reading and thinking on his theatrical style deepened, he noted in his journals the provenance of the realistic style in its earlier Romantic impulse:

> 8 Jan 1948: The first time the desire to please, to make one's presentation agreeable or exciting, to hold the public's attention, actually manifests itself to me is in the schi[iller]-g[oethe]-correspondence. that [sic] stance of opposition to the audience which i adopted as a playwright, extended to matters of form; in fact it began with them. the [sic] "well-made play," following as it did the aesthetic which enabled the

theatre to perform its notorious social function, employed a misleading organization of the material; from that position you could not achieve realism (as formal realism, namely naturalism, shows). the [sic] representation of reality merely served to trigger certain emotion (which had gone rotten) and did not need to be right for this particular purpose. . . .[15]

Brecht's interests lay in the social and political realm. He wished to discuss forces of history because he saw those as deciding human behavior far beyond the powers of any individual's will. His structuring of the epic theatre stages those historical forces in order to force the audience to criticize them. He takes deliberate aim at the bourgeois theatre, which he named the Dramatic Form, opposing each facet of it with its Epic opposite.[16]

For Brecht, action produces character, the exact reversal of the realist formula.[17] Brecht's actors were to be aware of the audience and to show that awareness as part of their performances. They were to distance themselves from their roles; "instead of embodying the characters, they were to *demonstrate* them."[18] Although his interest in the acting process was minimal, Brecht designed exercises for his actors to help them acquire the distance he required. This creation of distance was part of his famed *verfremdungseffekt,* or strange-making. The exercises included speaking the lines in the third person instead of the first person and trading roles temporarily with other actors. While emotion was permitted, it was so only in realistic demonstration of a character's behavior; it was certainly not the goal and aim of a performance. Physical and sensory details, the bread and butter of the realistic Method, were in Brecht entirely secondary. Where in Stanislavski the text was secondary to the character's inner truth, Brecht's interest was in social truth. Instead of drawing a spectator into an event, consuming his capacity for action, and provoking feelings in an instinctual way, Brecht sought to make the spectator a critical observer of an event, to awaken his capacity for action, to demand decisions from him, and to consciously propel feelings into perceptions. Brecht wanted the house lights to remain lit during performances and the spectators to sit and smoke and talk, as if they were at a sports event.[19] Critic Margaret Eddershaw says: "The focus in 'epic' theatre is transferred from the actor to the script, or from performer to what is performed."[20]

As a corrective to the spell casting of realism, this model of character was historically groundbreaking and much needed. In forcing the audience to confront the oppression of the suffering other, it satisfies the biblical calling Middleton and Walsh point to. However, this approach to character also often erases the gift quality of the self. At the very moment a character engages our empathy, Brecht often moves to make her strange to us once more. Brecht's self-aware distancing of himself from his characters and of his characters from the actors performing them was deliberate and intended to produce in us, his audience, a dialectic, critical attitude.

This brief survey of the varying features of dramatic character in theatrical history makes clear the principle that worldview is decisive for performance in modeling a vision of the human self. What, then, would a biblical approach to theatrical character be like? If the Method makes too much of the gift character of selfhood, and Brecht makes too much use of the calling aspect of the self, then some third way must be found. If the realists focus on the actor, and the Brechtians on the script, a biblical model will focus on the gifts of the Holy Spirit, on interpreting with clarity the vision of the performance for performers and the audience alike.

Middleton and Walsh critiqued the modernist view of self, *cogito ergo sum,* by offering a biblically conditioned *sum amatus ergo sum.* I would point to the First Question and Answer of the Heidelberg Catechism:

> Q What is your only comfort in life and in death?
> A That I am not my own, but belong—
>   body and soul, in life and in death—
>   to my faithful savior Jesus Christ. . . . [21]

It is in the emptying of the self, and in the recognition that even my self is not my own, that I find my only comfort. Let me suggest *sum amatus ergo amo.* Faith itself is a gift from God, yet its confirmation can only be in the act of returning that Perfect Love. We must be fully present in performing the role of being God's obedient, loving children, and we must reflect on and learn from that experience. It is as we love that we know.

First Principles

In moving toward a method for Christians to approach performance, we need to grasp performance's creational nature and function. One definition of performance's function can be found in Timothy Hoare's "Pulling the Siamese Dragon: Performance as Theological Agenda for Christian Ritual Praxis":

> Performance is a symbolic expression that rehearses, celebrates or shapes the consciousness and identity of a particular community or the human community at large. Liturgically, theatrically, politically, or socially, performance informs us as to who we are, reminds us who we have been, and envisions who we are capable of becoming as human beings living in relational tension with one another, with history, with the environment and with the Holy. [22]

This view of the function of performance makes clear its multidimensional, comprehensive nature. The cultural implications of this view of performance are obvious. Performance connects directly with history. Certainly the aesthetic is an important aspect of theatrical performance, but equally, its roots in ritual place performance in the same class as other institutions of cultural formation such as education and ecclesial worship. This observation has its clearest implications in the relationship between the performance and its audience. Performance must remind us truthfully of who we have been, who we are, and who we hope to become as God's people; and it must acknowledge the contingency of our relations with God and each other.

The means by which theatre engages with and reflects human culture must be grounded in the relationship between performer and audience. The thing that occurs on stage is not a fixed plastic object or the mere representation of some prior text, but rather is an event in space and time, performed by actors in roles. The heart of the theatre, therefore, is symbolic action. Winston Neutel, in his "Dooyeweerd on Stage? Reformational Aesthetics and Theatre Theory," points out that the belief that the actor's identity is suspended or somehow erased in performance is a rationalist reduction, which reduces signification to the empirically observable.[23] Rather, performance is creative work that performers do and before which they must be fully present, as the audience is. Neither part of the transaction can be subsumed by the other. Of course, performers are changed by the work they do, and so too are the audience members; that is the whole point of the endeavor. But to suggest that they literally erase themselves while performing or that they take on themselves the character's sins as if they were their own is to misunderstand the nature of performance work. To accept performed events as real is to venture into psychosis.

Hoare approaches the nature of performance from a stance that acknowledges the separation of performer and performance and the integrity of both:

> Performance conveys a time and space that is both "here and now" and "there and then." It presents an actor who is both a self and a role, or it invites an audience to be at once present and remote. . . . Performance is, by its very nature, a symbolic form, but not in the discursive sense of leading directly or conceptually to a fixed unequivocal referent. Rather, performance is a nondiscursive symbol that has no referent beyond its own embodiment; by virtue of the relational tension of the elements that constitute it, performance is expressive in and of itself.[24]

Put simply, performance doesn't *do* something; it *is* something. Performance functions in a way that Calvin Seerveld would describe as allusive, pregnant with meanings. Its meaning cannot be exhaustively described in any other way than to witness to it, to be present before it. In that sense, biblically obedient performance is performance that brings performers and audience together, fully present before a symbolical event.

The above analysis of performance has yielded three principles: performance connects directly with human history; performance is symbolic action; and performance is inescapably contingent and relational. These principles fit very well with the biblical view of human identity developed earlier. God has given us the gift of an identity as his children and called us to serve him directly in redeeming his creation. We can do that by telling the truth about who we are, have been, and hope to become. As we strive to speak the truth, we remain accountable to him and to each other, on a moment-to-moment basis. Our task is to be image-bearers of Christ.

As workers in the arts seek to imitate Christ, we should consider the role of the Holy Spirit in evoking our creative vision. Since Pentecost, the Spirit has remained the means by which our hearts are moved to know Jesus. To image Jesus, then, is to witness his presence in our lives by means of the Holy Spirit, whose temple is the body, our physical being. As human creativity mirrors divine creativity represented in the Incarnation, so artists can, through God's grace and the Spirit's guidance, be given eyes to see and ears to hear the Spirit's testimony, and they in turn can witness bodily to truthful visions about human experience.

On the day of Pentecost the Spirit came down like the blowing of a violent wind. The apostles saw ". . . what seemed to be tongues of fire that separated and came to rest on each of them. All of them were filled with the Holy Spirit and began to speak in other tongues as the Spirit enabled them" (Acts 2:3, 4). As witnesses to the Spirit's presence, God's servants were lifted beyond their own experience; they saw strange sights and spoke in unfamiliar tongues. The gathering crowd, the audience, is amazed and perplexed. As Peter explains to them, the apostles, by the Spirit's leading, have begun to see visions and dream dreams.

In the same way, Daniel accepts responsibility to be an interpreter of dreams. In Daniel 4:1–27, Daniel interprets Nebuchadnezzar's dream about a tree being cut down and stripped of its leaves. As he comes to understand the dream, Daniel is perplexed and terrified, yet he recounts to the king what he has seen. And his vision comes true: Nebuchadnezzar loses everything and wanders in the desert for "seven times." He learns by his trial to see what he had failed to see clearly in Daniel 2—the vision of the glory of the King of Heaven in the here and now.

A performance is like a dream, and as a faithful witness the performer is enabled to be the dream's interpreter. Daniel is given eyes to see each detail of the dream, even though it was not his own dream but Nebuchadnezzar's. Though, like Daniel, performers are often afraid of and perplexed by the dream, by trusting in the Holy Spirit they can avoid being consumed by the flames. In giving ourselves fully to the work of witnessing to the experience of another, we find ourselves renewed, able to see and hear things we could not see or hear before.

That offering of the self must happen in every dimension of the performer's experience, as Paul makes clear in Romans:

> Therefore, I urge you, brothers, in view of God's mercy, to offer your bodies as living sacrifices, holy and pleasing to God—this is your spiritual act of worship. Do not conform any longer to the pattern of this world, but be transformed by the renewing of your mind. Then you will be able to test what God's will is—his good, pleasing and perfect will. Romans 12:1, 2

Theatre both illustrates and helps us to realize this transformation: when we allow ourselves to be wholly present in body and spirit before the symbolic event performed, our minds can be transformed. To be fully present before this event—neither subsumed by it nor disengaged from it—is to witness passionately in body and mind, as if through flames, to a dream or a vision that is not of our own experience. This kind of performance happens in the immediacy of the present tense, and in the experience of a symbolic "other" event we discover something about ourselves. The faithful witness testifies to the details of the vision, but does not become the vision; by the Spirit's promptings, the witness gains renewed eyes and ears and can speak in unfamiliar tongues. God has given us the talent to do this work as image-bearers of Christ and the example in him of how to do it.

Theatre Performance: Christ our Prophet, Priest, and King

Theatre performance inevitably mirrors human experience. That mirroring is deceptive; from the performer's point of view, performance is always—indeed must be—a heightened state arrived at through the judicious use of craft. It is the reverse of the mundane, the everyday. To the extent that Christians have written about performance, they have first and foremost called for excellence. In *Christianity and the Theatre,* Murray Watts writes, "[e]very Christian actor will approach his work with the utmost professionalism, that he will bring glory to God by the excellence of his artistry."[25] However, the markers of that excellence are seldom clearly defined. I propose that we think about performance excellence in terms of Spirit-led imaging of Christ's model as prophet, priest, and king.

Christ's kingly example is instructive of the discipline necessary to shape our lives and to contain theatrical performance. Before Christ began his ministry, which would end in his ascension, he first had to learn to submit himself to his Father's will. He withdrew into the desert to fast and pray and overcame temptation. Without a disciplined faith life, there is no experiential vessel in our lives to bind our wills with the will of God. Likewise, without a disciplined performance technique and disciplined habits, we will not be able to capture those moments when all in the room are present before a shared vision. In teaching theatre, therefore, my primary goal is to develop an approach to acting technique that is grounded in Christian discipline.

Daniel's interpretation of Nebuchadnezzar's dream may serve as a model for this Christian theatrical discipline. Daniel recounts all the details of the dream and explains their significance with great clarity. He is careful to maintain his awareness of his audience and speaks his interpretation in the manner most likely to be clearly heard by the king. He is at once fully immersed in the dream and fully present to the king. He has a strong sense of timing; he allows each section of the dream to be exactly as long as it needs to be for it to be fully disclosed to the king. In mastering his fear and perplexity, Daniel arrives at clarity, simplicity, a penetrating imagination, and effective delivery.

The prophetic element of performance appears in its use of dramatic characters and events to perform something of the conflict in human life. Dramatic characters always struggle between opposites, and the audience responds to that struggle. The performer's task is to remain consistently present before the extremes of the struggle, even though doing so, as the very human Old Testament prophets like Isaiah, Jeremiah, and Amos found, can be profoundly difficult. To be a faithfully prophetic witness, the performer must be able to communicate honesty and utter deceit, courage and complete cowardice, love and hatred. That struggle must be understood, felt, reflected upon, and made physical in the work of the performer. As performers seek to be present before all the various aspects of a character, their personal inhibitions can be a bar to their commitment. Emotional and physical freedom is therefore another goal of effective performance training. Performers may have scruples concerning their characters' action or may simply dislike the characters they are asked to play. That is a challenge good craft will overcome; research will reveal the root of that antipathy, and compassion in Christ can turn that very problem into the source of a strong performance. Any remaining antipathy will hinder the imaginative work as it forces the performer to perform only from within her own experience.

Performance captures a heightened view of our lives; it draws imaginative attention to aspects of our experience that normally go unexamined. They go unexamined often because we really don't want to look at them. The Christian performer must be encouraged to play a performance with the highest degree of loving commitment possible. This is the goal of playing with fire: to play as if your very life is at stake, to immerse yourself in the dream of the performance, and to trust that your faith in Christ will keep you safe in the flames and that the Spirit will grant you sufficient clarity about the dream that you can signal to those outside the furnace. Performance occurs in heat and generates light. To prepare the Christian performer to be present before those moments requires teaching him to play with an inner fire, a transforming passion.

The danger of playing with fire is of course that one can burn oneself if one isn't careful. As teacher and director, it is my responsibility to protect my students from harm and to give them the tools to avoid harming themselves. In Daniel 3, Shadrach, Meshach, and Abednego are not consumed in the furnace precisely because they trust in God to protect them, and they announce that trust to Nebuchadnezzar before being thrown in the fire. The fire is so hot that it consumes the soldiers who throw them in, but the three are unharmed, not because of any strength of their own, but because they trust in the Almighty One to save them. That trust is reinforced by public declaration; Daniel's three friends confirm their roles, confessing and identifying themselves as his servants. Clearly the biblical model for avoiding lasting damage is to create a disciplined process that reminds us of who we are and obliges us to declare that identity fully.

Studies have demonstrated that student actors need the ability to clearly separate themselves from their roles. This is particularly true for college-aged students because of where they are in the process of personal maturation. In their paper "The Impact of Acting on Student Actors: Boundary Blurring, Growth, and Emotional Distress," Burgoyne et al. studied the inability of student actors to separate self from role:

> Overall, our respondents reported two major types of potentially distressing boundary blurring. In the first type, the actor's personal life may take over in performance, leading to the actor's loss of control on stage. . . . Conversely, the actor's character may take over offstage, with the actor carrying over character personality traits into daily life.[26]

Burgoyne points out that this blurring was greatest when an "inside/out" method, a term frequently used to describe psychological Method acting, was most prevalent. In that model, students are encouraged to use their own experiences as the grounds of characterization and to adopt the character's personality as their own while in role. The mere use of the term "personality" is a clear signal of the psychologizing of the performance process, and Burgoyne's article also discusses some of the benefits to be had from boundary blurring. Her only suggested method of combating the blurring of boundaries was therefore limited to simply making newer students aware of the possibility that blurring might occur; no routines were suggested as part of an overall approach to the discipline.

A biblical model for performance will hold the actor's sanctity in high regard and will offer the student actor a clear technique for preserving selfhood. The processes I have used include regular company devotions, prayer partners, pre- and postrehearsal discussion and analysis, and the inclusion of the acting company in cross-disciplinary studies linking our production work with study in other departments. I seek to refine and augment these procedures, as they have not yet reached maturity in an organized performance discipline.

In reflecting on the work after it is done, we can remember who we are as God's obedient children; we can use words and commit actions onstage that we would never choose off-stage, without damaging our own faith commitments, as long as we are careful to reinforce the separation of actor and role. Hoare's work supports a clear separation of actor and role:

> The performer is not him/herself but is also *not not* him/herself, for the self as identity is never simply erased; it always exists in tension with the role. It is through this ambiguous relational tension of [actor and role], of self-possession and being pos-

sessed, that the illusion of character is generated, that the otherness of the divine or demonic is sustained.[27]

The separation between actor and role should be made all the clearer because of its communal focus. If realist Method acting is driven by an oracular, psychological view of the performer, a biblical vision of the acting process must hold the performer in the communal, relational, performative moment. Sinful behavior in character is a structural feature of the performance and of our creation; it is not attributable to the performer herself.

However, sometimes actors simply aren't able to complete that separation. Each performer must learn to make her own decisions about what will and what will not damage her faith commitment and must have a safety net she can trust to hold her accountable. The relational tension between actor and role is built by the actor, working with the director, on the basis of the actor's choices. This act of choosing is what separates the actor from the role and needs to be underlined in the process of generating a performance.

By the quality and nature of the choices he makes, the actor constructs a performance that will be rich, multilayered, and compelling. By the ability of the actor to be personally present before those choices, they will be filled with the actor's love for his character, for his audience, and for his art. That courageous ability to be present and yet not present, to be both self and other in a committed way, is precisely the vehicle that draws the audience out of themselves and into the presence of the other. If we are to speak the truth to ourselves fully about who we are, it will fall to someone's role to enact sin. By the performer's relentless discipline in not letting go of the truth, he is compelling himself and his audience to acknowledge that truth. The audience doesn't want to do it, yet in the end they are grateful for it; it is far easier to be comforted by the trite, the cliché, but is also much less satisfying.

In following Christ's priestly example, Christian performers will both give themselves passionately to the performance of a character and hold the audience always in loving view as part of the production process. On occasion, that will mean that a performance ends without offering hope, just as some of the testimony of the Old Testament ends in condemnation. We need to learn, as Ezekiel does, to grieve and lament over the detestable things done in the city. However, we are also accountable on a moment-by-moment basis both to our audience and to God. We must ask ourselves why and how a truth needs to be spoken. To do that, we must know our audiences very well indeed; the whys and hows are particular to each community. Performers must hold onto the truth of the dream with great persistence; but they must also speak the dream in such a way that it will be fully heard. The Christian performer in rehearsal holds her fellow performers and her audience up in prayer and uses the reflective return to herself after the work is over to meditate thoughtfully on how the work is affecting her and how it might be received by an audience. In that way the rehearsal process advances both the performer's understanding of and commitment to the work, and also the potential for the work to engage and transform its audience.

This view of performer-audience relations differs from the more Nietzschean view current in our culture. Most theatre artists are today taught that their work is paramount and that their audiences must unconditionally accept their performances for the mere sake of the art itself. This separation of artist and audience is one of the forces engendering the oracular stance of realist acting. The oracular stance is also grounded in the lived quality that realist performance aims at. Meisner devotees are taught by means of repetition exercises to live through actions as if they were occurring entirely in the moment, for the first time. Stanislavski's Method uses the principle of the "as if" to ask actors to live through the character's actions as if they were their own. Both methods conflate the actor's experience with the character's and encourage the actor's subconscious life to replace that of the character. There are other means to encourage the imagination to witness truthfully to the experience of the "other," means that will better respect the integrity of both character and performer.

A performance is like a dream, and the performer is the dream's interpreter. To capture that vision for a few fleeting moments requires craft, courage, discipline, and passion. Passion is human fire; it is born of love and empties and transfigures the self. It is the power with which God gifts the artist performer. May we use it to his glory.

Notes

1. Mark Fortier, *Theory/Theatre: An Introduction* (London: Routledge, 1997), 49.

2. J. Richard Middleton and Brian J. Walsh, *Truth Is Stranger Than It Used To Be* (Downers Grove, IL: InterVarsity Press, 1995), 140.

3. Ibid., 164.

4. Ibid., 183.

5. Ibid., 183, 184.

6. Ibid., 149.

7. Ibid., 140, 141.

8. Elinor Fuchs, *The Death of Character* (Bloomington: Indiana University Press, 1996).

9. Evert Sprinchorn, *Ibsen: Letters and Speeches* (New York: Hill and Wang, 1964), quoted in Elinor Fuchs, *The Death of Character*, 68.

10. F. Schleiermacher, quoted in Fuchs, *The Death of Character*, 17.

11. Fuchs, *The Death of Character*, 138.

12. Timothy J. Wiles, *The Theatre Event: Modern Theories* (Chicago: University of Chicago Press, 1980), 34–35.

13. Ibid., 32.

14. Fuchs, *The Death of Character*, 28.

15. Bertolt Brecht, *Bertolt Brecht: Journals 1934–1955,* trans. John Willett (New York: Routledge, 1993), 385.

16. John Willett, *The Theatre of Bertolt Brecht* (New York: New Directions, 1968), 170.

17. Ibid., 171.

18. Margaret Eddershaw, *Performing Brecht* (London: Routledge, 1995), 136.

19. Willett, *The Theatre of Bertolt Brecht*, 144–46.

20. Eddershaw, *Performing Brecht*, 137.

21. Emily R. Brink, ed., *Psalter Hymnal* (Grand Rapids: CRC Publications, 1987), 861.

22. Timothy D. Hoare, "Pulling the Siamese Dragon: Performance as a Theological Agenda for Christian Ritual Praxis," in *Theatre and Religion* 2 (Goshen, IN: Theatre and Religion Forum Group (ATHE), 1996): 49.

23. Winston Neutel, "Dooyeweerd on Stage? Reformational Aesthetics and Theatre Theory," online at http:www.uovs.ac.za/arts/phil/nuances, 3.

24. Hoare, "Pulling the Siamese Dragon," 2–3.

25. Murray Watts, *Christianity and the Theatre* (Edinburgh: Handsel, 1986), 21.

26. Suzanne Burgoyne, Karen Poulin, and Ashley Rearden, "The Impact of Acting on Student Actors: Boundary Blurring, Growth, and Emotional Distress," *Theatre Topics* 9, no. 2 (1999): 163.

27. Hoare, "Pulling the Siamese Dragon," 5.

On Musical Excellence

Karen A. DeMol[*]

. . . .

Excellence and music seem to go hand-in-glove. Excellence is an essential part of the territory in which musicians work, the *sine qua non* of their field. Indeed, musicians do have a good time making music, shaping expressive things out of the created world of sound, and being playful about it. But they are also serious about it, working very hard and committing much time and intense effort to being very good composers, performers, and teachers. Usually they spend more time producing excellent music than talking about it.

Excellence is also the territory of *academia*. A glance at the college advertisements in *Campus Life* magazine, for instance, reveals many proclamations of excellence. Taylor University says we'll find academic excellence there. So do Messiah College, Toccoa Falls College, Malone College, The King's College, and Houghton College. Southern California College claims that study there leads to excellence in the workplace. Sterling College is devoted to excellence in teaching. LeTourneau states that Christianity plants within us the desire to excel. And at Wheaton College the faculty demands musical excellence.[1] Not one of them proclaims the pursuit of mediocrity!

---

[*] Dr. DeMol is Professor of Music at Dordt College. This article was originally presented at the Conference of Christian College Coalition Music Faculties in March 1992, on the campus of Anderson College, Anderson, Indiana. It was also published in *Pro Rege* in June 1992.

But what is excellence in music? It is difficult to define. Part of the difficulty is that in conversation or in articles, we must resort to words for discourse about music, and words don't do well for music. Words may be adequate for discussing politics or philosophy or even poetry, but they are quite inadequate for music. To communicate what excellence means in music, one can best present examples of the best, and of merely good, and of downright poor in music, whether classical, jazz, or folk. But that cannot be done in print. In conversation or in teaching we can communicate best by playing examples; we sing the little lick, play the fragment on a nearby piano, put on the compact disc, saying, "*This* is what I mean." We use the materials of music itself to "talk" about music. When we do try to use words, we often tend to talk about structure (and end up missing the aesthetic essence), or we talk about emotions and effect (and end up sounding subjective and sloppy). However, when our discourse consists of the music itself, when we use examples, we find that quality is identifiable. Across the centuries and even across cultures, there is music about which people say, "Aha! That's it! That's really good!"—even if they can't identify why or find words for it.

Another part of the difficulty is that a sense of quality in music is built over time through experience, not simply appropriated from a statement, a definition, or even a well-written article. Discernment is developed gradually by repeated exposure to good and less good music.

Nevertheless, I am going to discuss what musical excellence is, to explain with mere words the concept of excellence in *music,* to explain what excellence is in the *music* itself, and to explain what excellence is for *Christian* musicians. I am going to try to identify what excellence is so that we can be more aware of what we do in music and so that we can better understand musical excellence in the light of our call to Christian servanthood. Such understanding is needed for professionals and future professionals in music and also for "lay" people such as seminary students, church worship committee members, and curriculum committee members of a school board; in fact, it is valuable for all Christians, for music touches all our lives.

I am assuming, of course, that seeking excellence is valid and appropriate. It is worth taking a moment to reaffirm this, for we live in a time when some question such a search in many and various ways. They view advocating quality as elitism and seeking "good music" as snobbery. They consider values—moral, political, aesthetic—mere opinion and taste. Their individualism ("I like what I like") has made questioning another's taste a breach of manners; they may even see criticism as libel! Then, too, in some quarters accepting people has become so important that accepting all they do is thought to be not only considerate, but necessary. Those who worry about the self-esteem of performers hesitate to identify quality because doing so implies some musicians or compositions don't have it, certainly a damaging blow to the artists' self-esteem! Evidently, low self-esteem is more serious than certified mediocrity. Also, people today express concern if something is racist or sexist or Euro-centric or all sorts of other "ists" (and in many instances rightly so), but not if something is mediocre. In fact, in some arenas "mediocre" may not be an acceptable word; soon it may be politically correct only to say that something is "aesthetically challenged"!

But Christian schools don't seem to buy into that, at least not according to their published stances. Those college advertisements in *Campus Life* certainly advocate excellence.

And they are in good company, for the Bible doesn't seem shy about excellence, either. The building of the tabernacle, for example, was entrusted to the gifted and the skilled (Exodus 26:1; 35:30–36:1). The training of the musicians in the Old Testament Israelite community was specific and demanding and under the direction of head musicians (Chronicles 6:31–42; 16:3–6, 42). The New Testament even charges us to think about those things that are lovely, excellent, and of good report (Philippians 4:8).

Let us assume, then, that the pursuit of excellence is worthy and that we all seek it, and now go on to discuss what comprises excellence in music.

I think there is a tension in the Christian community between musical excellence (which musicians learn in lessons and graduate schools and in the so-called "professional" world) and Christian service (on which we focus in church, chapel, and private devotions), as if they are mutually exclusive: either we are very, very good at music-making, or we are in Christian service. This tension exhibits itself in doubt about the propriety for a Christian to have a career in "professional performance"; we wonder if a concert career is valid as service—unless, of course, the music has Christian words. It exhibits itself in many of the dilemmas of church music: as for example, in the perceived conflict between excellence and the participation of many members. It exhibits itself in our fear of elitism and in conflicting perceptions and worries about what constitutes "Christian music" and "Christian service."

I suggest that servanthood and musical excellence belong together, that both are components of true Christian experience, along with some other components, and that all of them are necessary and work together.[2] In discussing the integrity of these components, I will focus on the music itself, the use of music, the attitude of the heart, and the result in the total fabric of the community. Along the way, a definition of excellence will be constructed.

Excellence in the Music Itself

Of what does excellence in the music consist?[3] How do we perceive goodness and badness, quality and mediocrity in music? And where do we get our standards?

In all our concerns, we should always look first to the Bible. Here, however, we do not find directions for the actual notes of music. The Bible does not tell us which chord to use, or what scales are ordained, or how many steps should be in an octave. What we find here are general admonitions to quality. Here we find norms for our attitude and for the use of music (and everything else) for the building of the body of believers. And here we get our concept of who we are, what kind of world our music is part of, and whose world it is. But the Bible does not help us in choosing notes.

Then we look to God's other revelation, the creation. In the natural world, however, we find no inherent music.[4] We might infer some general principles about variety and about the union of form and function. Some people, in fact, have worked at finding aesthetic principles for music in the natural world, but they find it easier to do so in terms of the visual arts than the sound arts. However, to my mind, they have not yet found specific musical guidelines.

Where then do we derive our guidelines for composition? The norms for composition come from the art of music itself.[5] Common general norms for all music include craftsmanship; unity and variety; aesthetic expressiveness; integratedness of materials, shape, and use; and authenticity, all of which apply in a rich variety of national, historical, and cultural styles. Of these, let us here consider especially three: craftsmanship, expressiveness, and the integrity of materials and function. These criteria apply to all music, be it Western high art music, Western pop, or music of non-Western cultures. The examples I use here, however, come from Western classical music, simply because that is what I know best.

It is often said that music is a great gift of God. However, while I admire the spirit of gratitude and worship in which this statement is made, I believe it should be clarified, for music is not a direct gift of God. It is the potential for music, the raw materials—the overtone series, the resonating qualities of larynx, wood, and metal—that are the great gift of God, as is our ability to shape something of them. But music itself is a cultural product, something humankind has made with God's raw materials. An unfortunate consequence of asserting that music is a gift of God is that music is set beyond criticism. This claim becomes a barrier to discernment and necessary judgment in a world that contains both musical trash and musical masterpieces.

Excellence Consists of Good Technique

In performance, excellence is technique, getting all the notes right and playing them in tune with good articulation on an instrument of superb quality. As we get better, technique becomes more multilayered. It includes scholarly insight, so that we play not only on a good instrument, but also on a historically accurate instrument;[6] not only with a balanced orchestra, but with a historically appropriate size of orchestra; not only in tune, but according to the tuning system of a given style or time. Music teachers and scholars spend their lives at this, teaching students from the bottom up to play the right notes, to develop an appropriate and lovely tone, to understand the style, and to improve all the other components of technique.

In composition, excellence is craftsmanship. Craftsmanship includes consistency in the handling of the musical materials (the themes, harmonies, rhythms). Craftsmanship includes observing the specific compositional practices associated with certain styles. For example, in certain traditional styles, composers avoid parallel fifths, particular note doublings, and bumpy chord connections. In jazz, certain scales are to be used. In any style, craftsmanship includes writing within the capabilities of the instruments chosen, even writing idiomatically for them. In any style, good craftsmanship requires writing with a coherence of materials.

Then there are technological accompaniments in the area of technique. The instruments themselves are well in tune. The performance space—hall, church, room—is acoustically live and balanced. The sound system, if used, is working, of good quality, and monitored carefully. The recording technology and equipment are of fine quality.

So: *excellence consists of good craftsmanship, good technique.* But not only of that.

Excellence Also Consists of Expressiveness

Excellence is not only getting all the correct notes. It also consists of expressiveness. We have all heard flawless performances that are wooden and have sensed that something essential to music was missing. And while a certain amount of proficiency is foundational to expressiveness, technique does not have to be flawless before expressiveness can begin. Excellence is not merely technical perfection. I wonder how many young musicians have been discouraged from music by an overemphasis on technical perfection, which can be manifested in a no-mistakes approach in piano lessons or in a diligent hunt for technical errors in written music exercises and a neglect of the gracious bits of melody in the same exercises. And I wonder about the extent to which we have bought into flawlessness by the flawless but false recordings made possible by the patching techniques of recording technology, a flawlessness rarely possible in live music-making. There is a telling story related by William Edgar:

> When the great pianist Artur Schnabel finished his monumental recordings of the complete Beethoven sonatas, the studio engineer came to him and explained that there had been a number of mistakes here and there. If Schnabel would come down to the studio he could play those measures and they could be dubbed in. Schnabel refused the offer. He even offered to do the entire thirty-two sonatas again, incorporating whatever new mistakes might be involved! But under no circumstances would he allow the studio to spoil the unity of the original performance, with the mood and ambience he had created.[7]

So excellence in music requires expressiveness. What is it? Here words falter while examples would flourish. However, we can say briefly that in performance, expressiveness is knowing, after getting all the notes in tune, when to bend a pitch, and how much, and why. It is knowing how much to stretch a yearning note upward, how far to flat a blue note. It is knowing, after getting all the rhythms right, when to stretch a note, and how much, and why. It is that moment in a recent rehearsal of the orchestra I play in, a rehearsal when we were all tired and perfunctory, so tired that all we wanted was to get the right notes and then go home, when the bassoonist shaped a brief solo so exquisitely that all heads turned and all eyes brightened.

In composition, expressiveness is nuance, subtlety. It is suggestiveness, shape. It is the choice of all the right materials at a given moment to achieve the desired musical effect.

It is the expressive aspect of music that aestheticians try to capture and explain—confined, again, to words. Calvin Seerveld says it is allusiveness, suggestiveness.[8] William Edgar calls it "metaphor," signifying a way of experiencing time and space.[9]

Expressiveness is hard to define, because, again, words are not suited to the task. Nevertheless, it is expressiveness that is at the aesthetic heart of that shaping of sound we call music. We assert this while at the same time acknowledging the role of function (for dance or liturgy or celebration), the connection to emotion (music to express or correlate with our deep feelings), the importance of textual content, and the political and social implications and context of music. The aesthetic is central. Even when music is present in a situation where the emphasis is on something else, the aesthetic is paramount. Music may have a didactic purpose: we may find or devise a tune to help us remember the letters of the alphabet or the books of the Bible or the names of Jesus' disciples or the directions for sailing across the Pacific; but if that tune is not aesthetically rich, we will have a good mnemonic device but not good music. Music may have a liturgical or ceremonial purpose; but even if the music enables all the graduates or the bridesmaids to walk in step, or the ballerinas to dance together, or the congregation to proclaim the words of a Psalm together, if the music is not aesthetically rich, we will not have good music. Music may have emotional significance in expressing our joy, loneliness, or grief, or a political purpose in uniting the patriots of a cause or a country, but if the music itself is not aesthetically rich, we will not have good music. Even when we write or choose music to carry a Christian text, we need musical expressiveness. For if the music isn't aesthetically good, we may as well dispense with it and use a poem or a speech instead.

That expressiveness is difficult to pinpoint, however; we catch the idea more than we are taught it. Performers catch it from great performers, teachers, and artists who model and instruct. Listeners both to traditional

Western music literature and to compositions and styles that are new to us
learn to discern it only under the tutelage of those with an ear to hear. Rules
don't help much; it seems that within an hour of formulating a tidy set of
rules or guidelines about what makes, say, a good melody, one can find half
a dozen examples that mist the eyes and catch the throat—and escape the
guidelines. We learn quality in musical expressiveness not from a lecture,
but from exposure to good music, under the tutelage and/or encouragement of an expert in the field. One needs a friend who says, "Listen to this
now. Hear how the little twist in the melody here fits the hidden suggestion
in the text, or sets us up for the next section, or keeps the harmony the
same yet different. Here right now, in this piece, this is evidence of expressiveness." And by discerning the same in numerous different instances, we
build up a sense of expressiveness and become sensitive to pieces and
performances that are both well-crafted and richly expressive, beginning to
distinguish them from those that are well-crafted but devoid of expressiveness, from those whose craftsmanship is flawed and yet are expressive, and
from those that are both shoddy and soulless. Because this tutelage, this
entry into the perception of musical quality, is best guided by an insider in a
style, requires musical examples, and takes considerable time, I cannot here
articulate much further what creates aesthetic expressiveness.

So let us summarize what we have so far:

Excellence is

> *superb craftsmanship*
> *in composition and technique in performance*
> *wedded to aesthetic expressiveness.*

Acknowledging that excellence exists in performance and in composition,
in both technique and expressiveness, we should press on to see it, to
encourage others to seek it, to show them where and how to find it.

Excellence Works in Stages toward an Ideal

Yet we also take note of levels of excellence. We acknowledge a sort of
absolute or ideal excellence: the finest compositions performed with outstanding technique and superb artistic/aesthetic expressiveness. It is the
best that has yet been done, the best that can be done. This excellence is an
ideal, a goal, a destination. I suppose that we would admit that this being
the limited and imperfect world that it is, the highest level of excellence
experienced in our world is still not the best possible, the best that we will
experience in the new heaven and the new earth. I like the words of Stanley
Wiersma: "It sounds as though we expect and A+ from [our] life, when all
we have ever achieved is a C."[10]

But it is appropriate also to acknowledge a relative excellence. When I
judge a junior high festival, for instance, if I were to hold to standards of
absolute excellence, I would give everyone a "poor" rating. Instead, I use a

standard of excellence related to what younger adolescents are capable of. This excellence is a way station on the road of excellence, a point on an infinite line. I must point out quickly, however, that affirming relative excellence does not at all mean affirming anti-aestheticism or the lowest common denominator or tolerating lack of growth.

We also acknowledge and work for personal excellence. Actually, all of us are operating in a context of relative excellence, limited by our own ability, training, and resources. This is true even of world-class artists and of the great masters of composition. Excellence is doing my best, my best at this point. All of us are finite, and all of us are flawed; all of us also are, or should be, in progress.

Our conception of excellence thus includes a sense of the best possible and of a point of development, both a destination and a journey. Part of the challenge and the difficulty of discernment in music is that we must constantly be judging the appropriate level of excellence to expect in each situation.

What, then, is excellence in music?

Excellence is

> *superb craftsmanship*
> *in composition and technique in performance*
> *wedded to aesthetic expressiveness,*
> *pursued toward the ideal*
> > *at the presently appropriate level.*

All of it. For it won't do to perform with technical virtuosity but with no soul, or to hamper expressiveness with inadequate technique, or to lavish performing excellence, both technical and expressive, on mediocre music. Excellence requires all of it.

A question that arises here is this: obedience to the cultural mandate, either knowingly or unknowingly, has resulted in the development of sound in a multiplicity of musical ways and styles, a multiplicity that is legitimate and rich. But are some of these styles capable of greater aesthetic richness? I suggest that the concept of relative excellence applies here, that some styles lend themselves to a higher level of excellence than others. It is possible and appropriate to say that two pieces of music are each excellent among their kind, but that one style is capable of a higher, broader, or deeper level of craftsmanship or expressiveness. It is worth considering if there are ceilings on what we can expect in the quality of certain styles of Christian Contemporary, for instance, or rock, or even classical. It could also be debated whether certain styles only appear to be limited, until later or deeper masters show the higher quality of which they are capable. Was the classical symphony, for example, excellent in the hands of Stamitz and Sammartini, or did that seem to be a musically modest genre only until the masters Haydn and Mozart set their hands to it?

162

Other questions also arise. One is the question of worldview and music. Surely excellence includes consistency with a Christian worldview. Other questions concern the power of music to move us, to influence our emotions and behavior. However, although both issues are important, they are beyond the scope of the present article.

Finally, we must be aware of some traps as we pursue musical excellence. One is discouragement. If we focus on ideal excellence out of balance with contextual excellence, we may intimidate or discourage others or ourselves. However, if we focus on relative excellence out of balance with ideal excellence, we hinder growth. "Good enough for now" can too easily become "good enough." We need both to set and seek high standards and to do so in a spirit of encouragement.

Another trap is to worship excellence and those who exhibit it and to feel superior to those whose level of discernment and appreciation is "below" ours. Related to this is a sort of idolatry of the artist and a belief that the artist's pursuit of excellence is such a high and exclusive calling that it exempts him or her from other duties in the Kingdom.

Excellence in the Use of Music

Secondly, let's consider the use of music. For music does not just hang on the wall. It functions in life. It is for use. Music is for life, and life is not limited to sitting quietly and listening, to what Wolterstorff has called "aesthetic contemplation," although that is indeed one fine use of music.[11]

For most of us, music functions in a variety of ways. In a given day, we may put the Canadian Brass on the stereo during breakfast and turn it up loud, too, to encourage a cheerful attitude. During chapel time we sing as we worship communally. At dinner we sing, in assorted family voices, "Happy Birthday" to a chortling one-year-old and shortly after, put him to sleep with lullabies. Then we're off to help chaperone a junior high skating party, where the music is to skate with. Or we might attend a concert or listen to a compact disc, where for the first time this day we simply sit and take it in, engage in "aesthetic contemplation." Is the concert the only valid use of music? I don't believe so.

Music is appropriately used with actions and activities, such as liturgy and dancing. It highlights ceremonies such as weddings, parades, birthdays, and inaugurations. It is a partner of theatre and dance. It is used in and for therapy.[12]

Music is used for personal things too. Whether or not some "purists" approve, music is used for relaxation. (Is that invalid? It would be curious if we approve the use of music for therapy but not for regaining our own serenity through relaxation.) It is used to make work more pleasant and more efficient. (Is that okay? Again, it would be curious if, while teaching historic work songs such as sea chanteys and railroad songs to our grade school children, we pull up our noses about the idea of music in offices.) It is used for entertainment and amusement. (We might theoretically doubt the validity of that, but it is difficult to tell where aesthetic enrichment leaves off and good entertainment begins.)

These associations come in part because music partners well. It is a ready and appropriate companion to many other activities and functions in life. The dimension we call rhythm, that shaping of the time element of creation, goes well with other activities that work in time, such as drama and dancing and parades and processionals, which leads to its role in celebrations such as graduations and inaugurations. It can enhance the efficiency and pleasure of work, as the heritage of sea chanteys and railroad songs attests. Its expressiveness partners well with whatever carries emotion, be it funerals or celebrations. These partnerships are valid, and, I would suggest, not less worthy than music for pure listening.

And herein lies a further criterion in the evaluation of quality: how well does the music join that which it is partner to? How well does the music fit and serve the liturgical action? How well does it help carry the play? Can one march well with the parade music and dance well with the dance music—not to, but with?

If its function is aesthetic contemplation—pure listening—it is only the technique and expressiveness, both in composition and performance, that count. If, however, the music is for an activity or function, it is not only technique and expressiveness, but also fittingness to the situation that count.[13]

Once again, we need it all. For if we focus only on the function and forget about technical and expressive quality, music becomes only a tool. We could claim that as long as we dance to the dance music, or as long as the offertory music matches the time it takes the deacons to pass the plates, or as long as the choir music stirs an audience or congregation to religious feelings, or as long as the advertising ditty sells the product, or as long as people are entertained by the performance, the music "works" and is therefore good; what else could one want? What we want, of course, is also aesthetic and technical excellence.[14]

Contrarily, if we consider only aesthetic excellence, we may not have a good fit to the occasion. I think here of church music: one of Bach's masterpiece preludes and fugues just might not make the best offertory for a given congregation on a given Sunday.

It is not either/or, but both/and. To be good, music should serve its purpose well and at the same time exhibit high musical quality, both technical and expressive. When we say music is bad, it may be because it is poorly crafted, or expressively barren, or unsuited to its use, or all of these.

Some concerns and questions arise here too:

(a) If well-crafted and aesthetically expressive music fits its use well, will it necessarily also be suitable for sheer listening? Mozart's background music for garden parties—his *divertimenti*—make charming concert pieces. Should that be true of all music with specific functions?

(b) Some may claim that music for pure listening (such as a symphony) is higher or better than music to relax by or work to. But is that true, or is that simply elitism?

(c) We should consider whether music is indeed needed for every situation. For example, given the long association of music with work, we ought to consider what sort of music (if any at all) is *good* as office/work music. Office music, store music, and elevator music can well be questioned. Often such music is bad or unnecessary or both. I confess that I frequently feel depressed when I must endure grocery store or elevator music. It's not only that the music is there, but that it's aesthetically depleting rather than aesthetically enriching. Yet sometimes the music is also unnecessary. While we acknowledge that music is an appropriate partner of many actions, I question whether every activity and place must be bathed with music of some sort. We should be able to shop or wait for the dentist or be on hold on the phone without always being immersed in music. The continual presence of music works against both discernment and enjoyment, for we learn simply to tune it out.

(d) A question for schools to ponder is the relation of the music department and its curriculum to the role of music in the total life of the school. If the use of music is an important and legitimate concern, shouldn't the study and performance of music go beyond that normally associated with the recital hall? By concentrating only on concert presentations we forget that music has many uses. But if music is important in all of life, our focus should be broadened. We should work for excellence whenever music touches life. We should be willing to offer our expertise to work for good music that fits other situations, too.

So what is excellence in music?

Excellence is
>*superb craftsmanship*
>*in composition and technique in performance,*
>*wedded to aesthetic expressiveness,*
>*pursued toward the ideal*
>>*at a presently appropriate level,*
>*together with an integrity of the materials and their shape*
>>*with the use for which the music is intended.*

Excellence in Servanthood

Excellence in music also means having our purposes straight. Here especially we can look for guidance to the Bible, God's rule for faith and life. We are to make music as creatures and as servants.

As God's creatures we make music in obedient, humble, and joyful response to the cultural mandate, the invitation and command to tend and develop God's good world of sound. We make music in awareness that we are tending God's garden in the area of sound. It is in response to this command that we are not only interested in but also committed to writing high-caliber music and performing it at the best possible level. All the qualities of musical excellence are related to this command. We do this in response to God and his creation.

As servants we make music in obedient, humble, joyful, and loving service to our neighbor, in concern for our neighbor's well-being. To respond to the command to serve our neighbor we work not only to develop quality in the music itself, but also to develop and exercise pastoral judgment in music. We do this first of all—and we would do it even in an unfallen world—because all God's gifts of talent and ability are to be used that way. For there is a wonderful match: each person, created in the image of God, has many aspects and many needs, including an aesthetic side and therefore aesthetic needs. Others have been gifted to meet and to serve those needs. These gifts have been given, not to mark us as superior, or to give us private pleasure, but to equip us for service. My neighbor, the dietitian, helps me tend my nutritional needs and looks after my physical well-being. I, the musician, tend her aesthetic needs and look out for her aesthetic well-being.

Let me pursue the analogy with my neighbor the dietitian. For dietitians, service means serving food that is both delicious and nutritious: both/and. A good dietitian serves the best. A good dietitian also refuses to serve the bad and does some teaching about why it is bad. A good dietitian won't just serve what is wanted if it is not also good for us. A good dietitian (like our mothers) also expands our repertoire of foods as we grow, from one good (milk and cereal) to other goods, as we are able. Likely we get stuck at times, refusing to eat eggs when we are four and disdaining all but pizza and potato chips when we are fifteen. But our good dietitian never thinks that we can't grow beyond that. Likewise, we musicians are to tend and nurture our neighbor's well-being in the aesthetic area, to serve up music that is both "delicious and nutritious," both enjoyable and aesthetically building. Serving as dietitian means serving quality food. Serving as an automaker or mechanic means seeing to it that our neighbor's brakes do not fail. Serving as musician means seeing to it that music does not fail our neighbor aesthetically. Serving as musician means choosing to do that which edifies our neighbor musically. We cannot do that with sloppy performance, ill-chosen music, mediocre instruments, or trite composition. Choosing music of high quality and performing it well *is* a way of being our neighbor's keeper.

We would do this even in an unfallen world. But it is a fallen world, and there is musical mediocrity and musical trash as well as musical greatness. Since sin has spoiled everything, including our aesthetic artifacts and our aesthetic perceptions, we have the added task of helping to sort out the good from the mediocre and the downright poor. Seeing to the well-being of my neighbor includes providing some guidance in musical discernment.

I referred earlier to a perceived tension between musical excellence and Christian service. The apparent tension occurs when we do not keep a balanced picture in mind. We can become so focused on the "serving" that we ignore the other components of excellence we've been outlining here. We like to say, "It's the heart that counts." And it is. But the truly serving heart will serve up quality, not aesthetic stones. For example, some would hesitate to deny a questionable musical offering in church because the well-meaning but unprepared singer "is so sincere." And it's true that sincerity of the heart of the giving musician is necessary. But that does not make good workmanship unnecessary. It is not true that sincerity of heart is so important that poor compositional craftsmanship, bad tuning, and unbalanced ensemble don't matter. Yet, at the same time, without sincerity of heart, our most perfect music is but a "sounding gong."

A balanced approach that understands aesthetic excellence and true service to be mutually inclusive helps us out of the sticky wickets that would be there if we considered only musical excellence or only usefulness or only (superficially) pleasing our neighbor. Having the genuine well-being of our neighbor and community in mind will help us stand up for excellence and against mediocrity with no more fear of elitism than the nutritionist who advocates a low-fat diet. Seeking the genuine well-being of our neighbors may help achieve the balance between usefulness and aesthetic concerns when a church or a wedding party or the PTA want music for a "function." Seeking the genuine well-being of our neighbors helps to match the type and level of excellence to the situation—a balancing act of musical and pastoral judgment.

All, says Paul, is to be done for the building of the Body of Christ (1 Corinthians 12). We champion music of high technical and expressive quality not as an end in itself, but for the well-being of our neighbors and for the well-being of the community. We make music well not as a badge of our own skill and achievement, but to tend our neighbors' well-being in the world of sound, for we are our neighbors' keepers in the area of musical aesthetics.

So what is excellence in music?

Excellence is

superb craftsmanship
in composition and technique in performance,
wedded to aesthetic expressiveness,
pursued toward the ideal
    at a presently appropriate level,
together with an integrity of the materials and their shape
    with the use for which the music is intended,

undertaken in joyful and obedient response to God's commands
to develop his good creation of sound
and to serve our neighbor.[15]

Excellence within the Total Fabric of the Community

Because we are called to serve, every area of life is an appropriate neighborhood. We may be set in a neighborhood, or we may choose one, matching it to our gifts, expertise, and sense of calling. Some persons, because of their gifts and opportunities, may be called to the concert world of high art, others to the local school or town, their neighbors in each case being those in that world. Our neighbors may be the audience at Carnegie Hall or the child in our care, the worshippers in a church or the children in an elementary school, the students in the small college or those in a great university. All these neighborhoods—local, national, or even international—have equal status as arenas of Christian service.

The result will be a total fabric of life of which music is an integral part and in which music contributes to a wholeness of life, a whole cloth with health and well-being in every aspect of personal and collective life. In this fabric, good music is an integral part of the whole of life, not reserved for moments of high worship or high-art concert life, nor regarded as optional entertainment. Wherever music appears, it is excellent and appropriate.

In the total fabric of life, music will interact with other areas of life, such as business (as in the music industry) and politics. As it does so, music must not lose its integrity. Integrity includes maintaining its essential nature: aesthetic expressiveness. Integrity also includes not being bumped off-center or compromised by the dilemmas and problems of the other areas of life with which it interacts. For example, as music interacts with business, its aesthetic integrity must not be compromised by any concerns of business that are sinful. As music interacts with and is influenced by political concerns, it must not be compromised by them. In short, wherever music interacts with other areas of life, musicians must be on the lookout lest the problems, imbalances, and "fallennesses" of those areas "leak over" into the world of music.

For what we are working toward and looking for is a whole and wholesome culture in which, as Scripture says, even the cooking pots and the bells on the horses will be inscribed "holy unto the Lord" (Zechariah 14:20), and the lullabies, too, and the symphonies, and the dance music, and all the songs, a culture that exhibits "life under the covenant, life in relation to Jehovah,"[16] a culture that is, to use and Old Testament term, a community of *shalom.*

Summary

So what is excellence?

Excellence is

composing and using music of the highest compositional craftsmanship and aesthetic richness and performing it superbly,
matching music with function,
doing both in gratitude to God and in service to our neighbor,
doing it all toward the end of *shalom*.

Excellence is

superb craftsmanship
in composition and technique in performance,
wedded to aesthetic expressiveness,
pursued toward the ideal
at a presently appropriate level,
together with an integrity of the materials and their shape
with the use for which the music is intended,
undertaken in joyful and obedient response to God's commands
to develop his good creation of sound
and to serve our neighbor
toward the end of the glory of God and of the well-being of the total fabric of the
community.

May God bless our work to that end.

Notes

1. *Campus Life*, ads from various issues from 1990.

2. Note that the summary of the law instructs us both to love God with all our *mind* and to
love our neighbor as ourselves (Matthew 22:37–40).

3. For more on musical excellence, see Harold M. Best, *Music Through the Eyes of Faith* (San
Francisco: HarperSanFrancisco, 1993).

4. There are bird songs, of course; but although they are a sort of incipient music, I have not
yet found an aesthetic of music based on them.

5. In *Rainbows for a Fallen World*, Calvin Seerveld writes:

When you want to find out how God ordered plants to grow, you don't go study the synoptic
Gospels: you go examine plants with a sharp knife and microscope. If you need to discover
what chinks in a person's emotional makeup are apt to crack wide open in later life and how
you should put an arm around such a one to help hold them together so they can heal, you
don't read Proverbs for details on neuroses and psychoses: you study the case histories of emotionally disturbed people and examine others who display psychic health, make notes, reflect,
and bite your fingernails as psychotherapist lest you mess up the life of somebody Christ died
for. If you must decide, so you can give leadership, on whether Chagall's stained class window
honouring the late Mayor Daley in the Art Institute of Chicago is more or less significant than
the striking piece by Abraham Rattner that takes a whole wall of the downtown loop synagogue, you don't go read Paul's letters, the Psalms, or even Isaiah 40 to look for information
on 'beauty': instead, you go study the art for hours, learn the composer or artist's whole oeuvre

169

to get context, examine the history of music, memorial and cult artistry, take a considered stand on the nature of art and slowly begin to discern what counts. All of this scrutiny is exceedingly difficult, because cultural artifacts complicate creation by slipping in also the committed slant of a man or woman's heart; but you make, perhaps in a communion with others, an aesthetic judgment that will bring relative blessing or a curse to those whom it influences.
Calvin Seerveld, *Rainbows for a Fallen World* (Toronto: Tuppence Press, 1980), 13–14.

6. By this illustration I do not wish to assert the necessity of using historical instruments, but only point out that certain matters of scholarship are matters of technique rather than of expressivity, although they should be undertaken for the purpose of enhancing musical expressivity.

7. William Edgar, *Taking Note of Music* (London: SPCK (Thirdway Books), 1986), 14.

8. Seerveld, *Rainbows for a Fallen World*, 128–135.

9. Edgar, *Taking Note of Music,* chapter 3.

10. Stanley Wiersma, *Adjoining Fields* (Grand Rapids, MI: The English Department of Calvin College, 1987), 33.

11. Nicholas Wolterstorff, *Art in Action* (Grand Rapids, MI: Eerdmans, 1980).

12. Dale Topp presents these various "uses" of music in connection with various areas of life: music and serenity (therapy and relaxation); music and friendship; music and declaration (political statement); music and action (liturgy, dance, play); music and amusement (entertainment); music and education (cultural understanding). Dale Topp, *Music in the Christian Community* (Grand Rapids, MI: Eerdmans, 1976).

13. It could be said, of course, that pure listening is also an activity. I make here a distinction between music for pure listening and music with another function to highlight some of the issues involved in this discussion.

14. Some Christians see Genesis 2:9 as presenting a model for both aesthetic value and usefulness in the arts: "And the Lord God made all kinds of trees grow out of the ground—trees that were pleasing to the eye and good for food." Genesis 2:9.

15. See "Our World Belongs to God: A Contemporary Testimony," in *Psalter Hymnal* (Grand Rapids, MI: CRC Publications, 1989), 1022: "As God's creatures we are made in his image to represent him on earth, and to live in loving communion with him. By sovereign appointment we are earthkeepers and caretakers: loving our neighbor, tending the creation, and meeting our needs. God uses our skills in the unfolding and well-being of his world."

16. Edgar, *Taking Note of Music,* 49.

Worldview and Leadership:
A Reformed Perspective on Country Development

John R. Visser[*]

....

Introduction

Millions of poor people around the world are waiting for skilled, vision-ary leaders with an integral worldview who can help lift them out of their poverty. Democracy is often seen as the answer to poverty, but millions of dollars have been wasted in futile efforts to plant democracies in political and economic soils unenriched by the kind of civil society and political/economic leadership that grow out of a consistent, integrated moral world-view. In addition to skills and vision, effective country leaders need the kind

[*] Dr. Visser, Professor of Business Administration, joined the faculty at Dordt College in 1976. His M.B.A. is from DePaul University and his Ph.D. is from the University of Alabama. Over the years his research and writing interests have evolved from the mathematical modeling of stock prices to the impact of culture, civil society, and religious beliefs on the health of organizations and economies. This essay is a shortened revision of his chapter "Worldview and Global Leadership," in *Leadership: Succeeding in the Private, Public, and Not-for-Profit Sectors*, edited by Ronald R. Sims and Scott A. Quatro (forthcoming).

of beliefs and worldviews that adequately address structural questions related to morality, equity, and justice. Further, they cannot afford to have large numbers of their citizens view these values as personal, relative, or subjective since effective leadership is a communal process that demands as much from the followers as from the leader.

Scholars have been writing about leadership for decades without agreeing on its definition. Moreover, a preoccupation with empirical measurement often restricts researchers from dealing with the most important (but difficult to quantify) aspects of leadership.[1] A third quandary evident from the research is some writers' refusal to refer to people such as Hitler or Stalin as leaders because of the damage they inflicted on millions of people. From a Reformed Christian perspective, these and similar differences of opinion are inevitable, given the writers' varied worldviews, one component of which is often the assumption that the only good way to know something is through empirical verification. Differences represent an inability to admit that before good *leadership* can be defined, the meaning of "good" must be determined. This discussion takes us back to worldviews and "habits of the heart."[2]

Leadership Literature

Stogdill, Mann, and a host of others have noted that from ancient times and still today, a massive amount of time and energy has been devoted to studying "great men" in the hope of discovering the traits of great leaders.[3] Charisma is probably the most studied of these traits, but other more easily measured traits, such as confidence, drive, intelligence, empathy, self-control, or creativity, have also been studied extensively and have come to form the backbone of modern personality tests.[4] The limitations of the traits approach are well documented; in fact, in its failure to address underlying worldview questions, the traits approach remains unconvincing to people with a long history of suffering under leaders who were probably charismatic, confident, and ambitious.

On the other hand, proponents of situational and contingency approaches to leadership point out that good leaders, regardless of their traits, need to use different approaches in different situations.[5] Still, the task of leading a country, let alone the myriad situations in which leaders find themselves, has not been well defined in leadership literature. The Path-Goal[6] and Leader-Member Exchange theories,[7] on the other hand, place special emphasis on leader-follower interaction. Together, these theories point out the importance of focusing on follower needs and goals, recognizing that these goals and needs may be affected by the nature of the tasks at hand and that they are different for individual followers. Unfortunately for country leaders, focusing on the needs of subordinates for clarity, direction, or freedom and choosing the right style (e.g., participative or directive) seems beside the point when they must work with a parliament or millions of citizens. Psychodynamic approaches to leadership also seem relatively unhelpful when it comes to defining effective country leaders. Although self-knowledge is always beneficial, insight into one's worldview and the dominant worldview components of the citizenry would seem more critical than insight into individual psychological tendencies.

Transformational leadership (TL) theories come the closest to having the breadth and depth needed to address worldview concerns.[8] Many popular business writers, such as Covey and Peters,[9] and a host of writers in the field of educational leadership, such as Bergquist, Bogue, McDade and Lewis, and Wilcox, subscribe to the basic tenets of TL.[10] In addition to critical traits such as confidence, TL focuses on the leader's vision, values, and ability to articulate those values to effect change by serving as a role model and catalyst in the process of transforming followers and organizations. All of these capacities are needed in poverty-stricken countries suffering from corruption, nepotism, strife, and thought patterns that have tied them to their poverty. Some scholars have been tempted to reduce TL to charismatic leadership,[11] but this reduction does not recognize the importance of transformational leaders' worldviews or the possibility of those worldviews becoming institutionalized with the infusion of the visionary leaders' values and vision into their organizations.[12]

More recently, servant leadership and leadership ethics have been the focus of Western literature. As Robert Greenleaf has ably noted, leaders who excel at seeing and focusing on followers' needs are more effective.[13] Along the same lines, Brady highlights the importance of an ethic of caring in building the trust and cooperation that promotes change.[14] Block, Covey, De Pree, Gilligan, and a host of others make nearly the same point: effective leadership requires a willingness to serve, which goes hand in hand with an emphasis on honesty and justice, respect for the dignity of the individual, and an emphasis on building community.[15]

This focus on ethics and serving has given impetus to a recent flurry of writing on spiritual leadership. Three somewhat distinct groups of writers have focused on the spirituality of leaders: those interested in the psychological aspects, those considered new age (popular) writers, and those interested in the traditional religious aspects of spirituality (e.g., Christian or Buddhist). A growing number of books draw leadership lessons from biblical accounts.[16] Others attempt to draw leadership lessons from the lives of people like Bonhoeffer, Ghandi, or Mother Theresa, who have made a significant impact through their "spiritual engagement" with the world.[17] The logical conclusion of this heightened interest in spirituality is the coinage of the term "*spiritual* intelligence"[18] and the expectation that it will carve out a spot in the mainstream literature as "Emotional Intelligence" did in the 1990s.[19] As useful as all these perspectives are, they do not carry the same potential as those that focus on worldviews.

Worldview and Country Leadership

Countries and entire cultures develop ways of seeing the world that are unique and are passed from generation to generation through child-rearing practices, religious beliefs, and educational systems. For example, by 1991 almost everything in the Soviet Union had been touched by its predominant religion. We are not talking about Russian Orthodoxy but rather atheistic communism, the (initial) victor in the seventy-year religious war that so ruthlessly sterilized Orthodoxy. Marxist-Leninist doctrine left its mark everywhere. Single-family homes were nowhere to be seen. Apartment buildings, jammed with pint-sized apartments and claustrophobic elevators, stretched as far as the eye could see. Abortion helped keep families from outgrowing their apartments, and prices were controlled on everything. The architectural uniformity of state-owned buildings complemented the one-color-fits-all overcoats filling the store racks inside, all in the name of attaining sanctifying equality and avoiding the carnal sin of individuality. Statues of the new saints—Lenin, Stalin, Dresinsky, the Cosmonauts, and the other heroes—stood everywhere, providing icon-like evidence of the core beliefs of leaders intent on molding the worldview of the Soviet citizens into their image.

The beginning of this era can be traced to Lenin's official Declaration of the Separation of Church and State. At first "purely religious" sermons were allowed, and registered churches were permitted to remain open, but by the time Stalin was finished interpreting the meaning of "separation," 98 percent of the Russian Orthodox churches had been closed, Bible printing was prohibited, children were not permitted to attend worship services, attendees of unregistered church services were given twenty-five-year prison sentences, and tens of thousands of priests had been killed. Khrushchev extended this assault to evangelical Protestant churches when he took over in 1959. In addition, the Marxist worldview held that wealth was created primarily by labor (rather than, for example, by management, marketing, finance, or ethics). Inevitably, the economy finally imploded under the weight of moral and political corruption, widespread shortages, and the lack of incentives. It wasn't until March of 1985 that Mikhail Gorbochev severed the official link that had been forged between Marxist/Leninist political and economic philosophy and atheism. Interestingly, this turnaround, important to the eventual breakup of the country, was only lightly covered in the Western press, probably because the press didn't understand the importance of subtle shifts in a country leader's worldviews.

However, leaders do not have to be Marxists to have fatal flaws in their worldviews. Many leaders of developing countries and many Westerners think that the world's wealth is so fixed that if one person ends up with more wealth, someone else will end up with less. Many people believe, for example, that a profit must be at the expense of employees' salary or wages or that when a business buys goods from another country, the foreign country is necessarily being exploited. Of course, part of the reason for this belief is that sometimes one person's gain is another person's loss, as is obviously the case in outright stealing or war and pillage. Exploitation is less obvious with unproductive workers, corrupt governments, poorly run companies, or complex international contracts. In fact, distinguishing wealth creation from redistribution is so difficult that entire nations have wrongly confused the two for hundreds of years. European powers established colonies on the assumption that exploiting resources and trading manufactured goods for raw materials would make them rich. Pre-WWII Japan believed the same, only to learn after the war (and beyond the shadow of a doubt) that a nation does not need to be endowed with great supplies of natural resources or use imperialism to dominate another's natural resources in order to thrive. Resource endowments can either help or hurt a nation, depending on the worldview of the people and their leaders. Many resource-rich African nations, like Nigeria, Sierra Leone, and Angola, have seen far more political upheaval than wealth accumulation from their oil, gold, or diamonds. In fact, recent research by Michael Woolcock of the World Bank makes the case that in the absence of critical moral and ethical beliefs, natural resource windfalls may hurt real progress by trapping nations in the lure of easy money, inviting corruption and financing political conflict.[20]

These findings have led some to assume that the most important component in a country leader's worldview is a belief in free markets and democracy. However, it doesn't take long to realize that Asian nations like Korea, Thailand, Indonesia, and Malaysia experienced phenomenal wealth increases for decades even though their *markets* were distorted by tariffs, other import barriers, cartels, and government interference. Likewise, China has grown remarkably for nearly three decades despite a lack of democracy, whereas many countries in Africa, where hundreds of millions of dollars have been spent on democratization, have made little or no progress in the past twenty-five years. Experiences in Russia and other former Soviet Block countries also hint that effective country leadership requires much more than an understanding of the potential benefits of freedom and democracy.

Clearly, worldview makes a difference. Beliefs that an economy is a zero sum, Darwinian jungle where labor, business, and government fight each other or a collection of co-conspirators who feather each others' nests at the expense of the average person are all very different from the belief that progress is ultimately rooted in service, cooperation, and fairness. Only a worldview containing the latter belief will succeed in implementing, for example, an efficient voluntary tax system, a truly civil society, or pluralistic approaches to building consensus. Scholars like Lawrence Harrison and Joel Kotkin, via study of the historical development of countries and ethnic groups, credit the importance of religious and cultural variables to country economic outcomes.[21] Other scholars and organizations, like the World Bank, although reluctant to abandon their empiricism, have complemented or extended this work by showing how incompetence in government and the absence of civil society are often the primary barriers to progress.[22] Not much development will take place where people fear the revenge of spirits or witches that oppose change, believe in the fundamental unworthiness of whole groups of people, see no reason to hope, refuse to move to where jobs are, don't trust each other, or choose revenge and retribution over cooperation and compromise.

Country Leadership, Wealth, and Well-being

Economists as a group have pointed out that *wealth* is important in the process of meeting needs because little or nothing can be produced in the future without some accumulation of wealth in the present. The farmer depends on accumulating wealth in the form of seed, equipment, and money to sow next year's crop. The factory accumulates *retained earnings* to purchase new equipment or production facilities. The young couple accumulates a down payment in order to purchase their first house. A psychiatrist accumulates knowledge to diagnose and treat his patients correctly. Still, what is wealth and how is it measured? The Bible makes it clear that both wealth and the ability to create it are gifts from God (Deuteronomy 8:18). We've been given an earth weighing approximately six sextillion tons, surrounded by an immensely useful atmosphere, receiving a steady supply of energy daily, filled with hundreds of different elements with millions of potential uses. Through the individual and collective work of ancestors, societies have living quarters, work places, places of worship, material objects, aesthetic creations, services, and perhaps most importantly, ideas, technologies, principles, and codes of conduct that create, preserve, and renew wealth.

Adam Smith argued that people need to create institutions that encourage citizens to act in morally and socially responsible ways. He considered the market to be one of the institutions that would do this, and he wrote about the ways that self-interest could serve the public good. However, he also noted that effective markets need other institutions that foster respect for life, property, a concern for the common good, and virtues like self-control, prudence, and farsightedness. Oddly (given perceptions of him today), Smith believed that government would naturally get larger as civilization advanced, and he wrote *Wealth of Nations* in part to convince politicians and officials to recognize their responsibility to seek the public good and to create an atmosphere where people would have incentives to do what was in the best interest of all people. His desire for limited government reflects, more than anything, both his belief that institutions other than the government are better qualified to provide the moral and ethical training that undergirds the creation of wealth and his conviction that government officials are often neither positioned well to micromanage economic exchanges nor inclined to promote the public good. Markets, he believed, had the potential to pit selfish competitors against each other, forcing them to promote the public good and produce better products and services and resulting in greater wealth overall.[23]

Smith clearly understood that ideas and beliefs are the foundation of a country's well-being. A major theme of his first book, *The Theory of Moral Sentiments,* was the need for people to create institutions and structures that would transform their natural inclination toward self-love and self-interest into altruistic and benevolent behavior. He also noted that excessive attention to commerce could result in the neglect of other important aspects of culture and that excessive dependence on reason has the potential to create a moral vacuum. Although opposed to religious monopoly and the idea that any one group of clerics could corner the truth, he clearly felt that moral teaching, aimed at inculcating proper beliefs about what constitutes moral behavior, is at the core of creating a good society. He supported laws, for example, discouraging divorce, since he understood innately what we know today through exhaustive empirical study: that the breakdown of the family is bad for children, for moral behavior, and for economic well-being.[24] Oriented by a Calvinist religious heritage, and in stark contrast to his caricature, Smith quietly gave away much of the wealth he had been instrumental in creating during his lifetime.[25]

Worldview and Country Leadership

In addition to knowing people's needs and wants, visionary country leaders understand that the well-being of people and the usefulness of material (tangible) and nonmaterial (intangible) things are interdependent. A machine, for example, will increase in value not only when moved to a factory where it will be used more intensively but also when operated in a responsible manner by a moral, wise, socially connected, stable individual who is trusted and valued by a team of solid managers in a financially responsible company operating in a politically and economically stable country. Likewise, a person will command a higher wage and capital will command a greater return because both are more productive in that environment. Both wealth and well-being, then, flow out of communal activity that depends as much on knowledge and ethics as on machines and money. The diagram below best illustrates this interconnection; it is my extension of a diagram that Bill Essig, Steve Hoffmann, and I introduced in the book *Civil Society: A Foundation for Sustainable Economic Development.*[26]

Development Wheel

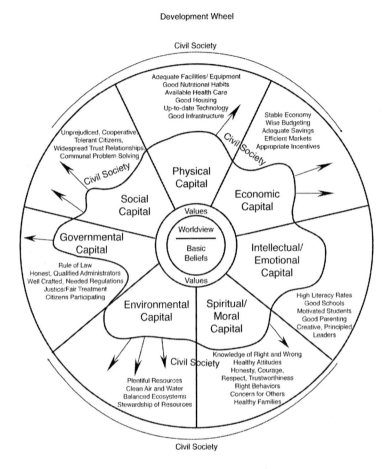

Wheel segments represent the different types of capital needed for development. The misshapen wheel illustrates capital impairment resulting from shortages of critical components of capital. Civil society enables countries to round out the wheel by acquiring or building essential forms of capital. The ultimate shape, structure, and strength of the wheel depends on the prevailing worldviews in the country.

As the diagram indicates, economic development is a productive process that resembles a wheel; its development is like the continuous movement of the wheel over time. Before a wheel can function properly, *material* must be gathered for the building process; in this case, seven types of resources (wheel segments) must be in place before the Development Wheel can be *rounded out* and function well. The word *capital* is used to describe these segments since we are already accustomed to identifying land, machines, and financial investments as forms of capital. Here, the traditional under-standing of capital is broadened to include communal and nonphysical things that must also be available before meaningful economic activity can take place. Clearly, healthy quantities of these things, such as infrastructure, systems, knowledge, trust, morality, and the like, are as important as physical and financial capital for productive activity to take place (i.e., for the wheel to be *rounded out* and for people's lives to improve).

All seven of these asset categories, like traditionally defined assets, take time to accumulate (i.e., they represent some endowment or *savings* from the past), need to be developed (i.e., we can and should *invest* in them), and have the potential to be either overutilized (depleted) or undersupplied. Since a round wheel will cover far more distance (more development, wealth creation, or well-being) with less waste than a misshapen wheel, the model presumes that an effective country leader needs to understand intuitively the importance of giving people incentives to build up, preserve, and replenish all seven forms of wealth/capital. A shortage in one or more of the needed inputs will result in something akin to the misshapen inner wheel in the diagram and reduce citizen satisfaction appreciably, in the short run or the long run. Furthermore, a lack of intangible (e.g., spiritual/moral or social) capital may be the most damaging shortage since the story of modern wealth creation is, in many ways, the story of the discovery and development of increasingly intangible forms of capital. In ancient times, people thought of wealth in terms of natural resources and hoarded things like gold and silver. Later, especially at the time of the industrial revolution, they began to see the value of transforming these resources into machines and other forms of physical capital. Later still, financial, intellectual, and governmental capital moved to the forefront. Future development—movement toward *shalom*—requires the buildup and exchange of social and spiritual/moral capital, which, for Reformed Christians, includes both discipleship and evangelism.

Shalom implies balance. Our modern overemphasis on the physical and economic segments has led to an excessive emphasis on material things and the depletion of environmental capital. However, just as overproduction can exhaust topsoil or mining can deplete scarce mineral resources, so an overemphasis on profit can exhaust a workforce and damage other forms of capital. For example, an overemphasis on labor productivity can erode social, governmental, or spiritual/moral capital, as evidenced when burned-out shift workers are too exhausted to interact with their children or neighbors, participate in the political process, or attend a church or synagogue. In an imperfect world, every society, community, organization, or individual requires a unique effort to restore shalom since each has greater or lesser problems in different sectors of the wheel. Still, it cannot be denied that country leaders who understand the nature of the creation and its Creator will be the leaders most likely to translate a vision for shalom into structures that bring balance, wholeness, and well-being into the different aspects of life. Among secular scholars, who prefer not to be explicit about a Creator, such a framework is often referred to as a *civil society*.

An Introduction to Civil Society

The modern attention given to civil society can best be traced back to December 1948, when the General Assembly of the United Nations unanimously adopted the *Universal Declaration of Human Rights*.[27] Most of the thirty articles in the declaration focus on rights such as the right to life, liberty, and freedom of religion; the right to freedom from arbitrary arrest, presumed guilt, slavery, or torture; the right to equal protection under the law, impartial public hearings, and privacy; and the right to freedom of movement, association, employment, and equal pay for equal work. The declaration also underscored the importance of marriage, family, and property ownership. However, it dealt more with the beliefs guiding a state's policies than with the thousands of institutions, laws, processes, and values needed to make it truly civil.

A useful definition of civil society for our purposes is *a set of institutions, processes, and attitudes that promote cooperation among individuals, private associations, and government agencies to produce practical solutions to common problems*. Some writers have described civil society as the "third leg" of a three-legged stool upon which society rests. In this way they distinguish civil society from government and markets (the other two legs) while simultaneously acknowledging the dependence of government and markets on civil society. Remove any one of the three legs, and the stool cannot stand.

Robert Bothwell's summary of the approaches to the subject is helpful in this regard.[28] He argues that the degree to which civil society exists in a country can be assessed in four fundamental ways:

1. Observing behaviors: Do we see lots of evidence in the society of trust, openness, participation, public debate, etc?
2. Inspecting societal foundations: Are freedom of speech, religion, association, the rule of law, educational opportunity, capable government, and political processes in place?
3. Examining broad outcomes: Is income widely distributed, are literacy rates or life expectancy high?
4. Examining institutions: How many religious organizations, community-based organizations, clubs, voluntary groups, consumer groups, unions, professional associations, etc. are there?[29]

The Absence of Civil Society

George B. N. Ayittey, in his book *Africa in Chaos*, describes the way much of Africa became a textbook illustration for why countries without healthy civil societies are not able to compete.[30] He notes that even in fairly large countries like Nigeria, with solid natural resource endowments, foreign investors became tired of bribes, extortion, permission fees, confiscatory exchange rates, petty and not-so-petty crime, and the threat of serious conflict, and they exited the country through much of the 1990s.

A brief foray into the problem of corruption will enlighten us as to the importance of the worldview of a country's leader. Corruption is many-faceted, often including bribery, extortion, nepotism, favoritism, black market activities, patronage, conflicts of interest, official theft, falsification of records, and the widespread expectation of excessive and often illegal "service fees" to get things done. Corruption makes economic activity less efficient, for these reasons:

- It reduces spontaneous cooperation with government because trust relationships are damaged as citizens come to see government not as a servant but as a predator. This condition greatly reduces the ability of government to exercise its legitimate authority and carry out its objectives, increasing, for example, the nonpayment of taxes, rent seeking, theft, and other economically damaging behaviors among citizens.

- It lowers the return on investment for government projects because of a tendency for officials to choose infrastructure projects that benefit them personally or consolidate their power in some way. Such projects are usually lower quality or provide lower return than do others with less tangible but widespread and public benefits.[31]

- It results in a society-wide focus on short-term gains since a corrupt environment is one in which the future is often unpredictable. This focus impedes the kind of long-term investing and risk-taking that is associated with the development of new industries and the economy as a whole.

- Corrupt countries attract the least efficient and least reputable foreign companies (since these companies would otherwise have trouble competing and therefore have the most to gain by paying bribes). Overall foreign investment is reduced because costs associated with corruption function like a tax. Likewise, capital tends to flee from uncertain environments (since people are concerned that their savings will be jeopardized by arbitrary actions), and less private/public foreign aid and so forth flows in, depressing the country's currency.

- Corruption slows the growth of small businesses (the engines of grassroots economic growth) via bureaucratic sclerosis and the imposition of unaffordable payments.[32]

- It causes talented people and ethical, efficient companies to become frustrated and seek to locate outside of the country (if they are able).

- Corruption results in inefficient resource allocation since arbitrary choices by government distort economic decisions throughout the society. Some public and private goods and services remain priced well above world prices and others well below, which leads to other inefficient decisions.

A current example is the damage being done to the country of Zimbabwe by Robert Mugabe.[33] By the end of 2003, life expectancy had slipped to thirty-five years (from fifty-six years thirty years earlier), and humanitarian agencies were feeding or planning to feed nearly six million people, approximately half of the population. Less than five years earlier, the country was exporting copious amounts of grain to feed people outside their country. To be sure, drought was one culprit, HIV infected more that a quarter of the adults, and many trading partners imposed sanctions. But the "jewel of Africa" had (and still has) excellent soil, natural beauty (such as Victoria Falls), good infrastructure, and a literacy rate of nearly 90 percent. What Zimbabwe did not have was a leader who understood the interconnections among the seven forms of capital in our illustration; this lack of understanding is at the root of the country's implosion. Under Mugabe's leadership, nearly 5,000 farms have been confiscated in the past several years and turned over to his political supporters. At the end of 2003, fewer than 3 percent of these were still functioning fully, unemployment was over 60 percent, and inflation had reached nearly 800 percent.

Mugabe's most obvious mistake was to take land away from the people who knew how to combine this resource with the other six forms of capital to make it productive. In doing so, he also impaired other forms of capital. He ran roughshod over justice (damaging government capital) since two-thirds of these farmers had titles that had been issued not by some colonial repressor but by Mugabe's government itself. Alarmed at the inflation rate caused by his own bungling, he fixed grain prices at a fraction of the market-clearing price, damaging economic capital. Farmers chose not to grow grain at a loss, further impairing both economic and physical capital (corn production was down by two-thirds and wheat by nearly 90 percent when compared to 2000). If people tried to export to avoid a loss, he forced them to convert their foreign money to Zimbabwean dollars at an exchange rate that left them with pennies on the dollar, further impairing economic capital. Roving bands of thugs tore down fencing and stole, dismantled, or sold equipment as scrap, impairing physical capital. Rejecting the humility and honesty that would characterize a servant leader, he tried to hide the truth about the shortages, rigged the election, shut down opposition newspapers, kept foreign journalists from exposing the truth, and jailed and abused opponents, thus impairing spiritual/moral and intellectual/emotional capital. As his power slipped, he indoctrinated the youth of the country through his National Youth Service Training Program and gave preferential treatment in civil-service jobs and university admissions to loyal followers, further impairing these forms of capital. Amazingly, he *saw* the need for this beehive of unproductive government activity while being unable to *see* the significance of nearly 10 percent of the county's population becoming orphaned because of his unwillingness to tackle the beliefs and attitudes at the root of his country's AID's epidemic.

Time and money spent on damage control is time and money not spent solving more perplexing problems. The same tradeoff applies to the care and maintenance of infrastructure, political processes, psychological health, moral values, ecosystems, and every other component of the seven segments of our wheel. Clearly, Mugabe's perceptions that accountability stops at the law (and he is the law), that authority is license (rather than an obligation to serve), that people are expendable (rather than priceless), and that public property is his treasure trove (rather than a sacred trust) conflict directly with the idea of servant leadership. Inevitably, these off-base foundational beliefs lead to other stultifying beliefs such as "the ends justify the means," "my needs and wants come first," or "it's only a problem if it is exposed," all of which tend to perpetuate corruption and inefficiency. In light of his record, Mugabe's leadership techniques deserve less attention than his misguided worldview.

The Need for Reformation at the Core

As much as civil society can do for development, its potential benefit (and very existence) depends on the values that undergird it. There are limits even to good things like transparency and participation. Without trust and integrity, transparency can degenerate into snooping and inefficiency, and without honesty and a sense of community, participation can lead to disinformation and chaos. The values at the core of the wheel determine whether countries prosecute fraud, enforce labor laws, or try to outlaw or regulate activities such as telemarketing scams or the illicit drug trade. Those values determine whether countries encourage charitable giving, volunteer activity, or family stability. Core values determine whether a leader sees economic policy as inextricably tied to political and social policy. They determine whether a leader focuses primarily on differences in gender, race, or ethnicity, or on the important things, such as justice, the promotion of good values, and the development of civil society organizations (CSOs). The Development Wheel captures this relationship by placing people's beliefs and values at the core of both civil society and the capital-building process. This placement is appropriate because beliefs and values form the core of trust relationships,[34] democracy,[35] effective governing,[36] the rule of law,[37] and a "good society."[38] They provide the social cohesion needed for a country to risk the kind of transparency and participation that leads to civil society.[39] They are critical to the economic success of countries[40] and form the root of the unusual accomplishment of communities and subcultures all over the world.[41]

Beliefs influence social organization, aesthetics, and education. Researchers long ago established links between even external (and obviously imperfect) proxies for what people believe (like church attendance) and family stability,[42] poverty,[43] teen pregnancy, suicide,[44] drug abuse,[45] crime,[46] mental and physical health,[47] and longevity and happiness.[48] And when *intrinsic* beliefs are distinguished from *extrinsic* behavior, the impact of beliefs becomes even more striking.[49] Much more could be said, of course. Perhaps it is enough to say that very little in the Western world, from our limited liability corporations to our financial institutions to our efforts to eradicate productivity-sapping diseases, remains untouched by our core beliefs. The same is true elsewhere.

For Reformed Christians, simply noting that all actions are ultimately rooted in beliefs is not enough. The minds and hearts of people with differing religious beliefs are wired in very different ways, and people will have values that are both good and bad. As Himmelfarb puts it, values "do not have to be virtues; they can be beliefs, opinions, attitudes, feelings, habits, conventions, preferences, prejudices, even idiosyncrasies—whatever any individual, group, or society happens to value, at any time, for any reason."[50] Unfortunately, many academics are only too willing to associate bad values with religious beliefs and are too unwilling either to discern the critical differences between belief systems or to allow faith and religion out of the little box into which they've gradually been crammed (by Western thinkers) over the past few centuries. They see religion as primarily related to the afterlife and acts of worship in large magnificent buildings or as useful for helping uncover so-called moral principles or as caring for the poor and performing acts of mercy but as little else. However, we Reformed Christians, for all our faults, know dualism and reductionism when we see them. Secular culture will continue to assault Christianity, but history is also replete with examples of the impact of Christianity on culture. In fact, the effects of Christianity are so pervasive and so thoroughly intertwined with Western culture that they are often indistinguishable to the untrained eye. Even people who have not darkened the door of a church for decades still breathe the air of their religious forebears. In the United States or Europe, this legacy means that even those who seldom open a Bible assume as normal and right what the Bible teaches about justice, righteousness, obedience to authority, law, property, work, accountability, favoritism, integrity, respect, tolerance, human rights, or compassion. Still, secular belief systems are equally complex and extensive. Those who put their faith in freedom, money, or technology are as religious as those who put their faith in Buddha, Allah, or Christ.

Conclusion

The Reformed Christian approach to country leadership presented here is closely related to the transformational approach in its emphasis on mission and vision and on leaders and followers raising one another to higher levels of motivation, ethics, and commitment. Moreover, it explicitly recognizes the need to balance seven essential forms of capital as essential to the transformation process. It also relates to the holistic, stewardship, and "new paradigm" approaches that others have emphasized,[51] but calls more attention to the critical importance of how a leader *sees* the world. Our approach also has some commonality with the "spirituality school" of leadership effectiveness, but with two important differences. We do not see spirituality as a kind of intelligence, like emotional or traditional measures of intelligence, but rather as a lens through which we view the world and that radically changes our answers to fundamental questions, assumptions, problem identification, and strategies for making things better. Additionally, we do not think of spirituality as either generic or necessarily good or beneficial. Its impact on leaders, countries, citizens, or employees can range from extremely positive to horrific, depending on the integrity of the beliefs. Trying to integrate a kind of generic (inoffensive) spirituality into an organization is more likely to result in settling for the lowest common denominator than in reaching for the highest human possibilities.

Research cited here makes it clear that worldviews and beliefs are critical to the development of a civil society and will determine the ebb and flow of countries and their leaders. Threads of this understanding run through sociology, psychology, philosophy, and theology literature. Although they may not use the same language, the writers of many popular leadership books and the leaders about whom they write also recognize the importance of beliefs and worldview in their talk about spirituality, values, teamwork, and transparency. In spite of this awareness, much of the scholarly research on leadership has too often sidestepped the importance of a leader's worldview.

In contrast, we think that the economic development experiences of many countries urge us to tackle the difficult tasks of defining major worldview groups and their components, parsing leaders into these groups, and studying their tendencies and effectiveness in different situations. A concerted effort is needed to study the ways that the nonnegotiable issues framing a leader's life—the *habits (and desires) of his heart*—interact with his traits and style, the tendencies of and relationships among his followers, and the contingencies associated with differing situations. It may just turn out that leaders whose worldviews lead them to diagnose problems correctly and to care deeply about meeting people's needs will be most effective in inspiring others in a variety of cultures, organizations, and situations.

Discussions of worldviews and their undergirding beliefs have been avoided in the past, in part because of Western scholarship's long tradition of privatizing beliefs in general and religious beliefs in particular. The predominant perspective in leadership research is that a little bit of religion is okay, as long as it doesn't challenge other (religious and secular) belief systems to the level of examining or undermining their assumptions or implications. We do not mean to imply that this avoidance of a belief's significant role has necessarily been intentional. In a commendable attempt to be inclusive and tolerant of all belief systems, leadership scholars have stepped gingerly around them all and, in the process, have (unfortunately) made them all but irrelevant by assumption.

The experiences of countries and their leaders are relevant for all kinds of organizations. People expect many of the same things from their employers that they expect from their countries, i.e., to have their basic needs met, to be secure, to have the opportunity to develop, to be part of a community, to reach important goals, to strive for the greater good, and so on. Organizations, then, like countries, need a balanced supply of all seven forms of capital to reach peak effectiveness. To reach this peak, leaders need an integral worldview, organizations need to be transformed over time into miniature civil societies, and civil societies need to progress to reflections of shalom. But even civil societies cannot be ushered in at will. The prerequisites of a civil society—participation, transparency, and a commitment to peaceable change—are themselves values that are rooted in religious beliefs. Truly ethical and transformational leaders, from William Wilberforce and Martin Niemoller to Martin Luther King and Mother Theresa, drew their strength and courage from a Source much greater than themselves. Reformed Christians, and particularly those called to public service, must do the same.

Notes

1. Bernard M. Bass, *Bass & Stogdill's Handbook of Leadership: Theory, Research, and Managerial Applications,* 3rd ed. (New York: The Free Press-Macmillan, 1990), 6.

2. Robert N. Bellah, *Habits of the Heart: Individualism and Commitment in American Life,* with R. Madsen, W. M. Sullivan, A. Swidler, and S. M. Tipton (Berkeley: University of California Press, 1986).

3. See Ralph M. Stogdill, *Handbook of Leadership: A Survey of Theory and Research* (New York: Free Press, 1974); and R. D. Mann, "A Review of the Relationship Between Personality and Performance in Small Groups," *Psychological Bulletin* 56 (1959): 241–70.

4. Isabel Briggs Myers and Mary H. McCaulley, *Manual: A Guide to the Development and Use of the Myers-Briggs Type Indicator* (Palo Alto, CA: Consulting Psychologists Press, 1985).

5. Robert R. Blake and Jane S. Mouton, *The Managerial Grid* (Houston: Gulf Press, 1964); F. E. Fiedler and J. E. Garcia, *New Approaches to Leadership: Cognitive Resources and Organizational Performance* (New York: John Wiley, 1987); F. E. Fiedler, "A Contingency Model of Leadership Effectiveness," in *Advances in Experimental Psychology,* Vol. 1, ed. L. Berkowitz (New York: Academic Press, 1964), 149–90; and F. E. Fiedler, *A Theory of Leadership Effectiveness* (New York: McGraw-Hill, 1967).

6. M. G. Evans, "The Effects of Supervisory Behavior on the Path-Goal Relationship," *Organizational Behavior and Human Performance* 5 (1970): 277–98; and R. J. House, "A Path-Goal Theory of Leader Effectiveness," *Administrative Science Quarterly* 16 (1971): 321–28.

7. F. Dansereau, G. G. Graen, and W. Haga, "A Vertical Dyad Linkage Approach to Leadership in Formal Organizations," *Organizational Behavior and Human Performance* 13 (1975): 46–78; and G. B. Graen, "Role-making Processes within Complex Organiza-

tions," in *Handbook of Industrial and Organizational Psychology*, ed. M. D. Dunnette (Chicago: Rand McNally, 1976), 1202–45.

8. James V. Downton, *Rebel Leadership: Commitment and Charisma in a Revolutionary Process* (New York: Free Press, 1973); J. M. Burns, *Leadership* (New York: Harper and Row, 1978); and Bernard M. Bass, *Bass and Stogdill's Handbook of Leadership: Theory, Research, and Managerial Applications*, 3rd ed. (New York: The Free Press-Macmillan, 1990).

9. Steven R. Covey, *Principle-Centered Leadership* (New York: Summit Books, 1991); and T. J. Peters and R. H. Waterman, *In Search of Excellence: Lessons from America's Best-Run Companies* (New York: Harper and Row, 1982).

10. William H. Bergquist, *The Four Cultures of the Academy: Insights and Strategies for Improving Leadership in Collegiate Organizations* (San Francisco: Jossey-Bass, 1992); E. G. Bogue, *Leadership by Design: Strengthening Integrity in Higher Education* (San Francisco: Jossey-Bass, 1994); S. A. McDade and P. H. Lewis, eds., *Developing Administrative Excellence: Creating a Culture of Leadership* (San Francisco: Jossey-Bass Publishers, 1994); and J. R. Wilcox and S. L. Ebbs, *The Leadership Compass: Values and Ethics in Higher Education* (Washington, DC: The George Washington University's ERIC Clearinghouse on Higher Education, 1992).

11. See Jay Alden Conger, Rabindra Nath Kanungo, and Associates, *Charismatic Leadership* (San Francisco: Jossey-Bass, 1988); and G. Yulk, "Managerial Leadership: A Review of Theory and Research," *Journal of Management* 15 (Fall 1989): 59–68.

12. For example, J. C. Collins and J. I. Porras, *Built to Last: Successful Habits of Visionary Companies* (New York: HarperBusiness-HarperCollins, 1994); and J. C. Collins, *Good to Great: Why Some Companies Make the Leap . . . and Others Don't* (New York: HarperBusiness, 2001).

13. Robert K. Greenleaf, *The Servant Leader* (Newton Center, MA: Robert K. Greenleaf Center, 1970), and *Servant Leadership: A Journey into the Nature of Legitimate Power and Greatness* (New York: Paulist, 1977).

14. F. N. Brady, "A Systematic Approach to Teaching Ethics in Business," *Journal of Business Ethics* 19, no. 3 (1999): 309–19.

15. Peter Block, *Stewardship: Choosing Service over Self-Interest* (San Francisco: Berrett-Koehler, 1993); Covey, *Principle-Centered Leadership;* Max De Pree, *Leadership Is an Art* (New York: Doubleday, 1989); and Carol Gilligan, *In a Different Voice: Psychological Theory and Women's Development* (Cambridge, MA: Harvard University Press, 1982).

16. Kenneth H. Blanchard, Bill Hybels, and Phil Hodges, *Leadership by the Book: Tools to Transform Your Workplace* (Colorado Springs: WaterBrook Press, 1999); Laurie B. Jones, *Jesus, CEO: Using Ancient Wisdom for Visionary Leadership* (New York: Hyperion, 1995); and Charles C. Manz, *The Leadership Wisdom of Jesus: Practical Lessons for Today* (San Francisco: Berrett-Koehler Publishers, 1998).

17. G. B. Kelly, B. F. Nelson, and R. Bethage, *The Cost of Moral Leadership: The Spirituality of Dietrich Bonhoeffer* (Grand Rapids, MI: Eerdmans, 2003).

18. R. Emmons, *The Psychology of Ultimate Concerns: Motivation and Spirituality in Personality* (New York: Guildford Press, 1999), and "Spirituality and Intelligence: Problems and Prospects," *International Journal for the Psychology of Religion* 10, no. 1 (2000): 57–64.

19. Daniel Goleman, *Emotional Intelligence* (New York: Bantam Books, 1995).

20. Michael Woolcock, L. Pritchett, and J. Isham, "The Social Foundations of Poor Economic Growth in Resource-Rich Countries," in *Resource Abundance and Economic Growth*, ed. R. Auty (New York: Oxford University Press; World Bank, July 2001), 76–92.

21. Lawrence E. Harrison, *Underdevelopment Is a State of Mind* (Landham, MD: Madison Books, 1985), and *Who Prospers? How Cultural Values Shape Economic and Political Success* (New York: Basic Books, 1992); and Joel Kotkin, *Tribes: How Race, Religion, and Identity Determine Success in the New Global Economy* (New York: Random House, 1992).

22. World Bank, *World Development Report* (New York: Oxford University Press, 1997).

23. Adam Smith, *An Inquiry into the Nature and Causes of the Wealth of Nations*, ed. Laurence W. Dickey (Indianapolis: Hackett Publishing, 1993).

24. Ibid.

25. Jerry Z. Muller, *Adam Smith: In His Time and Ours* (Princeton, NJ: Princeton University Press, 1993).

26. Bill Essig, Steven Hoffmann, and John Visser, *Civil Society: A Foundation for Sustainable Economic Development*, ed. Melissa Rose (Portland, OR: Mercy Corps International; Coalition for Christian Colleges and Universities, 1998).

27. Ian Brownlie, *Basic Documents on Human Rights*, 3rd ed. (Oxford, England: Clarendon Press, 1992).

28. Robert Bothwell, "Indicators of a Healthy Civil Society," in *Beyond Prince and Merchant: Citizen Participation and the Rise of Civil Society*, ed. J. Burbidge (Brussels: Institute of Cultural Affairs International/New York City: Pact Publications, 1997), 249–62.

29. Ibid., 249–51.

30. George B. N. Ayittey, *Africa in Chaos* (New York: St. Martin's Press, 1998).

31. See, for example, Rose-Ackerman's research on the quality of public services, in Susan Rose-Ackerman, *Corruption and Government: Causes, Consequences, and Reform* (New York: Cambridge University Press, 1999).

32. Hernando de Soto, *The Mystery of Capital: Why Capitalism Triumphs in the West and Fails Everywhere Else* (New York: Basic Books, 2000).

33. S. Power, "How to Kill a Country: Turning a Breadbasket into a Basket Case in Ten Easy Steps—The Robert Mugabe Way," *The Atlantic Monthly* (January 2003): 87–100.

34. Francis Fukuyama, *Trust: The Social Virtues and the Creation of Prosperity* (New York: The Free Press, 1995).

35. Mary Ann Glendon and David Blankenhorn, eds., *Seedbeds of Virtue: Sources of Competence, Character, and Citizenship in American Society* (Lanham, MD: Madison Books, 1995).

36. V. Braithwaite and Margaret Levi, *Trust and Governance* (New York: Russell Sage Foundation, 1998).

37. Daniel R. Coats, *Mending Fences: Renewing Justice between Government and Civil Society*, ed. James W. Skillen (Grand Rapids, MI: Baker, 1998).

38. A. Etzioni, *The Golden Rule* (New York: Basic Books, 1996).

39. Don Eberly, *America's Promise: Civil Society and the Renewal of American Culture* (Lanham, MD: Rowman and Littlefield Publishers, 1998); and David G. Green, *Reinventing Civil Society: The Rediscovery of Welfare without Politics* (London: IEA Health and Welfare Unit, 1993).

40. D. S. Landes, *The Wealth and Poverty of Nations: Why Some Are So Rich and Some So Poor* (New York: Norton, 1998); Lawrence E. Harrison, *Who Prospers? How Cultural Values Shape Economic and Political Success* (New York: Basic Books, 1992); and Ayittey, *Africa in Chaos*.

41. Harrison, *Who Prospers?;* Joel Kotkin, *Tribes: How Race, Religion, and Identity Determine Success in the New Global Economy* (New York: Random House, 1992).

42. A. E. Bergen, "Values and Religious Issues in Psychotherapy and Mental Health," *The American Psychologist* 46 (1991): 394–403.

43. R. B. Freeman, "Who Escapes? The Relation of Church-Going and Other Background Factors to the Socio-Economic Performance of Black Male Youths from Inner-City Poverty Tracts," *Working Paper Series No. 1656* (Cambridge, MA: National Bureau of Economic Research, Inc., 1985).

44. D. B. Larson, S. S. Larson, and J. Gartner, "Families, Relationships, and Health," in *Behavior and Medicine,* ed. Danny Wedding (Baltimore: Mosby Year Book), 135–47.

45. M. Daum and M. A. Lavenhar, "Religiosity and Drug Use," *National Institute of Drug Abuse* DHEW Publication, ADM (1980): 80–939.

46. J. Rohrbaugh and R. Jessor, Institute of Behavioral Science at the University of Colorado, "Religiosity in Youth: A Personal Control against Deviant Behavior," *Journal of Personality* 43, no. 1 (1975): 136–55.

47. G. W. Comstock and K. P. Partridge, "Church Attendance and Health," *Journal of Chronic Disease* 25 (1972): 665–72.

48. B. Beit-Hallami, "Psychology of Religion 1880–1939: The Rise and Fall of a Psychological Movement," *Journal of the History of Behavioral Sciences* 10 (1974): 84–90.

49. Richard D. Kahoe, "Personality and Achievement Correlates on Intrinsic and Extrinsic Religious Orientations," *Journal of Personality and Social Psychology* 29 (1974): 812–18; and Ken F. Wiebe and J. Roland Fleck, "Personality Correlates of Intrinsic, Extrinsic and Non-Religious Orientations," *Journal of Psychology* 105 (1980): 111–17.

50. Gertrude Himmelfarb, *The De-moralization of Society: From Victorian Virtues to Modern Values* (New York: A. A. Knopf/Random House, 1994), 12.

51. Block, *Stewardship: Choosing Service over Self-Interest;* and Warren G. Bennis, Jagdish Parikh, and Ronnie Lessem, *Beyond Leadership: Balancing Economics, Ethics, and Ecology* (Cambridge, MA: Blackwell Press, 1994).

Development, Capabilities, and *Shalom*

Jonathan Warner[*]

· ·

What Is Development?

Economic growth, which has traditionally been seen as a good proxy for development, has the merit of being easy to define—it is simply an increase in national income, or Gross Domestic Product (GDP). It is (in principle, at least) easy to measure, and an increasing GDP at least implies that resources are available that might be used to improve the lot of people living in the country.

But GDP leaves a lot of room for improvement. For example, what might matter at least as much as aggregate GDP is its distribution. Even in rich countries, there are often pockets of poverty. Increasing the aggregate income per capita might do little to help those at the bottom of the income scale. If the United States were to annex Equatorial Guinea (one of the world's poorest countries), the GDP per capita of the new state would

[*] Dr. Warner is Associate Professor of Economics at Dordt. He studied at Oxford and Birmingham Universities before earning his Ph.D. at the University of Wales.

greatly exceed the current average in Guinea. But the annexation in itself would not increase the income of the Guineans by a cent. In addition, using GDP as the sole measure of a country's well-being neglects all aspects of life except the economic.

Economic development is less easy to define. While it is clear that not all increases in GDP constitute development (for example, the plundering of natural resources increases GDP, but can devastate a country and its people), people will differ as to how they view the outcomes of particular growth episodes. One definition of economic development, from a leading textbook, reads as follows:

> In addition to being concerned with the efficient allocation of existing scarce (or idle) resources and with their sustained growth over time, [development economics] must also deal with the *economic, social, political* and *institutional* mechanisms, both public and private, necessary to bring about *rapid* (at least by historical standards) and *large-scale improvements* in levels of living for the masses of poverty-stricken, malnourished, and illiterate peoples of Africa, Asia, and Latin America.[1]

But even this is too narrow. Rather than talking only of increases in the standard of living, a holistic approach to development needs to deal with the quality of life, the ability of people to flourish. While there is likely to be some correlation between income and life quality, it is not appropriate to see the one as a substitute for the other. Growth in the general health of the population, in the levels of literacy, and the years of schooling are good things, but they do not necessarily correlate well with income. The merit of looking at standard of living alone, though, is that it avoids difficult questions of trade-offs: how is one to decide, for example, what is the appropriate trade-off between more health and more education when resources are so limited that it is impossible to do both?

The United Nations Development Programme (UNDP) Human Development Index (HDI) is a "cheap and dirty" attempt to do this. The HDI is a weighted index of three factors: GDP per capita, education (defined in terms of literacy and years of schooling), and life expectancy. To some extent, this index will tend to capture the effects of inequality—a country with a few rich and many poor will tend to have lower average scores on the longevity and education axes. A country that wishes to increase its HDI score could do so by taxing the rich and using the proceeds to increase spending on health care and education, for example. Although this would probably reduce total GDP (higher taxes tend to discourage wealth-creation), the gains in literacy and longevity could improve a country's standing on the HDI scale.

But the HDI still suffers from a number of drawbacks. Human development is about more than just economics. A rich country can be culturally, socially, and religiously impoverished. Bob Goudzwaard refers to this phenomenon as overdevelopment.[2] John Visser stresses that for economic development, all forms of capital or wealth (including noneconomic forms such as social and cultural capital, the stock of "civic virtues," and networks of civic engagement and trust) need to be enhanced and developed together.[3]

Some may question introducing topics like religious poverty and civic virtues to an analysis of development. Generally, economists have tried to suggest that the discipline is value-neutral. That is, economic analysis holds regardless of the ethical views or worldview held by the economist. Of course, one's ethical views may well affect one's choice of research topics, but the tools of the trade are held to be unbiased. In reality, in the history of economics, a materialist conception of utilitarianism has been particularly strong. The aim of society, according to this norm, is to achieve the greatest happiness of the greatest number. Thus, if happiness, or utility, is measurable, it is, in theory, possible to construct a social welfare function that takes into account the effects of all influences (material goods, level of wealth, environmental quality, and so forth) that affect people's happiness and then "simply" maximize that function.

From the 1970s, the ideas of John Rawls have led to the development of theories based on maximizing the welfare of the least well-off representative group.[4] As the achievement of these maxima would almost certainly involve the use of the redistributive power of taxation and subsidy, these norms seem to imply an active role for government. Those who feel that individual liberty is of greater value than some maximization of happiness tend to believe that policies of this sort are inappropriate.

More recently, writers concerned with the interaction of the environment and economics have made analysis of values a more integral part of economic analysis. If economic growth threatens the possibility of the long-term survival of human beings as we push up against environmental limits, then certain questions need to be addressed—urgently. There would not seem to be any obvious reason that free markets will automatically prevent our attempting to run the economy at a rate beyond the earth's carrying capacity. Therefore, a more holistic account, one that limits economic growth and development to an appropriate sphere, is needed. Here, as elsewhere, the vision of *shalom* has potentially powerful analytical value.

Development in its broadest sense, I would suggest, is the building of shalom. The biblical norm of shalom is the vision of a state of everything-being-right, of peace and justice, of a society where human beings can truly flourish and use their God-given gifts and talents to fulfill the cultural mandate to develop, care for, and rule over the earth. One component of shalom is that people have access to the opportunities and resources necessary to be able to achieve their potential, to be able to flourish. A promising recent proposal in development theory, the capabilities approach, explicitly takes human flourishing to be the goal of development.

The Capabilities Approach

At the root of the capabilities approach is a concern about human flourishing: the aim of human development is to give to all people those things that are necessary for them to fulfill their own conception of the good life. The roots of the idea are Aristotelian: it is concerned with ends, with a *telos* (a pursuit of a vision of an end, the good). A person's conception of the good could be almost anything (in the classical liberal tradition, anything that doesn't adversely affect anyone else). The capabilities approach, then, is concerned with enabling people to realize their conceptions of the good. As such, it provides a common ground on which all people of good will can meet: certain fundamental preconditions are necessary for people to be able to live a good life, as they see it, regardless of what that conception is. Thus the ability to have access to food, clothing, and shelter are necessary preconditions to living a fulfilled life; without them, a person would not survive to be able to pursue her concept of the good.

Some proponents of the capabilities approach see it as almost value-neutral; at least, it is neutral between competing encapsulations of the good. Whatever your view of the good is, you will accept that there are certain things necessary for you to be able to pursue it. Alternatively, the approach might be seen as a framework, creating space for discussions of the nature of the good, or perhaps as a political platform on which people of widely differing beliefs can agree.

The Nobel Prize-winning economist Amartya Sen gave a series of lectures to the World Bank in the late 1990s, seeking to broaden the bank's vision of what constituted development.[5] While policies such as those advocated by the Washington Consensus might, if successful, lead to increases in growth in developing countries and restore macroeconomic stability, their failure to reduce poverty or to improve the lot of many people in poorer countries had led to questions about the efficacy of this approach. The time was propitious for a paradigmatic change in development models.

As Sen pointed out, both utilitarianism and GDP maximization are deficient as decision rules for society. Both take no account of distributional effects or of rights that might trump considerations of collective good. Utilitarianism takes no account of how happiness comes about; it ignores the fact that extraneous forces, such as advertising, can easily sway perceptions of well-being. GDP takes no account of things other than marketed goods and services. If the quality of life (and the elimination of poverty) is at all important, these deficiencies are troubling.

However, to ignore output of goods and services entirely or to say that happiness has no role in distinguishing a good life from a bad or indifferent one would be bizarre. Professor Sen is right to stress the need for an integrated approach to the problem of development and poverty elimination. By advocating the importance of freedom and, specifically, the capabilities entailed and conducive to the growth of substantive freedoms, both the overemphasis on GDP and/or happiness and considering them to be relatively unimportant are avoided. The freedoms that Sen picks out as especially important for development (or as integral parts of what development, in its fullest sense, is) are:

- Political freedoms
- Economic facilities
- Social opportunities
- Transparency guarantees
- Protective security.[6]

Each of these reinforces the others. All are good things in themselves, but also have instrumental value in leading to other good things and a constructive role in strengthening commitment to these freedoms and the values that underlie them. For example, Sen argues for democracy as not only a good thing in itself, but also because democratic regimes tend to produce greater economic and social opportunities than the alternatives and because democracy tends to create norms and values that are conducive to the further enhancement of freedoms.

Sen also stresses the importance of agency freedom—the ability of people to make their own decisions and pursue their own goals. Although an all-knowing benevolent dictator might reach the outcomes of the choices that people make more efficiently (or even achieve outcomes that they would agree to be superior), Sen believes that there is value in the making of choices that more than compensates for any inefficiency.

It is important, argues Sen, to distinguish between capabilities and functionings. Each capability implies a functioning—the exercise of that capability. But someone might legitimately choose not to make use of the capabilities she has; the important thing is that she is able to make that choice. As Sen points out, there is a big difference between someone who chooses to fast and someone who has no food available. The latter person has no choice but to go hungry.

Capabilities can be regarded as a claim: a certain level of capability possession is necessary for living a fulfilled life. A viable theory of development needs to take into account the importance of securing at least this minimal level of functioning. As Martha Nussbaum describes, "The basic intuition from which the capability approach begins, in the political arena, is that certain human abilities exert a moral claim that they should be developed."[7]

Classical liberalism places great emphasis on "negative" freedoms—the right not to be prevented from doing certain things. The capabilities approach takes the conception of development a stage further by emphasizing the importance of various forms of positive freedoms—the ability, or the potential, to do certain things or to pursue one's own conception of the good life. As Nussbaum points out, women, especially in poorer countries, have traditionally been denied opportunities available to men.[8] When family resources are limited, it tends to be the male children, rather than the females, who receive the bulk of attention and opportunities. While boys are viewed as an asset to the family, girls are seen as a liability—their adult working lives will be spent in the service of their future husband's family, rather than their own. And then there is the question of providing an appropriate dowry . . . In short, in many societies, women have traditionally been treated as second-class citizens or, worse, as chattels of their fathers or husbands.

While Sen's version of the capabilities approach stresses the primary importance of freedom (the freedom to be able to lead the life one wants and to pursue the goals that one sees as valuable), Martha Nussbaum takes the process further by producing a list of central human functioning capabilities that, she argues, are necessary for leading a worthwhile life. The list is not to be seen as definitive; it is subject to modification and revision in the light of experience and discussion. She does claim, though, that the list—or something like it—embodies a set of universal values, and when she sets out to defend her approach, she refutes arguments that deny the possibility, or the desirability, of universal values.

The current version of the list is this:

CENTRAL HUMAN FUNCTIONAL CAPABILITIES

1. Life. Being able to live to the end of a human life of normal length; not dying prematurely, or before one's life is so reduced as to be not worth living.

2. Bodily Health. Being able to have good health, including reproductive health; to be adequately nourished; to have adequate shelter.

3. Bodily Integrity. Being able to move freely from place to place; having one's bodily boundaries treated as sovereign, i.e. being able to be secure against assault, including sexual assault, child sexual abuse, and domestic violence; having opportunities for sexual satisfaction and for choice in matters of reproduction.

4. Senses, Imagination, and Thought. Being able to use the senses, to imagine, think, and reason—and to do these things in a "truly human" way, a way informed and cultivated by an adequate education, including, but by no means limited to, literacy and basic mathematical and scientific training. Being able to use imagination and thought in connection with experiencing and producing self-expressive works and events of one's own choice, religious, literary, musical, and so forth. Being able to use one's mind in ways protected by guarantees of freedom of expression with respect to both political and artistic speech, and freedom of religious exercise. Being able to search for the ultimate meaning of life in one's own way. Being able to have pleasurable experiences, and to avoid non-necessary pain.

5. Emotions. Being able to have attachments to things and people outside ourselves; to love those who love and care for us, to grieve at their absence; in general, to love, to grieve, to experience longing, gratitude, and justified anger. Not having one's emotional development blighted by overwhelming fear and anxiety, or by traumatic events of abuse or neglect. (Supporting this capability means supporting forms of human association that can be shown to be crucial in their development.)

6. Practical Reason. Being able to form a conception of the good and to engage in critical reflection about the planning of one's life. (This entails protection for the liberty of conscience.)

7. Affiliation. A. Being able to live with and toward others, to recognize and show concern for other human beings, to engage in various forms of social interaction; to be able to imagine the situation of another and to have compassion for that situation: to have the capability for both justice and friendship. (Protecting this capability means protecting institutions that constitute and nourish such forms of affiliation, and also protecting the freedom of assembly and political speech.)

B. Having the social bases of self-respect and non-humiliation; being able to be treated as a dignified being whose worth is equal to that of others. This entails, at a minimum, protections against discrimination on the basis of race, sex, sexual orientation, religion, caste, ethnicity, or national origin. In work, being able to work as a human being, exercising practical reason and entering into meaningful relationships of mutual recognition with other workers.

8. Other Species. Being able to live with concern for and in relation to animals, plants, and the world of nature.

9. Play. Being able to laugh, to play, to enjoy recreational activities.

10. Control over One's Environment. A. Political. Being able to participate effectively in political choices that govern one's life; having the right of political participation, protections of free speech and association.

B. Material. Being able to hold property (both land and movable goods), not just formally but in terms of real opportunity; and having property rights on an equal basis with others; having the right to seek employment on an equal basis with others; having the freedom from unwarranted search and seizure.[9]

Nussbaum proposes her list as a platform for political action, grounded on beliefs that we all do, in fact, share. Any legitimate government, she believes, can be expected to sign up for the program, to guarantee and enhance the capabilities of its citizens. The list is not neutral (wife-beaters and slave owners would not find it attractive), although Nussbaum argues that it provides a set of necessary conditions for anyone to achieve their conception of the good. She argues that there are certain universal values and defends that claim against charges of paternalism, cultural imperialism, and lack of sensitivity to the value of diversity. Her reply is that the universal values she is arguing for transcend all reasonable, ethical visions of the good.

Her aim is to produce what she calls a Thick Vague Theory of the Good. That is, the list of desired qualities produces a rich account of what human flourishing entails; but at the same time recognizes that the way in which people flourish (the institutions, relationships, and conditions of life) can—and should—be very different in different human communities.

There is a trade-off between thickness and vagueness. As the theory becomes clearer and less vague, it becomes thicker in the sense that more conceptions of the Good are ruled out. If it remains vague, then it becomes thinner, and the richness of the capabilities approach, in allowing for diversity, diminishes.

In her recent work, Nussbaum has linked the idea of capabilities more explicitly to a notion of social justice.[10] A society where capabilities are not guaranteed is, she believes, fundamentally unjust. But as her thinking on capabilities and justice develops, she needs to be careful to walk a fine line between under- and overspecification of the theory. Her attempt to develop principles of global justice from the capabilities approach produced a list that many people would not agree to. Overspecification reduces the amount of common ground available for people of different traditions and societies share. Political platforms that grow into sets of specific proposals reduce the vagueness of the theory, but in so doing sacrifice consensus. On the other hand, underspecification makes the theory thinner: greater consensus is achieved at the cost of leaving certain critical issues unresolved. (For example, Nussbaum's bodily health capability, as it stands, says nothing on the abortion issue.)

But the major advantage of the capabilities approach is that it draws attention to important aspects of human flourishing that are absent from a mechanical attempt to maximize GDP or some other aggregate. The drawback is that it is impossible to measure capabilities in dollar terms, which is the preferred way in economics of making values commensurate with each other. The capabilities approach does allow some comparisons in ranking between countries: those with high levels of capabilities (or a high proportion of capability-endowed citizens) would count as superior to ones where capabilities are absent or where a substantial proportion of the population are not so endowed. Nussbaum speaks of a threshold effect—that there is a certain level of capability-endowment below which human flourishing is impossible.[11] In other words, for certain very basic capabilities, people ought not be given the choice not to function, because to do so impoverishes their lives so much that they are unable to make rational choices in other areas. One needs to be literate before one can rationally decide that illiteracy is better.

One attractive feature of Nussbaum's approach is that she takes religion seriously. Instead of condemning societies where, for religious reasons, women decide to adopt traditional modes of life and dress, she asks only that the women be given the opportunity not to adopt this lifestyle if they so choose. For rich countries such as the United States, with its diverse cultural and religious beliefs and practices, she argues (as does the U. S. Constitution) that government interference in religious practices should be limited to matters where there is an overwhelming issue of public policy at stake. There are, admittedly, difficult cases: Should Amish girls be required to attend school after age fourteen, when their parents and Amish tradition dictate otherwise? Should Native American use of marijuana in religious ceremonies be permitted, despite Federal anti-drugs laws?

Martha Nussbaum describes herself as an Enlightenment Jew. After experiencing the racism of the Episcopalian church in which she was raised, she was attracted to Reform Judaism because of its openness to argument and to the questioning of traditions and of Scripture.[12] This worldview influences her ideas: the Enlightenment trumps Judaism. The values underlying her version of the capabilities approach, while often sharing common ground with the Scriptural tradition, are humanistic, and toleration (the right of people to pursue any conception of the Good that does not demean others) is high among them.

Other criticisms have been made of Nussbaum's approach:

- One problem with the list is that each of the elements seems to be independent of the rest. No trade-offs are allowed. If a choice has to be made between enhancing various capabilities to the detriment of others, this is a tragic situation, but Nussbaum offers no guidance as to how to avoid the tragedy. The result is that all elements on the list are treated as having equal status, whereas it is surely the case that there is some rank ordering of them.

- The status of the items on the list is problematic. If people really should be guaranteed a life of normal length, this has huge implications for the allocation of resources: spending vast sums of money to extend the life of terminally ill (but young) patients would seem to be required, for example. The opportunity cost of this (what else society might use these resources for) is not considered, for there can be no trade-offs.

- The ahistoric nature of the theory is also potentially problematic. For real people, the sort we're interested in, history is important. One's perception of one's history (or the history of one's community) colors one's view of the present, one's hopes for the future, and the way in which one's conception of the Good is stated and developed. Resentment and a lack of closure of previous wounds, hurts, and injustices will impair current functioning. History matters! As Lesslie Newbigin claims, "No human life can be rightly understood apart from the whole story of which it is part";[13] so too, no life is lived independently of the past.

- As David Clark points out, the Aristotelian origins of the capabilities approach may well surprise us—that a basis in timeless Greek myth should provide an adequate basis for a twenty-first-century theory of human flourishing.[14] People don't live in social vacuums. Societal traditions (peer pressure) affect the way people think and behave, what they want, and, importantly, what the value of particular freedoms might be to them.

As Amartya Sen has recently argued, the capabilities approach does not produce a full account of justice and morality.[15] At best, it is a partial theory that can form an element of a more comprehensive account of how we ought to live. The capabilities approach is helpful in thinking about individual choices, human development, and perhaps even sustainability in development (if we assume that capabilities are universal in time, so that future generations will value them as we do). But the outcomes of individual choices and the process of development do not (together) give a full account of what life should be like. The relationship between capabilities and human rights is not fully developed; an analysis of the causes and means by which bad (and good) affect us is left open; and there is no apparatus within the capabilities approach that allows us to judge outcomes. The ingredients for flourishing may be there, but further steps are necessary before we can declare that people are truly flourishing. As Sen points out, a death from SARS is doubtless tragic, but we evaluate it differently from a death as a result of murder. To the capabilities approach, all deaths are equal. All free choices are equal. All conceptions of the good are equal.

It is this attempt to claim neutral, as opposed to common, ground that is also a major weakness of the capabilities approach. We can agree that the capabilities approach has value in achieving one's conception of the good— but only because the conception of the good that we actually have happens to be advanced by the capabilities approach. The force of the capabilities approach is that people with widely differing conceptions of the good can agree on some (flexible) version of the elements of Martha Nussbaum's list and agree, with Sen and Nussbaum, that the ability to make informed, real choices about things that affect aspects of one's well-being is desirable. But the acceptance of the political platform depends crucially on seeing it as a means to an end—not, as all too readily happens, as an end in itself. What is necessary is a more comprehensive account of what it is to be a flourishing human being.

Shalom provides a more comprehensive view, a more holistic view of what development, and flourishing, might mean. Human flourishing is a part of shalom but does not exhaust the concept, in the same way as capabilities do not exhaust the concept of what it is to lead a good life.

Capabilities and Shalom

The Hebrew word *shalom* is generally translated as "peace" but covers a rather broader idea. Nicholas Wolterstorff puts it this way:

> Shalom is the human being dwelling at peace in all his or her relationships: with God, with self, with fellows, with nature. . . . But the peace which is shalom is not merely the absence of hostility, nor merely being in right relationship. Shalom at its highest is *enjoyment* in one's relationships. A nation may be at peace with all its neighbors and yet be miserable in its poverty. . . . [J]ustice, the enjoyment of one's rights, is indispensable to shalom. . . . If individuals are not granted what is due them, if their claim on others is not acknowledged by those others, if others do not carry out their obligations to them, then shalom is wounded.[16]

In Wolterstorff's view, then, justice and the elimination of poverty are prerequisites for the achievement of shalom.

The following quotation from the prophet Isaiah (writing around 700–680 B.C.) illustrates the contrast between a vision of desolation and a vision of shalom:

> The fortress will be abandoned, the noisy city deserted; citadel and watchtower will become a wasteland forever, the delight of donkeys, a pasture for flocks, till the Spirit is poured upon us from on high, and the desert becomes a fertile field, and the fertile field seems like a forest. Justice will dwell in the desert and righteousness live in the fertile field. The fruit of righteousness will be peace; the effect of righteousness will be quietness and confidence forever. My people will live in peaceful dwelling places, in secure homes, in undisturbed places of rest. Though hail flattens the forest and the city is leveled completely, how blessed you will be, sowing your seed by every stream, and letting your cattle and donkeys range free. Isaiah 32:14–20

Another biblical picture of shalom is that of all families having their own allotment of land and resources and the ability to enjoy them in peace. The prophet Micah (around 700 B.C.) foresaw a time "in the last days" when "every man will sit under his own vine and under his own fig tree, and no one will make them afraid" (Micah 4:4), a vision also shared by Zechariah (Zechariah 3:10). This was a return to what was, for the ancient Israelites, the Golden Age of the Davidic kingship. "During Solomon's lifetime Judah and Israel, from Dan to Beersheba, lived in safety, each man under his own vine and fig tree" (1 Kings 4:25). Thus shalom implies a situation where material and security needs are met, a sustainable state of dwelling giving the opportunity for economic, societal, and cultural advances.

In 701 B.C., when Sennacherib threatened Jerusalem, he offered, "Make peace with me . . . then every one of you will eat from his own vine and fig tree and drink water from his own cistern" (2 Kings 18:31)—a tempting prospect for the besieged defenders of the city, but one that was ultimately unattractive as the peace proffered was to be in the context of a life of service to an alien ruler.[17] Shalom requires more than material security; that is, it is wider than economic justice and the elimination of poverty.

The book of Hebrews describes life within God's Kingdom as a Sabbath rest. Entering the Kingdom is entering God's rest. The word-picture is from Psalm 95: because the Israelites were unfaithful, people whose hearts went astray, the whole generation died in the deserts of Sinai. God declared on oath, in his anger, "They shall never enter my rest" (Psalm 95:10–11). But the promise still stands: we can enter his rest (Hebrews 4:1). Access is as a result of the sacrifice of himself made by Jesus, our great High Priest. The result is to enter into a realm of peace—the peace (or shalom) of God that passes all understanding, as Paul puts it (Philippians 4:7).

Shalom is thus broader than the capabilities approach. The capabilities approach is, at base, an individualistic way of viewing flourishing. At best, it would see community, for example, as a means of increasing individual flourishing. Any "third-generation" community rights are inferior to, and trumped by, considerations of (negative or positive) freedoms. Third-generation (or group) rights are such things as national rights of self-determination, minority language rights, and the right to such public goods as environmental integrity.[18] Similarly, the capabilities approach will tend to underplay the significance of social capital and other good things that have public good elements to them. Just as a market economy will tend to under-provide public goods, so the capabilities approach will downplay their importance. A society of shalom will not have these defects.

Shalom, as an ideal, might be conceived as a description of the end-state of creation following the consummation of redemption at the second coming of Christ. The capabilities approach is part of a process that might move us in the direction of that goal, although it is something that cannot be fully realized in a fallen world. Because of the depraved nature of human beings, it is evident that the use of capabilities will not necessarily tend toward shalom: evil people can use the freedoms that they have to further evil ends.

The capabilities approach formally leaves open the question of whether a society where individual capabilities are established at a high level will be unambiguously superior to one where capabilities are less prominent, but where the provision of certain collective goods is greater. It is here that the individual bias of the capabilities approach can be best contrasted with the communal aspects of shalom.

For example, there could be a trade-off between capabilities and social goods, such as security or public health, especially if these social goods are unevenly distributed. There is no guarantee that a society consisting of people who are endowed with a low level of capabilities would rationally choose to enhance capabilities at the expense of certain collective goals. Sen engages this issue in his critique of the "Asian values" argument (that Asians are significantly different from Europeans and Americans, that a theory born in Europe or the United States will not necessarily apply to them); his argument, however, is largely that Lee Kwan Yew's views on authority and freedom are not the only Asian views to emerge, rather than that the argument itself is flawed.[19] The thrust of the capabilities approach is to suggest that individual capabilities are prior to any collective goals.

Although the capabilities approach implies a "thick vague" view of the good in that it is consistent with widely divergent visions and conceptions of the good, it is still too thin to allow a full theory of social justice to be derived from it: a capable society could still be unjust. Historical injustices might remain (African Americans, Cypriots, and, generally, all refugees can relate to this). Systemic social evils could still exist. For example, opponents of globalization point out that although the World Trade Organization gives formal equality in trading practices between nations, the global south still finds it hard to harness the benefits of trade. People within the global south might be capable at an individual level and yet still be unable to enjoy a fair share of the world's wealth because of structural evil.

A society where everyone has a high level of capabilities might still fail to flourish because other elements of shalom are missing. Russia in the 1990s was a society where the growth of a form of mafiaization led to fracture, despite the (relatively) high level of capability fulfillment. Another example might be that of African Americans, whom history seems to hold captive in striking ways. In the United States, despite forty years of Civil Rights legislation and affirmative action, the Supreme Court still thinks that another generation will be necessary before compensatory discrimination can be ended.[20] The Turkish Cypriot community in Cyprus has been in a state of uneasy peace for the past thirty years since the 1974 invasion of Cyprus separated them from their Greek Cypriot neighbors and persecutors. The "Cyprus Problem," with the perceived Turkish Cypriot need for security, has dominated politics on the island and has warped development. Economic growth has concentrated on exploiting loopholes in Turkish law (the growth of universities and casinos are good examples); depleting natural resources (the overpumping from aquifers is particularly alarming); and government restrictions on various forms of personal freedom on the grounds of security. By regional standards, the Turkish Cypriots are rich, but many seek to leave the island as they see no prospect of reconciliation between the two peoples of Cyprus.

Toward a Fuller Account of Shalom

It is relatively simple to envisage elements of a utopian society. But most utopian novels actually describe frightening visions of control and of a society that is happy but unfulfilled. The more the details of a particular utopia are filled in, the less utopian it appears to be. The Bible gives us only a few hints of what heaven is like; we know little more than that it will be a place of great happiness and rejoicing. People, such as David Lawrence, who have tried to imagine the details are generally stronger on envisioning a largely agricultural society, where crafts predominate over mass production and there is work for all. But the development of creation—through industrial to postindustrial modes of production—is neglected in this approach.

Articulating a vision of shalom in anything more than vague terms is difficult. Scripture gives a picture of shalom in a garden, and the hints in the Old Testament are primarily agricultural. It is perhaps indicative of the problems that most pictures of heaven-on-earth, the consummation of God's Kingdom, are largely agricultural. Scripture ends with a picture of a city—a city of skyscrapers with a river flowing along its major artery. But there are fewer details of the functioning of the city than of life in the garden.

There is a deeper issue here: to what extent can we speculate about a state of shalom through the effects of the Fall? How much of the vision of Paradise shines through the wall of separation our sin has erected between us and God? Although Jesus' mediation and propitiatory death removed the wall, the effects are still all too evident. Human minds, warped by sin, envision structures and relationships that seek to be God-glorifying but are warped by the effects of sin. For example, sinful products often satisfy real desires, but do so in an inappropriate, warped, or inefficient way. Therefore, even being able to articulate a fully developed vision of shalom might be impossible.

Even if we can recognize what shalom is (or, better, what marginal redemptive improvements on the structures of society can increase shalom), how is shalom to be achieved? The outline of some parts of it might be clear. In the Old Testament, God sent prophets to call the leaders of the people back to the ways of the Lord. The kings were to practice justice and righteousness (Psalm 72); when they did not, they were condemned by the prophets. Fred Kammer argues that "the cycle of Baal" led, inevitably, from forgetting about the poor (the disintegration of community) to spiritual adultery that led to the exile.[21]

Seeing shalom as right relationships takes us beyond peace-with-justice. Loving one's neighbor as oneself is not a requirement of justice, nor are other relationships between people. The ethic presented by Jesus' Sermon on the Mount is more a catalog of reaction to injustice than a call for justice. Perhaps it is necessary to make a set of distinctions between justice, compassion, and love.

	Actor	Patient
Justice	should	deserve
Imperfect Obligation	grace	deserve
Compassion	should	grace
Love	grace	grace

In the table, the "actor" is the person who is in a position to initiate the relationship; the "patient" is the recipient. (Thus in the story of redemption, God is the actor, we are the patients.) If a relationship is a matter of justice, it is one where the patient deserves the relationship and the actor is required to fulfill his obligations. Paul points out, "When a man works, his wages are not credited to him as a gift, but as an obligation" (Romans 4:4). The view of writers such as Martha Nussbaum and Ron Sider is that aid to developing countries is a form of compassion: they have no claim on us as a matter of justice, so their receiving is an act of grace, but there is an obligation on us to help, so we should do it.[22] Or, as Ram Gidoomal puts it, justice is about the restoration of rights; compassion is about the giving (or ascribing) of rights.[23] Love is a relationship of grace on the part of both people. True shalom would take account of these relationships as well as those based solely on justice.

But, instead of trying to fill out the vision, it is probably easier to identify those things that prevent the realization of shalom.

True development, the building of shalom, requires both a community aspect and a personal aspect. Without a Christ-nature (given by redemption through Jesus), human beings will inevitably be enticed away into sin-broken relationships, uncompassionate dealings with others, and lack of neighbor-love. At best, the devising of institutions that work toward shalom will make it harder for the worst of depravity to manifest itself, but their efforts will not produce a full shalom. For that, we shall have to wait until Christ returns.

Conclusion

The capabilities approach is useful in helping to fill out the importance of human flourishing. As an account of what is necessary to allow people to make real choices about how to live their lives, it is in accord with shalom. But shalom is so much more than this: it requires also that there be justice and compassion in relationships between people—in short, genuine love. Jesus said that on the two commands of loving God and loving neighbor hang all the law and the prophets. In addition, the structural arrangements within society can contribute to, or subtract from, the advancement of shalom.

In short, capabilities are an important part of an overall vision of shalom, of peace and fulfillment, of being able to follow one's own conception of the good and flourishing, but they are not, in themselves, a guarantee of shalom. By focusing solely on capabilities, one may lose sight of this broader vision. Capabilities imply a mechanistic view of relationship that is thin on the importance of community, compassion, and love. As a step toward a more holistic vision of development, the capabilities approach is a useful and helpful step, but it does not exhaust what it is to be a flourishing human being, at peace with God, his world, and with other people.

Notes

1. Michael P. Todaro and Stephen C. Smith, *Economic Development,* 8th ed. (Boston: Addison Wesley, 2003), 9.

2. Bob Goudzwaard, *Aid for the Overdeveloped West* (Toronto: Wedge, 1975), 1.

3. John Visser, William R. Essig, and Stephen P. Hoffmann, "Foundations: Development and Civil Society," in *Civil Society: A Foundation for Sustainable Economic Development* (Portland, OR: Mercy Corps International and Coalition for Christian Colleges and Universities, 1998), chapter 1.

4. John Rawls, *A Theory of Justice* (Cambridge, MA: Harvard University Press, 1971).

5. See Amartya Sen, *Development as Freedom* (New York: Anchor, 2000).

6. Ibid., 38ff.

7. Martha Nussbaum, *Women and Human Development* (Cambridge, MA: Cambridge University Press, 2000), 83.

8. Ibid., 1ff.

9. Ibid., 78–80.

10. For an example, see Martha Nussbaum, "Beyond the Social Contract: Capabilities and Global Justice" (Paper presented at the 3rd Conference on the Capabilities Approach in Pavia, Italy, September 2003).

11. Nussbaum, *Women and Human Development,* 12.

12. Martha Nussbaum, "Judaism and the Love of Reason," in *Philosophy, Feminism, and Faith,* ed. Marya Bower and Ruth Groenhout (Bloomington, IN: Indiana University Press, 2003).

13. Lesslie Newbigin, *The Gospel in a Pluralist Society* (Grand Rapids, MI: Eerdmans, 1990), 164.

14. David Clark, *Visions of Development: A Study of Human Values* (Cheltenham, UK: Edward Elgar, 2002).

15. Amartya Sen, "Preliminary Reflections on Freedom and Justice" (Paper presented at the 3rd Conference on the Capabilities Approach in Pavia, Italy, September 2003).

16. Nicholas Wolterstorff, *Until Justice and Peace Embrace* (Grand Rapids, MI: Eerdmans, 1993), 69–71.

17. As Vaclav Havel has pointed out, it is possible for a society to have an outward appearance of peace, but if conformity is the result of fear, there is no real peace. See his letter to the then Czech President Gustav Husak in 1975 and his essay, "The Power of the Powerless" in Jan Vladislav, *Vaclav Havel: Living in Truth* (London: Faber and Faber, 1989).

18. Interestingly, John Alexander includes "peace" as a public good and a third-generation right. See John Alexander, "Capabilities, Human Rights and the Moral Pluralism," *The International Journal of Human Rights* 8, no. 3 (2004).

19. Sen, *Development as Freedom,* 231–38.

20. *Grutter v. Bollinger,* U.S. Supreme Court ruling handed down 23 June 2003.

21. Fred Krammer, *Doing Faith Justice* (New York: Paulist Press, 1991), 29–40.

22. For an example, see Ronald Sider, *Rich Christians in an Age of Hunger* (Nashville: Word, 1997).

23. Ram Gidoomal, *How Would Jesus Vote?* (London: Monarch, 2001), 94. Nussbaum argues that charitable giving is an example of imperfect obligation: the poor deserve (have a right) to aid, but the obligation to provide does not fall on any one identifiable person, but on people in rich countries in general. I would want to resist this, as it seems to suggest that the mere fact of being poor gives one claims against those who are rich.

Is the Newer Deal a Better Deal?
Government Funding of Faith-Based Social Services

Jim R. Vanderwoerd[*]

. . . .

Introduction

President Franklin Roosevelt's New Deal in the 1930s is widely heralded as the harbinger of the extensive federal role in the twentieth-century American social welfare state. Since then there has been active debate about the proper role of government in solving social problems.[1] The lines between government and private responsibility became blurred in the 1970s when the federal government increasingly contracted with nonprofit organizations to provide federally mandated social services. It has been particularly in the past two decades that increasing recognition is being given to the role of nonprofit organizations[2]—and specifically faith-based

[*] Dr. Vanderwoerd is Associate Professor of Social Work at Dordt College. His M.S.W. is from Wilfrid Laurier University and his Ph.D. from Case Western Reserve University.
This article was published previously in the Spring 2002 *Christian Scholar's Review* (vol. 31).

organizations (FBOs)—in solving social problems.[3] However, FBOs have always been actively involved in meeting human and social needs,[4] and much of the current discussion of the role of the voluntary and religious sector arises from a reconsideration of the merits of nineteenth-century approaches to social provision in response to the real and perceived failures of twentieth-century welfare state expansion.[5] Nevertheless, this recent attention represents one of the major changes in the social welfare landscape since the New Deal and has been referred to by at least one observer as the "newer deal."[6] Particularly in the past several years the issue has garnered national attention well beyond academic and policy circles, as evidenced in the 2000 presidential campaign[7] and in January 2001 by the establishment by executive order of the White House Office of Faith-Based and Community Initiatives (OFBCI).[8]

A unique feature of current discussions is a growing sense of legitimacy—albeit not without controversy and opposition—of FBOs receiving public money to provide various social services under religious auspices. This legitimacy has been enhanced both by legislation and by the active support of the Bush White House, through the OFBCI, to expand and strengthen government partnerships with faith communities providing social services. Beginning with section 104 of the Personal Responsibility and Work Opportunity Reconciliation Act (PRWORA) of 1996,[9] so-called "Charitable Choice" provisions have been extended via legislative amendments to several other federal programs including Welfare to Work, Community Services Block Grants, juvenile justice, drug and mental health services, and children's and public health programs in the fall of 2000.[10] Spearheaded by the White House OFBCI, efforts have continued in the spring and summer of 2001 to expand Charitable Choice legislation to virtually all federal funding relationships with nongovernmental organizations.[11] When states use federal funds that are subject to Charitable Choice legislation to contract with nonprofits, states may not exclude any organizations, including churches, simply on the basis of religion. Further, if states do contract with FBOs, they may not require them to "secularize" their services. In other words, FBOs using public money under Charitable Choice may continue to use explicitly religious language, programs, and activities and to hire staff on the basis of adherence to religious tenets. At the same time, clients seeking services from such agencies must be given the choice whether to participate in religious activities, and the state must ensure that the client has access to other similar providers if he or she so chooses.[12]

Charitable Choice legislation is an attempt to allow FBOs to receive public money without having to "water down" their religiosity and, hopefully, not also violate the First Amendment restrictions on free expression and government establishment of religion. However, many unresolved issues remain. This paper will attempt to address some of these questions first by tracing recent work by nonprofit scholars to recast the theoretical terrain of the welfare state in a way that accounts more completely for the active role of the nonprofit sector.[13] Second, this paper will summarize theoretical and legal advances that—despite opposition and continued challenges—have allowed for increasing participation of people of faith in the public arena of social welfare. Beyond these theoretical and legal issues, this paper will also address three outstanding questions regarding the effectiveness, capacity, and unanticipated consequences of increased government–FBO partnerships. It is hoped that a consideration of these questions may add some clarity to a timely but complex issue and provide a better position from which Christians and others can assess the "newer deal."

The Nonprofit Sector in the Welfare State

Scholars of the nonprofit sector bemoan the lack of recognition accorded to the nonprofit sector by many social welfare analysts.[14] As Lester Salamon put it, "According to widespread beliefs, the social welfare programs of the New Deal and Great Society effectively displaced voluntary agencies in the United States and led inevitably to their decline."[15] Similarly, Stephen Monsma noted that "the American nonprofit sector is alive, growing, and plays a vital role in many key areas of American life," while at the same time, "[r]esearchers usually pay little attention to the nonprofit sector and its role in providing public services."[16] Eleanor Brilliant described how social workers focus almost exclusively on the role of government in providing social services and tend to downplay or even disparage the role played by the nonprofit sector.[17]

The reason for the inattention to the nonprofit sector does not appear to be a lack of information, although researchers frequently point out that much is unknown about the extent and activities of nonprofits.[18] It is rather that observers are blind to the importance of the nonprofit sector largely because modernity provides a conceptual framework of the welfare state that overemphasizes the public sector and individual citizens at the expense of what Peter Berger and Richard Neuhaus called the "mediating structures: those institutions standing between the individual in his private life and the large institutions of public life."[19] These and other scholars argue that the inability to perceive fully the intermediary role of nonprofits between state and individuals harks back to classical Enlightenment ideas. When European liberalism was exported across the Atlantic and adapted in the new American colonies, it set the stage for the elevation of the individual above all other societal structures. Further, it conceived of the individual, and his liberty,[20] as being the supreme value, and thus saw the state as a threat and an adversary to the individual. In this conceptualization, the existence of intermediary institutions, such as churches, schools, and other associations, was minimized.

In addition to minimizing the role of mediating institutions, polarized interpretations of the history and development of the welfare state pose problems for understanding the current potential of the nonprofit sector as well.[21] At one end of the spectrum is a version that claims that voluntary organizations run by concerned citizens successfully addressed all social problems until government stepped into social service delivery in the 1930s. As the government role expanded in the 1960s and 1970s, the voluntary sector was either crowded out or co-opted. This perspective views government expansion—and the growth of the welfare state—as anathema to volunteerism and personal responsibility. Although many who hold this view generally acknowledge that some minimal level of government intervention is necessary,[22] more extreme proponents argue that there is a latent potential for all social needs to be met by the voluntary sector, if only the government would get out of the way.[23] This has typically been the stance of those who wish to minimize the role of government and dismantle the welfare state, assuming that once it is dismantled, voluntary agencies will be freed to step into the gap.[24] On the other end of this spectrum are those, usually classified as liberals, who view government-provided, science-guided, technology-driven, and professionally delivered social services as the best hope for solving social problems, and they therefore interpret nineteenth-century efforts as inadequate for the challenges of modern industrialized societies. Thus, they tend to regard the expansion of the welfare state and the "withering away" of the nonprofit sector as a positive sign of the progressive evolution of civilization and view attempts to resurrect[25] the voluntary sector with suspicion and even hostility.[26]

Careful historical scholarship of the nonprofit sector has shown both interpretations to be simplistic and inaccurate[27] and has prompted nonprofit scholars to search for an alternative framework to account for nonprofit-government relations.[28] While these efforts are preliminary, the theoretical work of Lester Salamon, a leading nonprofit scholar, has been among the most influential. Salamon argues that many policy analysts view the welfare state from models developed in some European counties in which the state is both the funder and provider of social services. To replace this model, Salamon proposes a "third-party government" in which the funding and provision functions are separated.[29] In this view, government's primary responsibility is to provide adequate funding for services, but not to provide them. The provision of services, Salamon argues, has historically been the responsibility of private organizations; where these services are for the general welfare, this typically has resulted in provision by the nonprofit sector, but with public financing. In Salamon's conception, government and the nonprofit sector are equal partners: government provides the funds and the nonprofit sector provides the services.

This concept of partnership is clearly an advance over previous frameworks that minimized either the nonprofit sector or the public sector. However, more recent work has shown that the partnership idea is also too simplistic and does not accurately address the way in which government, as the funder, has the power to dictate and influence nonprofit activity.[30] Peter Frumkin has recently argued, for example, that new challenges must be addressed in the wake of mounting evidence that nonprofits are not independent and equal partners at all, but turn out to become increasingly "quasi-public" organizations that gradually lose their uniqueness and autonomy.[31] The outstanding issue now, according to Frumkin, is the importance of developing a style of public management that can balance two competing goals: to preserve the independence of nonprofit organizations and to meet the appropriate need to provide public accountability.

Religion: Private or Public?

Although these theoretical formulations are helpful in understanding the role of nonprofits and their relationship to government, they are focused broadly on the nonprofit sector as a whole and not specifically on that subset of nonprofit organizations that are specifically religious. The role of FBOs has been limited in part because of the contention that the public and private sectors are limited respectively to government and individuals and that faith issues are only relevant to individuals, while public issues are neutral. Some authors have pointed out that this conventional neutrality is really not neutral at all, but a particular version of Enlightenment American neo-liberalism that has become ensconced as the sole and best value-free, rational position from which all public decisions and discussion ought to be based.[32] That is, rational and free individuals do not and should not let their own religious convictions influence their deliberations regarding public issues. This is because religion is thought to be a private, individual matter, which has no bearing on public life. Indeed, the separation of church and state dictated in the First Amendment is interpreted by some to mean that one should keep one's personal religious convictions separate from one's public participation. The First Amendment was seen to be a way to protect people's rights to personal religious belief and practices without having these interfere with public life. Public life, on the other hand, was to operate from a religion-free stance, a so-called nonsectarian position that is supposedly free from personal religious biases, and thus neutral.

In contrast to a political order that assumes the public to be secular and neutral and religion to be private and biased, many authors argue for a stance that takes into account people's religious convictions without separating them from public life and that recognizes the legitimacy of social structures—many of which are religiously based—beyond the state and the individual.[33] Monsma for example, states:

> Communities and associations—whether religiously or secularly based—are best seen, not as creatures of government and subordinate to it, but as prior to and existing independently from government. Thus, they possess an autonomy that is theirs by right and not at the sufferance of the state. . . . Pluralism insists that human associations and communities are natural, necessary features of human society that exist independently of and have as much right to exist as does government.[34]

Skillen, building on the Protestant Reformed tradition developed in the Netherlands in the nineteenth and early twentieth centuries,[35] takes the concept of pluralism further in order to articulate a framework that creates the legitimacy for people's religious convictions to shape their public participation and that also provides clarity and boundaries for the roles of government and the myriad associations and institutions that make up society. Structural pluralism, he argues, is the recognition that society consists of different entities, including, of course, government and individuals, but also including an infinite multitude of organizations, institutions, and associations. These other institutions have the same legitimacy as the state and the citizen, and thus the political order should recognize and protect such rights. Skillen puts it this way: "Justice for the commonwealth requires just treatment not only of persons *as citizens* but also of all non-governmental institutions and relationships through which people constitute their lives."[36]

But pluralism is more than just the recognition of the diversity of social structures. Skillen also suggests that pluralism entails recognition of the legitimacy of individuals' and organizations' religious convictions and practices, which he calls confessional pluralism. Thus the protection of religious expression in the First Amendment is an acknowledgement of confessional pluralism. But the interpretation of religion as being confined to the church relegates confessional pluralism to only one area of structural pluralism, that is, the formal church. In reality, Skillen argues, people's religious convictions shape their activities in all social structures—family, job, school, church, political office, recreation, and so on. True pluralism, therefore, means recognizing both that people are free to express their religion and that this expression is permitted in all the variety of structures in which social life takes place, not merely relegated to one social realm, the institutional church. Skillen summarizes this point this way:

> The Constitution does not give government the right to confound religion with, or to confine religion to, institutional churches. . . . If . . . citizens are given legitimate protection under the Constitution to practice their religions freely (confessional pluralism), then all citizens should be free to conduct family life, schooling, and other social practices (structural pluralism) in ways that are consistent with the obligations of their deepest presuppositions and faiths.[37]

The implication of structural and confessional pluralism is that a new relationship between government and FBOs becomes possible. Rather than regarding government aid to FBOs as a violation of the First Amendment, this kind of pluralism would mean that FBOs be given the same opportunity for access to public dollars as other nonprofit organizations. In other words, organizations should not be prevented from accessing public funding on the basis of their religious beliefs or because the services for which they seek funding are explicitly religious. Rather, the principle of structural and confessional pluralism would enable various organizations to maintain the integrity of their particular religious beliefs and still participate in particular aspects of public life.

Esbeck and Monsma argue that the concept of neutrality or equal treatment provides a legal interpretation that acknowledges this pluralism compared to earlier separationist interpretations of "no aid to religion."[38] The neutrality principle allows for individuals and groups to participate fully in the public square without having to leave their personal religious or secular viewpoints at home. The concept of neutrality, therefore, is seen to provide a legal framework that opens the way for government funding of FBOs while remaining true to the intentions of the First Amendment. Esbeck for example, arguing that the Charitable Choice legislation does not violate the constitution, suggests that

> . . . the neutrality principle rejects the three assumptions made by separationist theory: that the activities of faith-based charities are severable into "sacred" and "secular" aspects, that religion is "private" whereas government monopolizes "public" matters, and that governmental assistance paid to service providers is aid to the providers as well as aid to the ultimate beneficiaries.[39]

With the rejection of these first two assumptions, neutrality theory is consistent with the concept of structural and confessional pluralism. Further, this principle suggests an approach that does not violate the intentions of the First Amendment, namely, that government neither advance nor restrict religious belief, but allow its citizens and groups autonomy regarding religious conviction and practice. Finally, in the interest of protecting religious autonomy, the neutrality principle improves on the separationist interpretation that attempted to divide religious organizations' activities into secular and "pervasively sectarian" categories. Recognizing that religious beliefs are expressed across the spectrum of human life—and not just constrained to either private life or to the church—the neutrality principle allows FBOs to receive public money and still maintain their religious integrity in the particular work they do.

Although there has been a shift in recent jurisprudence from a separationist to a neutrality interpretation,[40] this discussion should not be interpreted to suggest that there is widespread consensus on this issue. Many groups and organizations, both explicitly religious and secular, have voiced vigorous opposition to increasing partnerships between government and religious groups.[41] Lawsuits have challenged the constitutionality of

Charitable Choice, and much of the debate surrounding this issue is acrimonious.[42] At the same time, there has been movement toward consensus among those who disagree,[43] and the principle of neutrality—grounded as it is in the concept of pluralism described above—appears to offer an alternative which satisfies the First Amendment and takes into account the diversity of twenty-first-century America.

Unresolved Issues

As the discussion above reveals, there are theoretical and legal alternatives to the conventional ways of thinking about FBOs and nonprofits that create conceptual and legal space, if not consensus, for their more extensive partnership with government in addressing social problems. While this provides a necessary foundation, it does not provide specific answers to some unanswered questions about the practical implications of these partnerships. At least three such questions will be addressed.

Are faith-based organizations really more effective at solving social problems?

The recent attention to the role of FBOs has been due in part to claims of their superior effectiveness in solving social problems compared to conventional programs. Some of these claims have garnered widespread publicity and have increased the pressure on politicians to make greater use of faith-based providers.[44] For example, the recent expansion of Charitable Choice legislation included in the reauthorization of funding to the Substance Abuse and Mental Health Services Administration[45] was likely due in part to the publicity of claims made by faith-based programs such as Teen Challenge, an international program addressing drug and alcohol addiction. Teen Challenge has reported success rates that are much higher than other government-funded drug rehabilitation programs.[46] However, the evidence for the improved success of religiously oriented social services is preliminary at best and misleading at worst. A 1998 review of the literature on faith-based social service providers concluded that "We have been unable to locate a single credible study assessing the relative effectiveness of religion-sponsored social services that meets the minimum requirements for evaluations."[47] That finding was confirmed by a more recent review of the empirical evidence sponsored by the Progressive Policy Institute. The researchers concluded:

> Despite the fact that the empirical data is mixed, existing studies seem to indicate two conclusions: (1) that religiosity appears to deter some behaviors, but not others, and (2) that FBOs might be more effective at rehabilitation than deterrence. Given this limited evidence, however, policy makers should ensure that government support of FBOs is conditioned on the same standards of accountability and performance that are applicable to secular organizations. . . . At best, religion can be credited with deterring some deviant behaviors, although its effect is not as strong as some would predict. Although the empirical record is somewhat more positive for religiously oriented programs aimed at rehabilitation, they are hardly a panacea.[48]

The statements and announcements from the White House Office of Faith-Based and Community Initiatives suggest that these recommendations for rigorous evaluative standards are being heeded.[49] Nevertheless, some observers have claimed that: ". . . the rhetoric and follow-up activity to the President's 'faith-based' initiative clearly demonstrates a desire to redirect federal grants to religious congregations whenever possible."[50] It is exactly this possibility of religious favoritism that has led opponents to challenge the Charitable Choice legislation and White House initiatives as both unconstitutional and as an unjust mismanagement of public resources.

The claims for increased effectiveness of religiously based social services compared to traditional public programs seem to rest on three areas. First, there is the spiritual component. Proponents argue that when social service programs include spirituality as part of their change strategy, they are able to get below the surface of the problem and bring about deeper, inner change in clients. For example, in a study of the Teen Challenge program, successful program graduates cited "the Jesus factor" as the most important program characteristic responsible for their success.[51] Second, proponents of increased FBO participation in social services focus on the personal relationships developed between religiously motivated helpers (whether paid employees or volunteers) and clients that are crucial in helping struggling persons make substantial lifestyle changes to overcome social problems. For example, Amy Sherman argues that the most important "added value" of religious organizations is their ability to reach people through extensive personal contacts.[52] Finally, FBO advocates, along with those supporting an increased role for all nonprofits, argue that small private-sector organizations are generally more flexible, with more highly committed staff and more ability to innovate and be responsive to client needs, than large government-run bureaucracies. As noted above, however, more evaluative work is needed to substantiate these claims across the breadth of religiously based social programs. There is a convincing body of literature that suggests that there is a positive relationship between spirituality and varying measures of well-being, including physical healing, mental health, coping, family functioning, and marital satisfaction.[53] This evidence alone, however, is simply not enough to conclude that FBOs provide more effective social services than their secular counterparts.

A number of serious obstacles impede the ability to design credible evaluations to test FBOs against other programs. First, it is often the case that clients served by FBOs seek and intentionally choose exactly the type of explicitly faith-based services that are offered. Thus, it is extremely difficult to determine whether differences in outcomes are due to the program or to the different motivations of those who seek faith-based approaches compared to those who do not. The best evaluation designs to overcome this selection bias require clients to be randomly assigned to different programs. However, it is not hard to see that most clients would not consent to being assigned to either explicitly religious or secular services against their wishes.

Second, it is notoriously difficult to pin down exactly what it is about the services FBOs provide that make them unique compared to secular services.[54] Some of the characteristics to which FBOs attribute their success may be simply the characteristics of any successful nonprofit: flexibility, commitment of staff, ability to innovate, a supporting constituency, lack of bureaucracy, personalized services, and personal relationships. Many of these characteristics typify FBOs, but apply to many non-faith-based nonprofits as well. Or, as concluded by two commentators, "The idealism that supports social commitment comes in many forms."[55] In fact, Lisbeth Schorr has argued persuasively that the failure of many traditional social service approaches has been due to their lack of attention to these very characteristics.[56] After reviewing hundreds of the most promising programs she concluded:

> . . . the programs that succeed . . . are intensive, comprehensive, and flexible. They also share an extra dimension, more difficult to capture: Their climate is created by skilled, committed professionals who establish respectful and trusting relationships and respond to the individual needs of those they serve.[57]

Similarly, the literature on the effectiveness of social support approaches suggests that the best help occurs when persons struggling with multiple social problems receive a combination of professional services and informal, long-term social relationships that are appropriate to their unique circumstances.[58]

In addition to the difficulties in identifying the unique characteristics of FBO effectiveness compared to secular programs, there is often an unclear link between program activities and hoped-for outcomes. This, of course, is not just a challenge for faith-based programs. Scholars in the social sciences are all too aware that many social programs are based on theory and evidence that is tentative, preliminary, and at times, contradictory.[59] All of this suggests that, until better evidence is available, the success attributed to FBOs may be confounded with the characteristics that we already know make for good programs, religious or otherwise. It seems prudent, therefore, to proceed with caution and to subject faith-based services to the same evaluative rigor demanded of all programs. Put another way, a concern for effectiveness, using the best available knowledge, theory, and methods, should supercede religiosity as a criterion by which to decide between programs.

Can faith-based organizations meet all the social needs out there?

A second unresolved question concerns the capacity of religiously based organizations to step into the gap vacated by a retreating federal government. The devolution trend of the past decade or two has seen federal responsibility for social programs decrease in favor of state and local

216

autonomy. This has had a substantial impact on nonprofits, including FBOs, since it is often these organizations that are expected to pick up the slack.[60] If devolution means that "religion is overpromoted as a way to argue for a return to state's rights, small government, and lower taxes,"[61] then one must ask whether it is realistic and feasible to expect that religious organizations and churches can do what the federal government will not.

Current evidence suggests that expecting FBOs and churches to take up the mantle of responsibility for solving social problems is wishful thinking. For one thing, this hope rests on the assumption that there is a large un-tapped reservoir of faith-based providers waiting for an opportunity to step into the arena of social programs. But a number of researchers have found that there is already a high amount of involvement of churches in social service provision. Ram Cnaan's review of the literature and studies con-ducted by he and his colleagues suggest that 60–90 percent of all congregations already provide some type of social services to persons who are not members of their congregation.[62] Further, it has been estimated that if churches were really to replace the government as the provider of social services each congregation in America would have to raise an additional $200,000 to $300,000 annually over and above their current average budget of $100,000.[63] Nor does it appear that the promise of federal funding provided through Charitable Choice legislation will spur vast increases in the number of churches and FBOs to get into the social service business. The Center for Public Justice, a Christian policy and research organization that supports and monitors Charitable Choice, found that the initial re-sponse in nine states of churches to the legislation was somewhat lower than expected.[64] More recent monitoring of the impact of Charitable Choice shows only modest rates of implementation, with most states failing the Center's "report card."[65] Finally, a 1998 nationally representative survey of over 1,200 congregations estimated that only one-third of all congregations would be willing to apply for government funds given the new opportuni-ties of the Charitable Choice legislation.[66] This finding was confirmed by a recent White House report, which concluded that only a small number of religious organizations were choosing to apply for federal funds, in part because they worried about losing their religiousness.[67] Regarding the ability of FBOs and churches to replace government, Cnaan argues,

> There is no way that the religious community can play more than a stepped-up util-ity role in supporting the public and nonprofit agencies in their communities. Our social problems are far too intricate and expansive and our public and private non-profit system of services, including the current system of services offered by religious congregations, is too structured and vast to expect a major redesign that would make religious-based social service organizations the main providers of our country's social services.[68]

It seems safe to conclude that the motivation for increased FBO access to public dollars should be based on facilitating better—and perhaps, limited[69]—partnerships between government and the religious sector, rather than as a means to reduce or eliminate government's responsibility for addressing social problems.

Will faith-based organizations become secularized or corrupted by partnering with government?

Clichés such as "government shekels bring government shackles" and "he who pays the piper calls the tune" capture the widely held fear that FBOs will be forced to give up their specific sense of mission and uniqueness as a condition of accepting public dollars. These are legitimate concerns that have been raised by both opponents and advocates of Charitable Choice.[70] However, few studies have specifically examined the impact of government funding on FBOs' autonomy using generally accepted methods of empirical inquiry.

A small number of studies have addressed this question.[71] These studies suggest that many agency representatives report only minor encroachments on their religious activity or mission when they receive public money. At the same time, a small number of agencies reported fairly stringent restrictions and interference; further, those agencies with the clearest articulation of their mission appeared to be the most resilient to government influence. However, these conclusions must be considered with a good deal of caution owing to some serious methodological limitations. Small and nonrandom sample sizes, poor response rates, and participation from a narrow range of social service agencies make it virtually impossible to reach beyond the samples and make inferences about the state of affairs for other FBOs. Another critical limitation is the relatively simple—or worse, nonexistent—attention to carefully defining and measuring important concepts such as the religiousness of an organization, organizational autonomy and mission, and even government funding.[72]

The lack of attention to factors other than the receipt of public money that might threaten agencies' autonomy is also a limitation. Although some researchers have noted that constraints can come from other funders and other sources,[73] much of the research does not adequately investigate the range of factors that influence an organization's religious identity and mission. One possibility is that agency directors—who were the primary respondents in the studies reviewed—are so influenced by the broader trends in society that they no longer recognize their own agency's secularization. For example, Glenn points out that an underestimated source of "mission creep" may be due to FBO administrators themselves: "...government interference is not the only threat to the integrity of faith-based organizations. They are also faced with the more subtle danger of self-betrayal."[74] If this is the case, subsequent

research is needed to identify and explicate the attitudes of FBO stake-
holders regarding distinctions between secular and sacred, roles of
government and nonprofits, the influence and role of religion in public and
private life, and so on. Finally, a lack of longitudinal data makes it difficult
to know whether actual constraints to FBOs' autonomy are anomalies or
part of a longer trend resulting from government funding or other variables.
Thus, while these few studies consistently point to a minimal impact of
government funding on agency autonomy, these conclusions must be
tempered by the methodological limitations and therefore must be taken as
preliminary at best, and at worst perhaps concealing or distorting what may
actually be going on.

Conclusion

Increased partnerships between the federal government and the religious
community in addressing social problems may be a "newer deal," but it is
not yet clear that they are a better deal. Charitable Choice legislation represents a level of recognition and space for religious expression in public life
that is overdue. Reducing the religious barriers to accessing government
funds acknowledges that faith is more than just the private beliefs of individuals, but that it also centrally directs a society's public life. Further, in a
diverse country, space must be allowed for the public expression of many
faiths, rather than the imposition of either the majority's faith perspective
or an allegedly neutral secular perspective. Charitable Choice, therefore, is
an important improvement over past social policy that has restricted the
participation of some religious groups in social provision. On this basis
alone, the newer deal is better.

Despite this promise, unanswered questions remain. First, the claims of
superior effectiveness of FBOs in addressing social problems compared to
secular alternatives must be subjected to more rigorous evaluation. Appropriate social science techniques must be employed to identify and test the
unique characteristics of faith-based services. Such evaluation is particularly
necessary to avoid uncritically favoring FBOs over secular services absent
other criteria for effectiveness. Second, it would be a grave mistake to
imagine that increasing the participation of faith-based providers with
government funds can substitute for a governmental responsibility. Social
problems have never been due solely to personal failures or personal sin,
and individually focused solutions will never solve the deeper-seated structural and systemic failures that are also implicated in social problems.[75]
When God calls his people to be ambassadors of reconciliation it is clear
that this reconciliation is not reserved just for personal and individual
brokenness, but for *all* creation (2 Corinthians 5:17–6:2). Government–
FBO partnerships should be part of the solution, but can never be the
whole solution. Finally, it remains to be seen whether FBOs will be able to

withstand external or internal pressures to wander from their missions. If FBO–government partnerships are to become an important part of the social welfare landscape, care must be taken to preserve the character of religious organizations so that they do not, over time, lose their ability to make a unique contribution.

None of these or other limitations, however, should detract from the pursuit and defense of public policies, such as Charitable Choice, that create space for public participation of society's infinite groups and associations. Rather, the appropriate rationale and motivation for increasing the participation of faith-based and other groups in the messy public life of social problems should be based on the principles of biblically informed structural and confessional pluralism. It seems prudent to agree on that point now and turn our energies to the difficult work ahead posed by the many specific unanswered questions that are necessary to make the "newer deal" better.

Notes

1. Phyllis Day, *A New History of Social Welfare,* 3rd ed. (Boston: Allyn and Bacon, 2000); Walter Trattner, *From Poor Law to Welfare State: A History of Social Welfare in America,* 6th ed. (New York: The Free Press, 1999); Bruce S. Jansson, *The Reluctant Welfare State: American Social Welfare Policies—Past, Present, and Future,* 4th ed. (Belmont, CA: Wadsworth/Thomson, 2001).

2. Elizabeth Boris and C. Eugene Steuerle, eds., *Nonprofits and Government: Collaboration and Conflict* (Washington, DC: The Urban Institute, 1999); Lester Salamon, *Partners in Public Service: Government-Nonprofit Relations in the Modern Welfare State* (Baltimore: Johns Hopkins University, 1995).

3. Mary Jo Bane, Brent Coffin, and Ronald Thiemann, eds., *Who Will Provide? The Changing Role of Religion in American Social Welfare* (Boulder, CO: Westview Press, 2000); Derek Davis and Barry Hankins, eds., *Welfare Reform and Faith-Based Organizations* (Waco, TX: J. M. Dawson Institute of Church-State Studies, Baylor University, 1999); Charles Glenn, *The Ambiguous Embrace: Government and Faith-Based Schools and Social Agencies* (Princeton, NJ: Princeton University Press, 2000); James Ellor, F. Ellen Netting, and Jane Thibault, *Religious and Spiritual Aspects of Human Service Practice* (Columbia: University of South Carolina Press, 1999); Peter Dobkin Hall, "Religion and the Post-Welfare State: An Untold Story," *Religion in the News* 1, no. 1 (1998).

4. Ram Cnaan, "Recognizing the Role of Religious Congregations and Denominations in Social Service Provision," in *Social Work in the 21st Century,* ed. Michael Reisch and Eileen Gambrill (Thousand Oaks, CA: Pine Forge, 1997), 271–84; Martin E. Marty, "Social Service: Godly and Godless," *Social Service Review* 54, no. 4 (1980); F. Ellen Netting, Jane Thibault, and James Ellor, "Integrating Content on Organized Religion into Macropractice Courses," *Journal of Social Work Education* 26, no. 1 (1990).

5. Joel Schwartz, *Fighting Poverty with Virtue: Moral Reform and America's Urban Poor, 1825–2000* (Bloomington: Indiana University Press, 2000); Steven Davies, "Two Conceptions of Welfare: Voluntarism and Incorporationism," in *The Welfare State,* ed. E. F. Paul, F. D. Miller, and J. Paul (New York: Cambridge University Press, 1997), 39–68.

6. Ram Cnaan, *The Newer Deal: Social Work and Religion in Partnership* (New York: Columbia University Press, 1999), 18.

7. Dennis Hoover, "Charitable Choice and the New Right," *Religion in the News* 3, no. 1 (2000); Jennifer Moore and Grant Williams, "Gore Vows New Partnership with Religious Groups," *Chronicle of Philanthropy* 12, no. 17 (2000); David Nather, "Funding of Faith-Based Groups Spurs New Civil Rights Debate," *CQ Weekly* 58, no. 24 (2000).

8. See President George W. Bush, "Rallying the Armies of Compassion" (Washington, DC: The White House, January 30, 2001).

9. David Sherwood, "Charitable Choice: Opportunity and Challenge for Christians in Social Work," *Social Work and Christianity* 25, no. 3 (1998).

10. Stanley Carlson-Thies, "Charitable Choice 101" (Washington, DC: Center for Public Justice, 2000). Available at http://www.cpjustice.org/charitablechoice/handouts.

11. Lewis D. Solomon and Matthew J. Vlissides, Jr., *In God We Trust? Assessing the Potential of Faith-Based Social Services* (Washington, DC: The Progressive Policy Institute, February 2001), 12.

12. Center for Public Justice, *A Guide to Charitable Choice* (Washington, DC: CPJ, 1997). See also John J. DiIulio, Jr., "Compassion 'In Truth and Action': How Sacred and Secular Places Serve Civic Purposes and What Washington Should—and Should Not—Do to Help," (speech delivered to the National Association of Evangelicals, March 7, 2001). Available at www.whitehouse.gov/news/releases.

13. See Eleanor Brilliant, "Nonprofit Organizations, Social Policy, and Public Welfare," in *Social Work in the 21st Century,* ed. Michael Reisch and Eileen Gambrill (Thousand Oaks, CA: Pine Forge, 1997), 68–79; Boris and Steuerle, *Nonprofits and Government;* Salamon, *Partners in Public Service;* and Steven R. Smith and Michael Lipsky, *Nonprofits for Hire: The Welfare State in the Age of Contracting* (Cambridge, MA: Harvard University Press, 1993).

14. Boris and Steuerle, *Nonprofits and Government;* Ralph Kramer, "Public Fiscal Policy and Voluntary Agencies in the Welfare States," *Social Service Review* 53, no. 1 (1979): 1–14.

15. Salamon, *Partners in Public Service,* 33.

16. Stephen V. Monsma, *When Sacred and Secular Mix: Religious Organizations and Public Money* (Lanham, MD: Rowman and Littlefield, 1996), 3, 15.

17. Eleanor Brilliant, "Nonprofit Organizations, Social Policy, and Public Welfare," 69.

18. Boris and Steuerle, *Nonprofits and Government;* Susan Ostrander, "Voluntary Social Service Agencies in the United States," *Social Service Review* 59, no. 3 (1985): 435–54.

19. Peter Berger and Richard Neuhaus, *To Empower People: The Role of Mediating Structures in Public Policy* (Washington, DC: American Enterprise Institute, 1977), 2.

20. These liberties were not extended to women at first, thus the use of the male pronoun. See Rosemary Putnam Tong, *Feminist Thought: A More Comprehensive Introduction,* 2nd ed. (Boulder, CO: Westview Press, 1998); and Mary Wollstonecraft, *A Vindication of the Rights of Women* (Rutland, VT: Charles E. Tuttle/Everyman's Library, 1992 [1792]).

21. Berger and Neuhaus, *To Empower People,* 4–6.

22. Schwartz, *Fighting Poverty with Virtue,* see especially chapter 8.

23. See Brilliant, "Nonprofit Organizations, Social Policy, and Public Welfare," 72–74, for a description of this perspective. A well-known proponent is Marvin Olasky, *The Tragedy of American Compassion* (Washington, DC: Regnery Gateway, 1992). Note, however, that President George W. Bush has clearly stated that his "compassionate conservatism" and

his administration's faith-based initiatives clearly include a role for the state. See President George W. Bush, "Rallying the Armies of Compassion."

24. Carol De Vita, "Nonprofits and Devolution: What Do We Know?" in Boris and Steuerle, *Nonprofits and Government*, 213–33; E. F. Paul, F. D. Miller, and J. Paul, eds., *The Welfare State* (New York: Cambridge University Press, 1997).

25. Of course, the term *resurrect* itself reveals the bias, for it assumes that the nonprofit sector was dead and must be brought back to life.

26. Brilliant, "Nonprofit Organizations, Social Policy, and Public Welfare"; Salamon, *Partners in Public Service.*

27. Peter Dobkin Hall, "A Historical Overview of the Private Nonprofit Sector," in *The Nonprofit Sector: A Research Handbook,* ed. Walter Powell (New Haven, CT: Yale University, 1987), 2–26; Theda Skocpol, "Religion, Civil Society, and Social Provision in the U.S.," in *Who Will Provide? The Changing Role of Religion in American Social Welfare,* ed. Mary Jo Bane, Brent Coffin, and Ronald Thiemann (Boulder, CO: Westview Press, 2000), 21–50.

28. Ralph Kramer, "A Third Sector in the Third Millennium?" *Voluntas: International Journal of Voluntary and Nonprofit Organizations* 11, no. 1 (2000): 1–23. See also Lester Salamon, "Of Market Failure, Voluntary Failure, and Third-Party Government: Toward a Theory of Government-Nonprofit Relations in the Modern Welfare State," and Stuart Langton, "Envoi: Developing Nonprofit Theory," both in *Shifting the Debate: Public/Private Sector Relations in the Modern Welfare State,* ed. Susan A. Ostrander and Stuart Langton (New Brunswick: Transaction Books, 1987).

29. Salamon, *Partners in Public Service,* 17–52. It is worth noting that Salamon's concept of third-party government is essentially the same as what John J. DiIulio, former director of the White House Office of Faith-Based and Community Initiatives, refers to as "government-by-proxy." See DiIulio, "Compassion 'In Truth and Action.'"

30. Boris and Steuerle, *Nonprofits and Government.*

31. Peter Frumkin, "After Partnership: Rethinking Public-Nonprofit Relations," in Bane et al., *Who Will Provide?,* 198–218.

32. Carl Esbeck, "A Constitutional Case for Governmental Cooperation with Faith-Based Social Service Providers," *Emory Law Journal* 46, no. 1 (1997): 1–41; James Skillen, *Recharging the American Experiment: Principled Pluralism for Genuine Civic Community* (Grand Rapids, MI: Baker, 1994); Timothy Sherratt, "Rehabilitating the State in America: Abraham Kuyper's Overlooked Contribution," *Christian Scholar's Review* 29, no. 2 (1999): 323–46.

33. See for example Bane et al., *Who Shall Provide?;* Glenn, *The Ambiguous Embrace;* Timothy Sherratt and Ronald Mahurin, *Saints as Citizens: A Guide to Public Responsibilities for Christians* (Grand Rapids, MI: Baker, 1995); Gerald Vandezande, *Justice, No Just Us: Faith Perspectives and National Priorities* (Toronto: Public Justice Resource Centre, 1999); and Brian Walsh and J. Richard Middleton, *The Transforming Vision: Shaping a Christian World View* (Downer's Grove, IL: InterVarsity, 1984).

34. Monsma, *When Sacred and Secular Mix,* 18.

35. Sherratt, "Rehabilitating the State"; James Skillen, "Going Beyond Liberalism to Christian Social Philosophy," *Christian Scholar's Review* 19 (March 1990): 220–30.

36. Skillen, *Recharging the American Experiment,* 84.

37. Ibid., 86–87.

38. Esbeck, "A Constitutional Case"; Monsma, "Substantive Neutrality as a Basis for Free Exercise–No Establishment Common Ground," *Journal of Church and State* 42, no. 1 (2000): 13–35. Other similar terms include "substantive neutrality" or "positive neutrality." See Monsma, *When Sacred and Secular Mix* and *Positive Neutrality: Letting Religious Freedom Ring* (Grand Rapids, MI: Baker, 1993).

39. Esbeck, "A Constitutional Case," 21–22. It should be noted that Esbeck was one of the authors of Section 104 of the Personal Responsibility and Work Opportunity Reconciliation Act, also known as the "Charitable Choice" legislation, and thus is not a neutral observer.

40. Note, however, that despite the shift in court interpretations toward neutrality and equal treatment, in practice the "no-aid-to-religion" principle is still widely followed, according to a recent White House report *Unlevel Playing Field: Barriers to Participation by Faith-Based Organizations* (Washington, DC: The White House, August 2001).

41. See, for example, the careful and excellent essays by Melissa Rogers, Sharon Daly, and Derek Davis in *Welfare Reform and Faith-Based Organizations,* ed. Derek Davis and Barry Hankins (Waco, TX: J. M. Dawson Institute of Church-State Studies, Baylor University, 1999). In addition to these challenges, several secular organizations have led lobbying efforts against Charitable Choice, including the American Civil Liberties Union and Americans United for the Separation of Church and State (see their respective websites: www.acul.org/congress/gfr.html and www.au.org).

42. Bane et al., *Who Will Provide?;* Davis and Hankins, *Welfare Reform;* David Sherwood, "Charitable Choice: Still an Opportunity and Challenge for Christians in Social Work," *Social Work and Christianity* 27, no. 2 (Fall 2000): 98–111.

43. See the report *In Good Faith: A Dialogue on Government Funding of Faith-Based Social Services* (Philadelphia, PA: Feinstein Center for American Jewish History, March 2001). Available at www.pewcharitabletrusts.org.

44. Wendy Kaminer, "Unholy Alliance," *The American Prospect* 35 (November–December 1997).

45. Carlson-Thies, "Charitable Choice 101."

46. Andrew Kenney, "Teen Challenge's Proven Answer to the Drug Problem," Teen Challenge World Wide Network, http://www.teenchallenge.com/tcreview.html (accessed December 7, 2000).

47. John McCarthy and Jim Castelli, *Religion-Sponsored Social Service Providers: The Not-So-Independent Sector* (Washington, DC: Nonprofit Sector Research Fund, The Aspen Institute, 1998), 53.

48. Solomon and Vlissides, *In God We Trust?*, 4, 6.

49. For example, President George W. Bush, in his forward to the "Rallying the Armies of Compassion" announcement (January 30, 2001) of the White House OFBCI said, "We must be outcome-based, insisting on success and steering resources to the effective and to the inspired."Similarly, John J. DiIulio, former director of the OFBCI said in a March 7, 2001, address to the National Association of Evangelicals, "Compassionate conservatism challenges Washington to work overtime and in a bipartisan fashion to ensure that social programs taxpayers fund, and the networks of nonprofit organizations that help to administer those programs, are performance-managed, performance-measured, and open to competition from qualified community-serving organizations, large or small, young or old, sacred or secular."

50. OMB Watch, "Analysis of Bush Administration's Charitable Choice Initiatives" (Washington, DC: OMB Watch, April 23, 2001). Available at www.ombwatch.org.

51. Kenney, "Teen Challenge's Proven Answer," 8.

52. Amy Sherman, "A Survey of Church-Government Anti-Poverty Partnerships," Welfare Policy Center, Hudson Institute, www.welfareformer.org/9stsurvey.htm.

53. David R. Hodge, "Welfare Reform and Religious Providers: An Examination of the New Paradigm," *Social Work and Christianity* 25, no. 1 (Spring 1998).

54. Thomas Jeavons, "Identifying Characteristics of 'Religious Organizations,'" in *Sacred Companies: Organizational Aspects of Religion and Religious Aspects of Organizations*, ed. N. J. Demerath, Peter Dobkin Hall, Terry Schmitt, and Rhys H. Williams (New York: Oxford University Press, 1998), 79–96.

55. Isaac Kramnick and R. Laurence Moore, "Can the Churches Save the Cities? Faith-Based Services and the Constitution," *The American Prospect* 35 (November–December 1997): 4.

56. Lisbeth Schorr, *Within Our Reach: Breaking the Cycle of Disadvantage* (New York: Anchor Books/Doubleday, 1988), and *Common Purpose: Strengthening Families and Neighborhoods to Rebuild America* (New York: Anchor Books/Doubleday, 1997).

57. Schorr, *Within Our Reach*, 259.

58. Gary Cameron and Jim Vanderwoerd, *Protecting Children and Supporting Families: Promising Programs and Organizational Realities* (New York: Aldine de Gruyter, 1997).

59. See, for example, Peter M. Kettner, Robert M. Moroney, and Lawrence L. Martin, *Designing and Managing Programs: An Effectiveness-Based Approach*, 2nd ed. (Thousand Oaks, CA: Sage, 1999); Eileen Gambrill, "Evidence-Based Practice: An Alternative to Authority-Based Practice," *Families in Society: The Journal of Contemporary Human Services* 80, no. 4 (July–August 1999); and Paul E. Meehl, "Credentialed Persons, Credentialed Knowledge," *Clinical Psychology: Science and Practice* 4, no. 2 (Summer 1997).

60. Ram Cnaan, *The Newer Deal: Social Work and Religion in Partnership* (New York: Columbia University Press, 1999), specifically chapter 1, "The Challenge of Devolution and the Promise of Religious-Based Social Services: An Introduction"; Jennifer Alexander, "The Impact of Devolution on Nonprofits: A Multiphase Study of Social Service Organizations," *Nonprofit Management and Leadership* 10, no. 1 (Fall 1999); and Carol J. De Vita, "Nonprofits and Devolution: What Do We Know?" in *Nonprofits and Government: Collaboration and Conflict*, ed. Elizabeth Boris and C. Eugene Steuerle (Washington, DC: The Urban Institute, 1999).

61. Kramnick and Moore, "Can the Churches Save the Cities? Faith-Based Services and the Constitution," 8.

62. Cnaan, *The Newer Deal*, see especially chapters 8, 10, and 11.

63. Cnaan, *The Newer Deal*, 17; and Tony Campolo, *Revolution and Renewal: How Churches Are Saving Our Cities* (Louisville, KY: Westminster John Knox, 2000), 50.

64. Stanley Carlson-Thies, "'Don't Look to Us': The Negative Responses of the Churches to Welfare Reform," *Notre Dame Journal of Law, Ethics and Public Policy* 11, no. 2 (1997).

65. See Center for Public Justice, "Charitable Choice Compliance: A National Report Card" (October 5, 2000), available at www.cpjustice.org; Amy L. Sherman, *The Growing Impact of Charitable Choice: A Catalogue of New Collaborations between Government and Faith-Based Organizations in Providing Social Services in Nine States* (Washington, DC: Center for Public Justice, March 2000); Amy L. Sherman, "Tracking Charitable Choice: A Study of the

Collaboration between Faith-Based Organizations and the Government in Providing Social Services in Nine States," *Social Work and Christianity* 27, no. 2 (Fall 2000): 112–29.

66. Mark Chaves, "Religious Congregations and Welfare Reform: Who Will Take Advantage of 'Charitable Choice'?" *American Sociological Review* 64 (December 1999).

67. The White House, *Unlevel Playing Field.*

68. Cnaan, *The Newer Deal,* 17.

69. This point is argued persuasively by Bob Wineburg, *A Limited Partnership: The Politics of Religion, Welfare, and Social Service* (New York: Columbia University Press, 2001).

70. Some of the opponents of Charitable Choice raising concerns are: Citizens Against Government Waste, "Phony Philanthropy: How Government Grants Are Subverting the Missions of Nonprofit Organizations," CAGW, www.cagw.org/publications (accessed July 28, 2000); Derek Davis and Barry Hankins, *Welfare Reform and Faith-Based Organizations* (Waco, TX: Dawson Institute of Church-State Studies, Baylor University, 1999); Joe Loconte, *Seducing the Samaritan: How Government Contracts Are Reshaping Social Services* (Boston: Pioneer Institute, 1997); Lisa Oliphaunt, "Charitable Choice: The End of Churches as We Know Them?" *Policy and Practice of Public Human Services* 58, no. 2 (2000): 8–12; Marvin Olasky, "The Corruption of Religious Charities," in *To Empower People: The Role of Mediating Structures in Public Policy,* ed. Peter Berger and Richard Neuhaus (Washington, DC: American Enterprise Institute, 1977), 94–104.

Some of the advocates of Charitable Choice raising concerns are: Bane et al., *Who Will Provide?*; Glenn, *The Ambiguous Embrace*; Ralph Kramer, *Voluntary Agencies in the Welfare State* (Berkeley: University of California Press, 1981); Amy Sherman, "Cross Purposes: Will Conservative Welfare Reform Corrupt Religious Charities?" *Policy Review* 74 (Fall 1995).

71. The author searched the literature for empirical studies that used generally accepted social science methodology to examine this question. Using such criteria, the following studies were identified and reviewed: Bernard Coughlin, *Church and State in Social Welfare* (New York: Columbia, 1965); Diana Garland, *Church Social Work: Helping the Whole Person in the Context of the Church* (St. Davids, PA: North American Association of Christians in Social Work, 1992); John Hiemstra, *Government Relations with Religious Non-Profit Social Agencies in Alberta: Public Accountability in a Pluralist Society* (Calgary: Canada West Foundation, 1999); Thomas H. Jeavons, *When the Bottom Line Is Faithfulness: Management of Christian Service Organizations* (Bloomington: Indiana University Press, 1994); Monsma, *When Sacred and Secular Mix;* F. Ellen Netting, "Secular and Religious Funding of Church-Related Agencies," *Social Service Review* 56, no. 4 (1982): 596–604; Felice Perlmutter, "The Effect of Public Funds on Voluntary Sectarian Services," *Journal of Jewish Communal Services* 45 (1968): 312–21.

72. Monsma, *When Sacred and Secular Mix.*

73. Kramer, *Voluntary Agencies in the Welfare State;* Netting, "Secular and Religious Funding."

74. Glenn, *The Ambiguous Embrace,* 241.

75. See John Mason, "Biblical Teaching and the Objectives of Welfare Policy in the U. S.," in *Welfare in America: Christian Perspectives on a Policy in Crisis,* ed. Stanley Carlson-Thies and James Skillen (Grand Rapids, MI: Eerdmans, 1996), 145–85; Sharon Daly, "Common Sense and the Common Good: Helping the Poor and Protecting Religious Liberty," in *Welfare Reform & Faith-Based Organizations,* ed. Derek Davis and Barry Hankins (Waco, TX: J. M. Dawson Institute of Church-State Studies, Baylor University, 1999), 139–52; Bane et al., *Who Will Provide?*

Disestablishment a Second Time:
Genuine Pluralism for American Schools

Rockne M. McCarthy[*]

....

The Central Question

Controversy surrounding the appropriate relationship between the state and schools is a regular part of American life. Often the debate is centered around a sense of lack of justice in public policies that affect education. When the conflict is not primarily over educational opportunity or quality, it is often focused on equity and the public funding of education. The contemporary debate over faith-based schools, vouchers, tax credits, and scholarships is a case in point. The roots of this debate reach back into the eighteenth and nineteenth centuries.

[*] Dr. McCarthy came to Dordt College in 1979. He is Vice President for Academic Affairs and Professor of History and Political Studies. His Ph.D. is from St. Louis University. This contribution is a revision and update of chapter four, "The Public School Institutionalized," taken from the out-of-print publication *Disestablishment a Second Time: Genuine Pluralism for American Schools* (Grand Rapids, MI: Christian University Press (Eerdmans), 1982). The title of this publication is used because it summarizes the thesis of the revised chapter and the central argument of the original scholarly contribution of the author and his colleagues James W. Skillen and William A. Harper.

In 1779 political reformers in Virginia supported a comprehensive set of democratic initiatives designed to do away with the economic privilege of the landed aristocracy, to separate the church from the state, and to establish a system of public schools. The last two objectives took the form of Thomas Jefferson's "Bill for Religious Freedom" and "Bill for the More General Diffusion of Knowledge." In Jefferson's mind the two bills, introduced before the General Assembly, would help to establish a more democratic order for Virginia.[1] The companion bills demonstrate Jefferson's awareness that if the Anglican church were to be disestablished, then another institution had to be found (established) to provide for the common (moral) unity that he assumed was necessary for the preservation of society. Jefferson's "Bill for Religious Freedom" passed the Virginia Assembly in 1786 by an overwhelming (74 to 20) majority. The effort at "disestablishment a first time" succeeded, but Jefferson's effort to establish a system of public primary and secondary schools in Virginia was not successful.

The vision for public education was to be taken up by the generation that came to maturity during the first decades of the nineteenth century. It was during this period that the original eighteenth-century educational vision of Jefferson, Benjamin Rush, and Daniel Webster developed into the institution known as the public school.[2] In order to understand the purpose and structure of the common school, it is important again to emphasize, along with Bernard Bailyn, that nineteenth-century public schools did *not* emerge from the mind of seventeenth-century New England Puritans. Bailyn makes the point this way:

> The modern conception of public education, the very idea of a clean line of separation between "private" and "public," was unknown before the end of the eighteenth century. Its origins are part of a complex story, involving changes in the role of the state as well as in the general institutional character of society. It is elaborately woven into the fabric of early modern history.[3]

Before the emergence of a clean line of separation between private and public education, the established pattern for financial support for schools—whether in the middle colonies, the South, or New England—was the English practice of multiple sources. The actual colonial practice of school financing was usually a combination of private donations, student tuition, and, in some cases, public funding in the form of land grants and taxes. Schools receiving money from the government were considered "public" even though they were managed by private individuals or religious groups that acted, not as officers and agencies of the government, but as trustees responsible for the preservation of their institution's educational program and goals. The reason was simple enough: such schools were considered public schools because their education was providing a public service.

Only in the nineteenth century did public education become limited exclusively to nonsectarian, government-run and -financed schools. The question that needs answering is whether this development was consistent with a just public order for a society that was increasingly pluralistic. To help answer this question it is necessary to review briefly the development of the common school as it came into existence in Massachusetts and New York City. These two examples clearly illustrate how a monopolistic educational model came to be established as the basis for all public education. Eventually this model spread through the rest of the United States.

Massachusetts

Although there are many contrasts between the role and place of schools in the Bible commonwealth of the seventeenth century and the eighteenth-century republican Commonwealth of Massachusetts, the underlying concern for education remained the same. The 1780 Massachusetts constitution clearly stated that "the duty of legislators and magistrates, in all future periods of this Commonwealth, [is] to cherish the interests of literature and the sciences," and "to encourage private societies and public institutions" in the promotion of agriculture, sciences, commerce, the trades, and the arts.[4]

According to this constitution, both private societies and public institutions were to be encouraged in their educational enterprise. Private societies or academies played an important educational role in Massachusetts and in many other states in the late eighteenth and early nineteenth centuries.[5] The academy was organized as a corporate entity with its own board of trustees, which hired a schoolmaster and teachers and raised funds for the institution. Michael Katz has labeled this model of public education "corporate voluntarism."[6] Because the academy's role in secondary education was widely recognized as serving a public interest, many states actively promoted its growth and development through grants of land and money. This was the case, as Katz points out, because in the early republican period "'public' implied the performance of broad social functions and the service of a large, heterogeneous, nonexclusive clientele rather than control and ownership by the community or state."[7]

In this respect the practice of the Massachusetts legislature, beginning in 1797 and lasting well into the nineteenth century, of offering land grants to academies to promote their establishment in every county was similar to government support for academies in other areas of the country. The actual curricula, size, interests of promoters, location (urban/rural), and quality of the academies defy any generalization. However, in an effort to bring some order and to guarantee some standards, the common school movement developed in Massachusetts in the 1820s. Common schools, first elementary and later secondary, challenged and eventually replaced the academies as the dominant educational institutions of the state.

The common school movement, referred to by Katz as "incipient bureaucracy," attacked both the "corporate voluntarism" of the academies as well as the "democratic localism" of early community schools.[8] The structure of "democratic localism" was the district system in which each ward of a city or small town managed its own school. The district system emerged in the colonial era when it was assumed that an essentially homogeneous people could agree on basic religious and cultural values. The growth of an increasingly pluralistic society challenged the viability of this structure, because the rivalry between groups within most communities, city wards, or neighborhoods fostered political competition for control of the local school "in order to ensure the propagation of particular points of view, or, at least, the exclusion of rival ones."[9]

Leading figures such as Horace Mann and Henry Barnard attacked democratic localism for the reason that it permitted "51 per cent of the local parents to dictate the religious, moral, and political ideas taught to the children of the remainder."[10] One of the ironies of this criticism, however, is that the bureaucratic control of local schools at the state level, as envisioned by the reformers such as Mann and Barnard, presupposed the same majoritarian political principle. Under the common school plan it was possible for 51 percent of voting adults (if not a small dictatorial, educational elite) to determine the religious, moral, and political ideas taught to everyone in the entire state, not just a local community.

One of the chief concerns of the common school reformers was to articulate and bring to bear the Enlightenment's messianic belief in nonsectarian public education for their own day. The public school movement did not develop in a vacuum—it was created by heirs of the Enlightenment. And what they created, as David Tyack has pointed out, was not "a 'private' school affected with the public interest, not a 'public' school supported in part by private charity—(but) a school controlled by publicly elected or appointed officials, financed from the public treasury."[11] And, it should be added, this public system came to provide a statewide, nonsectarian, though still largely Protestant, education.

Horace Mann (1796–1859), the organizer and first secretary of the Massachusetts State Board of Education, was the preeminent apostle of religious nondenominationalism in the public schools.[12] Strongly influenced by Unitarianism, Mann was concerned that the theological differences that divided the numerous sects should remain in the home and church, while in the public schools the "common" Christian beliefs should provide the basis for the child's moral and religious development. In his mind "the Religion of Heaven should be taught to children, while the creeds of men should be postponed until their Minds were sufficiently matured to weigh Evidence and Arguments."[13] This is in fact the familiar Jeffersonian distinction between religion as a common moral code and religion as a private promotion of sectarian dogmas and beliefs. Mann's "Religion of Heaven" referred to the nonsectarian ethical standards of Protestantism, while the "creeds of men" were the sectarianism that divided people into many and often hostile denominations. Mann's goal was to create, through the public schools, a homogeneous community based upon a common morality.

The success of educational innovators such as Mann was not assured at the outset. In the 1840s the proponents of democratic localism attempted to check the influence and as yet limited power of the Massachusetts Board of Education and the state's normal schools.[14] A Committee on Education of the House of Representatives recommended in 1840 the abolition of both the Board of Education and the normal schools because of the danger of attempting to base all schools and teachers upon one perspective or model as was done in France and Prussia.[15] The House committee argued:

> Undoubtedly, common schools may be used as a potent means of engrafting into the minds of children, political, religious and moral opinions; —but, in a country like this, where such diversity of sentiments exists, especially upon theological subjects, and where morality is considered a part of religion and is, to some extent, modified by sectarian views, the difficulty and danger of attempting to introduce these subjects into our schools, according to one fixed and settled plan, to be decided by a Central Board, must be obvious. The right to mold the political, moral and religious opinions of his children, is a right exclusively and jealously reserved by our own laws to every parent; and for the government to attempt, directly or indirectly, as to these matters, to stand in the parent's place, is an undertaking of very questionable policy. Such an attempt cannot fail to excite a feeling of jealousy, with respect to our public schools the results of which could not but be disastrous.[16]

The House committee challenged the position of the educational reformers that public education could avoid feelings of jealousy by being neutral toward all perspectives. The committee pointed out that religion and politics so permeated all subjects that neutrality was never possible and went on to argue that even if neutrality were possible it would not be desirable, because "A book, upon politics, morals, or religion, containing no party or sectarian views, will be likely to leave the mind in a state of doubt and skepticism, much more to be deplored than any party or sectarian bias."[17] In the end, however, the critics failed by a narrow margin to abolish either the Board of Education or its normal schools. Nevertheless, the Massachusetts House committee report is upheld, in part, by such twentieth-century educational historians as Katz, who concludes:

> Schoolmen who thought they were promoting a neutral and classless—indeed, a common—school education, remained unwilling to perceive the extent of cultural bias inherent in their own writing and activity. However, the bias was central and not incidental to the standardization and administrative rationalization of public education. For, in the last analysis, the rejection of democratic localism rested only partly on its inefficiency and violation of parental prerogative. It stemmed equally from a gut fear of the cultural divisiveness inherent in the increasing religious and ethnic diversity of American life. Cultural homogenization played counterpoint to administrative rationality. Bureaucracy was intended to standardize far more than the conduct of public life.[18]

There is little question that there was a pressing need in Massachusetts and elsewhere for more educational opportunities for the countless numbers of urban children. Expanding educational opportunities for every person and upgrading professionalism, however, did not have to be synonymous with the establishment of government control over all public education. The fact that it was established is more a demonstration of the power of a majoritarian ideology than of the undisputed normativity of the structure.

New York City

The same majoritarian imposition that led to the establishment of a public school system in Massachusetts also occurred in New York City, although under somewhat different circumstances. Unlike Massachusetts, with its heritage of public support for schools, education in New York lacked community support until late in the eighteenth century.[19] In 1795 the state legislature appropriated $50,000 annually for five years as matching funds for towns that organized their own schools. Within a few years more than a thousand schools teaching almost 60,000 students dotted the state.[20] Encouraged by this development, the state legislature in 1805 set up a permanent school fund to support a public school system.[21]

For a time the educational history of New York City took a different course than the rest of the state. Rather than supporting district common schools as in upstate areas, moneys from the permanent school fund were used to support the city's existing church schools and the four charitable organizations that provided free education.[22] The allotment to both the denominational and charitable institutions was divided in proportion to the number of students given free education and was only to be used for teachers' salaries.[23] This system of subsidized educational pluralism was unique in the state, but it did not survive the growing pressure of the common school movement.[24]

During New York City's early history the immigrant population was made up primarily of American-born white Protestants of Dutch or English descent. In 1800 New York was more than 95 percent Protestant divided into many denominations and sects. This comparatively homogeneous population remained stable until the early 1820s, when large-scale immigration of poor Irish began.[25] By 1830 the Irish of New York City comprised a significant ethnic community with its own newspapers, social clubs, professional elites, and schools.

The expanding presence and growing significance of Catholics challenged the Protestant majority in New York City. In 1831 the directors of a Roman Catholic orphan asylum pressed the Catholic claim for a proportional share of the public school fund before the common council.[26] The petition went before the board of aldermen, and after a great deal of debate, by the margin of one vote, the board decided to include the asylum in the list of schools entitled to receive public funds. It then sent the measure on to the board of assistants.[27]

Protestants and supporters of the Public School Society were outraged. The board of assistants was acutely conscious of the political pressure from all sides and on September 5, 1831, referred the whole question to a law committee to report on the constitutionality of the ordinance. The report of the committee was important not only for the fate of the Catholic claim but also as a clear indication of the future direction of the legal debate surrounding education.

The report concluded that Catholic schools were not entitled to public funds because they were not "common" schools. A common school was defined as one open to all in which "those branches of education, and those only, ought to be taught, which tend to prepare a child for the ordinary business of life."[28] The report continued by arguing that, "if religion be taught in a school, it strips it of one of the characteristics of a common school, as all *religious* and *sectarian* studies have a direct reference to a future state, and *are not necessary* to prepare a child for the mechanical or any other business."[29]

Such a moral judgment about the relevance of religion to everyday life was itself clearly a religious judgment, though a judgment made on supposedly neutral, nonreligious, "secular" grounds. While a vast majority of Protestants in the city would *not* have agreed that religion was irrelevant to everyday life, they were content to support a supposedly neutral, nonreligious, "secular" argument if it meant that Catholics would be excluded from participating in the common school fund. Years later this legal argument would be championed by secularists who rejected traditional religion but who are nevertheless deeply religious in their secular worldview. The origin of the secularist argument, however, dates from a time when defenders of orthodox Christianity were in the majority.

The duplicity of Protestants supporting a supposedly neutral, nonreligious, secular argument is highlighted by the declaration in the Law Committee's report that the schools of the Public School Society were legitimately common schools and thus had a just and legal claim to the school fund even though "a portion of the Scriptures is read in the morning by the teachers, without comment."[30] Actually, the Society's schools required far more than the reading of a portion of Scripture without comment. In 1830 the board of trustees published a "manual" that was to be used by teachers in the primary departments at the beginning of school. The opening exercise for the youngest children contained in part the following recitation:

> *Teacher.* My dear children, the intention of this school is to teach you to be good and useful in this world, that you may be happy in the world to come. What is the intention of this school? . . .
>
> *T.* We therefore first teach you to "remember your Creator in the days of your youth." What do we first teach you? . . .

T. It is our duty to teach you this, because we find it written in the Holy Bible. Why is it our duty to teach you this? . . .

T. The Holy Bible directs us to "train you in the way you should go." . . .

T. Therefore, my children, you must obey your parents.

Scholar. I must obey my parents.

T. You must obey your teachers.

S. I must obey my teachers.

T. God always sees you. (*Slowly, and in a soft tone.*)

S. God always sees me.

T. God hears all you say.

S. God hears all I say.

T. God knows all you do.

S. God knows all I do. . . .

T. May all you, dear children, learn, while attending this school, to be good and useful in this world.

S. May we all, while attending this school, learn to be good and useful in this world.

T. And, with God's blessing, may you be happy in the world to come.

S. And, with God's blessing, may we be happy in the world to come.[31]

In light of this required "profession of faith" in the schools of the Public School Society, it is difficult to accept the Law Committee's finding that Catholic schools failed but the Society's schools passed a "secular" test for determining what constitutes a common school. The secular/religious distinction is only understandable as a self-serving definition used by Protestants with political power to exclude Catholics from participating in the common school fund.

Roman Catholics argued that the law committee's report established an unjust system of public funding for schools because "Jews, Christians of every denomination, deists, and unbelievers of every description, contribute their due portion to the school fund, and it ought to be so distributed and disposed so that all may participate in the benefits."[32] The Catholic argument continued:

> It would be but a poor consolation to an individual to know that he may entertain whatever religious opinion he pleases, and attend any church he may select, and at the same time be legally compelled to contribute a portion of his property to the support of a school in which religious doctrines diametrically opposed to those he entertains are taught.[33]

Thus, from the Catholic point of view, the consolidation of the public school in the hands of Protestants who insisted upon the inculcation of their perspective in education was a violation of a minority's religious rights. They stressed that the very reading of Scripture in school without comment was a sectarian Protestant practice. It was, therefore, impossible for them in good conscience to send their children to such institutions. But the law committee's report rejected this Catholic argument and set forth a basically secular/religious test as the norm for determining what qualified as a public school.

234

By the late 1830s the school issue became embroiled in the growing anti-Catholic agitation and the complex party struggles of New York politics. While the increasing numbers of Irish immigrants were welcomed as needed toilers in a growing industrial society, their presence aroused the nativist sentiments of that era's swelling American nationalism. The clannishness of the Irish, their habits, their poverty, and above all their intense religious loyalties to the Catholic Church were interpreted by nativists as a threat to an established way of life. The nativist movement in New York was mirrored in other parts of the country as immigrants experienced the plight of a minority in a majoritarian-minded society.[34]

In New York City the Democratic party attracted the bulk of the Irish vote,[35] while the beleaguered conservative and aristocratic Whig organization identified itself with the growing nativist movement. A group of young upstate Whigs, on the other hand, decided on a different course. For reasons of politics (to break the Irish-Democratic party coalition) and justice, Whigs led by William Henry Seward began championing the immigrant cause.[36]

As a result of the Panic of 1837 and divisions within the Democratic party, the Whigs won the governorship in 1838. Encouraged by the victory, the party hoped to broaden its base of political support. In 1839 Seward, in his inaugural message as governor, responded to the needs of the vast number of immigrants. He was particularly concerned about the state's role in education, and one of the educational reforms he proposed dealt specifically with the plight of the German and Irish immigrants. There should be, he said, "schools in which their children shall enjoy advantages of education equal to our own, with free toleration of their peculiar creeds and instructions."[37]

In 1840 Governor Seward followed up this general statement with a more specific recommendation calling for "the establishment of schools in which they [immigrant children] may be instructed by teachers speaking the same language as themselves and professing the same faith."[38] The Catholics in New York City responded to the governor's message by pressing their long-standing claim to a proportional share of the common school fund. The cause was led by the newly appointed Bishop John Hughes.[39]

In a petition to the New York board of aldermen, Bishop Hughes argued that a monopoly of state fund for education was controlled by a private corporation that had as one of its goals the "early religious instruction" of children.[40] He went on to point out the obvious bias expressed toward Catholics in the "early religious instruction" and insisted that correction of the errors could not be possible *without giving just ground for exception to other denominations.*[41] In this argument Hughes clearly set forth the fundamental dilemma created by every effort to maintain a majoritarian, monopolistic public school system in a religiously pluralistic society. He pointed out that it was impossible for professing Christians to teach the "essentials of religion" without offending the conscience of some other

Christians, because there would always be differences among Christians as to what the "essentials of religion" should be. And if it was assumed that religion could be completely dismissed from education, then students would be left "to the advantage of infidelity."[42] The fundamental dilemma of a majoritarian, monopolistic educational structure was plain. Since education would always be religious (never neutral) in some form, whether Protestant, Catholic, secular, or something else, a majoritarian system would always offend the religious conscience of those in the minority.

The Public School Society and a group of Protestant clergymen replied that Hughes's charges were absurd. Pratt documents the fierce counterattack launched to depict the Catholic Church as a despotic monster and an un-American institution.[43] The press and city Whigs joined in the anti-Catholic crusade and attacked Governor Seward for his position on the school question. Democrats in turn used Whig attacks "to convince Irish voters that Seward was deceiving them, that he could not deliver on his school proposals because his party was not behind him."[44]

The proposed solution by the Catholics to the educational imposition of cultural, class, and religious values on their children would have returned New York City to its original practice of dividing the public school money proportionally among all the schools offering free education. The common council rejected this solution, arguing that such action would compromise the separation of church and state. While there was a willingness on the part of the council and the Public School Society to see changes in some of the most offensive passages in school textbooks, the assumption continued to reign supreme that nonsectarian religious education did not violate the civil or religious freedom of any patriotic American. Flagrant nativism, combined with religious/philosophical assumptions about the nature of religion, led many to reject the Catholic argument.

With the common council's sustained rejection of Catholic demands for justice in education, Catholics decided to take their case before the state legislature. Although they were unsuccessful in getting funds for their schools, they were able to exert enough political pressure to convince politicians that some kind of solution to the issue had to be found.[45] The times were changing, and politicians, particularly Democrats (in true Jacksonian fashion), began attacking the New York Public School Society as a dangerous private monopoly over which the public had no direct control. The political debate resulted in a new school law that passed the legislature in 1842. The law allowed the Society to continue to operate its schools, but only as district public schools under the supervision of an elected board of education and state superintendent of common schools. In districts where a *majority* did not want to support the Society's schools, the people could establish new district schools supported by public funds.[46]

A crucial provision of the law prohibited the granting of public funds to any school in which "any religious sectarian doctrine or tenet shall be taught, inculcated, or practiced."[47] While Catholics thus failed to achieve their original demand for the incorporation of their schools into the public system, the law did break the citywide monopolistic hold of the Public School Society. The structural consequences of this political development, however, meant little for the future of public education. In reality the only change, to use Katz's categories once again, was that the monopolistic structure of a paternalistic voluntary school system was transformed into a professional, bureaucratic, monopolistic structure of state government.

Catholics realized that the majoritarian, monopolistic structure would remain. Since they were in the minority, the only way for them to have schools that reflected their worldview was to build and operate them at their own expense while continuing to pay taxes for the support of a majoritarian school system. Once Bishop Hughes became convinced that parents' and children's rights to a proportional share of the educational funds would not be realized, he decided to abandon public education and devote much of his remaining life to the building of a privately financed parochial school system in New York.[48] The Bishop was so convinced of the need for Catholic education that whenever he appointed a new pastor he insisted that the priest "proceed upon the principle that, in this age and this country, the school is before the church."[49] Vincent Lannie credits Hughes with being one of the first bishops to urge the development of a Catholic school system as an integral part of the American Catholic Church.[50] The bishop's educational vision was officially implemented by The Third Plenary Council of Baltimore in 1884, which required every pastor to establish a school within two years and all Catholic parents to send their children to a Catholic school whenever one was available.[51]

An irony of the Protestant/Catholic educational struggle in New York is that in the end education for both Protestants and Catholics was defined by an essentially Jeffersonian-Enlightenment public-legal structure for schools. It must be emphasized that the victory did not come easily. But what eventually emerged was a majoritarian, monopolistic public school establishment that would have delighted Jefferson and his Enlightenment visionaries. Protestants paved the way for this development. In their effort to avoid allocation of public funds to Catholics they championed a non-pluralistic conceptual framework for education that satisfied their immediate political objectives and religious prejudices.

Consequences of the Struggle over School Funding

It is important to make clear exactly what can be learned from the Massachusetts and New York school controversies. Educational historians have often used Massachusetts and New York as paradigm cases for the triumph of secularism in public education. Most often such works reflect less the actual historical situation than the authors' commitment that schooling *should* be secular, managed by professionals, and supported and funded by the state.[52]

Fortunately such biased historical interpretation has been corrected by recent scholarship. Timothy L. Smith, David Tyack, and others have demonstrated the significant nineteenth-century evangelical Protestant influence and control in the common school movement.[53] This was particularly the case in the new western communities where Protestant ministers were often the founders, teachers, and directors of the common schools.[54] Lyman Beecher's *Plea for the West* is a classic statement of missionary concern for schooling and a clear demonstration that schools and churches were allies in the quest to establish the Kingdom of God in America.[55] The continuing Protestant influence in the common school movement is thus important to keep in mind.

While there is the danger of wanting to conclude too much from the Massachusetts and New York school controversies, it is clear that the 1842 New York and 1855 Massachusetts laws prohibiting the granting of public funds to sectarian schools were extremely important. Both in Massachusetts and New York the variety of public educational structures that originally existed in the first half of the nineteenth century gave way to the common school movement, which in turn led to the governmental centralization and monopolization of all funding for public primary and secondary education.

In contrast to this development, England settled its religious/educational controversy in the 1840s by extending state grants to educational societies representing Wesleyans and Roman Catholics. Thus in England, while a monopolistic, Anglican ecclesiastical establishment continued, a system of subsidized pluralism emerged to support schools. This principle of multiple establishment was rejected in the United States during the eighteenth-century debate over multiple church/state establishment.[56] In the new republic all churches were disestablished, but they were replaced by monopolistic public school systems in the several states that tolerated other schools only if they paid their own way.

To be sure, this was a historical process that came slowly in some states and more rapidly in others. By the time of the Civil War, five states—Wisconsin, Michigan, Indiana, Oregon, and Minnesota—had constitutional provisions against the use of public funds for sectarian purposes.[57] These constitutional provisions were in part a Protestant response to the school conflict in New York; the nativist reaction had indeed spread throughout the country.

Many of the western states that came into the Union after the Civil War also constitutionally prohibited religious instruction in public schools. This reflected a continuation of prewar nativist sentiments at the federal level.

President Grant used the occasion of his annual message to Congress in 1875 to help gain nativist support for the Republican party. Grant proposed a constitutional amendment that would specifically prohibit any public funds for the direct or indirect aid of any religious sect and prohibit the teaching in public schools of any "religious, atheistic, or pagan tenets."[58] Grant's proposal led to a Republican drive in the House of Representatives to change the First Amendment of the Constitution.

The Republican national convention followed the lead of Grant and the Republican leadership in Congress. A specific plank in the Republican platform contended that

> The public school system of the several States is the bulwark of the American Republic; and with a view of its security and permanence, we recommend an amendment to the Constitution of the United States forbidding the application of any public funds or property for the benefit of any school or institution under sectarian control.[59]

Although the Republicans were eventually successful in the 1876 presidential election, their desire for a constitutional amendment failed to achieve the necessary two-thirds support in the Senate. Congress was successful, however, in passing legislation that required all new states admitted to the Union after 1876 to adopt an irrevocable ordinance that not only guaranteed religious freedom but required the states to include provision "for the establishment and maintenance of systems of public schools, which shall be open to all the children of said States and free from sectarian control."[60] The legislation was applicable to North Dakota, South Dakota, Montana, and Washington. The same provision was contained in the Enabling Act of Utah, Oklahoma, New Mexico, and Arizona. The Idaho and Wyoming constitutions contained similar provisions.[61]

By the end of the nineteenth century, the United States Congress had not yet provided funds for public education. It had determined through federal legislation, however, that specific states were required to establish and control nonsectarian public schools. In the twentieth century the federal government finally secured the preferential fiscal rights of majoritarian, monopolistic public schools in every state of the union. It did so by means of decisions of the Supreme Court.

Concluding Reflections

The Supreme Court enshrined for the first time a strict separationist interpretation on the First Amendment Establishment Clause in *Everson v. Board of Education* (1947) and *McCollum v. Board of Education* (1948). It did so by setting forth the standard of "absolute separation" of church and state in disallowing state aid to religious schools.[62] The Court thus read Jefferson's call for a "wall of separation between church and state" as the necessary meaning of the First Amendment.

The legal doctrine of strict separation essentially remained unchallenged from 1947 to 1989. According to John Witte:

> In nearly forty cases, the Court largely removed religion from the public school and largely removed religious schools from state patronage. In *Lemon v. Kurtzman* (1971), the Court demanded that all laws must (1) have a secular purpose; (2) have a primary effect that neither advances nor inhibits religion; and (3) foster no excessive entanglement between church and state. This constitutional reification of separationist logic rendered the First Amendment Establishment Clause a formidable weapon for lower courts to outlaw many remaining forms and forums of church-state cooperation.[63]

Professor Witte goes on to point out that more recently the Supreme Court "has abandoned much of this strict separationism in favor of other principles of religious liberty—neutrality, accommodationism, noncoercion, equal treatment, and nonendorsement most prominently."[64] It is therefore reasonable to suggest that there are legal as well as other signs to indicate that, just as the original church-state establishment succumbed to forces of diversity and erosion of ideological underpinnings, disestablishment a second time is well underway in reference to the preferential fiscal rights of majoritarian, monopolistic public schools in the United States. And if history is a worthy instructor, it is also reasonable to conclude that just as a greater measure of public justice emerged from the first disestablishment it is very likely to do so again in the wake of this second disestablishment. This would mean a return to an earlier nonexclusivistic definition of public education that did not limit public funding to schools owned and operated by the state. The argument of this paper is that such a development would be consistent with this country's earliest history and also with a contemporary view of a just public order for our highly pluralistic society.[65]

Notes

1. This point is made clear by Jefferson in his autobiography. See Paul Leicester Ford, ed., *The Writings of Thomas Jefferson* (New York: G. P. Putnam's Sons, 1899).

2. For a more detailed discussion of the educational vision of Jefferson, Rush, and Webster, consult Rockne M. McCarthy, James W. Skillen, and William A. Harper, *Disestablishment a Second Time: Genuine Pluralism for American Schools* (Grand Rapids, MI: Christian University Press (Eerdmans), 1982), 30–51.

3. Bernard Bailyn, *Education in the Forming of American Society: Needs and Opportunities for Study* (Chapel Hill: University of North Carolina Press, 1960), 11. See also John S. Whitehead, *The Separation of College and State: Columbia, Harvard, and Yale, 1776–1876* (New Haven, CT: Yale University Press, 1973).

4. "Massachusetts Constitution of 1780, Chapter V, Section II." Reprinted in Francis Newton Thorpe, ed., *Federal and State Constitutions* (Washington: Government Printing Office, 1909), 5:467.

5. Theodore Sizer's study of the growth of academies in the United States reports that there were at least 6000 such institutions by the middle of the nineteenth century. Theodore Sizer, *The Age of Academies* (New York: Columbia University, Teachers College Press, 1964).

6. Michael B. Katz, *Class, Bureaucracy, and Schools: The Illusion of Educational Change in America* (New York: Praeger, 1971), 22. Katz defines "corporate voluntarism" as the conduct of *single* institutions as individual corporations. This is one of the four alternative patterns of public education that received support from state governments in the first half of the nineteenth century. Three other patterns analyzed by Katz are "democratic localism," "incipient bureaucracy," and "paternalistic voluntarism." Katz has made a significant contribution to a better understanding of the history of American education by uncovering and analyzing these different organizational patterns of early nineteenth-century public schools.

7. Ibid., 23.

8. Ibid., 15–22.

9. Ibid., 28. For other defects in democratic localism, see 15–22; 28–30.

10. Ibid., 28.

11. David B. Tyack, *Turning Points in American Educational History* (Waltham, MA: Blaisdell Publishing, 1967), 125.

12. A most insightful and penetrating analysis of Mann's worldview and educational philosophy is in Charles L. Glenn, *The Myth of the Common School* (Amherst: University of Massachusetts Press, 1988).

13. "Horace Mann to Frederick Packard, July 22, 1838," in Raymond B. Culver, *Horace Mann and Religion in Massachusetts Public Schools* (New Haven, CT: Yale University, 1929), 267.

14. For a detailed analysis of the political battles between supporters of district schools and the educational reformers, see Michael B. Katz, *The Irony of Early School Reform: Educational Innovation in Mid-Nineteenth Century Massachusetts* (Boston: Beacon Press, 1968), especially Part I, "Reform Imposition: Social Origins of Educational Controversy," 19–112. For a discussion of the struggle at the turn of the century in other parts of the country, see David B. Tyack, "City Schools: Centralization of Control at the Turn of the Century," in *Building the Organizational Society: Essays on Associational Activities in Modern America,* ed. Jerry Israel (New York: The Free Press, 1972).

15. The use of schooling to inculcate values and political order was a feature of both European liberalism (French educational writers after the 1780 revolution) and European conservatism (Prussia in the nineteenth century).

16. "Report of the Committee on Education of the House of Representatives, March 7, 1840," in Rush Welter, comp., *American Writings on Popular Education; The Nineteenth Century* (Indianapolis: Bobbs-Merrill, 1971), 91. Orestes Brownson also opposed the establishment of a centralized state school system. He warned his fellow Massachusetts citizens that "We may as well have a religion established by law as a system of education, and the government educate and appoint the pastors of our churches, as well as the instructors of our children." Katz, *Class, Bureaucracy, and Schools,* 18.

17. "Report of the Committee," 92. The House committee's argument also included the following:

> That must, indeed, be an uninteresting course of reading, which would leave untouched either of these subjects [religion and politics]; and he must be a heartless writer, who can treat religious or political subjects, without affording any indication of his political or religious opinions. Books that confine themselves to the mere statement of undisputed propositions, whether in

politics, religion, or morals, must be meager indeed; nor is it possible to abstract, from treatises on these subjects, all that would give offence, without abstracting at the same time, the whole substance of the matter. Mere abstract propositions are of very little interest—it is their practical application to particular cases, in which all readers, and especially young readers, are principally interested. It is not sufficient, and it ought not to be, that a book contains nothing which we believe to be false. If it omit to state what we believe to be true; if it founds itself upon vague generalities, which will equally serve the purpose of all reasoners alike, this very omission to state what we believe to be the truth, becomes, in our eyes, a fault of the most serious character.

18. Katz, *Class, Bureaucracy, and Schools,* 39. The issue of motivation is crucial to a proper interpretation of the educational reformers. It is not being suggested, as many radical historians do, that a "conspiracy of class or self-interest" was the primary motivation of the nineteenth-century urban schoolmen and their supporters. For the most part the reformers sincerely believed that their culture, values, and religion were best for all people and thus should be the norm for all of society. The habit of overriding the rights of minorities became institutionalized, defended, and perpetuated, not so much as a planned "conspiracy" than as a consequence of the "imposition of majoritarian beliefs." The schoolmen and their supporters succeeded not because of a cunningly conceived strategy but because their Anglo-Saxon, Protestant, class commitments were shared by a majority of Americans. The power of the state was used by the majority to establish a way of life judged to be normative for every citizen.

19. For an overview of the educational scene in New York City before the nineteenth century as well as a statistical accounting of the educational opportunities available between 1638 and 1782, see Lawrence Arthur Cremin, *American Education: The Colonial Experience, 1607–1783* (New York: Harper and Row, 1970), 534–41; and C. J. Mahoney, *The Relation of the State to Religious Education in Early New York, 1633–1825* (Washington, DC: Catholic University of America Press, 1941), chapter 1.

20. Diane Ravitch, *The Great School Wars, New York City, 1805–1973* (New York: Basic Books, 1974), 7.

21. Ibid.

22. By the legislative act passed on March 12, 1813, the Commissioners of School Moneys were directed to pay the moneys received by them to "the trustees of the Free School Society in the city of New York and to the trustees of teachers of the Orphan Asylum Society, the Society of the Economical School in the city of New York, the African Free School, and of such incorporated religious societies in said city as now support, or hereafter shall establish, charity schools within the said city, who may apply for the same." Quoted in W. M. Oland Bourne, *History of the Public School Society of the City of New York* (New York: W. M. Wood and Co., 1870), 725.

23. The 1813 law stated that the "distribution shall be made to each school in proportion to the average number of children between the ages of four and sixteen years taught therein the year preceding such distribution, free of expense." Ibid, 68.

24. John Webb Pratt offers the following explanation for the development of New York City's subsidized, pluralized structure of education:

> The explanation for the arrangement, seemingly contradicted by the policy of publicly managed schools enacted for upstate in 1812, was that the idea of public education did not yet include a clear-cut distinction between 'public' and 'private' means of education. The state saw as its objective the encouragement of teaching in good citizenship. Schools as physical entities were but means to this end, requiring the public's serious attention only where such buildings were nonexistent, as was the case upstate but not in New York City. To a government of limited means, there were also obvious economies in such a policy.

John Webb Pratt, *Religion, Politics, and Diversity: The Church-State Theme in New York History* (Ithaca, NY: Cornell University Press, 1967), 165–66.

25. The standard work on immigration in this period is M. L. Hansen, *The Atlantic Migration, 1607–1860* (New York: Harper and Row, 1961).

26. Bourne, *History of the Public School Society of the City of New York*, 124.

27. Ibid., 132.

28. Ibid., 134.

29. Ibid., 136 (italics added).

30. Ibid.

31. Portions of "Manual" reprinted in ibid., 642–44 (italics in original).

32. Bourne, *History of the Public School Society of the City of New York*, 139.

33. Ibid.

34. For an analysis of the nativist movement see Ray Billington, *The Protestant Crusade, 1800–1860* (Gloucester, MA: Peter Smith, 1964).

35. The details of the political struggle in New York are discussed by John Webb Pratt, *Religion, Politics and Diversity*, especially chapter 7, "Church, State and Education."

36. For research that demonstrates Seward's true commitment to minority rights, see Henry J. Browne, "Public Support of Catholic Education in New York, 1825–1842: Some New Aspects," *The Catholic Historical Review* 39 (1953); and Vincent Lannie, *Public Money and Parochial Education: Bishop Hughes, Governor Seward, and the New York School Controversy* (Cleveland: Case Western Reserve University, 1968), 1–28.

37. William Henry Seward, quoted in Glyndon G. Van Deusen, "Seward and the School Question Reconsidered," *The Journal of American History* 52 (1965): 313.

38. Ibid., 314. As to exactly what Seward had in mind with his proposal, Van Deusen points out that "It is clear enough what sort of teachers he wished for the children of foreigners, but he did not indicate whether he wished them to teach in public or parochial institutions. A few years later he told a friend that what he had in mind was 'to let the Catholics support schools of their own and receive their own share of the public monies,' but this may have been in hindsight." Ibid. John Webb Pratt's research supports Seward's contention that he "was suggesting that the state support sectarian schools, more specifically Catholic schools." Pratt, *Religion, Politics and Diversity*, 176.

39. For a discussion of the Catholic position before the arrival of Bishop Hughes, see Browne, "Public Support," 1–11. John R. G. Hassard has written a biography of Bishop Hughes, *Life of the Most Reverend John Huges* (New York: Appleton and Co., 1865).

40. Petition quotes from the Public School Society's 1827 Report. The entire petition is printed in Welter, *American Writings*, 98–109.

41. Ibid., 104 (italics added).

42. Ibid., 105. Hughes formulated the dilemma in the following way: The Public School Society members

> profess to exclude all sectarianism from their schools. If they do not exclude sectarianism, they are avowedly no more entitled to the school funds than your petitioners, or any other denomination of professing Christians. If they do, as they profess, exclude sectarianism, then your petitioners contend that they exclude Christianity; and leave to the advantage of infidelity the tendencies which are given to the minds of youth by the influence of this feature and pretension of their system." Ibid.

43. Pratt, *Religion, Politics and Diversity*, 178.

44. Ibid., 179. For an important theoretical defense made in 1841 by the New York secretary of state, John C. Spencer, in support of the Catholic claim that justice demanded a proportional share of public funds for their schools, see Rockne McCarthy et al., *Society, State, and Schools: A Case for Structural and Confessional Pluralism* (Grand Rapids, MI: Eerdmans, 1980), 90–92.

45. For a discussion of the direct Catholic venture into politics (the Catholic ticket of 1841) see ibid., 183–86.

46. Ibid., 183.

47. Quoted in ibid., 187. The Massachusetts school struggle culminated in a similar law. A constitutional amendment of 1855 stated:

> All moneys raised by taxation in the towns and cities for the support of public schools, all moneys which may be appropriated by the state for the support of common schools, shall be applied to, and expended in, no other schools than those which are conducted according to law, under the order and superintendence of the authorities of the town or city in which the money is to be expended; and such moneys shall never be appropriated to any religious sect for the maintenance, exclusively, of its own school.

Eighteenth amendment to the Massachusetts constitution, adopted 1885; see Francis Newton Thorpe, ed., *Federal and State Constitutions* (Washington, DC: Government Printing Office, 1909), 1918.

48. Lannie, *Public Money and Parochial Education*, x.

49. Quoted in ibid.

50. Ibid.

51. Ibid., xi.

52. Ibid., 193. Lawrence Cremin discusses this historiographical tradition in *The Wonderful World of Ellwood Patterson Cubberly* (New York: Teachers College Press, 1965).

53. Timothy L. Smith, "Protestant Schooling," and David Tyack, "The Kingdom of God and the Common School: Protestant Ministers and the Educational Awakening in the West," both in *Harvard Educational Review* 36 (1966): 447–69; Robert Michaelsen, *Piety in the Public Schools: Trends and Issues in the Relationship between Religion and the Public School in the U.S.* (New York: Macmillan, 1970); Donald Pitzer, "Christianity in the Public Schools," in *Protest and Politics,* ed. Robert G. Clouse, Robert D. Linder, and Richard V. Pierard (Greenwood, SC: The Attic Press, 1968), 151–81.

54. Presbyterian and Congregational ministers representing New England missionary societies or the American Home Mission Society combined with Baptist and Methodist preachers to guarantee that frontiersmen did not escape Christian civilization by falling victim to Romanism, barbarism, and skepticism.

55. Lyman Beecher, *Plea for the West* (New York: Leavitt, Lord, & Co., 1835).

56. Before the American Revolution, in New York, Maryland, and South Carolina the traditional pattern of establishment of a "single" church had evolved toward a "multiple" form of Christian establishment. See Cushing Strout, *The New Heavens and the New Earth: Political Religion in America* (New York: Harper and Row, 1973), 83–84; and R. Freeman Butts, *The American Tradition in Religion and Education* (Boston: Beacon Press, 1950).

57. Wisconsin (1848), Article 1, section 18, 4078–79; Michigan (1850), Article 4, section 40, 1950; Indiana (1851), Article 1, section 6, 1074; Oregon (1857), Article 1, section 5, 2998; and Minnesota (1857), Article 1, section 16. Found in Thorpe, *Federal and State Constitutions*.

58. President Grant, quoted in R. Freeman Butts, *The American Tradition in Religion and Education* (Boston: Beacon Press, 1950). Grant urged there be a complete and absolute

separation between church and state. This included doing away with tax exemptions for church property.

59. Ibid., 143.

60. Illinois ex rel. McCollum v. Board of Education, 333 U.S. 203 (1948), 469.

61. Ibid., 470. State constitutional provisions related to the funding of schools are many and varied. See James R. Brown, "State Constitutions and Religion in Education," in *Educational Freedom and the Case for Government Aid to Students in Independent Schools,* ed. Daniel D. McGarry and Leo Ward (Milwaukee: Bruce Publishing, 1966), 163–83.

62. See, for example Anson Phelps Stokes and Leo Pfeffer, *Church and State in the United States,* revised one-volume edition (New York: Harper and Row, 1964).

63. John Witte, Jr., "That Serpentine Wall of Separation," *Michigan Law Reviews: 2003 Survey of Books Related to the Law* 101, no. 6 (2003): 1904. Witte's essay reviews Daniel L. Dreisback, *Thomas Jefferson and the Wall of Separation between Church and State* (New York: New York University Press, 2002) and Philip Hamburger, *Separation of Church and State* (Cambridge, MA: Harvard University Press, 2002). The Dreisback and Hamburger works offer a penetrating critique and alternative to the Stokes/Pfeffer strict separationist interpretation of the First Amendment. For an overview of Witte's First Amendment Perspective see *Religion and the American Constitutional Experiment: Essential Rights and Liberties* (Boulder, CO: Westview Press, 2000).

64. Ibid., 1904.

65. For a much more in-depth public justice argument consult James W. Skillen, "Religion and Education Policy: Where Do We Go From Here?" *Journal of Law and Politics* 6, no. 3 (1990); and James W. Skillen, *The School-Choice Controversy: What Is Constitutional?* (Grand Rapids, MI: Baker Books, 1993). See also Charles L. Glenn, *The Ambiguous Embrace: Government and Faith-Based Schools and Social Agencies* (Princeton, NJ: Princeton University Press, 2000).

Me, My Students, and the I of Psychology:
Bridging the Gaps between Us

Sherri B. Lantinga[*]

....

As a social activity, teaching shapes selves in ways beyond adding knowledge of facts and theories. Good teaching, perhaps especially in psychology, should cause students to examine and develop their basic beliefs: Who am I? What is my place in this world? Christian teaching should go even further: students should develop a deepened awareness of how and who people were created to be and how sin taints our thinking, behavior, relationships, calling, and culture. Students' examined beliefs shape their social behaviors, which in turn will influence others' beliefs and actions. In the long run, psychology students at a Reformed college should be equipped to distinguish between who we are and who we should be;

[*] Dr. Lantinga is a Professor of Psychology at Dordt College. This essay is based on work done as part of the Pew-funded Calvin Summer Seminar program in 2001 and a Dordt College Studies Institute leave in 2003. Revised portions of this essay have been presented at the Midwest Institute on the Teaching of Psychology, at two Christian Schools International conferences, and in a book edited by Paul C. Vitz and Susan Felch, *The Self: Beyond the Postmodern Crisis* (Wilmington, DE: Intercollegiate Studies Institute, forthcoming).

between created norms and sinful distortions; between the pulls of a King-dom culture and a fallen culture. In short, they should be equipped to not just score well on standardized psychology tests but to also carry out dis-cerning pastoral and prophetic service in the larger Kingdom.

Why is good Christian teaching in psychology so difficult? I can think of at least two reasons. First, psychology has neglected its disciplinary mother: philosophy. Psychology texts and professors' graduate training programs tend to emphasize the "logy" (methods of study) of "psychology" that were inherited from our discipline's father: biology. In fact, psychologists are sometimes downright defensive about psychology being primarily a science; we continually fight the stereotype of psychology just being a fancy way of listening to and helping people with their problems. Perhaps because of our defensive stance on "logy," we rarely discuss what is meant by the "psyche" in psychology. Discussing such concepts falls outside the accepted scientific way of knowing in psychology; we cannot directly observe or measure the psyche, so it is not important to study. This neglect could also be caused by the strong secularism in psychology; discussing the "psyche" comes too close to discussing the soul.[1] Whatever its cause, the neglect of the *psyche* (or soul or self) for the sake of the *logy* shortchanges students and the larger community. As a discipline dedicated to studying the crown of creation, psychology has much to contribute to the discussion of who we are. This is especially the case for Reformed Christians interested in discerning how sin affects every area of human life.

A second reason for the difficulty of effective Christian teaching in psy-chology is the gap between student and teacher beliefs about the nature of people. As a Reformed Christian professor, I know that my basic beliefs about the nature of people and reality shape how I relate to students, how I decide what is important for them to know, and how I teach. As a psy-chologist, I know that students' basic assumptions influence what they see as important or interesting, what they ignore, and even what gets distorted to fit their preexisting framework of beliefs. I also know that Christians are strongly influenced by their faith and, perhaps equally strongly, by their culture. Therefore, even at a Christian college, my basic beliefs about people and those of my pop-culture-savvy students might not be the same. How can an effective teacher hope to bridge that gap?

In this essay, I will first describe data collected from Christian college students that reveal a relatively narrow understanding of the human self. To put this data in context, I will next present a biblically-based model of the human self that is also consistent with psychological research and theories.[2] I will end with suggestions for using the model as a way to teach psychol-ogy students torn between the pulls of their faith and Western cultural values.

College Student Understandings of the Self

I surveyed 221 undergraduates from four Christian liberal-arts schools (in Iowa, Illinois, Kentucky, and Oklahoma) to learn how students understand the self.[3] Almost every responding student self-identified as Christian and reported attending at least one religious service in the last month (the average student attended about two services per week).

Students were instructed to "write an essay on what you mean by the word 'self,'" and most students seemed to have difficulty articulating what they meant. Many students appealed to synonyms ("My self is my identity") or resorted to vague statements like "self is who I am," followed by a list of characteristics ("personality, beliefs, emotions"). Overall, however, the essays reflected Baumeister's observation that over the centuries "the concept of self [is] something increasingly hidden, abstract, and elusive. The self ceased to be equated with observable behavior and commitments, and it came to be understood as the cause and owner of the visible phenomena."[4] The students saw the self as a relatively static, subjective individuality: the self is the "inner core of one's being" known through internal reflection rather than through observable behaviors, relationships, or external commitments. Although many essays included the words "body" or "relationships," these were typically part of a laundry list of characteristics that merely influenced but were not integral to that inner being called the "self."

What was missing from the essays is striking given the strong Christian affiliation reported by the students: 72 percent of the essays did not even mention God or Jesus. Only one mentioned any form of religious process in connection to the self (e.g., profession of faith, baptism, sanctification). Not even a single essay mentioned the Holy Spirit, fruits of the Spirit, or the Bible. For professing Christians, it is odd (at best) that none of these central ideas was included in an explanation of the self. From a historical perspective, student essays reflected a late-modernist ideal of the self (Romantic era), but did not include early modernist ideas that would fit with a biblical perspective, such as the concepts of responsibility, reason, virtue, or morality. The historical retreat of the self from observable behaviors to the inner core may remove a sense of responsibility for things that are outside the inner self.

It is possible that the nature of the essay prompt itself shaped or limited students' responses. After all, a logical, coherent essay on an abstract concept is not an easy task. Further, students may never have taken the time to examine their beliefs about the self, so that what appeared in their essays was not a full description of their implicit beliefs. Therefore, I asked two other groups of Dordt students to respond to somewhat different prompts. One group (thirty-four students) wrote an essay "on what constitutes (e.g., makes up, composes) your 'self.'" This prompt personalized the concept of self rather than making it an abstract concept. The other group (thirty-nine students) drew "any sort of diagram that shows what you mean by the word *self*"; explanatory statements accompanied most of the resulting pictures. The diagrammed self and the personal self essays both revealed a richer understanding of the self than shown by the abstract "self" essays. Students still tended to focus on the internal, subjective self (e.g., "We are like presents. You don't know what is the true thing until you . . . slowly peel away layers and catch glimpses of the present inside"), but they were more likely to include religious ideas (e.g., image of God, faith, Bible), relationships, social roles, and physical contexts (e.g., body, the farm, United States).

In the end, Christian students tend to believe in a core, internal self that is hidden from other people unless they intentionally choose to reveal it. Some students' essays also indicated that the self is influenced by other people, God, and the physical body. Taken together, students' essays reflect an eclectic assortment of traditional religious views and late-modernist or Romantic views. Some call this emerging trend of religiously based, postmodern beliefs about the self "transmodernism" in order to distinguish it from the relativistic, secular stream of postmodernism.[5] There is much good in transmodernism, but how well do students' views of the self fit with a biblical perspective or one based on psychological research?

A Biblical Model of the Self

The Scriptures tell us that people are made in the image of God. But what does that mean? What makes us human rather than angels or monkeys or sea cucumbers? The model that I have developed to answer that question as I teach psychology is based on Scripture and is consistent with psychological research. This model is certainly not the only way to think about the human self; a popular time-management book suggests a somewhat similar framework[6] and the bio-psycho-social model explains many health-related behaviors.[7] However, my four-part model has been very useful in teaching psychology to Christian college students. It helps believers to make explicit their implicitly held beliefs and allows them to examine and deepen those beliefs as they learn about psychology.

As described below, the model's four aspects of the self are our embodied nature, our embedded or relational nature, our reflective ability, and our responsibility. Throughout my description, I assume (at least) three things. First, I assume that God is the creator and sustainer of everything that exists, including people; we did not make ourselves and we did not evolve from apes. Second, I believe that sin has wormed its way into every aspect of human life, tainting our bodies, our minds, our behaviors, and our multifaceted relationships. Third, I assume that all four parts of this model are heavily intertwined; they are artificially separated here to allow for closer examination of each.

We Are Bodies

We do not just have bodies, attached to or encasing ourselves, but we *are* bodies. The Bible has uncountable references to the body, sometimes using it as an allusion to the state of the person's relationship with God or with his/her culture. The most obvious references are the Genesis creation account, the Song of Solomon, and the passion story of Christ. But there are others, too: the physical beauty of Sarah, Rachel, and Queen Esther; King Eglon's great fatness (and apparent history of constipation) and deliverer Ehud's left-handedness (Judges 3); the prophet Eli's many physical ailments (1 Samuel 3–4); the sick persons whom Jesus heals; the footwashing before the Last Supper. At the transfiguration of Jesus, disciples Peter, James, and John do not just hear the voices of Moses and Elijah—they *see* the men; even the succinct Gospel of Mark takes time to mention this (Mark 9:2). The Apostle John reports seeing the angels and creatures and elders; he doesn't just hear voices or describe ghostly apparitions or disembodied souls (e.g., Revelation 5). I believe that the only disembodied voices in the Bible are God's [e.g., Moses on Mt. Sinai (Exodus 19); upon Jesus' baptism (Matthew 3:17)], and even God occasionally assumes a physical form (e.g., the burning bush, Jesus).

The body helps define what is "me." The way we talk about pain suggests that we assume the body is an integral part of who we are: we say "I hurt myself." People whose appearance has changed through injuries or scars can become different people. For example, "Burn patients who see themselves in a mirror for the first time . . . typically feel alien from their appearance. And yet they do not merely "get used" to it; their new skin changes them. It alters how they relate to people, what they expect of others, how they see themselves in others' eyes."[8] Persons who use wheelchairs may come to see the wheelchair as a part of themselves, somewhat like an experienced driver "wears" her car as she navigates it out of the garage. Neurologist and writer Oliver Sacks describes intriguing clinical tales of people whose sense of self is changed by nerve damage (including his own[9]). In one story, Sacks writes about a young patient who awoke in a hospital to find someone else's dead leg in bed with him. He was initially disgusted, then decided that the leg had been stolen from the autopsy room as a ghastly joke by the nurses. He attempted to throw the leg out of his bed but discovered to his horror that "when he threw it out of bed, he somehow came after it—and now it was attached to him. 'Look at it!' he cried. He seized it with both hands, with extraordinary violence, and tried to tear it off his body."[10] The young man's nerve damage made his brain unable to sense his own leg, and things we cannot sense are usually not a part of ourselves; thus, the man concluded that the insensate leg in his bed was not his own.

The very perspective from which we see the world, the ways that we anticipate acting in it, and our actions themselves are invariably shaped by our

251

bodies. Our height, our degree of physical fitness or physical disability, and our appearance influence how we act and how others act toward us. For example, give a three-year-old a camera, then notice how the pictures show a different world than the one you live in. If you have ever woken up with a cold sore or some other facial blemish, you know that that physical aspect of you influences your interpersonal behavior and your thoughts about yourself. Tall people are often given more status and respect by others than are short people. Because of their smaller size and strength, women are generally more likely to interpret ambiguous interactions with men as threatening. Our bodies reflect and help us enact our gender, which is the only demographic characteristic included in the Genesis creation account.

Consider nonverbal communication without a body. Can you do it? We constantly use our faces, hands, and posture to gesture, pray, hug, or hurt others, to welcome or to reject others. Even with e-mail, perhaps the most impersonal form of modern communication, we use "emoticons," which are typographical characters that allude to how our bodies would express our feelings. Our bodies are not just means of expression but *are* the expressions; they are the emotions themselves. Memory, personality, and emotions are all firmly connected to the body; injury to specific parts of the brain or the adrenal glands can dramatically alter a person's sense of self and behavior. Having a body allows one to experience and develop in the world.

We Are Relational

Antoine de Saint-Exupery, dying of thirst after crashing his plane in the Libyan desert in the 1930s, reflected in his diary that humans are utterly dependent on the world around them: "I had no notion that our self-sufficiency was so circumscribed."[11]

As St.-Exupery and others in extreme situations have discovered, humans cannot live in isolation; we are utterly and thoroughly connected to things that are outside of ourselves. In other words, we are embedded in a context of relationships. David Novak comments on Hermann Goering's son's decision to enter a monastery: ". . . so much of our being-in-the-world is not our own decision. Hermann Goering's son did not choose to be Hermann Goering's son; he did not choose to be born a German in the 1930s."[12] The Genesis account makes it clear that to thrive as humans we must be in proper relationship with our Creator God, with this place where we have been put, and with other people. We are not our own.

In relationship with God. Scriptures, creeds, and traditions attest to our relationship with God. God made and sustains us. God's love brings our selves into existence, and denying him does not negate the relationship: God sustains even avowed atheists by giving them food and water and love (as a Middle Eastern saying has it, "For the sake of the rose, the thorns get watered"[13]). Christians believe that God richly endows us with gifts and talents, so that recognizing our strengths is a way of "bragging on God" rather than bragging about oneself. Being self-aware also allows us to know our limits, to avoid taking on more than we can bear; we cannot properly worship God or care for others if we are burned out.[14] If faith is the activity by which we relate ourselves to God, then what affects the self will affect our faith. Pastor and psychologist Dale Ellens notes that childhood abuse may form a self that shuns a punitive God while a childhood of encouragement and respect can form a self that seeks out a loving God.[15]

Mainstream psychology almost completely ignores the God-person relationship, probably in part because it is not scientifically measurable. The rare consideration of this topic usually tries to relate religious beliefs to prejudice, altruism, do-not-resuscitate orders, or counseling strategies. Although this aspect of the self is probably the most foundational for believers, it is the most ignored by psychology.

In relationship with the creation. We are made out of God's good earth and we cannot live as humans apart from its gifts and its responsibilities. People are called to rule over the creatures as we name and care for them. God initially gives people plants and fruits to eat (Genesis 1:28–29) and after the Flood he also gives us the animals to eat (Genesis 9:3). Beyond just their food value, Job reminds his friends that the animals can teach us and remind us of God the Creator (Job 12:7–10). The creation can also serve as a means to relate to other people. For example, until the development of symbolic forms of wealth (money), people measured wealth with fish or sweet potatoes or pigs; because all three of these die and rot, wealth could not be hoarded but needed to be shared with others.[16]

We live in and are profoundly influenced by a background of geography, of history, of culture. Where we live, when we live, and the people amongst whom we live all shape how we view the good life, what we perceive to be important, and how we see ourselves.[17] Students from the Great Plains feel claustrophobic in forests or big cities; students from coastal cities prefer the bustle and hectic pace of crowded urban areas. The physical place of our background provides an inner "map" that tells us about who we are and whether we are in the right place, whether we are "at home." Some aspects of relating to place are individual: I think of a college student who missed caring for her family farm's baby pigs and another who missed caring for the gardens back home. Some aspects are more universal: we breathe deeply the after-rain smells outside, calling it fresh air and finding excuses to remain outside in it.

Our full relationship with creation is not possible without our body's sensory technologies, perhaps especially the eyes and skin.[18] For example, light energy that has bounced off from my son's dirty face enters my eye and is transduced into electrical-chemical energy that eventually gets matched with my memories (neural networks) of previous experiences in the world (this is my son, this is not how his face usually looks). The world that was outside my brain is now represented inside of it; the brain in its dark bunker never directly experiences the external creation but relies on messages sent from the body's front lines.

The way we interact with the creation gives us information about ourselves. We learn that as we move forward, everything near us visually appears to stream backward. Experiencing this visual flow is usually a dependable cue that I am moving. We also learn to see objects outside of ourselves as relating to us in terms of possible actions we could take. If I am hiking, I have a sense of whether I can use a fallen log to cross the stream; if I am very young or old, I will probably not perceive the log as affording me passage and will probably find another route. The way we consider the outside world tells us something about who we are: I am a person who is physically fit or a risk-taker or in a hurry.[19]

In relationship with other people. In the Genesis creation account, the litany of pronouncements "it was good" is interrupted by God saying, "It is not good for the man to be alone" (Genesis 2:18). God makes woman from man, and together they form the image of God (Genesis 1:27). A biblical view of the nature of persons suggests that relationships are perhaps more fundamental to persons than individuality. Indeed, the Bible does not describe any faithful "Lone Rangers" (indeed, even the Lone Ranger was never far from his faithful sidekick). Biblical figures who tried to make their own rules, who tried to live outside of obedient relationships with a community or with God, were punished. Consider Achan, who stole from Jericho things devoted to God (Joshua 7); King David's treacherous strategy to take Bathsheba as his wife (2 Samuel 11); or Ananias and Sapphira's deadly lie to the new church (Acts 5).

Many non-Western cultures recognize that family members are essential parts of the self: "To be without family is to be dead."[20] The historic punishment of exile was the equivalent of a death sentence in its finality of separation from a community of meaning. That we are conceived at all requires some sort of human relationship; even scientific-medical means of reproduction still require at least a team of lab technicians. Other people provide the context of our lives, even before our birth: as we grow and develop inside another human being's body, fathers, farmers, truckers, grocers, medical professionals, and neighbors provide social and material support and love for our mothers that sustain them as they care for us. From the moment of our conception until we die, we are surrounded by people, their language and tools, and their various cultural beliefs. St.-Exupery said it this way, "When the body breaks apart, the essential is revealed. Man is only a knot of relationships."[21] As our culture relies more heavily on technology, we actually become more dependent on other (invisible) people to support us; perversely, we are perhaps more likely than ever to think of ourselves as individuals and isolate ourselves from others.[22]

Although slow to recognize that the self is fundamentally interpersonal, psychological research has increasingly demonstrated that to be the case. Harry Harlow's revolutionary research with monkeys in the mid-twentieth century demonstrated that social creatures, including people, require at least one good relationship in order to survive. He found that monkeys without any companionship (even a dog) ". . . could not make it alone."[23] Harlow's work opened the door for research on human relationships. Recent research shows that relationships affect brain functioning and social health. Indeed, "...the human child is hardwired . . . for close attachments to other people, beginning with their . . . relatives, and then extending out to the broader community. Research also shows that people are 'hardwired' for meaning, born with a built-in capacity and drive to ask the ultimate questions about life's purpose."[24] Parts of our brain are dedicated to quickly recognizing other people (the so-called "grandma cells" in the brain's right temporal lobe) or to decoding complex nonverbal, emotion-laden messages in split-second snapshots.[25] Italian researchers reported on "mirror neurons" in our brains that are not only activated when we do something (e.g., reach for an apple) but when we see someone else do the same thing.[26] In other words, some patterns of brain activity may not distinguish between my actions and those of others, giving us the ability to imitate others or to empathize with them.

A great deal of research on group influence shows the profound and often subconscious effects that others have on us. For example, compared to when we are alone, we perform well-learned tasks better if other people are around—even if the other people are blindfolded (the same facilitation effect is also true of cockroaches running mazes). Our opinions and attitudes subtly shift, depending on who is doing the asking. When situational factors make us feel individually anonymous (e.g., being in a group of people), we tend to act worse than we would if we were alone. We feel less likely to get caught and we feel distanced from our internalized, communal values, which together makes antisocial mischief more likely. As a final example, if we are working on a team and our individual output cannot be measured, we tend to loaf more than if we were individually accountable. All of these examples suggest that we are keenly attuned to the presence and evaluations of others, so that we adjust our attitudes and actions accordingly.

In summary, God, the creation, and the human community continually shape our understanding of the world and of ourselves. We are meaningfully embedded in spiritual, social, and physical contexts; to be abstracted from them damages our humanity.

We Are Reflective

Humans have the presumably unique ability to not only record incoming sensations or to act based on particular situations, but we can also internally reflect on our attitudes, desires, past actions, and future goals. We take this ability almost completely for granted (in contrast, imagine your cat saying to itself, "I just can't believe I ran from that pipsqueak dog when I've been working hard to remain calm. I am so embarrassed! What will the other cats think of me now?").[27] The Scriptures simply assume that we are able to discern and reflect upon our motives and actions. For example, Jeremiah grieves over Israel's exile and urges the people, "Let us examine our ways and test them" (Lamentations 3:40). The Apostle Paul corrects members of the early church by saying, "A man ought to examine himself before he eats of the bread and drinks of the cup" (1 Corinthians 11:28), "Examine yourselves to see whether you are in the faith" (2 Corinthians 13:5), and "Each one should test his own actions" (Galatians 6:4). Jesus cautions us to attend to the plank in our own eye before removing specks from others' eyes (Matthew 7:5). All of these references assume that people are not only capable of conscious self-analysis but that we ought to be doing so more carefully.

Scripture and psychological research agree that we have the ability to know ourselves, at least to some extent. We earlier saw that the college student essays emphasized the internal, self-reflective aspect of the self. Interestingly, the idea that the conscious self is (or is fully aware of) the "true" self is not consistent with psychological research; conscious processes direct relatively few of our actions or motivations. Indeed, very recent brain research suggests that the conscious decision to move actually occurs a few milliseconds *after* the signals have already been sent to the muscles.[28] Most of our perception of the outside world happens at a subconscious level. Many of our actions are directed by well-learned habits that allow us to drive or brush our teeth or take a shower without much conscious attention to these tasks; indeed, turning our attention to them may decrease effective performance. In short, we have the ability to be self-reflective, but what we are able to consciously perceive is not the whole story.

Beyond knowing something about ourselves, we are also able to evaluate what we know. Our self-image is a conscious reflection of who we believe ourselves to be, based in part on our experiences in the world, observations of our own behavior, and feedback from other people. Our self-evaluations, hidden though they may be from others, can be tainted by sinful distortions. We may either think of ourselves more highly than we ought (sinful pride) or more lowly than we ought (worthlessness).[29] Self-insight that is guided by our multifaceted relationships is key to more realistic self-evaluations: "The hermit who retires from the world in order to understand himself better is actually abandoning the set of mirrors—human society—from which he could best gain self-understanding."[30]

Our ability to reflect upon ourselves changes over time: it develops during the first two years of life and may disappear near the end of life. Babies must first learn that they are separate from other people, then they learn to distinguish their own image from others' faces, to use terms to describe themselves, and to respond emotionally to their own wrongdoing.[31] Wendy Shalit describes part of this process: "Before 'I think, therefore I am,' there is something else: 'I hide, therefore I am.' Because I can withhold myself, this proves I exist. This is why Peekaboo is so delightful to a baby— because it involves the discovery that there is a self to withhold."[32]

More mature self-reflection further requires the ability to connect what is presently happening to things we have learned before; without memory we cannot make sense of the world or ourselves, and therefore memory is foundational to self-reflection. An articulate victim of Alzheimer's disease reflected that, "Without memory you lose the idea of who you are. These memories become the last remnants of my search for who I am."[33] Alzheimer's disease is quickly becoming the most common ravager of adult human memory. As a result of this disease, the victims and their loved ones helplessly watch a breakdown in the sense of self as memory fails. They witness a gradual loss of self-identity (e.g., loss of work, withdrawal from relationships, deterioration of physical abilities); a decreasing ability to connect intentions with action ("what was I doing?"); increasing "failures to initiate action because the persons forgot that a given activity was one that they could perform based on memories of having done so in the past"; and a breakdown of higher-order thinking.[34] With loss of memory comes loss of the self-reflective aspect of the self.

The abnormal process of Alzheimer's highlights the fact that identity and memory are not just individually owned: they are communal projects. Caregivers of Alzheimer's victims help identify tasks that can still be performed, help to fill in lost memories, and provide reminders of the significance of life "so that their identities are not forgotten even when they can no longer remember those identities on their own."[35] In a modernist world, where geographic mobility is not only possible but preferred, individuals become disconnected from their communities of meaning. This is especially tragic for those experiencing dementia but can hurt us all: we resort to two-dimensional, static photographs or telecommunications to remind ourselves of who we are rather than having others breathe our lives back into us. Gilbert Meilaender reminds us that "the first years of our life become part of our own memory largely through the shared memory of others. One's life exists not only in the privacy of one's own memory but also in the stories others tell about us."[36] Over and over, God commands the wayward Israelites to remember; they are called not just to repeat the historical facts, but to remember their chosen community by recalling the shared experiences and history of walking with their God. Shared memories of common experiences bond together a community. Memories allow us to reflect on who we are and what we ought to be about.

We Are Responsible

As we have seen, humans have the ability to examine and evaluate themselves. Building on that aspect, humans also have the capacity to make and carry out meaningful, moral decisions. Our ability to act in the world goes beyond instinctive responses or learned habits. God has placed us in the role of steward. Therefore, we are capable of understanding his rules and expectations, and within those boundaries we are free to make decisions about the daily running of our lives and the creation that we tend. Because of our relational and self-reflective nature, we are response-able: we are designed with the ability to recognize where shalom is being destroyed and take steps to restore it.[37] We are called to recognize and root out the tendrils of sin in every good thing of God's. I think of the deeply rooted, invasive plants in my garden that are lovely in their own place, but which can quickly ruin other plants and the overall beauty of the garden if left to their own devices. We are called to make disciples, telling the good news of Christ and God's promises to all people so that they may share in the joy of salvation. We are called to and are able to respond instead of waiting by helplessly for fate or God or chaos to just take care of the matter.

In psychology, this responsible aspect is closest to what is called the executive function.[38] This is the interaction between the internal "me" and the external environment; it is what we call "I." The executive function enables us to exert self-control and control over our environment rather than merely observing and reflecting on the world around us.[39] For example, I can decide whether to spend my money now for a short-term pleasure (e.g., a new CD) or save it to help fulfill my longer-term goals (e.g., keeping my commitment to tithe every week or buying school supplies for my kids). In making this decision I consider my long-term goals, values, and beliefs and my particular present situation. I also recognize (at some level) what costs are involved for indulging in or forgoing the present pleasure. I then enact my decision and cope with its anticipated and unexpected consequences for myself and others.

However, not all of our behaviors require deliberate choices by a conscious, rational CEO in our heads. A rather substantial part of our decision-making goes on behind the scenes and is based on our past experiences, our goals and values, our fears. Although adult actions are not determined by childhood experiences, as Freud believed, we all have well-learned habits based on prior decisions that still guide today's behaviors without necessitating much thought (e.g., praying before meals, stopping at red lights). Although not every behavior is consciously chosen, we still hold people accountable for the consequences. People believed to be responsible for causing their own problems (e.g., losing a job because of drinking) receive far less sympathy and help than those believed to not be responsible (e.g., losing a job because of corporate downsizing).[40]

We began this section by wondering what it means to be made in God's image. One of my students defined a human as "an integral yet multidimensional creature who is embedded in a web of inter-relationships with God, other humans, and the non-human world."[41] We share some important aspects of the self with other earthly creatures (e.g., physical bodies, embedded in a physical context), and perhaps we share some aspects with the angels (e.g., responsibility and self-reflection). It is the particular combination of these aspects that make us different. We are well-suited to be caretakers of God's world, fallible and limited as we are.

Bridging the Gap

In their essays, college students clearly emphasized the self-reflective aspect of the self over the other three. In some ways, this postmodern perspective fits well with psychology as a discipline that is increasingly interested in internal cognitive and emotional processes. However, this view of the self is far too narrow. It would be irresponsible for a Christian teacher of psychology to just focus on the self-reflective aspect without showing students the importance of the other aspects as well. How can a Christian psychologist bridge the gap between Christian students' beliefs about the human self and the views of Scripture and psychology? In this final section, I offer several concrete recommendations for in-class demonstrations or assignments that help clarify the nature of the self.

The first step in bridging the gap is to articulate one's own perspective on the nature of the self. This task is related to developing a teaching philosophy in that it provides the underlying faith perspective that drives one's philosophy. How does one discern one's own implicit perspective? I have found it useful to begin with what I know—my daily behavior—and ask questions to work backward to my implicit beliefs. For example, I memorize and use all of my students' names within the first two weeks of each semester. Why is this important? I believe it shows respect for my students and fosters a relationship with them. Why are respect and relationships important? I believe that students learn best in a relationship of respect, where the professor is accountable to the learners and even open to learning from them. Why are these young people worthy of respect? In this particular domain, I have more knowledge and experience than students do, but as fellow servants in God's Kingdom, they also have gifts and skills and experiences from which I can benefit. As believers, we work together to discern goodness and evil as we attempt to bring redemption to sin-tainted relationships. Why do we believe that we have any authority to do this work? I believe that our work in this world is part of the "cultural mandate" in Genesis 2, where people are *together* called to care for the creation and to reproduce. We are therefore all communally responsible for that creation (and are therefore placed above animals). This creation has been distorted by sin, and in caring for it we need to understand it and bring about healing. In summary, I believe that God has created the world in such a way that people must communally care for and help one another as we together tend God's creation. This brief example shows how to use one's everyday actions to access the beliefs that guide behavior. It is not a static process, however. One's fundamental beliefs (e.g., that people are inherently responsible) may not relate to one's current behaviors (e.g., giving no penalties for students' late work). Teachers need to regularly think about the connection between their behaviors and their beliefs, both individually and communally.

Students also need to identify and reflect on their own and others' implicit beliefs. One useful assignment is to have students read their text's introductory chapter and write a paper about things in the chapter that "bug" them or are lacking from a Christian perspective. Many of my students identity the authors' assumption of evolutionary theory as fact, the lack of any mention of God or spirituality or religion, and the assumption that nearly all social behaviors are ultimately for one's own gain. Class discussion can then focus on what students' criticisms reveal about what they believe is important: God is the creator and sustainer, that self-gain reflects a sinful mindset rather than a redeemed one, and so on. Similarly, students can learn to evaluate other theories or historical shifts. For example, Sigmund Freud had a lot of wrong ideas from both a Christian and scientific perspective, but we can agree with him on some things, like the fact that people are pretty rotten at the core. Behaviorist B. F. Skinner got a lot wrong, too, but he correctly emphasized that our physical and social context strongly influences our everyday behavior. Thus, students are encouraged to compare their own basic beliefs with those of others to assess common ground and areas of fundamental disagreement.

Thought experiments can help students understand their individualistic assumptions. For example, I ask students to consider living an entire hour without relying on *anyone,* past or present, physically present or not. They quickly discover that the computers they use, the chairs on which they sit, and even the clothes they wear all connect them to other people. Insightful students realize that the very language they use to think about the question depends on a prior social context. The very stuff from which we try to create our individualistic self has been given to us by others.

Some topics highlight several aspects of the self at once. One example is that of eating disorders. Internalized cultural messages about the body affect behavior (e.g., choices about eating, consumption of diet pills), which in turn affects relationships with others. People with eating disorders become increasingly self-focused, withdrawing from others while trying to become the perfect person; they may question the love of a God who seems to assign defective bodies to some. In a psychology classroom, we can analyze the persuasive power of culture regarding eating and how those messages affect our physical self, our relationships, our self-evaluations, and our ability to make good decisions. We can also discuss the best means of combating such messages and how to bring healing to people already battered by them.

Another topic that highlights several aspects of the self is emotions, especially anger and stress. How one thinks about oneself and one's relationships affects how one interprets particular situations, which in turn affects how the body responds at a neurochemical and behavioral level. When teaching this idea, I emphasize our strong temptation to sin while angry, either by feeding oneself self-justificatory thoughts to maintain one's pride (self-reflective aspect) or by trying to hurt another person physically, emotionally, or socially (relational, responsible, and perhaps physical aspects). As a lively demonstration, I have students review a recalled situation of anger with a partner; they then rehearse ways to fix that situation by calming the body (e.g., counting to ten), taking time for honest self-examination (e.g., asking oneself what the real issue is), and using "the language of responsibility" to solve the problem.[42]

A postmodern culture where the subjective, inner self is emphasized is a lonely place. With relativism, we lose a common moral horizon so that I am supposed to find my own meaning and you yours. We stand quite alone, left with only the little worlds that we have made for ourselves. Signs that this loneliness is not normative are becoming obvious throughout our culture. The increasing number of communication technologies (e.g., Internet chat rooms) and "victim groups" testify to the felt need to connect with other people, warped as those connections might be.[43] Self-declared victimhood may be a covert means to establish some sort of social bond in a lonely, subjective world (a theme of the movie "Fight Club"). From a social psychological perspective, research shows that westerners are biased when judging responsibility for another's problems: we consistently underestimate the influence of uncontrollable factors, so that we tend to blame other people for their problems more than we should.[44] In other words, we are not as likely to judge others as victims as they may actually be, and as a result we may be angrier, less sympathetic, and less helpful to people than is just.[45] Therefore, our beliefs about responsibility (which are influenced by our culture) affect our feelings and interpersonal behavior in a way that tends to hurt relationships rather than bring healing. Christian students can then be challenged at a more personal level: are believers responsible for only helping people who seem to deserve it (recognizing that we are often too harsh in our judgments)? Or should we help everyone regardless of whether they caused their problem (which escapes the harsh judgment problem by offering grace to all but ignores justice)? In other words, should we lean toward justice or toward grace? A discussion based on these questions helps students to clarify their beliefs about human nature, including where and how sin plays a role.

Conclusion

Psychology is a joy to teach because of its immediate relevance to students' everyday lives. At the same time, teaching is made challenging by the array of unarticulated beliefs present in the classroom. As a discipline, psychology prefers to use the scientific methods adopted from biology while virtually ignoring questions of the self brought by philosophy. Christian students may simultaneously believe they are created in God's image but that they are in control of who they are. Christian teachers of psychology trained in a secular, postmodern context may feel pressure to cover the field's content and neglect a deeper discussion of the self. The assortment of unidentified and perhaps conflicting assumptions may cause students to leave a psychology course with their initial beliefs either reinforced or perhaps merely confused. Neither of these is an ideal outcome. Christian psychology students should be equipped to articulate a basic biblical understanding of the self. Further, they should be equipped to use their whole selves as they attend to service in the Kingdom.

Notes

1. A. Conner, "They All Answer to 'Psychologist,'" *Observer* 14, no. 1 (2001): 1, 8–9, 11.

2. I use the word *self* because it seems to present fewer problems than related terms like *soul* or *psyche* or *mind*. See also K. R. Popper and J. C. Eccles, *The Self and Its Brain* (New York: Springer International, 1977).

3. More detailed results are reported in Sherri B. Lantinga, "Social Psychology and the Self: Teaching and Research," in *The Self: Beyond the Postmodern Crisis*, ed. Paul C. Vitz and Susan Felch (Wilmington, DE: Intercollegiate Studies Institute, forthcoming).

4. Roy F. Baumeister, "How the Self Became a Problem: A Psychological Review of Historical Research," *Journal of Personality and Social Psychology* 52 (1987): 163–76.

5. For example, see Paul C. Vitz, "The Future of the University: From Postmodern to Transmodern," in *Rethinking the Future of the University*, ed. D. L. Jeffrey and D. Manganiello (Ottawa, ON: University of Ottawa Press, 1998), 105–16.

6. Stephen R. Covey, A. Roger Merrill, and Rebecca R. Merrill, *First Things First: To Live, To Love, To Learn, To Leave a Legacy* (New York: Simon and Schuster, 1994).

7. Richard O. Straub, *Health Psychology* (New York: Worth, 2002).

8. Atul Gawande, *Complications: A Surgeon's Notes on an Imperfect Science* (New York: Metropolitan Books, 2002), 158.

9. See Oliver W. Sacks, *A Leg to Stand On* (New York: Summit Books, 1984).

10. Oliver W. Sacks, *The Man Who Mistook His Wife For a Hat, and Other Clinical Tales* (New York: Summit Books, 1985), 53–54.

11. Antoine de Saint-Exupery, quoted in E. E. Leslie, *Desperate Journeys, Abandoned Souls: True Stories of Castaways and Other Survivors* (New York: Houghton Mifflin, 1988), 370.

12. David Novak, quoted in Gilbert Meilaender, "Why Remember?" *First Things* no. 135 (August/September 2003): 22.

13. Naguib Mahfouz, *Palace Walk* (New York: Anchor Books/Doubleday, 1991), 179.

14. Dale Ellens, "The Healthy Self: A Christian Perspective" (Address, presented at the annual Heartland Christian Educators' Convention at Dordt College, Sioux Center, IA, October 4, 2002).

15. Ibid.

16. Peter Illyn, "Theology of the Wild" (Paper presented in Dordt College's course "GEN 300: Calling, Task and Culture," Sioux Center, IA, November 5, 2002).

17. See also Kathleen Norris, *Dakota: A Spiritual Geography* (Boston: Houghton-Mifflin, 1993).

18. For more on the wonders of these technologies, see Michael Sims, *Adam's Navel: A Natural and Cultural History of the Human Form* (New York: Viking, 2003).

19. For more on this ecological awareness, see Ulric Neisser, "The Roots of Self-Knowledge: Perceiving Self, It, and Thou," in *The Self Across Psychology: Self-Recognition, Self-Awareness, and the Self Concept*, ed. Joan Gay Snodgrass and Robert L. Thompson (New York: New York Academy of Sciences, 1997), 18–33.

20. Mary Pipher, *The Shelter of Each Other: Rebuilding Our Families* (New York: Ballantine, 1997), 25.

21. Saint-Exupery, quoted in Leslie, *Desperate Journeys, Abandoned Souls*, 354.

22. Thanks to Jasper Lesage for this insight.

23. Deborah Blum, *Love at Goon Park: Harry Harlow and the Science of Affection* (Cambridge, MA: Perseus, 2002), 215.

24. American Values, "Press Release: 'Hardwired to Connect: New Scientific Case for Authoritative Communities,'" www.americanvalues.org/html/hardwired.html.

25. David Myers, "Intuition: Its Perils and Powers" (Keynote address, presented at the annual meeting of the Midwest Institute for Students and Teachers of Psychology, Glen Ellyn, IL, February 28, 2003).

26. See G. Rizzolatti and M. A. Arbib, "Language within Our Grasp," *Trends in Neurosciences* 21, no. 5 (1998): 188–94.

27. This self-reflective ability is a different form of relationship (one with ourselves) than the other three types in which we are embedded. Some believe that this person-self relationship is fundamental to the other three kinds (e.g., Anthony A. Hoekema, *Created in God's Image: The Christian Doctrine of Man* (Grand Rapids, MI: Eerdmans, 1986)), but others believe that we cannot set one type as more fundamental than the other three (e.g., Sydney Hielema, *Deepening the Colors* (Sioux Center, IA: Dordt College Press, 2003), 28). I agree with the latter view but have given this relationship a separate aspect to itself because of its importance in the field of psychology (e.g., Roy F. Baumeister, "The Self," in *The Handbook of Social Psychology*, 4th ed., Vol. 1, ed. D. T. Gilbert, S. T. Fiske, and G. Lindzay (New York: McGraw-Hill, 1998), 1680–740).

28. Angela Sirigu, Elena Daprati, Sophie Ciancia, Pascal Giraux, Norbert Nighoghossian, Andres Posada, and Patrick Haggard, "Altered Awareness of Voluntary Action after Damage to the Parietal Cortex Nature," *Nature Neuroscience* 7, no. 1 (2004): 80–84.

29. For more on these distortions in the Genesis account of the Fall, see Hoekema, *Created in God's Image.*

30. Howard Rachlin, "Self and Self-Control," in *The Self across Psychology: Self-Recognition, Self-Awareness, and the Self-Concept*, ed. Joan Gay Snodgrass and Robert L. Thompson (New York: New York Academy of Sciences, 1997), 86.

31. D. E. Papalia and S. W. Olds, *Human Development*, 6th ed. (New York: McGraw-Hill, 1995).

32. Wendy Shalit, *A Return to Modesty: Discovering the Lost Virtue* (New York: Free Press, 1999), 134.

33. Thomas DeBaggio, *Losing My Mind: An Intimate Look at Life with Alzheimer's* (New York: The Free Press, 2002), 42.

34. Glen Weaver, "Losing Our Memories and Gaining Our Souls: The Scandal of Alzheimer's Dementia for the Modern or Postmodern Self," in *The Self: Beyond the Postmodern Crisis*, ed. Paul C. Vitz and Susan Felch (Wilmington, DE: Intercollegiate Studies Institute, forthcoming).

35. Ibid.

36. Meilaender, "Why Remember?," 22.

37. Sydney Hielema, *Deepening the Colors: Life Inside the Story of God* (Sioux Center, IA: Dordt College Press, forthcoming).

38. Baumeister, "The Self," 165.

39. Ibid.

40. Bernard Weiner, *Judgments of Responsibility* (New York: Guilford, 1996).

41. Matt Bakker, personal communication, May 30, 2004.

42. Ronald B. Adler and Neil Towne, *Looking Out/Looking In* (New York: Harcourt Brace, 2002).

43. Philip Cushman, "Why the Self Is Empty," *American Psychologist* 45 (1990): 599–611; Kenneth J. Gergen, "Social Saturation and the Populated Self," in *Literacy, Technology, and Society*, ed. G. E. Hawisher and C. L. Selfe (Upper Saddle River, NJ: Prentice Hall, 1997), 12–35; and Paul C. Vitz, "Christian Theory of Personality," in *Limning the Psyche: Explorations in Christian Psychology,* ed. R. C. Roberts and M. R. Talbot (Grand Rapids, MI: Eerdmans, 1995).

44. Lee Ross, "The Intuitive Psychologist and His Shortcomings: Distortions in the Attribution Process," in *Advances in Experimental Social Psychology,* Vol. 10, ed. Leonard Berkowitz (New York: Academic Press, 1977), 174–221.

45. Weiner, *Judgments of Responsibility.*

Calvin and the Stars, Kuyper and the Fossils:
Some Historiographical Reflections

Keith C. Sewell*

. . . .

Preface

This article makes no claims to originality. My purpose is to emphasize the importance of the history of historiography—including the history of the writing of the history of science. By looking carefully at the history of the literature on a given topic, we can gain insights into the role of religious starting points in shaping the way that the story has been told. Moreover, a closer examination of the context from which contributions to the literature have emerged can enable us to discern undeclared starting points and unexamined or forgotten motivations. Furthermore, if we are familiar with the history of the historiography of a certain episode or idea, we are less likely to be taken in by the latest version or theory. Indeed, it may turn out that more "popular" works tend to perpetuate errors already exposed and discredited in the more

---

* Dr. Sewell is Professor of History and a specialist in the work of Herbert Butterfield. He came to Dordt College in 1998 from Australia. He received a M.A. from Victoria University in Wellington, New Zealand and a Ph.D. from Deakin University in Victoria, Australia.

specialized literature. Of course, these observations apply to all branches of historical study and not just to the history of astronomy and geology.

Calvin and the Stars

Of all British philosophers in the twentieth century, Bertrand Russell (1872–1970) probably achieved the highest level of public recognition. Russell received repeated exposure in the national media for his less-than-conventional views on conscription, pacifism, and sexual ethics and for his leadership role in the Campaign for Nuclear Disarmament.

Philosophically, his most decisive contribution was his articulation of the standpoint known as "logical constructionism," particularly in the *Principia Mathematica* (three volumes, 1910–13), co-authored with A. N. Whitehead, and in his lectures on *The Philosophy of Logical Atomism* (1918). After 1919, Russell became a much-sought-after lecturer, and many of his later and more accessible writings are the products of such speaking engagements. One such work is his *Religion and Science* (1935). Here we read, in the context of a discussion of the response to the heliocentric theory of Copernicus:

> Luther said that "People give ear to an upstart astrologer who strove to show that the earth revolves, not the heavens or the firmament, the sun and the moon. Whoever wishes to appear clever must devise some new system, which of all systems is of course the very best. This fool wishes to reverse the entire science of astronomy; but sacred Scripture tells us that Joshua commanded the sun to stand still, and not the earth." Melanchthon was equally emphatic; so was Calvin, who, after quoting the text "The world also is established, that it cannot be moved" (Psalm 93:1), triumphantly concluded, *"Who will venture to place the authority of Copernicus above that of the Holy Spirit?"*[1]

It is important to keep a number of points in mind when assessing these statements. First, Russell was deeply agnostic in his response to the claims of Christianity, and this agnosticism certainly influenced his view of the history of science.[2] Second, he generally adhered to the "warfare model" of the relationship between Christianity and science, as exemplified in the writings of John William Draper (1811–1882) and Andrew Dickson White (1832–1918).[3] Third, this approach was undoubtedly connected to the traditions in Protestant Christianity with which he was most familiar. According to Russell's daughter, Katherine Tait, "In . . . the only form of Christianity my father knew well, the life of this world was no more than a gloomy testing ground for future bliss."[4] In his formative years, Russell was exposed to Welsh Nonconformity and other British Protestant traditions that knew little of the positive Calvinian understanding and appropriation of the biblical teaching concerning the order of creation. For him, Christianity appeared ethereally other-worldly, intensely moralistic, and scientifically obscurantist.[5]

Finally, it should be noted that Russell provided no reference to the alleged statement by John Calvin, "Who will venture to place the authority of

Copernicus above that of the Holy Spirit?" The Luther statement was well known, appearing as it does in the *Tischreden*.[6] Not only was the Calvin assertion more problematic, but it was also repeated by Russell in his best selling *History of Western Philosophy* (1945), as follows: "Calvin similarly demolished Copernicus with the text, 'the world also is established, that it cannot be moved' (Psalm 93:1), and exclaimed: 'Who will venture to place the authority of Copernicus above that of the Holy Spirit?'"[7] In the absence of any supportive reference, Russell's readers were entitled to ask if Calvin ever said or wrote such a thing. Of course, the obvious first recourse would be to Calvin's own *Commentary on the Psalms*, and specifically to his discussion of the first verse of Psalm 93. These are Calvin's words:

> The heavens revolve daily, and immense as is their fabric, and inconceivable the rapidity of their revolutions, we experience no concussion—no disturbance in the harmony of their motion. The sun, though varying its course every diurnal revolution, returns annually to the same point. The planets, in all their wanderings, maintain their respective positions. How could the earth hang suspended in the air if not upheld by God's hand? By what means could it maintain itself unmoved, while the heavens above are in constant rapid motion, did not its Divine Maker fix and establish it?[8]

While it would be hard to sustain the thesis that Calvin was a Copernican from these words, there is no substantiation here of Calvin's explicit repudiation of Copernicus as asserted by Russell. There is no suggestion here of Copernicus being exalted by anyone above the Holy Spirit.

However, particularly in his *Religion and Science*, Russell had acknowledged a definite indebtedness to the American author Andrew Dickson White, historian and militantly secular first President of Cornell University. In the early 1890s, White wrote an article in which he stated the following: "Calvin took the lead, in his *Commentary on Genesis*, by condemning all who asserted that the earth was not at the center of the universe. '*Who*,' he said, '*will venture to place the authority of Copernicus above that of the Holy Spirit?*'"[9]

White later reworked and incorporated this passage in a book that became highly influential, his *A History of the Warfare of Science with Theology in Christendom*, as follows:

> While Lutheranism was thus condemning the theory of the earth's movement, other branches of the Protestant Church did not remain behind. *Calvin took the lead, in his* Commentary on Genesis, *by condemning all who asserted that the earth was not at the center of the universe. He clinched the matter by the usual reference to the first verse of the ninety-third Psalm, and asked, "Who will venture to place the authority of Copernicus above that of the Holy Spirit?"* Turretin, Calvin's famous successor, even after Kepler and Newton had virtually completed the theory of Copernicus and Galileo, put forth his compendium of theology, in which he proved, from a multitude of scriptural texts, that the heavens, sun, and moon move about the earth, which stands still in the centre.[10]

While these assertions broadened the possibilities by introducing Calvin's *Commentary on Genesis* into the discussion, White does not resolve our problem because he gives no footnote for his quotation from Calvin. However, White does say, "On the teachings of Protestantism as regards the Copernican theory, see citations in Cannon Farrar's *History of Interpretation*, 'Preface.'"[11]

In 1885, Frederick William Farrar (1831–1903), a leading clergyman in the Church of England in the latter part of the nineteenth century, gave the Brampton Lectures at the University of Oxford on the subject of "The History of Interpretation." In his *Preface* to the lectures, published the following year, Farrar cited Calvin as but one example of how churchmen have been in error over the centuries. Farrar's exact words were these: "*'Who,' asks Calvin, 'will venture to place the authority of Copernicus above that of the Holy Spirit?'*"[12]

Farrar was not singling out Calvin for special treatment,[13] for he continued with this statement: "'Newton's discoveries' said the Puritan John Owen, 'are against evident testimonies of scripture.' With what outbursts of denunciation has almost every new science been received by narrow literalists!"[14] The reference to "narrow literalists" is significant. Farrar contended that "Texts have been used a thousand times to bar the progress of science, to beat down the sword of freedom, to destroy the benefactors of humanity, to silence the voice of truth."[15]

However, as if to tantalize us further, Farrar also failed to substantiate this quotation of Calvin from the works of Calvin himself. His son, Reginald Farrar, in a book that he wrote about his father's life and work, nevertheless offers a clue to the puzzle. In his *The Life of Frederick William Farrar* (1904), Reginald wrote of his father as follows:

> In judging . . . all his books, it must not be forgotten that there are two orders of scholars, the "intensive" and the "extensive" school, both necessary to the world— those whose function is original research, and those whose function is to interpret and make available the labours of the former class, whose work would otherwise remain buried under its own weight. And it is to this latter class that my father unquestionably belonged.[16]

Moreover, the son portrayed the father as constantly engaged in pastoral work, reading, and a substantial correspondence. Nevertheless, the son adds,

> It may be safely said that my father *never* paused, as do some preachers, to *choose* a quotation which should illustrate his meaning. We cannot do justice to this aspect of his preaching unless we try to realize that quotation to him was entirely spontaneous, almost involuntary, because his marvelous memory was stored, nay, saturated with passages from poets which had become, as it were, a part of his very being, and which, when the appropriate association evoked them, came unbidden to his lips.[17]

In fact, at the beginning of his *History of Interpretation*, F. W. Farrar had forthrightly acknowledged that "In a work which covers such vast periods of time and which involves so many hundreds of references it would be absurd to suppose that I have escaped from errors."[18]

Escaped he had not. We may well come to the conclusion that Farrar's "quotation" was the product of an overburdened memory rather than deliberate falsification, and that the churchman had unwittingly provided fuel for Russell's anti-Christian fire. However, this conclusion hardly settles the matter. A. D. White had referred to Calvin's *Commentary on Genesis* in claiming that the Reformer had condemned Copernicus, while F. W. Farrar, whom White had read, made no such connection. So there remained a problem: Where then did A. D. White derive the belief that the *Commentary on Genesis* supported his assertion?

In order to answer this question, we must move from English Anglicanism to American Presbyterianism. More particularly, we must turn to another late nineteenth-century work to which A. D. White refers.[19] It is by Charles Woodruff Shields (1825–1904). Shields was a man of the Princeton School, no less than Professor of the Harmony of Science and Revealed Religion at Princeton University, New Jersey. Shields wrote as follows:

> Luther, with characteristic bluntness, denounced Copernicus as an upstart astrologer, who sought notoriety by trying to overturn the whole science of astronomy, as if the earth could revolve around the sun, when the scriptures tell us that Joshua commanded the sun to stand still, and not the earth. The mild Melanchthon, in his *Elements of Physical Doctrine*, not only reasoned against the Copernican theory with Scriptural and scientific arguments, but held that the civil authorities ought to suppress such a wicked and atheistical opinion. *Calvin introduced his commentary on Genesis by stigmatizing as utter reprobates those who would deny that the circuit of the heavens is finite and the earth placed like a little globe at the centre.* The orthodox Turretin, while yet Newton was completing the demonstration of Kepler, issued from Calvin's chair a *Compendium of Theology,* in which, with a scholastic array of proof texts, objections and answers, he argued that the heavens, sun and moon are in motion, but the earth is at rest.[20]

So, it was from Farrar that White derived the unsubstantiated Copernicus reference, and it was from Shields that he derived Calvin's assertion of geocentricity. Furthermore, it is hard to escape the conclusion that Shields, who certainly did not regard himself as anti-Calvinistic, had in truth misrepresented what Calvin said at the start of his commentary of the first book of Moses called Genesis. This is what Calvin actually says in his *Commentary on Genesis:* "We indeed are not ignorant that the circuit of the heavens is finite, and that the earth, like a little globe, is placed at the center."[21] Here is an assertion of geocentricity, and in this respect Shields is clearly following Calvin, but although Calvin is severe toward his adversaries in this passage, he does not stigmatize as reprobates those who embrace the position of Copernicus. In fact, he does not mention Copernicus at all.

The truth is that Calvin's astronomical understanding was pre-Copernican rather than dogmatically anti-Copernican. Moreover, while Calvin was definitely not antiscientific, his understanding of many things would appear to be clearly prescientific. It is in such terms that we should understand his preference for a geocentric viewpoint.[22] If what we would now call "science" disturbed him, it was not the endeavor itself but the possibility that it might detract from the worship and service of Almighty God.[23]

In this sense, science was like much else that is legitimate: it may be put to wrongful use by a fallen and disobedient humankind. If Calvin sensed the potential for secularization, the champions of secularization in the nineteenth century were among those who seized upon the false quotation because it all too clearly exemplified their image of what they saw as an obscurantist Christianity. The supposed quotation from Calvin was too good to pass up: Russell derived his false assertion from White, who could point to two Christian writers as authorities on the matter, namely Farrar and Shields.

In due course, many others were to follow White and Russell. For example, we find the following statement in the writings of the highly influential Thomas S. Kuhn: "Calvin, in his *Commentary on Genesis,* cited the opening verse of the Ninety third Psalm—'the earth also is [e]stablished, that it cannot be moved' and he demanded, *'Who will venture to place the authority of Copernicus above that of the Holy Spirit?'*"[24] The error disseminated by White and Russell on the foundations laid by Farrar and Shields seemed to have entered the common knowledge of scholars by the mid twentieth century.

The repetition of the error became much less excusable following the publication of three articles in *The Journal of the History of Ideas* in 1960 and 1961, namely Edward Rosen's "Calvin's Attitude towards Copernicus,"[25] Joseph Ratner's "Some Comments on Rosen's 'Calvin's Attitude towards Copernicus,'"[26] and Edward Rosen's rejoinder, "A Reply to Dr. Ratner."[27]

To Edward Rosen must go the honor of having unraveled the origins of the wrongful ascription to John Calvin of the now-familiar quotation. It was Rosen who traced the lineage of error outlined above. In due course, the spuriousness of the quotation became known and was noted by a variety of writers.[28]

Yet even here we must enter some caveats. First, there were always doubters, among them Reijer Hooykaas of the Free University of Amsterdam.[29] His work embodied an almost complete reversal of the "warfare" thesis of the relationship between Christianity and science. He presented a range of arguments supporting the view that the Christian religion, rightly understood, shorn of the influences of Aristotelianism, and particularly as exemplified by the Calvinian Reformation with its positive understanding of the order of creation, was proscientific and not antiscientific.[30] Moreover, just prior to the appearance of the *Journal of the History of Ideas* articles, John Dillenberger had reported that he was unable to locate an explicit reference to Copernicus in the writings of Calvin.[31]

Secondly, in his article in the *Journal of the History of Ideas,* Joseph Ratner challenged the concluding assertion made by Edward Rosen that Calvin never heard of Copernicus and could therefore never have condemned him in the explicit terms of Farrar's erroneous quotation.[32] This challenge opened up a more intractable problem. The focus shifted now from tracing the impact of a nineteenth-century error into the twentieth century to attempting to substantiate a negative proposition with respect to the six-teenth century—that Calvin did *not* know of Copernicus.

Copernicus published his *De Revolutionibus Orbium Caelestium* in 1543. The work was known to Luther, who died in 1546. Calvin died in 1564, close to two decades later. Rosen's argument is problematic—an argument from silence. On the other hand, Ratner's challenge came without substantiation.

There the matter remained until 1966, when the great Calvin scholar Pierre Charles Marcel published a short discussion in the French journal *La Revue Réformée*. Marcel argued that there was a strong presumption in favor of the view that Calvin did know of Copernicus, although there was still no firm evidence.[33] Then a further contribution was published in France by Richard Stauffer. This author argued that a passage in Calvin's *Sermons* on 1 Corinthians made clear that Calvin knew of the heliocentric theory of Co-pernicus and that he rejected it in the strongest terms.[34]

This view was challenged by both Rosen and Marcel.[35] For many, the passage adduced by Richard Stauffer was not overwhelmingly decisive, although it certainly supports the assertion that Calvin had some knowledge of the Copernican theory. The passage is as follows:

> [The Christian is not to compromise so as to obscure the distinction between good and evil, and is to avoid the errors of] those dreamers who have a spirit of bitterness and contradiction, who reprove everything and pervert the order of nature. We will see some who are so deranged, not only in religion but who in all things reveal their monstrous nature, *that they will say that the sun does not move, and that it is the earth which shifts and turns.* When we see such minds we must indeed confess that the devil pos-sesses them, and that God sets them before us as mirrors, in order to keep us in his fear. So it is with all who argue out of pure malice, and who happily make a show of their imprudence. When they are told: "That is hot," they will reply: "No, it is plainly cold." When they are shown an object that is black, they will say that it is white, or vice versa. Just like the man who said that snow is black; for although it is perceived and known by all to be white, yet he clearly wished to contradict the fact. And so it is that they are madmen who would try to change the natural order, and even to dazzle eyes and benumb their senses.[36]

Here we certainly see Calvin wrestling with the key concept of heliocentric-ity. He is clearly uncomfortable with a theory that seems to be at too great a variance with our ordinary experience of things. Yet there is no decisive repudiation of Copernicus by name. This statement by Susan E. Schreiner may therefore still stand: "Calvin presupposed a geocentric world view and regardless of the heated debate between Edward Rosen and Joseph Ratner, there is no real evidence that Calvin ever read Copernicus."[37]

Indeed, Calvin may never have read Copernicus, but the passage from the sermon on 1 Corinthians makes it particularly difficult to sustain the view that he never heard of the theory of heliocentricity. Supporting the idea that Calvin was familiar with the heliocentric theory, A. Mitchell Hunter, more than half a century ago, reminds us, "Though Copernicus had finished his treatise in 1530 . . . he did not publish it until 1543, six years after Calvin issued the first edition of the Institutes. It is almost incredible that he did not hear of it, for Beza had read it. . . ."[38]

So how are we to understand Calvin's stance, especially in view of his well-known cordiality toward astronomy as indicated in this passage?

> Moses makes two great luminaries; but astronomers prove, by conclusive reasons, that the star of Saturn, which, on account of its great distance, appears the least of all, is greater than the moon. Here lies the difference; Moses wrote in a popular style things which, without instruction, all ordinary persons, endued with common sense, are able to understand; but astronomers investigate with greater labor whatever the sagacity of the human mind can comprehend. Nevertheless, this study is not to be reprobated, nor this science condemned, because some frantic persons are wont boldly to reject whatever is unknown to them. For astronomy is not only pleasant, but also very useful to be known: it cannot be denied that this art unfolds the admirable wisdom of God. Wherefore, as ingenious men are to be honored who have expanded useful labor on this subject, so they who have leisure and capacity ought not to neglect this kind of exercise. Nor did Moses truly wish to withdraw us from this pursuit in omitting such things as are peculiar to the art; but because he was ordained a teacher as well of the unlearned . . . as of the learned, he could not otherwise fulfil his office than by descending to this grosser method of instruction. Had he spoken of things generally unknown, the uneducated might have pleaded in excuse that such subjects were beyond their capacity.[39]

In answering this question we do well not to forget that Luther is also part of this story. He was mentioned by White, Shields, and Russell, and his repudiation of Copernicus can be substantiated. Two considerations emerge when the context of Luther's responses is considered.

First, there can be little doubt that Luther was deeply attached to the *ipsissima verba* of Scripture, which may have predisposed him against astronomical and other scientific theses that challenged a literalistic approach to the understanding of the biblical text. Luther seems to have had a greater tendency toward literalism than Calvin. A deeply literal attachment to the words themselves may also be detected in Luther's reported strident repetition of the words "This is my body" at the Colloquy of Marburg in October 1529.[40]

The curious affair of the anonymous introduction to Copernicus' *De Revolutionibus* might be viewed in this light. Osiander, a Protestant of the Lutheran school, wrote an anonymous preface to *De Revolutionibus* in which he represented Copernicus as offering a calculation based on heliocentricity *as only a hypothetical exercise,* whereas Copernicus actually envisaged the objective correctness of the heliocentric proposition. Possibly Osiander considered himself driven to this course of action in order to save the authority of the Bible—literalistically understood—from the contradiction that would apparently arise if Copernicus' thesis was itself taken literally rather than hypothetically.[41]

Second, there was the issue of astrology. Here the observations of Heinrich Bornkamm are deeply pertinent:

> On no other branch of nature study did Luther have so much occasion to express himself as on astrology. . . . His entire century—including nearly all the humanists—shared in the belief in astrology. Copernicus and Kepler clung to it. In Luther's own circles horoscopes were cast and constellations were studied. Melanchthon kept dinning his evil forebodings and dismal prophecies into Luther's ears. Luther mockingly said that Melanchthon pursued the study of astrology "as I take a drink of strong beer when I am troubled with grievous thoughts." Thanks to thorough instruction in natural philosophy at Erfurt, Luther cast the superstition of his time aside. He admittedly also believed that comets, rainbows, and other phenomena in the heavens could be signs and hints from God, as everything in nature was a sign to him. But it seemed ridiculous and impious to him to try to make this a science. Events are not dependent on the stars but on God. "Our God does not consult the sky."[42]

If the truth be told, in this respect Luther was significantly in advance of his own more supposedly scholastically learned and sophisticated disciple Philip Melanchthon.[43] We must also not forget that in the sixteenth and seventeenth centuries, scientific astronomy and superstitious astrology could be united in the outlook of the same person. For some, the attraction of a more accurate astronomy was the casting of more accurate horoscopes.[44]

As for John Calvin, he took great pains to distinguish between astrology and astronomy. While he supported the latter, he wrote against astrology in a work from 1549 entitled *Avertissement contre l'astrologie judiciaire* (*Admonition against the Astrology that is called Judicial*).[45] Moreover, in his entire approach, Calvin seems to have been less inclined toward biblicism. Consider, for example, these statements drawn from his discussion of Psalm 136:

> Moses calls the sun and moon the two great lights, and there is little doubt that the Psalmist here borrows the same phraseology. What is immediately added about the stars, is, as it were, accessory to the others. It is true, that the other planets are larger than the moon, but it is stated as second in order on account of its visible effects. The Holy Spirit had no intention to teach astronomy; and, in proposing instruction meant to be common to the simplest and most uneducated persons, he made use by Moses and the other Prophets of popular language, that none might shelter himself under the pretext of obscurity, as we will see men sometimes very readily pretend an incapacity to understand, when anything deep or recondite is submitted to their notice. Accordingly, as Saturn though bigger than the moon is not so to the eye owing to its greater distance, the Holy Spirit would rather speak childishly than unintelligibly to the humble and unlearned.[46]

Here is an important statement about both the perspicacity and intention of Holy Scripture. It fully respects the divine inspiration and authority of Scripture, and in principle it sets aside any need for the kind of literalism that the twentieth century would associate with fundamentalism. Here is a view of the Scriptures that has no need to panic before the latest theories of a Copernicus, Kepler, or Galileo.[47] Calvin may well be best understood as pre-Copernican rather than anti- or pro-Copernican. Nevertheless, even if on occasions he was inclined to be anti-Copernican, his view of biblical hermeneutics was such that it did not dogmatically preclude the acceptance of heliocentricity.[48]

Nevertheless, writers such as Paolo Rossi still insist on representing Calvin as if he were some sort of naïve literalist.[49] More grievous still are those who cling to the erroneous quotation "Who will venture to place the authority of Copernicus above that of the Holy Spirit" for the purposes of treating the Christian religion as a discredited theory. A trace of this tendency may be found in Brian Silver's declaration: "The straight-laced Protestant John Calvin also blasted Copernicus. . . ."[50] More flagrant yet has been the use of the original erroneous quotation by philosophy popularizer and Russell-admirer Bryan Magee[51] in a glossy and heavily marketed publication, where we are confronted in large font with the now all-too-familiar quotation: *Who will venture to place the authority of Copernicus above that of the Holy Spirit? — JOHN CALVIN.*[52]

Beyond the obvious conclusion that old and entrenched errors die hard, especially when perpetuated by prestigious authors, what conclusions might we draw from all of this? First, we can conclude that a little historical knowledge is a dangerous thing. Reliance upon a single compendious text may serve to entrench the reader within a circle of mutually supporting misunderstandings. There can be no substitute for a detailed knowledge of the literature. This is not to lay upon everyone the absurd burden of being a specialist in everything. It is, however, to say that it is better to reflect upon the differing perspectives of a variety of authors than to place oneself in the hands of a single authority. Those who place themselves solely in the hands of Silver on science or Magee on philosophy will not have their minds disabused of a proven falsehood. For their readers, Calvin's reputation with respect to science remains tarnished. At the same time, we need to recognize that the best contemporary scholarship is much less likely to exhibit the smears and slurs to which Calvin has often been subjected in the earlier literature. For example, Kenneth J. Howell's *God's Two Books* treats Calvin with far greater fairness than did the secularized Protestants of the late nineteenth and early twentieth centuries.[53]

Second, the remedy lies not only in comparing authority with authority but also in analyzing the history of the historiography of each discipline and problem, along with the history of the discovery and appropriation of the sources. Such procedures not only uncover the frequently undisclosed starting points and half-acknowledged agendas of primary and secondary authors but also serve as a salutary reminder of our relative position in the course of human history.

Third, the complexity of issues surrounding Calvin's supposed and/or probable outlook toward the Copernican thesis should have a cautionary effect on our assessment of comparable historical situations. This issue raised the important question of how the church, as the people of God with Bible in hand, is to respond to extrabiblical evidence.[54] If that question came to the first Protestants of the sixteenth century by way of the "astronomical revolution of the sixteenth century," it came to their mid to late nineteenth-century successors by way of the Darwin-Wallace evolutionary theory of the origins of species.

Kuyper and the Fossils

The two historical situations are more intimately related than might at first be thought. On Saturday, June 30, 1860, John William Draper, author of one of the key texts in the "warfare" literature referred to above, addressed the Zoology and Botany division of the British Association in Oxford, with what John Richard Green described as "an hour and a half of nasal Yankeeism."[55] The restiveness apparently thus engendered in the meeting seems to have exploded shortly thereafter in a confrontation that itself entered the annals of the "warfare between science and religion." I refer to the alleged exchange between Samuel Wilberforce, then (Anglican) Bishop of Oxford, and Thomas H. Huxley, assuming unto himself the role of defender and advocate of the theories of Charles Darwin. According to the legend that had built up by the end of the nineteenth century concerning this exchange,

> Wilberforce turned to him [Huxley] and "with smiling insolence begged to know whether it was through his grandfather or his grandmother that he claimed to be descended from a monkey." Huxley exclaimed to his neighbour, "The Lord hath delivered him into my hands." He ended his speech with these words, "If I am asked whether I choose to be descended from the poor animal of low intelligence and stooping gait, who grins and chatters as we pass, or from a man endowed with great ability and a splendid position who should use these gifts to discredit humble seekers after truth, I hesitate what answer to make."[56]

Shrewd historians have always had doubts about this story, noting that it took many decades for the "received version" to appear.[57] More recent research has served to unmask falsehoods, place all concerned more effectively in their context, and so help to set the record straight.[58] There can be little doubt that this exchange, or more correctly, perceptions of this exchange and its implications, helped fuel and bolster the "warfare" literature that gave rise to the misrepresentation of Calvin already discussed.[59]

At the same time, Christians themselves may adopt a warfare model in discussing religion and science, especially if taking a fundamentalist stance regarding the inspiration and authority of scripture when seeking to combat "evolution." Here, not least, the Calvinian understanding of the scope of Holy Scripture is definitely needed. Without such insight, we may well find ourselves committing to the world-picture of the biblical authors in the name of being obedient to the biblical message, even though the latter transcends the cultural and prescientific circumstances in which the Scriptures were inspired in the first place.

Moreover, these considerations come into play when we consider Anglophone literature on Abraham Kuyper. For many years, readers of English had to content themselves with the hagiographic work of F. Vander Berg, latterly supplemented by the writings of McKendree R. Langley and Louis Praamsma.[60] In recent years the situation has changed considerably, with the publication of a number of substantial volumes.[61] However, a portion of this more recent output seems to tend toward the evangelicalization of Kuyper's neo-Calvinian standpoint. There seems to be an inclination to set aside Kuyper's strictures toward "Methodism."[62] References to Kuyper as an evangelical are unhelpful, arguably obscuring more than they ever clarify.[63]

Such an approach opens up the way to an appropriation of Kuyper by the more fundamentalistically minded wing of evangelicalism. For example, James E. McGoldrick states,

> Not only did Kuyper object to evolution as an explanation for life in the universe, he assailed it because its proponents made it the basis for an anti-Christian worldview. They argued that they had found an absolute, all-embracing principle that is applicable to all of life and to every discipline of study, including religion.[64]

Such assertions need to be assessed with great care. Kuyper's objections were indeed to evolutionism—to what he frequently referred to as "the dogma of Evolution" or the "Evolution-dogma."[65] His opposition was to any *theory* that purported to be the explanation of all that is. Such totalization amounted to a dogma-driven reductionism that exceeded the bounds of science. For Kuyper, the problem with evolution did not lie so much with it *as a theory as such,* although there were problems there also, but with evolutionism advanced as the overarching, all-consuming worldview. This distinction is not altogether clear in McGoldrick, perhaps in view of the possible fundamentalist-inclined proclivities of his readership.[66]

The truth is that Kuyper stood much closer to the view of Calvin—with its rich appreciation of the order of creation—than to that of the fundamentalists. If Calvin and Luther could both reject the (at best) pseudoscience of astrology, and if Calvin recognized that the Bible speaks in terms of everyday experience and not abstract theory, so also Kuyper was no obscurantist. Here he proves that he was a long way from repudiating science as such or all of the science of his day:

> Who of us still capable of enthusiasm would conceal the ecstasy so often provoked by the profound insight these studies give into the essential structure of the world? But the knowledge of these unveiled facts may not be equated with the Evolution-dogma falsely distilled from them.[67]

> Every sincere person immediately agrees with that which is logically deduced from established facts, but before accepting these intertwined deductions as a well-rounded system, you must test the philosophical principles underlying these basic operations against the axioms of your own thinking. . . . This watchfulness is all the more urgent since our adversaries are inclined not only to establish the facts but also to construe them philosophically.[68]

In his approach toward science, Kuyper adheres to a position that arguably arises from the central and most basic doctrine of the Calvinistic Reformation: the sovereignty of God. His position suggests that once we recognize the sovereignty of God, our theorizing enjoys the widest possible range of hypothesis formulation and that it is not for us to presume to bind the Almighty so as to say that God could not have created in this, that, or the other way. For according to Kuyper,

> Of course it is an entirely different question . . . whether religion as such permits a spontaneous unfolding of the species in organic life. . . . This question must be answered affirmatively, without reservation. We will not force our style up on the Chief Architect of the universe. If he is to be the Architect not in name only but in reality, He will also be supreme in the choice of style. Had it thus pleased God not to create the species but to have one species emerge from another by enabling a preceding species to produce a higher following species, Creation would still be no less miraculous.[69]

In other words, Kuyper opposed the "system" of evolution*ism* because it required an "aimlessly and mechanistically constructed cosmos"—one that was somehow its own autonomous, yet blind, directing principle. Such a view was fundamentally inconsistent with a cosmos constantly and in every respect dependent upon its Creator.[70] In this respect, evolutionism exceeded the bounds of science and assumed the role of an ideologically constituted false religion. However, for all these misgivings, Kuyper rightly leaves many questions open. The range of possible hypotheses is not to be ideologically restricted but may be as wide as the sovereignty of the Creator is complete. Therefore, not only are we free to address questions pertaining to the emergence, diversity, distribution, and extinction of species in geological time, but we are also called to do so.

Both Calvin and Kuyper exceeded the limitations of a false biblicism in their own days. Disciplined and detailed historical work enables us to place both men in their historical contexts and thereby understand them more accurately. They and all other historical figures call for an effort of historical understanding on our part. Without such an effort, we stand perilously close to the prospect of bearing a false witness against them.

In our elucidation of these issues, the history of historiography has its part to play, especially when it takes into consideration the religious starting point of all historical theorizing. Insight into the functioning of such starting points enables us to unmask the basis of the various distortions that cloud our historical understanding and assists us in detecting the historical origins of those distortions. This unmasking and detection is certainly so in respect to the misrepresentations of Calvin. The history of historiography may also help teach us to be on the alert for any emerging tendency to present Kuyper primarily, or perhaps even exclusively, in evangelical or even fundamentalist terms.

Notes

1. Bertrand Russell, *Religion and Science* (New York: Oxford University, 1935), 23 (italics added).

2. Ibid., 43, 79–80, 194, 244. See also Bertrand Russell, *Why I Am Not a Christian, and Other Essays on Religion and Related Subjects* (New York: Simon and Schuster, 1957), in this context especially 3–22, 48–52, 72–87.

3. Russell, *Religion and Science*, 7–19. The most relevant works are John William Draper, *History of the Conflict between Religion and Science* (New York: Appleton, 1875), in this context especially 167–73; and A. D. White, *The Warfare of Science* (New York: Appleton, 1876), which paid only passing attention to Calvin. Of greater significance is his much more comprehensive two-volume *A History of the Warfare of Science with Theology in Christendom* (1896). This work has been variously reprinted (including New York: George Braziller, 1955). For the context of the latter, see A. D. White, *The Autobiography of Andrew Dickson White*, Vol. I (New York: Century, 1914), 422–26. For an important discussion of the "warfare" metaphor in this context, see James R. Moore, *The Post-Darwinian Controversies: A Study of the Protestant Struggle to Come to Terms with Darwin in Great Britain and America, 1870–1900* (Cambridge: Cambridge University Press, 1979), 19–100. For a further repudiation of the "warfare" metaphor, see David N. Livingstone, *Darwin's Forgotten Defenders: The Encounter between Evangelical Theology and Evolutionary Thought* (Edinburgh: Scottish Academic, 1987). For a discussion of the context within which the "warfare" metaphor arose, see Colin Russell, "The Conflict Metaphor and its Social Origins," *Science and Christian Belief* 1 (1989), 3–26.

4. Katherine Tait, *My Father Bertrand Russell* (New York: Harcourt, Brace, Jovanovich, 1975), 183.

5. The influence of fathers is not absolute. In later years Katherine Tait professed the Christian religion herself. Ibid., 185–89.

6. "So it goes now. Whoever wants to be clever must agree with nothing that others esteem. He must do something of his own. This is what the fellow does who wishes to turn the whole of astronomy upside down. Even in these things that are thrown into disorder I believe the Holy Scriptures, for Joshua commanded the sun to stand still and not the earth [Joshua 10:12]." Translated thus in the American edition of *Luther's Works*, Vol. 54, ed. and trans. Theodore G. Tappert (Philadelphia: Fortress, 1967), 359. The full entry appears at 358–59, and is headed "Luther rejects Copernican cosmology—June 4, 1539 # 4638." Cf. Wilhelm Norlind, "Copernicus and Luther: A Critical Study," *Isis* 44 (September 1953): 273–76.

7. Bertrand Russell, *History of Western Philosophy* (New York: Simon and Schuster, 1945), 528 (italics added). Russell was insistent that the new astronomical science of the sixteenth and seventeenth centuries prospered in Protestant rather than Catholic lands not because the Protestants were more supportive of science, but because of the relative weakness of the Protestant clergy (528–29).

8. John Calvin, *Commentary on the Book of Psalms,* 1557; last revised by Calvin, 1563; first English edition by Arthur Golding, 1571; here trans. James Anderson in the Calvin Translation Society edition (London, 1845; reprinted Grand Rapids, MI: Eerdmans, 1948), Volume IV, 6–7.

9. A. D. White, "New Chapters in the Warfare of Science," *Popular Science Monthly* 40 (1891/92): 587 (italics added).

10. White, *A History of the Warfare of Science with Theology in Christendom,* Vol. I, 127 (italics added).

11. Ibid., 128.

12. Frederick William Farrar, *The History of Interpretation* (London: Dent and Dutton, 1886), xviii (italics added).

13. This said, Farrar clearly favored "the titanic force" of Luther over "the remorseless logic of Calvin." F. W. Farrar, *The History of Interpretation*, 323. For Farrar on Calvin, see 3, 342–52.

14. Ibid., xviii.

15. Ibid., 41.

16. Reginald Farrar, *The Life of Frederick William Farrar* (New York: Crowell, 1904), 193.

17. Ibid., 255–56.

18. F. W. Farrar, *The History of Interpretation*, xxix.

19. White, *A History of the Warfare of Science with Theology in Christendom*, Vol. I, 127.

20. C. W. Shields, *The Final Philosophy, or System of Perfectible Knowledge Issuing from the Harmony of Science and Religion* (New York: Scribner, Armstrong, 1877, 1879), 60 (italics added).

21. John Calvin, *Commentary of the First Book of Moses called Genesis*, 1554; first English translation by Thomas Tymme; here trans. John King, Calvin Translation Society edition (London, 1847; reprinted, Grand Rapids, MI: Eerdmans, 1949), Vol. I, 61.

22. See Christopher B. Kaiser, "Calvin's Understanding of Aristotelian Natural Philosophy: Its Extent and Possible Origins," in *Calviniana: Ideas and Influence of Jean Calvin*, ed. Robert V. Schnucker (Kirksville, MO: Sixteenth Century Journal Publishers, 1988), 77–92, at 85–89.

23. Cf. John Calvin, *Institutes of the Christian Religion*, I. v. 5, ed. John T. McNeill, trans. Ford Lewis Battles (Philadelphia: Westminster, 1960), Vol. I, 57–58.

24. Thomas S. Kuhn, *The Copernican Revolution* (Cambridge, MA: Harvard University, 1957), 192 (italics added). Kuhn gives White as his source.

25. Edward Rosen, "Calvin's Attitude toward Copernicus," *Journal of the History of Ideas* 21 (1960): 431–41. Reprinted in *Copernicus and his Successors* (London: Hambledon, 1995), 161–71.

26. Joseph Ratner, "Some Comments on Rosen's 'Calvin's Attitude toward Copernicus,'" *Journal of the History of Ideas* 22 (1961): 382–88.

27. Edward Rosen, "A Reply to Dr. Ratner," *Journal of the History of Ideas* 22 (1961): 386–88.

28. For example, Marie Boas Hall, *The Scientific Renaissance, 1450–1630* (London: Collins, 1962), 127–28, and especially 355, note 31; and Harold P. Nebelsick, *Circles of God: Theology and Science from the Greeks to Copernicus* (Edinburgh: Scottish Academic, 1985), 204, and especially 262, note 13.

29. Reijer Hooykaas, "Thomas Digges' Puritanism," *Archives Internationales d'Histoire des Sciences* 8 (1955): 151; "Science and Reformation," *Journal of World History* 3 (1956): 136–38; and "Calvin and Copernicus," *Organon* 10 (1974): 139–48. Cf. Reijer Hooykaas, *Religion and the Rise of Modern Science* (Edinburgh: Scottish Academic, 1972), 117–22, 154. For an assessment of Hooykaas, see H. Floris Cohen, *The Scientific Revolution: A Historical Inquiry* (Chicago: University of Chicago, 1994), 310–14.

30. Hooykaas argued this case extensively, most accessibly in his *Religion and the Rise of Modern Science*, and *Robert Boyle: A Study in Science and Christian Belief* (Lanham: University Press of America, 1997). It might be argued that this viewpoint pays inadequate attention to the deistic tendencies of the Baconian position that it appears to privilege. In this context

see particularly Basil Wiley's chapter on "Bacon and the Rehabilitation of Nature" in *The Seventeenth Century Background* (London: Chatto and Windus, 1934), especially at 28–30.

31. John Dillenberger, *Protestant Thought and Natural Science* (New York: Doubleday, 1960), 38, note 33: "I have been unable to find the passage in Calvin and doubt that it exists."

32. J. Ratner, "Some Comments on Rosen's 'Calvin's Attitude toward Copernicus,'" 382.

33. Pierre Charles Marcel, "Calvin et la science: comment on fait l'histoire," *La Revue Réformée* 68 (1966): 50–51.

34. Richard Stauffer, "Calvin et Copernic," *Revue de l'Histoire des Religions* 179 (1971): 31–40.

35. Edward Rosen, "Calvin n'a pas lu Copernic," *Revue de l'Histoire des Religions* 182 (1972): 183–85; and Pierre Charles Marcel: "Calvin & Copernic, La Légende ou les Faits?" *La Revue Réformée* 31 (1980/81): 1–210. The latter appeared in a condensed English language version as "Calvin and Copernicus" in *Philosophia Reformata* 46 (1981): 14–36.

36. John Calvin's Sermon on 1 Corinthians 10:19–24, in the *Calvini Opera Selecta* [being Vol. 29 to 87] in the *Corpus Reformatorum* (Berlin, Leipzig and Zurich, 1863–1900), Vol. 49, 677, as translated by Robert White in "Calvin and Copernicus: the Problem Reconsidered," *Calvin Theological Journal* 15 (1980): 233–43, at 236–37 (italics added). Cf. John Hedley Brooke, *Science and Religion: Some Historical Perspectives* (Cambridge: Cambridge University, 1991), 96–97.

37. Susan E. Schreiner, *The Theater of His Glory: Nature and the Natural Order in the Thought of John Calvin* (Durham, NC: Labyrinth, 1991), 22.

38. A. Mitchell Hunter, *The Teaching of Calvin* (London: Lutterworth, 1950), 289.

39. John Calvin, *Commentaries on the First Book of Moses called Genesis* [1554], Calvin Translation Society edition, 1847, 1949, Vol. I, 86–87. The comment is on Genesis 1:16.

40. According to Richard Marius, in the matter of the Zurich view of the Lord's Supper in relation to Luther's consubstantiation standpoint, "When his Swiss foes Oecolampadius and Zwingli tried to answer him with mild language, Luther responded with unmitigated rage and railing." Richard Marius, *Martin Luther: The Christian between God and Death* (Cambridge, MA: Harvard University, 1999), 474. Cf. Bernhard Lohse, *Martin Luther: An Introduction to His Life and Work* (Edinburgh: T. and T. Clark, 1987), 69–77; and Heinrich Bornkamm, *Luther in Mid-Career, 1521–1530* (Philadelphia: Fortress, 1983), 505–51. For Zwingli in this connection, see George R. Potter, *Zwingli* (Cambridge: Cambridge University, 1976), 288–92, 309–16, 320–332; and Ulrich Gabler Huldrich, *Zwingli: His Life and Work* (Edinburgh: T. and T. Clark, 1986), 132–38.

41. Osiander's preface "to the Reader" stated, "the author of this work has done nothing blameworthy. For it is the duty of the astronomer to compose the history of the celestial motions through careful and skillful observation." Osiander then insisted,

> If any causes are devised by the imagination . . . they are not put forward to convince anyone that they are true, but merely to provide a correct basis for calculation. Now when from time to time there are offered for one and the same motion different hypotheses . . . the astronomer will accept above all others the one that is the easiest to grasp. The philosopher will perhaps seek the semblance of the truth. But neither of them will understand or state anything certain, unless it has been divinely revealed to him.

Stephen Toulmin and June Goodfield, *The Fabric of the Heavens* (London: Hutchinson, 1961), 177. According to J. L. E. Drayer:

> That Osiander and not Copernicus was the author of the strange preface, does not seem to have become generally known for a long time, although a careful reader might have noticed that the wording of it was hardly compatible with its having been written by the author of the book. Kepler found out the author's name from a learned colleague at Nürnberg and announced it in a very conspicuous place, on the back of the title-page of his book on Mars

issued in 1609; but it is certainly to be regretted that Copernicus had until then in the eyes of many people lain under the imputation of having proposed a startling hypothesis while believing it to be false.

J. L. E. Drayer, *A History of Astronomy from Thales to Kepler* (New York: Dover, 1953), 321. Cf. Pierre Duhem, *To Save the Phenomena: An Essay on the Idea of Physical Theory from Plato to Galileo* (Chicago: University of Chicago, 1969), 66–70 [French edition published in Paris in 1908]. For Johannes Kepler in this context see Edward Rosen, "Kepler and the Lutheran Attitude towards Copernicanism," *Vistas in Astronomy* 18 (1975): 225–31. The question of Osiander's Preface to *De Revolutionibus* is shrewdly discussed by Heiko A. Oberman in *The Dawn of the Reformation* (Edinburgh: T. and T. Clark, 1986) at 189–92.

42. Heinrich Bornkamm, *Luther's World of Thought* (Saint Louis, MO: Concordia, 1958), 185.

43. Which is not to say that Melanchthon repudiated Copernicus as some would suggest. Rather, he fashioned his own characteristic appropriation and utilization of Copernican theory. See Bruce T. Moran, "The Universe of Philip Melanchthon: Criticism and the Use of the Copernican Theory," *Comitatus* 4 (1973): 1–27, especially 8ff. and 13ff. Also, Robert S. Westman, "The Melanchthon Circle, Rheticus, and the Wittenberg Interpretation of the Copernican Theory," *Isis* 66 (1975): 165–93, especially at 172–74.

44. The great Johannes Kepler is prominent at this point. See John V. Field, "A Lutheran Astrologer: Johannes Kepler," in the *Archive for the History of the Exact Sciences* 31 (1984): 189–272. Field insists that "Kepler's concern with astrology was not peripheral to his cosmological theories," 222.

45. See the short but pertinent article by Christine McCall Probes on "Calvin on Astrology," in the *Westminster Theological Journal* 37 (1974/75): 24–33. Cf. A. Mitchell Hunter, *The Teaching of Calvin* (London: Lutterworth, 1950), 290–91. Long before Bertrand Russell had become a popular anti-Christian writer on science, Dorothy Stimson had wisely written that "Calvin . . . was apparently little touched by this new intellectual current [the rise of modern science]. He did write a semi-popular tract against the so called 'judicial' astrology, then widely accepted, which he, like Luther, condemns as a foolish superstition, though he values 'la vraie science d'astrologie' from which we understand not merely the order and place of the stars and planets, but the causes of things." Dorothy Stimson, *The Gradual Acceptance of the Copernican Theory of the Universe* (Hanover, NH: Baker and Taylor, 1917), 41. See also Bernard Cottrett, *Calvin: A Biography* (Grand Rapids, MI: Eerdmans, 2000), 1–7, 283–85.

46. John Calvin, *Commentary on the Book of Psalms* [1557] Calvin Translation Society edition (1849, reprinted Eerdmans 1949), Volume V, 184–85, concerning Psalm 136:7.

47. Cf. the words of Herman Ridderbos, *Studies in Scripture and its Authority* (St. Catharines, ON: Paideia, 1978), 23–24:

> We may not apply to the Scripture standards which do not suit it. Not only does it give no exact knowledge of mathematics or biology, but it also presents no history of Israel or biography of Jesus that accords with the standards of historical science. God speaks to us through the Scriptures not in order to make us scholars, but to make us Christians. To be sure, to make us Christians in our science, too, but not in such a way as to make human science superfluous or to teach us in a supernatural way all sorts of things that could and would otherwise be learned by scientific training and research. What Scripture does intend is to place us as humans in a right position to God, even in our scientific studies and efforts. Scripture is not concerned only with persons' religious needs in a pietistic or existentialistic sense of that word. On the contrary, its purpose and authority is that it teaches us to understand everything sub specie Dei— humanity, the world, nature, history, their origin and their destination, their past and their future. Therefore the Bible is not only the book of conversion, but also the book of history and the book of creation.

48. Cf. B. A. Gerrish, "The Reformation and the Rise of Modern Science," in *The Impact of the Church upon its Culture: Reappraisals in the History of Christianity*, ed. Jerald C. Brauer (Chicago: University of Chicago, 1968), 233, cf. 245–50.

49. Paolo Rossi, *The Birth of Modern Science* (Oxford: Basil Blackwell, 2000), 60. Rossi does not give the spurious quotation from Calvin repeated by Russell, but he seems to want a Calvin who would say such a thing and ignores Calvin's positive estimation of astronomy as a science.

50. Brian L. Silver, *The Ascent of Science* (New York: Oxford University, 1998), 53.

51. For Magee's philosophical development, see his *Confessions of a Philosopher: A Journey through Western Philosophy* (New York: Random House, 1997), especially Chapter 12, "Getting to Know Russell," at 203–12. Statements made in the British (Orton Books) edition of this work—but not the quotation here discussed—gave rise to civil litigation in England, in which the Queen's Bench Division of the High Court of Justice recorded a settlement in favor of the claimant and against Bryan Magee as codefendant. It transpired that Magee was unable to substantiate a leading statement. *The Guardian*, November 11, 1999.

52. Bryan Magee, *The Story of Philosophy* (London and New York: Dorling Kindersley, 1998), 65.

53. Kenneth J. Howell, *God's Two Books: Copernican Cosmology and Biblical Interpretation in Early Modern Science* (South Bend, IN: University of Notre Dame, 2003). In the present context, see especially 3–5, 139–44.

54. Cf. Davis A. Young, *The Biblical Flood: A Case Study of the Church's Response to Extrabiblical Evidence* (Grand Rapids, MI: Eerdmans, 1995), especially 306–13.

55. Leslie Stephen, ed., *The Letters of John Richard Green* (London: Macmillan, 1901), 44–45.

56. S. C. Carpenter, *Church and People, 1789–1889: A History of the Church of England from William Wilberforce to "Lux Mundi"* (London: Society for the Promotion of Christian Knowledge, 1933), 471.

57. See, for example, Owen Chadwick, *The Victorian Church*, Vol. II (London: A. and C. Black, 1970), 10–12.

58. See Moore, *The Post-Darwinian Controversies*, 60–62; J. R. Lucas, "Wilberforce and Huxley: A Legendary Encounter," *Historical Journal* 22 (1979): 313–30; and especially Sheridan Gilley, "The Huxley-Wilberforce Debate: A Reconsideration," in *Studies in Church History*, Vol. XVII: Religion and Humanism (Oxford: Basil Blackwell, 1981), 325–40. See also in this context, Livingstone, *Darwin's Forgotten Defenders* (Grand Rapids, MI: Eerdmans, 1987), 33–35. A later discussion by J. Vernon Jensen, "Return to the Wilberforce-Huxley Debate," *British Journal for the History of Science* 21 (1988): 161–79, is especially useful on the lead-up to the confrontation.

59. For A. D. White on this episode, see his *A History of the Warfare of Science with Theology in Christendom*, Vol. I, 70–71.

60. F. Vander Berg, *Abraham Kuyper* (Grand Rapids, MI: Eerdmans, 1960); McKendree R. Langley, *The Practice of Political Spirituality: Episodes from the Public Career of Abraham Kuyper, 1879–1918* (Jordan Station, ON: Paideia, 1984); and Louis Praamsma, *Let Christ Be King: Reflections on the Life and Times of Abraham Kuyper* (Jordan Station, ON: Paideia, 1985).

61. Peter S. Heslam, *Creating a Christian Worldview: Abraham Kuyper's Lectures on Calvinism* (Grand Rapids, MI: Eerdmans, 1998); Luis E. Lugo, ed., *Religion, Pluralism and Public Life: Abraham Kuyper's Legacy for the Twenty-First Century* (Grand Rapids, MI: Eerdmans, 2000); James E. McGoldrick, *Abraham Kuyper: God's Renaissance Man* (Darlington: Evangelical,

2000); and John Bolt, *A Free Church, A Holy Nation: Abraham Kuyper's American Public Theology* (Grand Rapids, MI: Eerdmans, 2001).

62. Cf. Abraham Kuyper, *The Work of the Holy Spirit* (Grand Rapids, MI: Eerdmans, 1956) xii–xiv.

63. "Kuyper Was an Evangelical Christian, But With a Difference," James D. Bratt, *Abraham Kuyper: A Centennial Reader* (Grand Rapids, MI: Eerdmans, 1998), 8.

64. McGoldrick, *Abraham Kuyper: God's Renaissance Man,* 104 (italics added).

65. Abraham Kuyper, "Evolution" [Rectoral Address delivered at the Free University of Amsterdam on October 20th, 1899], trans. Clarence Menninga, in Bratt, *Abraham Kuyper: A Centennial Reader,* 405–40. The expressions referred to here, as translated, appear with particular frequency in the initial portions of the address. The translation first appeared as "Evolution" in *Calvin Theological Journal* 31 (1996): 11–50.

66. It is perhaps noteworthy that McGoldrik's publishers have issued various fundamentalist antievolution titles over the years, the first of which was H. Enoch, *Evolution or Creation* (1967).

67. Abraham Kuyper, "Evolution" in Bratt, *Abraham Kuyper: A Centennial Reader,* 416.

68. Ibid., 416–17. Kuyper here does tend to suggest that "the facts as such" are neutral. Of course, various phenomena certainly exist independently of our knowledge of them; however, "the facts" that we may state concerning such phenomena are always known and viewed contextually. This said, Kuyper's distinction between the evidence discovered and addressed by special sciences such as geology and paleontology, and the broader conclusions drawn from such evidence, is nevertheless sustainable.

69. Ibid., 436–37.

70. Ibid., 438.

A Proposal:
Two Problems, A Single Solution

Russell Maatman[*]

··

When I came to Dordt in 1963, two problems particularly interested
Dordt faculty and other Christian academics: first, how Christian colleges
should deal with data from the natural sciences that seem to contradict the
Bible (most perceived contradictions were related to the question of biological evolution); second, whether there is a Christian way to teach the various
academic disciplines. Simplistic answers to both questions were available. The
first question evoked two responses: (1) conclusions in the natural sciences
can be verified in various ways, and if conclusions are perceived to conflict
with the Bible, the conflict is only a perception based on too literal an interpretation of the Bible; or (2) conclusions in the natural sciences can be wrong.
The second question was often answered by the claim that as long as a Christian teaches well, the result is Christian teaching. During the last half-century,
Dordt's faculty members were not satisfied with those answers. A Reformed
understanding was called for. Aided by interaction with other faculty members, I developed my ideas of a Reformed approach to the findings of science.

---

[*] Dr. Maatman is Professor of Chemistry Emeritus. He taught at Dordt College from 1963
to 1990. His publications include *The Bible, Natural Science, and Evolution* (1970), *The Unity
in Creation* (1978), and *The Impact of Evolutionary Theory* (1993).

In 1963, I knew the apparent contradictions between conclusions in the natural sciences and the Bible, and I knew that there had to be a uniquely Christian approach to the disciplines. In my first years at Dordt, I gave much more attention to the first problem than to the second.

The Problem of Contradictions

My approach, along with that of many other Christians, was to look carefully at the apparent contradictions between the conclusions in the natural sciences and the Scripture and remove them, one by one. In the 1960s, Dordt held formal and informal discussions about these apparent contradictions. Several of the subsequent ideas appeared in my book *The Bible, Natural Science, and Evolution.*[1] As the discussions continued, work in the natural sciences only added to the list of contradictions. The anti-evolutionists found more work to do to remove the contradictions.

Concerning human evolution, one possible contradiction existed. Natural scientists continued to find evidence suggesting that beings—hominids—lived a very long time ago and were humanlike in structure and behavior. The existence of these ancient beings seemed to contradict the biblical account of the origin of humans.

The two following lists present a sampling of the fossil and biochemical evidence suggesting that hominids lived tens of thousands to millions of years ago.[2] The first list consists of only two items taken from a much longer list by Pattle Pun, Associate Professor of Biology at Wheaton College:

- Fossils of 30,000–150,000 years ago were buried with elaborate rites; one, which had undergone elaborate arm surgery, was buried on a blanket with flowers.
- One-million-year-old fossils, which are believed by some to be pre-human, have been found.[3]

The second list, from geologist Glenn Morton, consists of fossil evidence and biochemical evidence. The fossil evidence is as follows:

- A being who lived 11,500 years ago and whose skull was found in Brazil is similar to that of a modern Australian aborigine, proving the ability to sail great distances at that time.
- Neanderthals produced sophisticated artwork 32,000–35,000 years ago.
- Head-bindings for "beauty" were carried out 50,000 years ago.
- Hand axes were manufactured 100,000 years ago.
- Stone tools were transported 200,000 years ago.
- Between 233,000 and 800,000 years ago, Homo erectus modified a stone to make it look like a female figure.
- The earliest wooden plank with polish existed at least 240,000 years ago.

- Idols existed 300,000 years ago.
- Between 350,000 and 424,000 years ago, Homo erectus built a village with campsite, shelters, hearths, workshops, paved area, small tools, and engraved sets of lines, indicating abstract thinking.
- Religious altars existed 400,000 years ago.
- "Industries" existed in northern Spain 400,000 years ago.
- The earliest ocean crossing occurred 780,000 years ago.
- At some sites 1.5 million years ago, hominids used fire.
- Woodworking was carried out 1.5 million years ago.
- Art existed 1.6 million years ago.
- Huts were built 1.8 million years ago.
- A tool factory existed 2.34 million years ago.
- Bones had been cut 2.5 million years ago and broken for a hominid, apparently a tool-user.
- Australopithecines of 2.6 million years ago could plan days ahead, as is suggested by the fact that they could butcher in places where they had not made the butchering tools and then later return the tools.

The biochemical evidence is as follows:

- Some pseudogenes (certain parts of DNA) are common to animals and man.
- Hominids of 200,000–400,000 years ago have been claimed, by analysis of a certain kind of DNA, to be related to us.
- Hominids of 400,000 years ago have been claimed, by analysis of hemoglobin data, to be related to us.[4]

How valid is this evidence? This evidence, only a sampling, is good enough for us to take seriously.

Some Christians have solved the problem of contradictions by making one of the following claims: (a) All humans have descended from Adam and Eve, but Adam and Eve descended from other beings, pre-Adamites; (b) All humans have descended from a mixture, Adam and Eve plus contemporary hominids; or (c) Adam and Eve were not real persons. In other words, in some way, animals are the ancestors of at least some people. For example, Francis S. Collins, Director of the Human Genome Research Institute, is a Christian who accepts human evolution: "From my perspective as a scientist working on the genome, the evidence in favor of evolution is overwhelming"; he refers to "the founder population from which we are all descended."[5] It seems, however, that a new approach must be called for.

A few points must be made before we take a new approach. First, some of the beings represented by the fossils referred to above might have been descendants of Adam and Eve.

Second, we should be able to claim that other ancient beings did not descend from Adam and Eve and therefore did not bear God's image, in spite of their activities, even apparently religious activities. Should we who are Reformed limit God and claim that somehow we know that he did not create beings similar to human beings, who, however, did not possess his image? There is no way to point to a fossil and claim that it was created in the image of God. In fact, some modern animals might possess traits once thought to be uniquely human traits.

Third, we should be wary of claiming that hemoglobin, DNA, and other biological evidence prove that human beings and other primates have common ancestry. In a universe in which everything fits together, we should expect the genetic makeup and the hemoglobin of one being to be similar to that of another being having similar physical characteristics. No wonder modern humans and some animals are close genetically and in other ways. (The fits-together concept is discussed further below.)

Fourth, the answer to the question "What is the difference between human beings and other created beings?" is actually obvious to everyone. When we look at our world, we observe that everything made by human beings—all aspects of human culture, such as art, literature, institutions, and even civilization itself—is uniquely human. No other created beings possess this kind of capacity to create.

As the evolutionistic mindset (evolutionism) continued to make progress in academia, it also influenced some developments outside the natural sciences. Consequently, President J. B. Hulst of Dordt challenged me, in the mid-1980s, to take another look at the problem. That project resulted in *The Impact of Evolutionary Theory: A Christian View*, published in 1993.[6] This book looks at the effect of evolutionistic thinking in the natural sciences and other disciplines. A Reformed approach demands that both the new evidence in the natural sciences and biblical teaching be taken seriously. This article amplifies the solution given in that book and points the way to the solution of the second problem—the matter of approaching academic disciplines in a Christian way.

A key to the argument presented here is the understanding that there existed no contemporaries of Adam who bore the image of God. Consider what happened when Adam was alone:

> So the man gave names to all the livestock, the birds of the air and all the beasts of the field. But for Adam no suitable helper was found. So the LORD God caused the man to fall into a deep sleep; and while he was sleeping, he took one of the man's ribs and closed up the place with flesh. Then the LORD God made a woman from the rib he had taken out of the man, and he brought her to the man. The man said, "This is now bone of my bones and flesh of my flesh; she shall be called 'woman,' for she was taken out of man." Genesis 2:20–23

Adam did not find a suitable helper, although the fact of his looking around suggests that there might have been some candidates. To us, it seems incredible that Adam would even have looked for a "suitable helper" in the animal world. In modern terms, his search would be like looking in a barn or a zoo for such a mate. Evidently, Adam was able to determine that no other being bore the image of God. Eve, who descended from Adam, did bear that image.

Some Christians, however, point to biblical passages that seem to suggest that early human beings did marry beings that were not descendants of Adam and Eve. For example, when Cain was banished because he had murdered Abel, he feared that he would be killed by "whoever finds me":

> Cain said to the LORD, "My punishment is more than I can bear. Today you are driving me from the land, and I will be hidden from your presence; I will be a restless wanderer on the earth, and whoever finds me will kill me." But the LORD said to him, "Not so; if anyone kills Cain, he will suffer vengeance seven times over." Then the LORD put a mark on Cain so that no one who found him would kill him. So Cain went out from the LORD's presence and lived in the land of Nod, east of Eden. Cain lay with his wife, and she became pregnant and gave birth to Enoch. Cain was then building a city, and he named it after his son Enoch. Genesis 4:13–17

Who was it that Cain feared? The beings Cain feared *out there,* in the land of Cain's banishment, could have been the kind of beings that Adam rejected when he could not find a "suitable helper"; in other words, beings that did not bear the image of God. If we accept even some of the fossil finds cited above, there were once beings that seemed much more like human beings than anything in the animal world today. Cain could indeed have feared such beings.

In the passage quoted, Cain's wife is mentioned. Who was Cain's wife? She bore the image of God and therefore was a descendant of Adam and Eve, possibly Cain's sister. The idea of his marrying a sister might surprise us. However in the first generations of the human family, there would have been no genetic problem with marriage between close relatives.

Another problem cited by those who question that all human beings were descendants of Adam and Eve is a passage mentioning the "sons of God":

> When men began to increase in number on the earth and daughters were born to them, the sons of God saw that the daughters of men were beautiful, and they married any of them they chose. Genesis 6:1–2

That the "sons of God" married the "daughters of men" has been suggested to mean that angelic beings married human beings. If such marriages had actually occurred, the descendants of these unions would have had angels among their ancestors. Rather, it seems that the "sons of God" were believing men who should, according to God's commands, have married the "daughters of God," or believing women. Although God told his covenant people not to marry unbelievers, many broke that law.

The overall biblical picture is this: Adam and Eve were created in the image of God.[7] Often it is claimed that the distinguishing characteristic between man and animals is that human beings possess souls while animals do not. However, using "image of God" for the subjects in this article seems more appropriate because the Bible links the phrase directly to the creation of human beings; the phrase suggests what human beings are like; and the phrase suggests what their behavior should be. Since Adam and Eve are the parents of the human race, being human means bearing the image of God, and bearing that image means being human.[8] Because Adam and Eve fell into sin, the image that every human being bears is broken. Redemption by Christ, who is God, consists of restoring the broken image of God in his people.[9]

John Calvin tells us to use the Bible as spectacles to be able to understand the natural world. Calvin's ideas become the starting point for Reformed scholarly work. The Bible provides the means to understand properly the discoveries in the natural sciences. Using the Bible as spectacles in the present case, we conclude that God did create beings that were similar to human beings but that did not bear God's image. This line of reasoning, providing us with an understanding of who human beings are, differs radically from the picture presented by modern-day evolutionists.

Using the Bible as spectacles allows us to propose the following: The solution to the problem of an apparent contradiction between the biblical account of the origin of human beings and the fossil record lies in the fact that all human beings bear the image of God, while supposed hominids did not. The defining difference is bearing God's image, not structure and behavior.[10]

Three questions arise concerning the image of God in human beings. First, what is the image of God? The Bible presents some of the elements of this image. God's image in human beings includes "knowledge" (Colossians 3:10), "righteousness," and "holiness" (Ephesians 4:24). Many Christians have described specific consequences of the image of God in human beings. David Tyler, of Manchester Metropolitan University, England, and Secretary of the Biblical Creation Society, gives eight "dimensions" to the image of God in man: "morality," "personal relationships," "dominion," "creativity," "rationality," "sanctity of life," "aesthetic appreciation," and "speech."[11] Other Christians suggest that human beings live in harmony with God to the extent that they can perceive that the parts of God's creation fit together. We not only discern but also depend upon order in creation. Taken together, all the elements of the image of God in human beings enable humans to form a human culture and even civilization itself, a capability no other living beings possess.

Second, why is it important to show that human beings are not related to animals? If we assume that human beings are related to animals, then humans become just another species. This position can lead to some version of affirmative action for the higher animals. According to some philosophers who take this position, a healthy animal is, under some conditions, more valuable than an unhealthy human being. In this line of thinking, infanticide becomes an option.[12] Humans have a special calling because they possess the image of God. Image-ing God means that humans do in a human way what God does in a divine way. As covenant partners, humans also respond to God. Adam and Eve broke but did not destroy the image of God in themselves when they sinned, or put themselves in the place of God. Redemption by Christ means being made over into his likeness.

Third, if the image of God is not transmitted from generation to generation genetically, how then is it transmitted? How this occurs is a mystery, although we know that it happens. A relevant truth in Reformed teaching is that the tendency to sin appears in each generation. We do not claim that there are genetic reasons for this tendency to appear in each generation. But this tendency to sin is the brokenness of—the flaw in—the image of God in man. The flawed image appears in each generation.

The Problem of a Christian Approach to the Disciplines

Discerning a Christian approach to the disciplines, which is very important in Dordt's history, is much more subtle than the problem of contradictions. But discerning such an approach is called for just because being Reformed means believing that Christ is the Lord of all creation. Before 1963, this problem had not been so prominent in my thinking, but by the time I came to Dordt, I had become impressed with how well things *fit together* in the basic physical sciences—chemistry and physics. For example, from the Periodic Chart of the Elements, one of the most ordered summaries in all of natural science, virtually all chemical properties can be derived. Given other assumptions, one can make similar statements for phenomena normally associated with physics. These conclusions in chemistry and physics are emphasized in *The Unity in Creation,* published in 1978.[13] The major point in *The Unity in Creation* is that human beings can perceive that the parts of creation fit together because they bear the image of God. Given a Reformed starting point, one would expect that God's works would fit together. To a certain extent, the image of God exists in harmony with God.

The Unity in Creation was written for readers who were becoming familiar with the physical sciences at the beginning college level. But chemists and physicists, working at a very sophisticated level, had been convinced for decades that the parts of the physical world fit together. For example, Fred Hoyle, a prominent atheistic astronomer, made a discovery concerning the energy levels in the nuclei of carbon and oxygen. He discovered that had there been only a slight difference in one of those levels, life would not exist. Those levels are exactly what they need to be. They had been "fine-tuned." Hoyle said, in what must be one of the most famous statements by an atheistic natural scientist during the twentieth century, that "[a] common sense interpretation of the facts suggests that a superintellect has monkeyed with physics. . . ."[14]

In the twentieth century, the fine-tuning concept became extremely important. It was pointed out that the so-called fundamental constants of the physical world had been fine-tuned. Examples of the fundamental constants are the speed of light and the strength of gravitational and electrical attractions. The fine-tuning of these constants means that if any of the constants had a slightly different value, the physical world (according to calculations) would not exist. Thus, the universe is the ultimate example of precision fitting. A person convinced that the physical world is *all there is*—there is a universe but not a creation—could conceivably write a book with the title *The Unity in the Universe,* without ever referring to a harmony between God's image and his works.

Perhaps the solutions proposed here to the two problems rest on the same underlying principle. A proposed solution to the first problem—a contradiction between the Bible and conclusions in the natural sciences concerning the origin of human beings—is that all human beings and only human beings bear the image of God, while ancient beings do not bear that image if they are not descendants of Adam and Eve. If the central fact about human beings is their bearing the image of God—the image that puts them at the head of God's creation and that is the reason for their making the components of human culture—then it is the image of God that enables them to investigate all of creation, including the components of human culture. Therefore, it is the image of God in human beings that makes scholarly work possible.[15]

A proposed solution to the second problem—how to develop a Christian approach to the disciplines—lies in the fact that all human beings bear the image of God. That image-bearing quality enables humans to investigate God's creation and the components of human culture.

A Christian approach to the disciplines is not possible without a Christian approach to all of life. What characterizes such an approach at the personal level? A person who bears God's image has, to the extent that he is conscious of bearing that image, a legitimate reason for realizing self-worth. The frequently spoken words "You are somebody!" are truly meaningful if the reason for the words is that the individual bears God's image. To image God in human interaction means to exhibit love for human beings according to the biblical instructions that God has provided in great number. The Bible shows that this love for others is specifically related to the image-ness of others: "With the tongue we praise our Lord and Father, and with it we curse men, who have been made in God's likeness" (James 3:9).

As we recognize that human beings bear the image of God, how should we do our scholarly activity? We should begin with these biblical teachings: God created the world, including human beings, who bear his image. Because they bear that image, human beings have the ability to investigate creation, but since sin has broken the image, the investigation will be flawed. Even so, because human beings bear that image, they will be able to create in the human sense, in a small way mirroring divine creation. Their human creations will never be able to overcome the effects of sin. However, Christ has redeemed the world, and therefore all human activity, including scholarly investigation, should anticipate the ultimate effect of this redemption.

Scholarly activity, and therefore the academic disciplines, usually rests on the bedrock of human logic. Secularists claim that for everyone, in all places and all times, the laws of human logic are the same: a syllogism is always a syllogism and the law of noncontradiction always holds. They therefore insist that whatever rests on the laws of logic is neutral ground: it does not matter which religion one adheres to—Christian, Hindu, Muslim, or any other.

In his book *Philosophy and Scripture,* John Vander Stelt shows how this concept of *neutral ground* played a role in American thought.[16] Influential American thinkers of the eighteenth century adopted Scottish "common sense philosophy." Thomas Reid taught common sense philosophy to John Witherspoon at the University of Edinburgh, who came to North America in the late 1760s and became the president of Princeton College. Witherspoon's importance lay in his teaching moral philosophy to Princeton students, who in turn helped shape American thinking for a very long time. The thinking of even some modern leaders can be traced to Witherspoon. Four principles summarize the basis of common sense philosophy: "the objective validity of sensory experience," "belief in original instincts," "intuitive awareness of the reality of sensed objects," and "the immediate conviction of the rationality of common rational truths." Such a set of philosophical assumptions could provide a "neutral ground," a starting point not dependent on Christian commitment.[17]

Vander Stelt and other careful thinkers who disagree with the concept of neutral ground have said, "Not so fast." For example, in discussing the concept of neutral ground in his book *The Myth of Religious Neutrality,* Roy Clouser points out that a proper definition of religion is required. Clouser argues that religion should not be defined by adherence to a liturgy, a behavior, or any other outward manifestation of belief. Religion in the ultimate sense is "religious belief": belief in the existence of an entity whose existence does not depend upon the existence of "anything else."[18] Christians believe in the uncreated Triune God, who created everything else that exists. Jews believe in the uncreated God of the Old Testament. Clouser shows that adherents of other religions, even though their belief is sometimes not in a specific god, believe in something that is ultimate, something that exists independent of anything else that exists.

Thus, when secularists claim that the existence of logical laws is the same for everyone, they imply that those laws have an existence independent of anything else that exists. They are actually expressing their ultimate faith in those laws. They live their lives and do their scholarly work resting on that faith. However, the Triune God, Creator of all, does exist, and human beings do bear his image. This belief applies even to the laws of logic: we image-bearers are not to assume or even seem to assume that the laws of logic are uncreated. In fact, these laws do not necessarily have universal application. The laws that human beings formulate, such as the laws of logic, and the laws that humans deduce from observed phenomena, such as the law of gravity, are merely human formulations and not created laws. How these considerations impact the disciplines is a problem for Christian scholars. A human being, who bears the image of God, should not assume part of the time that he does not bear that image. Human laws do not have an existence independent of God's creation. In fact, Christians take for granted that God did not create the heavens and the earth in the framework of preexisting laws.[19]

Those who work in the disciplines exhibit their image-ness by standing in awe as they become aware of the magnificence of God's creation. They will adopt a posture of humility. They will assume that progress is possible using laws formulated by human beings. They will praise God when these laws correctly predict future discoveries. However, they will not be surprised when such laws do not correctly predict future discoveries. They will once again thank God for these *failures,* which often open up new dimensions of God's creation. So many new dimensions have appeared in recent centuries that the understanding we now have of creation bears almost no resemblance to the understanding people had a few centuries ago.

At the same time, scientists who know that they bear God's image realize that scientific progress and discoveries have become intimately associated with the brokenness of God's image: every corner of the disciplines shows evidence of sin. Not everything that is achievable is right in God's sight. Those who know that they bear God's image attempt to counteract the effect of scholarly projects that have harmed creation. In other words, as these image-bearers devise projects that will help people care for God's creation, their activities will be God-praising activities.

A few of the problem areas that remain in the disciplines, as they are usually analyzed and taught, should be discussed. For example, the central law in biology, buttressed by laws of chemistry and physics, is Darwinian evolution. Darwinian evolution postulates that all living beings have descended from a single living being ("common ancestry"). Chemicals present on the primordial earth interacting according to chemical and physical laws formed this single living being. The driving force for the origin of both the original living being and all subsequent life forms is natural selection by the "survival of the fittest." In the minds of evolutionists, the law of natural selection and the laws of biology, chemistry, and physics, all deduced by human beings, account for all life. Evolutionists recognize that laws of biology, chemistry, and physics can be replaced by better laws. At any one time, however, evolutionists do their work as if the currently accepted laws are ultimately dependable.

According to Neal C. Gillespie, in *Charles Darwin and the Problem of Creation,* the physical sciences were already the "positive" sciences before Darwin:

> [P]ositivism signifies that attitude toward nature that became common among men of science and those whose intellectual lives were influenced by science in the nineteenth century, and which saw the purpose of science to be the discovery of laws which reflected the operation of purely natural or "secondary" causes.[20]

Gillespie says that when Darwin formulated evolutionary theory, he made biology a positive science, thereby completing the task of making all of natural science positive.[21] In other words, biological, chemical, and physical laws taken together in principle account for the existence of human beings and everything—living and nonliving—that they observe.

Darwin and those who preceded him in the physical natural sciences accomplished two things. Their work led to (a) the postulation of a general theory of evolution and (b) a scientific reason for placing human beings on a pedestal.

The general theory of evolution (GTE) extends from the origin of all life, as described above, to all aspects of human behavior. The emphasis in GTE is to be put on *general.* No longer do scientists find it necessary to build up the evolutionary structure piece by piece: it is now to be assumed *a priori* that evolution accounts for life and human behavior. Any suggestion that some life has not evolved has been opposed vigorously. For example, any suggestion that human life has not evolved, even if the suggestion does not utilize a biblical argument (such as the biblical argument presented above), meets with intense disapproval. Nothing previously postulated to have evolved may be removed from the general scheme.

An example of this mindset is provided by the reaction to those who have postulated Intelligent Design (ID) theory.[22] Discussions of ID usually focus on aspects of nonhuman evolution. ID theorists claim to have proved that Darwinian evolution cannot account for certain biological structures. Much of the fire they have drawn centers on the word "intelligent," which suggests to many that the theory invokes the work of a supernatural being. But anyone who has followed the intense and extensive argument over ID in recent years would probably conclude that the objections would be almost as vigorous if no hint of a supernatural being were made. Any idea that suggests that some life did not evolve must be prohibited from entering the academy: evolutionary theory must remain general.

In placing human beings on a pedestal, secularists put the central claim of the eighteenth-century Enlightenment on a scientific basis: *Man is autonomous.* For example, the achievements of Isaac Newton in physics and astronomy late in the seventeenth century made it possible to predict the motions of the planets for thousands of years into the future. Such predictions showed, said philosophers, what man could do and that God was at most a deistic God, one who set the universe, a machine, into motion and then left it alone.[23] In the late twentieth century Robert John Russell reflected on developments in physics and astronomy. The solar system could last five billion years, according to Russell, and the universe 100 billion years or perhaps forever. Therefore, "[life] can continue for countless billions of years into the far future. . . . If we do explore space and colonize the stars, as some envision, our role may indeed become that of the voice, the mind, even the spirit, of the universe."[24] Perhaps this statement is the ultimate example of putting man on a pedestal.

The late nineteenth and early twentieth centuries saw two opposite approaches to an understanding of how economics should function in human populations. One was an outgrowth of the evolutionary mindset, described above, which was associated with Charles Darwin and one of his contemporaries, Herbert Spencer. Economic relations in human populations could best be understood by using the principle of the survival of the fittest. There must be winners and losers. The "fittest," or winners, become rich. Others, depending upon how fit they are, do less well. The least fit are the losers in society. The other understanding about how economics should function seemed to be the opposite. But this opposite position also incorporated the idea that human beings had evolved and that left to themselves, the fittest would prevail. Therefore, said proponents of this interpretation, government should intervene. It should make the playing field level, thereby preventing the strongest from crushing the weakest. Unfettered capitalism and socialism were manifestations of these two extremes. Other systems seem to be some combination of these two.[25]

Other disciplines, such as sociology and psychology, have also been affected by the assumption of human evolution. For example, some leading psychology theorists claim that there is no alternative to evolutionary psychology. Evolutionistic approaches for these disciplines are inadequate. He who is conscious of bearing the image of God realizes that GTE is not consistent with what actually exists in God's creation. GTE is a straitjacket: it does not allow for the existence of anything that cannot be fit into GTE.

A person conscious of bearing the image of God will not accept this straitjacket. After all, God surprises us. To allow for a world that admits elements that simply do not fit into any overall scheme, especially a scheme like GTE, ignores God. In the face of such possibilities, researchers will stand in awe before God. They will be humble at the same time they realize that they have more freedom to investigate than does an evolutionist. This added freedom will enable them to discover things that the GTE enthusiasts, because of their prejudice, cannot find.

Putting man on a pedestal in the way that Darwinians and other futurists do is actually counterproductive. The Enlightenment—and later the Darwinian—view of an ever-improving human race, migrating (wandering?) for billions of years to other galaxies, is hardly an optimistic view. Those who are conscious of bearing the image of God will joyfully look forward to Christ's return, the redemption of creation, and the completion of their being made over into the likeness of Christ. Research in the disciplines, which are, after all, various ways of studying God's creation and human beings' responses to creation, should inspire hope, not visions of a dreary, almost endless future in the kind of world we live in now. Perhaps our hope will include hope that our work in this life will in some way continue when we have that perfect life with Christ, whose perfected image we will bear.

How should researchers, if they believe that human beings bear God's image, respond to the problems in the various disciplines? First, no procedure or law developed by human beings is to be a straitjacket. One example of what not to do is to use GTE to account for all aspects of human behavior. For example, some researchers have attempted to show that evolutionary theory accounts for human altruism.[26] This is stretching a theory meant to account for the development of new organs and new species. Such a stretch reduces selfless behavior to behavior brought about by physical causes. No longer is altruism God's gift to his image.

Second, researchers should recognize that some solutions already advanced are based on improper assumptions. In economics, for example, the winner/loser solutions described above rest on the assumption that human beings have evolved. Another solution, one that recognizes that all human beings bear God's image, is called for.

Third, researchers should avoid the assumption that each human being is born naturally good. The image of God that each human being bears has been broken. As a result, sin will be found throughout human endeavor. Several activities associated with materials used to obtain nuclear energy provide an example of making the wrong assumption about human goodness. Thus, developments in physics and engineering have led to the construction of nuclear reactors, nuclear weapons, and places to store used nuclear materials.[27] In all these cases, extreme measures have been taken to ensure safety. A requirement in all cases is that the nuclear materials be safe for a long time, perhaps for many centuries. One wonders what safety arrangements would be made if it were assumed that all the guardians of these nuclear materials in future generations will be naturally sinful, i.e., prone to cheat on the safety rules.

Fourth, researchers should anticipate in all scholarly work that Christ's return will bring about a qualitative change in human affairs. Christ's redemption will bring about the consummation of human history, for it will bring about a new heaven and a new earth. We know very little about the future. However, it does seem likely that in some way the activities we carry out in human history will relate to our activities in sinless, eternal life with our Savior.

Conclusions

The defining difference between human beings and other forms of life is that human beings possess the image of God. Only human beings, by reason of their activities, have constructed human culture or human civilization. No activities of other living things have had similar consequences. It follows, then, that we are called to reflect consciously our image-ness in all of our activities, both those that are uniquely human, related to culture- and civilization-forming, and those that are not. A subset of the uniquely human activities, work in the scholarly disciplines, must therefore be guided by image-ing God, utilizing the special capabilities God has given us.

Our activities should not be divided into biblically guided and culturally guided activities. If it were possible to make such a division legitimately, we could maintain that some activities have no relation to the image of God in us, which is manifestly an incorrect conclusion. The Bible does not provide us with one body of knowledge while our scholarly activities provide us with another body of knowledge. It is not enough to adopt the two-bodies-of-knowledge model along with the claim that properly understood, there is no contradiction between biblical teaching and scholarly teaching. That claim is valid, of course, but only because the Bible provides spectacles that enable us to understand scholarly investigation.

To use the phrase "the Bible and science" suggests the two-bodies-of-knowledge model. Of course, this phrase is often used along with the recognition that the Bible provides the spectacles. However, our calling as God's people is to put the matter in proper perspective, not to separate the Bible from scholarly activity.

Notes

1. Russell Maatman, *The Bible, Natural Science, and Evolution* (Grand Rapids, MI: Reformed Fellowship, 1970).

2. The discussion concerning contradictions is intended for those who accept the possibility that the earth is much older than a few thousand years. However, the main point of the article, the true nature of human beings and the consequences of having that true nature, is relevant regardless of the age of the earth.

3. Pattle P. T. Pun, *Evolution: Nature and Scripture in Conflict?* (Grand Rapids, MI: Zondervan, 1982), 112–17.

4. Glenn Morton, "Reply to Tanner," *Perspectives on Science and Christian Faith* 50, no. 3 (1998): 233–34; Glenn Morton, "Planning Ahead: Requirement for Moral Accountability," *Perspectives on Science and Christian Faith* 51, no. 3 (1999): 176–80. I am indebted to Morton for providing by e-mail communication some of the items on this list.

5. Francis S. Collins, "Faith and the Human Genome," *Perspectives on Science and Christian Faith* 55, no. 3 (2003): 151–52.

6. Russell Maatman, *The Impact of Evolutionary Theory: A Christian View* (Sioux Center, IA: Dordt College Press, 1993).

7. "Let us make man in our image, in our likeness" (Genesis 1:26–27); "made him in the likeness of God" (Genesis 5:1); do not shed the blood of man, "for in the image of God has God made man" (Genesis 9:6); "conformed to the likeness of his Son" (Romans 8:29); [in the resurrection] "so shall we bear the likeness of the man from heaven" (1 Corinthians 15:49); we are "transformed into his likeness" (2 Corinthians 3:18); renewed "in the image of its Creator" (Colossians 3:10); and "we curse men . . . made in God's likeness" (James 3:9). In both the Old and New Testaments, "likeness" and "image" are equivalent in the passages cited.

8. "Adam named his wife Eve, because she would become the mother of all the living" (Genesis 3:20).

9. "For those God foreknew he also predestined to be conformed to the likeness of his Son, that he might be the firstborn among many brothers" (Romans 8:29).

10. This is the position taken by Henri Blocher in his careful analysis of the opening chapters of Genesis: "For the Bible, man is neither angel nor beast, nor even a little of both; the prologue of Genesis defines him as a creature made *as the image of God.*" Blocher devoted an entire chapter of his book to the meaning of "image of God." Henri Blocher, *In the Beginning: The Opening Chapters of Genesis*, trans. David G. Preston (Leicester: InterVarsity Press, 1984), 79. For a summary of his argument, see Maatman, *The Impact of Evolutionary Theory*, 289, footnote 10.

11. David Tyler, *Creation: Chance or Design* (Darlington, England: Evangelical Press, 2003), chapter 4. No doubt these and other suggestions made by Christians do not exhaust the concept. But taken together, they do enable us to use the concept fruitfully.

12. See a discussion of the consequences of blurring the difference between species, involving the philosophical underpinnings of movements such as People for the Ethical Treatment of Animals (PETA) and Animal Liberation Front (ALF) in Maatman, *Impact of Evolutionary Theory*, 254–60.

13. Russell Maatman, *The Unity in Creation* (Sioux Center, IA: Dordt College Press, 1978).

14. For a discussion of Hoyle and fine-tuning fundamental constants see Maatman, *The Impact of Evolutionary Theory*, 45–46.

15. For Christian answers to this problem, see four articles in *Pro Rege* 31, no. 4 (2003): Roy Clouser, "Is There a Christian View of Everything from Soup to Nuts?" 1–10; John H. Kok, "Learning to Teach from within a Christian Perspective," 11–19; Calvin Jongsma and Hubert Krygsman, "The Educational Framework of Dordt College," 20–25; and Murat Tanyel, "We Have Heard It Said: Reflections on Christian Engineering Scholarship," 26–31.

16. John C. Vander Stelt, *Philosophy and Scripture: A Study in Old Princeton and Westminster Theology* (Marlton, NJ: Mack Publishing, 1978).

17. Ibid., 65–75.

18. Roy Clouser, *The Myth of Religious Neutrality* (Notre Dame, IN: University of Notre Dame Press, 1991), 18–19.

19. Interestingly, some modern physical discoveries concerning quanta of energy might, because they are counterintuitive, contradict human logic. George Johnson, in *A Shortcut through Time: The Path to the Quantum Computer* (New York: Alfred A. Knopf, 2003), pointed out that in ordinary computers a switch is either "on" or "off" while in a quantum computer a switch can be *both* on and off: "Defying all common sense, a single

particle [here, a quantum of energy] can be two places at the same time" (6). That this is so is proved by the fact that an extremely elementary quantum computer functioned as predicted (130–31). In addition, a photon, a quantum of light energy, has been observed to pass through two slits simultaneously (38–40).

20. Neal C. Gillespie, *Charles Darwin and the Problem of Creation* (Chicago: The University of Chicago Press, 1979), 8.

21. Ibid., 155.

22. For Intelligent Design (ID) theory see, for example, Michael J. Behe, *Darwin's Black Box: The Biochemical Challenge to Evolution* (New York: The Free Press, 1996); and William A. Dembski, *The Design Inference* (New York: Cambridge University Press, 1998). Phillip E. Johnson, now the acknowledged leader of the ID movement, referred to the concept of design approvingly in *Darwin on Trial* (Downers Grove, IL: InterVarsity Press, 1991) and in *Reason in the Balance: The Case against Naturalism in Science, Law, and Education* (Downers Grove, IL: InterVarsity Press, 1995), before Behe presented actual biological examples in *Black Box.*

23. The eighteenth-century predictions of planetary motion were, however, slightly inaccurate and were known to be inaccurate. Not until the twentieth century, with the development of Einstein's General Theory of Relativity, was this inaccuracy removed.

24. Robert John Russell, "Christian Discipleship and the Challenge of Physics: Formation, Flux, and Focus," *Perspectives on Science and the Christian Faith* 42, no. 3 (1990): 139–54, especially 153.

25. For a discussion of this problem in economics, see Maatman, *The Impact of Evolutionary Theory,* 233–38.

26. For efforts to give an evolutionary explanation for altruism, see discussions in Maatman, *The Impact of Evolutionary Theory,* 210, 217, and 256.

27. The argument presented here does not include the obvious problems associated with nuclear warfare, terrorists, and "rogue states."

Twenty-Five Years of *Plumblines*

Charles Adams[*]

....

Engineering at Dordt: Redeeming Technology
June 10, 1980

Dordt College is in the process of developing a four-year engineering program. This program, which aims to graduate its first class of engineers by the spring of 1983, will offer bachelor's degrees with emphases in mechanical engineering, electrical engineering, and engineering science.

Offering an engineering education to its students makes Dordt somewhat unique among liberal arts colleges, particularly among Christian liberal arts colleges. There are a number of reasons for this. But today I would like to focus very simply on the question, "Why should *Dordt College* offer a program in engineering?"

Dordt College sees itself as a biblically directed institution, standing in the tradition of the Reformation. One implication of this is that the sover-

---

[*] Dr. Adams is Dean of the Natural Sciences and Professor of Engineering. He has been teaching at Dordt College since 1979. These five contributions represent a small sample of *Plumblines* he has written and recorded for KDCR radio during the past twenty-five years. About 100 of those 250+ *Plumblines* have been collected in the booklet *Exercising Our World View*, under the pseudonym of D. Livid Vander Krowd, and are printed annually by the Dordt College Print Shop for use in two courses: EGR 390 Technology and Society and CMSC 390 Computer Technology and Society.

eignty of God is recognized over all areas of life. There is no area of life, no part of creation that can be called neutral. The Scriptures are very clear on this point. For example, Paul says this about Christ

> He is the image of the invisible God, the firstborn over all creation. For by him all things were created: things in heaven and on earth, visible and invisible, whether thrones or powers or rulers or authorities; all things were created by him and for him. He is before all things, and in him all things hold together. And he is the head of the body, the church; he is the beginning and the firstborn among the dead, so that in everything he might have the supremacy. For God was pleased to have all his fullness dwell in him, and through him to reconcile to himself all things, whether things on earth or things in heaven, by making peace through his blood, shed on the cross. Colossians 1:15–20

In these five verses the Lord Jesus Christ is described in three ways. First, he is the creator of all things, or as John says in the second and third verses of the first chapter of his gospel, "He was with God in the beginning [and] through him all things were made." Second, he is not only the Creator of all things, but he also holds all things together. We might say he sustains or upholds the creation and gives it meaning. Finally, Paul teaches us that Christ's death on the cross brings reconciliation to all things. This is most important to understand for often in our minds we tend to limit the atoning work of Christ to the hearts of men, and fail to see, as the Scriptures clearly teach, that the work of redemption involves all of creation. In summary then, Jesus Christ is the creator, sustainer, and redeemer of all things—the whole creation.

Engineering is an activity whereby humans, using their reasoning abilities, attempt to develop the creation. But that development cannot take place in a vacuum. It is God's creation that the engineer must work with since all things were created by Christ. And since Christ is the sustainer and the source of meaning for all things, engineering as an activity must have a direction. It is either done in submission and obedience to the will of God, or it is done in ignorance and rebellion against God's will.

The development activity in which an engineer engages can be traced to the original mandate given to Adam to tend the garden. Thus, engineering is a form of stewardship. The engineer has a task of conserving creation: that is, of taking care of our physical environment. He or she also has the task of unfolding creation. By this is meant, enabling creation to express itself in ways that would be impossible otherwise. Examples are the development of a synthetic fiber or the harnessing of wind energy by a machine that may convert it to usable electrical energy. There is a third aspect of the work of an engineer that is connected with our fall into sin and that is becoming increasingly important today: the work of healing creation. And for the Christian, it is here where we see concrete evidence of the redemptive work of Christ in all things.

Because we have turned away from God, we have rejected our task as stewards. Instead we have become exploiters of creation. Our greed and self-centeredness have damaged creation. Air and water pollution, nuclear waste disposal, the extinction of certain species of wildlife, the shortage of natural resources, the energy crisis: all of these problems are manifestations of humankind's failure to respond obediently to the Word of the Lord in our role as stewards over creation.

These problems have caused a great deal of uncertainty and unrest in our society. Many people have become disenchanted with technology, believing that technology itself is the source of our ecological and energy problems. Others have taken just the opposite stance, believing that only increased technological efforts will save us from our current problems. In either case, or in the case of the average citizen who is just baffled by technological developments and problems, there is recognition that we need answers; that the future will be shaped to a great extent by decisions that are now being made.

Into this situation of turmoil the Christian is called to bring the redemptive healing and the redirection of the gospel. But to speak to technological issues authoritatively, the Christian must know the Word of God for technology. The only way that Word can be known is by a careful study of creation in the light of the Scriptures. In other words, we need Christ-centered engineering schools that will graduate engineers who are equipped with a high degree of technical competency and directed by the conviction that their task is one of stewardship—conserving, unfolding, and bringing redemptive healing to the creation—in service to their fellow humans and to the glory of God.

Christian Teaching: Hiring for Perspective
April 7, 1989

One of the greatest problems with living in a Christian community, growing up in a Christian home, or attending a Christian school is the tendency to take for granted the defining characteristics of that community, home, or school—the qualities and attributes that set it apart as distinctively Christian. For example, what does it mean to be a Christian teacher? If you had the responsibility for hiring a teacher for your Christian school, what would you look for?

In the past few years, on a number of occasions, I've been involved in the process of hiring a Christian teacher. This occurred at the college level, here at Dordt, when we were searching for engineering professors. It also occurred on the high school level when I served as a member of a Board of Trustees and was involved in interviewing prospective teachers in areas such as English, music, art, and Spanish. What struck me on these and other occasions was, in contradiction to our profession as Reformed Christians, the ease with which it was taken for granted that a teacher who is a Christian is a Christian teacher.

Let's imagine that we are on the board of a Christian school. It could be a grade school, high school, or college. Imagine that we have the responsibility for interviewing and approving or disapproving a candidate for a mathematics teaching position in our school. It doesn't matter that we are not experts in mathematics or in math education. Determining the candidate's technical qualifications is not the job of board members; it's the job of the professionals on the school staff. As board members we have the responsibility to determine whether or not the candidate will be a truly Christian teacher. So what specifically will we be looking for? What kinds of questions ought we ask?

Unfortunately, the easy thing to do is to ask about the candidate's faith life and faith commitment. By listening to this Christian describe her faith in Christ, her church activities, and her commitment to the community of believers, we can easily be mistaken into thinking that the candidate is a Christian teacher, when all we have really ascertained is that she is a Christian. I don't mean to imply that the candidate is consciously deceiving us or that we as board members are consciously trying to avoid the real question. It's just that it's so easy to take for granted that a Christian who is trained as a teacher is a Christian teacher.

What kinds of questions ought we to ask our candidate for the position of math teacher in our Christian school? Let me suggest three.

First: "How will your mathematics class be different from the mathematics classes of your secular counterparts?"

Second: "How do you expect the lives of your students to be different from the lives of their contemporaries because they were in your class?"

And third: "What people and what books have been most influential in forming your ideas about a Christian approach to mathematics and to math teaching?"

The first question attempts to determine if the candidate has an understanding of what it means to teach Christianly. The second question gives the candidate an opportunity to tell you about her vision of what teaching math means for the Kingdom of God. The third question is, in a sense, a check. People don't suddenly become Christian teachers overnight. They have to develop. That development takes time and the influence of other Christians. Some of that occurs in school. But most of it—the most important part, anyhow—occurs when the potential student interacts with other Christian teachers—either directly or through books. Thus, a genuine Christian teacher is going to be enthusiastic about telling you who her teachers were and what they taught. She will also want to tell you about the books that have greatly influenced her. And if the candidate is a really sharp

Christian teacher, she will be able to tell you about books she is reading now and plans to read in the future. A serious Christian teacher is one who is immersed in and excited about his or her calling.

But let's go back to the first question: "How will your mathematics class be different from the mathematics classes of your secular counterparts?"

If your candidate tells you that 2 + 2 = 4 is the same for Christians and non-Christians and therefore the "facts" that she teaches will be no different from what is taught in the secular schools, then I think you ought to politely thank her for her time and go on to your next candidate.

When I ask that question to a prospective Christian math teacher I listen to hear three things. Those three things can be categorized as "content, purpose, and methodology," or phrased in even simpler terms, "what, why, and how."

First I want to hear that in this teacher's class students will learn that numbers, equations, and the like are creatures of the Lord. They are not mere neutral facts that simply exist or that humans have created. Rather, they, like stars, songs, elephants, and people, are servants of the Lord Jesus Christ, some of who have been here from the beginning and some of who have been unfolded in time by God's image-bearers. Perhaps she will even quote Psalm 119, where we read:

> Your word, O Lord, is eternal; it stands firm in the heavens.
> Your faithfulness continues through all generations;
> you established the earth, and it endures.
> Your laws endure to this day, for all things serve you. Psalm 119: 89–91

That brings me to the second thing I want to hear. In this teacher's class, students will be confronted with the reality that they are servants of God called to develop their insights and talents in obedience to his Word—and called to claim the world for the cause of his Kingdom. That means the purpose for studying math is not merely "to get a job" or "to become well-rounded persons," but to redeem a part of creation from the clutches of the evil one. In studying math with this Christian teacher, they will come to see themselves as "subversives-in-training"—being prepared to go out and turn the world upside down in the name of Jesus.

Finally, I want to hear how the teacher plans to do this. I look to see the teacher's eyes light up as she tells me how she would avoid the pitfalls of radically student-centered education where the individual is all-important and of subject-centered education where the student is made the slave of the curriculum. And if the teacher is really good, she will be telling us how to combat the effects of TV on the students by using the media to deepen the Christian perspective of the students and how she will integrate the learning of mathematics with the other learning experiences that the students will be undergoing.

If I hear all that, I will attempt to hire her on the spot. If I hear what sounds like the beginnings of that perspective, I will rephrase my questions in an attempt to enable the teacher to convey that perspective in her own language.

To close, let me say that there's only one thing worse than hearing no perspective at all from the candidate: it is hearing my colleagues or fellow board members say, "She may be a little weak on perspective now, but she is a solid Christian and is open to learning." For a Christian teacher, perspective is not something you learn while "on the job." Our responsibility to Christian students will not allow it.

The Creation as Art
August 3, 1990

For those who can see it, reality often appears as a majestic piece of artwork, a tapestry woven together with the finest of threads—"quantum threads," my physicist friend John might say—and containing an unimaginable assortment of jewels. These jewels sparkle, like the stars in the night sky, radiating a portion of the unfathomable creative imagination of the Master Artist to those who, as he said, "have eyes to see and ears to hear." In fact, some of those jewels in the fabric of reality *are* the stars—those distant nuclear furnaces whose light takes thousands of years to travel before it reaches and delights our upward gazing eyes. But the stars are only one kind of an infinite assortment of jewels that decorate this carefully woven tapestry we call creation. No less important are the moments and events that, when taken together, comprise the life of each one of us human creatures. Whether it be an extended event like that shared by two people who have pledged their troth to each other and kept it for over fifty years or a brief pleasure as in the smell of honeysuckle, when a gentle summer breeze wafts it across your face; each of the jewels is held fast in the fabric of the tapestry. Tied together by "quantum" threads, each has its place and significance—but again, to appreciate that significance you must have "eyes to see and ears to hear."

Without that special vision, reality will be perceived very differently from that which I've just described. There may be, now and then, a twinkling glimpse of the light radiated from each of the jewels, but the fabric as a whole is invisible. And when the threads that tie the fabric of reality together go unseen, then the jewels cannot be fully appreciated, and the whole beautiful tapestry disintegrates into a chaotic array of unrelated creatures and events. The stars become merely distant nuclear reactions whose only significance to one's life is related to the chance that you happen to be looking at them at a given point in time. Each event in one's life is disconnected from other events and from the events in the lives of other persons, none of them having any lasting significance. Shakespeare expressed it well when he had his tragic hero Macbeth say:

> And all our yesterdays have lighted fools
> The way to dusty death. . . .
> Life's but a walking shadow, a poor player
> That struts and frets his hour upon the stage
> And then is heard no more: it is a tale
> Told by an idiot, full of sound and fury,
> Signifying nothing.[1]

This past week I couldn't help being dazzled by the brilliance of a number of jewels in the fabric of the creation, and I was particularly struck by the way they were tied to each other. For three days, invited by relatives, my wife and I stayed at a rather plush resort in the Ozarks. We were involved in a number of activities while there, but two in particular gleamed brighter than the rest. The first was when four of us left the resort and traveled to a little, out-of-the-way state preserve, where we and perhaps a dozen other people, guided by a state conservation officer, explored a cave. The simple beauty of a relatively unspoiled cave, half a mile into a mountainside and a quarter mile underground, contrasted sharply with the noise of the busy lake resort. The intelligent and genuinely enthusiastic commentary of the conservation officer as she discussed the geology, biology, and history of the cave was totally different from the superficial vocabulary and "party" attitude of the resort workers, who, after teaching you to water ski, talked among themselves of the money to be made in the next month as the influx of tourists hit its yearly maximum.

The other activity occurred on the night before we left for home when my wife's brother-in-law took us out for an hour's spin around Lake-of-the-Ozarks in his boat. The night was softly illumined by moon and starlight filtering through a haze of clouds. The air was cool, and as the boat sped at 30 mph across the waves, I was immersed in a sea of sensations: the pounding of the waves just under my seat, the smell of fresh lake-water air as the breeze blew it across my face, the sight of lights on one shore of the lake contrasting with the darkness of the woods on the opposite shore; and then there was this exceptionally pretty girl sitting across from me in the bow, her brown hair blowing backward as she gazed ahead into the 30 mph breeze. For a fleeting moment I thought how nice it would be to own a boat on a lake like the one I was riding in. But then I began to see those threads in the fabric of reality, and other thoughts filled my mind. The boat was just a kind of lens that enabled me to see, with a little different perspective, things that the Lord had given to me to enjoy long ago. Its owner could take it home, but he also would have to be responsible for keeping it up, for paying the fees associated with using it on the lake, and for justifying his ownership of it when for weeks it went unused, just sitting in the dock.

I, on the other hand, would still have the moonlight and stars to appreciate. While the breeze in Sioux Center on a summer's night would rarely compare to that experience while crossing the lake, it is still something to enjoy and be thankful for. And the boat ride itself is not just one pleasurable but isolated past event. Rather, it is one of those creational jewels, tied neatly into the fabric of reality. In fact if you close your eyes you just might see that fine thread tying it, this *Plumbline*, and you the reader together. And best of all, while my friend may have had the satisfaction of knowing that his boat was safely docked a hundred feet from his house after the ride was over, that pretty girl I mentioned went home with me—as she's done now for the past twenty-three years.

What enabled me to perceive better the threads that tied these events into the fabric of reality was something that occurred shortly after we returned home to Sioux Center. After a long day's drive we unpacked, settled in, and began to go through the mail of the past few days. Under the usual mountain of junk mail, I found the latest issue of *The Reformed Journal*. In that issue was a gem of an article by Philip Yancey entitled *Ecclesiastes: The High Counterpoint of Boredom*. Reading the article reinforced my vision of the connecting threads that tied together our recent time spent at the resort, the cave exploration, the boat ride, the *Journal* article itself, and this *Plumbline* (which I began anticipating).

To many people Ecclesiastes is a strange book and seems to not belong in the Bible. Over and over the its writer is driven to give us the same discouraging advice that Shakespeare's Macbeth gave us:

> "Meaningless! Meaningless!" says the Teacher. "Utterly meaningless! Everything is meaningless." . . . All things are wearisome, more than one can say. The eye never has enough of seeing, nor the ear its fill of hearing. Ecclesiastes 1:2, 8

Yancey, in his *Reformed Journal* article, suggests that Ecclesiastes was written during a time of great material success in Israel.[2] Whether or not it was Solomon who wrote it, it was written to portray the kind of despair that comes to anyone who honestly looks at reality with eyes blinded by the success of power, wealth, fame, or intellectual prowess—eyes blind to the threads in the tapestry of the Lord's creation. Contemplating the events of the past few days in the light of Ecclesiastes, I was reminded of those words from the epistle of James:

> Every good and perfect gift is from above, coming down from the Father of the heavenly lights, who does not change like shifting shadows. James 1:17

If one cannot see that life's pleasures are an integral part of God's good creation, that they have lasting significance because they are gifts, referring back to the Creator who gives them, then even the best of those pleasures will fade quickly with time and be seen in retrospect as mere "chasing after wind," as the writer of Ecclesiastes describes.

I want to end this *Plumbline* by trying to make visible one other thread that the events at the lake and the *Reformed Journal* essay on Ecclesiastes enabled me to see. Chapter 12 of Ecclesiastes begins with these words:

> Remember your Creator in the days of your youth, before the days of trouble come and the years approach when you will say, "I find no pleasure in them." Ecclesiastes 12:1

Twenty-five years ago, when I first seriously studied the book of Ecclesiastes, I was troubled by those words. They almost seemed to reinforce that pagan notion that to be eighteen is better than to be eighty. Well, experience has taught me to disbelieve such nonsense. But reading that *Reformed Journal* article enabled me to better understand what the Lord is telling us in this strange Old Testament book. Oddly enough, that thread tied together the last chapter in Ecclesiastes with the words of a song written by Bob Dylan about thirty years ago. It's true that reading Ecclesiastes, chapter 12 troubled me many years ago. "Ah, but I was so much older then, I'm younger than that now."[3]

Postmodernism: Academic Fiddling While the World Burns
February 7, 1997

When I was a young child, I had a recurrent nightmare in which I observed a person slowly playing a violin in the front room of a house while, in the back room, violence was being done to another person. The violinist seemed blithely unaware of the trauma occurring only two rooms away. I call it my dissonance dream, and, although I had the role of a mere observer, it caused me greater distress than even the more typical "monster" nightmares, where one is being chased by a large animal while seemingly wearing boots of lead. I would wake from that dissonance dream trembling, wet with sweat, and unable to get back to sleep. Thankfully, my mother seemed to recognize my state of high anxiety and was ready with the cure: a glass of warm milk and a few comforting moments sipping it while seated on the couch in our living room.

I've recently had occasion to reflect on that dissonance dream. Although it was confined to my childhood, it is one of the few nightmares that accurately, if metaphorically, reflects a paradox of life in the twentieth century: the incongruous coincidence of tranquility and mayhem. At times I think that, in some mystical way, the dream is related to the circumstances of my birth. I've recently come to realize that in the month or so before my conception, my parents were enjoying the peaceful bliss of newlyweds while, on the other side of the world, more than 300,000 people were dead or dying from the atomic bombs that were dropped on Hiroshima and Nagasaki. Strange, isn't it—this confluence of joy and suffering that so often characterizes our world?

What brought this most recently to my—not usually so melancholic—mind, was a Dordt College Faculty discussion about postmodernism. Actually the discussion was about a book about postmodernism, a book entitled *Truth Is Stranger Than it Used to Be* by Richard Middleton and Brian Walsh.[4] In the book the authors do an excellent job of analyzing postmodernism from a Christian perspective and try to give some hopeful suggestions for how we, disciples of Christ, might live in a postmodern age.

For those of you listeners who are wondering just what in the world I am talking about, postmodernism might be described as a worldview. Its central tenet is a rejection of the Enlightenment faith in reason, science, and authority. In some respects it's not new. The Romantic poets like Blake and Wordsworth knew something was wrong with those "dark Satanic Mills"[5] of the early industrial revolution and with a "meddling intellect" that "Misshapes the beauteous forms of things:—we murder to dissect."[6] More recently the existentialist thought of Kierkegaard, Sartre, and Camus denounced the modernist worldview that glorified reason at the expense of individual freedom and responsibility. Even the flower children of the late sixties, with their rejection of structure and authority, might be seen as harbingers of postmodernism. In some sense the New Age movement is a kind of superficial expression of postmodernism.

The most positive thing that can be said about postmodernism is that it takes seriously the claim that all of one's life experiences are colored by one's worldview or perspective. There is no neutral area of life that we can retreat to and where we can all agree. Even Joe Friday's *facts* are shaped by a perspective. Even our simplest mathematical calculations are the product of a particular worldview. Of course, Reformational Christians have been saying that, at least, since Abraham Kuyper. And that has made it a little easier for us to communicate with our secular academic contemporaries.

But there is a negative side to postmodernism as well. For many postmodernists, not only can we not know the reality around us except through the system of our worldview, but it is often believed that *there is no reality except* that which we construct from out of our worldview. Thus, for example, everyone's point of view must be as valid as everyone else's. And anathema upon anyone who tries to impose his perspective on anyone else or, worse yet, suggests that his perspective might be the truth!

Still, the academic climate conditioned by postmodernism is exciting. It's fun to sit and discuss these issues with fellow Christians and sometimes even with non-Christians—for at least now they are willing to listen. Do you hear the violin playing?

The trouble with all this is that postmodernism, while certainly driving much of our culture, is not driving all of it. Its most obvious influences are in the humanities and social science divisions of major universities; among the artists who produce such cultural expressions as films, books, music, and television; and certainly among those members of the media who daily tell us about ourselves—the journalists and writers for major newspapers, magazines, and TV and radio news broadcasting. Perhaps you may ask, "Well, who is left?" Well, I will tell you who is left. The majority of scientists, business owners, engineers, financiers, and military leaders know nothing about postmodernism. And the few who do are largely unaffected by it. These are the power brokers, the people in our culture for whom there *are* absolutes—absolutes such as the scientific method, the law of supply and demand, the drive to rise to the top of one's field, the almighty buck, the faith that modern technology can solve all our problems, and the belief that democracy must be preserved—even if that preservation requires the destruction of other human beings. Is the violin still playing?

My dissonance dream today is that the masses in our wealthy American culture will be influenced by postmodernism into *tolerating* these power brokers. Thus economism, scientism, hedonism, and militarism will not be unmasked and seen as the evil spirits of our age that they are. And the poor will get poorer, the hungry will not be fed, the widow and the orphan will suffer injustice. And the masses will be kept content in their postmodern world by the mind-manipulating products of high technology—advanced versions of Nintendo and lots and lots of choice of TV programming. And the Word of the Lord that came to the prophet Hosea will come to our land:

> For the Lord has a case against the inhabitants of the land,
> Because there is no faithfulness or kindness
> Or knowledge of God in the land.
> There is swearing, deception, murder, stealing, and adultery.
> They employ violence, so that bloodshed follows bloodshed.
> Therefore the land mourns,
> And everyone who lives in it languishes
> Along with the beasts of the field and the birds of the sky;
> And also the fish of the sea disappear. Hosea 4:1–3[7]

All the while the postmodern violinist plays on . . . and I feel very much in need of a glass of hot milk.

Between Technicism and Bio-Romanticism
November 1, 2002

In the book of Genesis we read that the Lord creates the heavens and the earth, fills them with life, and then installs his image-bearing servants to oversee and manage it all as it develops throughout time. "Develops throughout time": I use that phrase deliberately, because the nonhuman creation has a dynamic, unfolding character to it—much like the way a child does, developing from infancy through childhood and adolescence, with all that is potential in the child being slowly and progressively actualized during different stages of maturation. And like the developing child who is in need of parents, the creation is in need of stewards for it to unfold and develop properly, according to the Word of the Lord. That is why the Lord charged his image-bearing servants with what Reformed Christians call today the cultural mandate.

But there is a problem, one that deeply affects the cultural mandate. God's image-bearer—humankind—rebelled and sought to live independently of God, independently of his fellow servants, and even independently of God's good creation—though such an attempt is absurd, since humans are finite and temporal creatures and very much an integral part of creation. The result of this rebellion, this fall into sin, has been a curse upon the relationship between humankind and the rest of creation. Creation resists humankind's attempts to steward it. And humankind, in turn, has attempted to subjugate the creation to its own selfish ends.

But the Lord, in his mercy, has provided a means for healing the brokenness that has resulted from this rebellion. In Christ not only are we humans restored to our right relationship with God, but also to our right relationship with the rest of creation. That's why Paul writes in Romans that

> The creation waits in eager expectation for the sons of God to be revealed. For the creation was subjected to frustration, not by its own choice, but by the will of the one who subjected it, in hope that the creation itself will be liberated from its bondage to decay and brought into the glorious freedom of the children of God. Romans 8:19–21

That liberation, however—that healing of creation and the rift between the human and nonhuman parts of creation—will not be completely accomplished until the Lord returns. Until that time Christians are called to be stewards, earthkeepers, concerned for being both agents of healing and reconciliation on the one hand and faithful stewards and culture-formers on the other hand. In other words, our task is to both help liberate creation from its bondage so that it can be what the Lord calls it to be and to unfold and develop creation according to the original cultural mandate so that creation can become what the Lord calls it to become. In simple everyday terms, we have the complimentary tasks of conservation and development.

But here lies a problem and the central point of this *Plumbline*. Due to our finitude and our sin, we Christians have developed a tension between these two aspects of our stewardship role. Some of us are motivated primarily (and perhaps triumphalistically) by a vision for the unfolding and developing of creation as we imagine how it may have occurred had the fall into sin not occurred. Claiming every square inch of creation for the King of creation, we seek to boldly develop it in whatever direction seems possible. Unconsciously influenced by the unbiblical spirits of technicism and economism—spirits that lie to us by saying that whatever is technologically possible ought to be pursued and that the accumulation of wealth is the

312

only road to happiness—we overlook our calling to heal and to conserve. On the other hand, some of us are motivated primarily by our awareness of the history of abuse that has characterized humanity's relationship to the nonhuman creation. Then, unconsciously influenced by the unbiblical spirits of naturalism and Romanticism, we deny our mandate as culture formers. For these spirits lie to us by saying that nature is good "in itself," independent from humankind, and that all development is inherently evil— an arrogant attempt to impose our selfish wills on something that would be much better off without us.

The only solution to this problem starts by listening to God's Word. And, of course, that means studying his whole Word, from Genesis to Revelation, and studying the creation in light of that Word. In concluding this *Plumbline*, however, let me refer to just those two key verses in Genesis where our role with respect to the nonhuman creation is first described. In Genesis 1 we read, regarding humankind:

> God blessed them and said to them, "Be fruitful and increase in number; fill the earth and subdue it. Rule over the fish of the sea and the birds of the air and over every living creature that moves on the ground." Genesis 1:28

But what is meant by "Be fruitful," "fill the earth and subdue it," or "Rule over?" We gain insight into what those phrases mean when we read the creation account in Genesis 2:

> The LORD God took the man and put him in the Garden of Eden to work it and take care of it. Genesis 2:15

To "work it and take care of it": the meaning here is clearly one that will not support our ravaging the creation for our own selfish wants. Neither, however, will it support our placing the nonhuman creation on a pedestal where it is best left untouched by human hands—or footsteps, as some are inclined to say. The nonhuman creation is given its proper due when, like an abused human child, it is treated with the tender care that brings healing and renewal and when it is enabled to flower and develop, before the face of the Lord—and according to his Word.

Notes

1. William Shakespeare, *Macbeth*, Scene 5, Act 5, lines 26–30.

2. Philip Yancey, "Ecclesiastes: The High Counterpoint of Boredom," *The Reformed Journal* 40, no. 6 (July 1990): 14–19.

3. Bob Dylan, "My Back Pages," Track 8 on *Another Side of Bob Dylan*, Columbia CK8993.

4. J. Richard Middleton and Brian J. Walsh, *Truth Is Stranger Than It Used to Be* (Downers Grove, IL: InterVarsity, 1995).

5. William Blake, "The New Jerusalem," in *Immortal Poems of the English Language*, ed. Oscar Williams (New York: Washington Square Press, 1952), 233.

6. William Wordsworth, "The Tables Turned," in *The Major English Romantic Poets*, ed. W. H. Marshall (New York: Washington Square Press, 1963), 129.

7. *The Holy Bible*, New American Standard Bible.

Sustainable Theocentric Agriculture

Ronald J. Vos[*]

....

Introduction

The famous Greek philosopher Anonymous stated that "Man, despite his artistic pretensions, his sophistication, and his many accomplishments, owes his existence to a six-inch layer of topsoil and the fact that it rains." When all the material things that surround us are stripped away to our basic physical needs, food is one of the most basic. As L. H. Bailey stated almost a century ago, "we must assuredly know how it is that all the peoples in all the places have met the problem of producing their sustenance out of the soil."[1] How we humans grow our food tells us a lot about ourselves, about how we view God, about how we view fellow humans, and how we view the rest of creation.

Headlines bombard us constantly with confusing items tangentially connected to agriculture. What is the appropriate reaction of Christians to the fact that 40,000 people die every day from starvation or hunger-related

---

[*] Dr. Vos is a graduate of Dordt College (1970) and Professor of Agriculture since 1985. His Ph.D. is from South Dakota State University. Ron operates a small family farm; promotes sustainable agriculture around the world including Russia, Honduras, Kenya, and the Ukraine; and works with policy and justice issues as they apply to agriculture.

causes?[2] Or what should Christians conclude when the Better Business Bureau berates the egg industry for advertising its products as humane while still promoting practices such as clipping hens' beaks, depriving birds of food and water to force molting, and caging the chickens in such a small area that they cannot flap their wings or turn around?[3]

Followers of Jesus Christ are not constrained by the culture in which they live. In fact, they should transcend that culture (James 4:4; 2 Corinthians 5:17; Romans 12:2). In this essay, I will focus on the "culture" of agriculture. Although often unrecognized, a culture is associated with how food and fiber are grown, consumed, and used. By culture, I am referring to a people's whole way of life: their ideas, objects, practices, and interactions. Culture can also be described as a way of living built up by a group of people that is then transmitted from one generation to another. It is also interesting to note that "culture" also refers to the action or practice of raising plants and animals. Considering all of these aspects is important as one examines the culture of agriculture. However, in North America today, the word *agriculture* with its agrarian roots is often replaced by the relatively new term *agribusiness*. Moreover, this new term is becoming widely used in other parts of the world. The implication of "agribusiness" is that culture is no longer part of agriculture, that all agricultural issues can be reduced to economic issues, and that narrow economic measures are the only way to assess the agricultural success.

If Christians are to live out their lives before the face of God, where should they look for guiding principles on how to conduct agriculture? While it is easy and thus tempting to look to contemporary culture for answers, the first place Christians should look to is the Bible. Although our culture contains many things that are noble and worthwhile, many others, when carefully scrutinized, are inconsistent with Scripture. Christians profess that they believe the Bible, so that is the first place to go for guidance and insight. However, Scripture must be interpreted carefully. Instead of simply tracking down one or two passages to reinforce a previously held position, one should look at Scripture as an organic whole.

The second source that Christians should explore for guiding principles is the rest of creation.[4] If one wants to find out more about the Creator, one of the best places to look is in his creation. To illustrate, if I want to find out more about great European painters, I should search out as many of their creations as I can. To find out more about Rembrandt or Van Gogh, I should extensively study their paintings. Moreover, I should learn from any written records that these painters left behind. Learning about these painters will involve in-depth study and reflection, not a quick perusal of one or two sketches. The writings of the famous painters are analogous to God revealing himself in Scripture, and their artworks are analogous to God revealing himself in creation. It is through both of these—Scripture and creation—that Christians can obtain guidance on how to interact with other humans and the rest of creation in the area of agriculture.

It is obvious from Scripture that God delights in the diversity of the nonhuman world that he made (e.g., Job 38–42; Genesis 1 and 2; Psalms 19, 50, 104, 150; and Luke 12:27–28.). In fact, he delights in things that humans may ignore or think insignificant. If we examine what he created, we also see rich diversity. From both of these sources, one can draw the conclusion that diversity in creation is normative. Consequently, humans are responsible for encouraging diversity in agriculture and the rest of creation in appropriate ways. This is a foundational principle for agriculture. Policies and practices that promote diversity should be encouraged because diversity is consistent with what we discover in Scripture and creation.

This principle raises an interesting question. Should Christians endorse all forms of agriculture? In reality, Christians do engage in all types of agriculture just as they practice almost all types of commerce. However, to be consistent with Scripture and creational revelation, Christians should endorse particular types of agriculture just as they should promote certain types of commerce. If Christians take seriously the concept of *coram Deo* (living out our lives before the face of God), they should reject many types of agriculture while embracing relatively few.

However, we need to raise more probing questions. As redeemed Christians, what is our role in agriculture? Do most evangelicals believe that Christianity is merely a personal experience relevant only to one's private life? Does faith have no relevance to agriculture or how we daily live out our lives before the face of God? Is it acceptable to follow popular culture during the week and then worship God on the special day that he set apart at the beginning of creation? These notions must be rejected. The prophet Jeremiah had harsh words for the people of Judah who practiced this dualism, for those who think they have their theology correct but live their lives in tune with the surrounding culture. Jeremiah 7:9–11 asks, "Will you steal and murder, commit adultery and perjury, burn incense to Baal and follow other gods you have not known, and then come and stand before me in this house, which bears my Name, and say, 'We are safe'—safe to do all these detestable things? Has this house, which bears my Name, become a den of robbers to you? 'But I have been watching!' declares the Lord."[5]

Many Christians believe that correct theology and proper Sunday observance are extremely important, as if that is all that the Lord requires of us. Doing right the rest of the week or living out their theology is less important in their minds. Worshipping, praying, and saving souls are of utmost importance. These Christians are not very concerned about what happens outside of church and in actuality leave the rest of the world to the devil. Some have referred to this as "upper story" Christianity, a focus on saving souls at the cost of shedding light on how Christ's disciples should live out their lives *coram Deo*. This upper-story view emphasizes personal piety and downplays the idea that the will of God must be discerned to determine how Christians should interact with their culture and the world. Others believe that their faith is only a personal matter between themselves and God; fellow Christians, these believers argue, have no right to suggest how to live life before God since this is a private matter.

This dualism is not found in Scripture but goes back to ancient Greek thought. Both the Old and New Testaments contain teachings that counter this dichotomy. In the New Testament, Matthew 4:23 states, "Jesus went throughout Galilee, teaching in the synagogues, preaching the good news of the kingdom, and healing every disease and sickness among the people." In the Old Testament, the prophet Isaiah encourages God's people to "Seek justice, encourage the oppressed. Defend the cause of the fatherless, plead the case of the widow" (Isaiah 1:17). Moreover, Micah 6:8 claims, "And what does the Lord require of you? To act justly, to love mercy, and to walk humbly with your God."

This same concept can be applied to agriculture. Instead of practicing proper theology on Sunday and following common cultural practices during the week, we need to transform the prevalent (agri)cultural situation. Doing so requires discernment. We need to return to the practice of the early Roman Christians. Tom Sine describes how Christians of the first century were not engaged in Roman culture during the week and then in church and proper theology on the weekend. There was no dualistic, compartmental-ized faith for them. Instead they were completely, radically changed in their relationship with the contemporary culture.[6]

A Brief History of United States Agriculture

The history of United States agriculture is extensive and complex. Few historians specialize in agricultural history. Consequently, agricultural history is not widely studied except at the graduate school level. While that history can be studied in many ways, here it will be described briefly in terms of the social contracts that existed between those producing food and fiber and those consuming these items. The term *social contract* refers to an unwritten understanding between groups within society.

Before European migration and settlement, Native Americans practiced agriculture on the continent. They had a complex agricultural system that was successful chiefly because it worked in harmony with natural cycles. The agricultural products and their uses varied considerably based on climate and tribal location. Indian agriculture practiced in the Southwest was considerably different than that practiced in the Northeast.

Despite this wide variation in agricultural practices, Native American ag-riculture shared some general characteristics. Indians viewed land as something that could not be bought, sold, or owned individually. It was

318

considered something sacred to be well cared for so that all might live well. In order for everyone in the village to be fed, crops were grown to supplement hunting and fishing. Game and crops were shared with everyone in the village based on elaborate systems that had developed over time, and work was limited to meeting family needs.

As early European settlers, the Puritans mark the next social contract related to agriculture on the continent. In many ways, their view of land and creation was the opposite of the Indian view. Their goal was to establish the Kingdom of God in the new world. God was a God of orderliness. Therefore, the Puritans believed that forests needed to be removed so that crops could be planted, whereas the Indians planted their crops in open spaces between trees. Land was viewed as something that could be owned, bought, and sold. A good example of the differences between these worldviews can be illustrated by the example of the sale of what is now Manhattan Island. One can only imagine what might have gone through the minds of the people involved. The Indians may have thought the Dutch buyers were quite foolish to think that they could actually buy and sell land. The Dutch might have thought that the Indians were quite dense to sell such a large amount of land for so little money. Perhaps both parties thought that they had tricked the other party.

A second example of the Puritan view can be found in a colonist's exultation that the epidemic of 1616–1619 cleared so many heathen from the path of the "chosen people." This Puritan chronicler linked the epidemic to "[t]he wonderful preparation of the Lord Christ by His providence wrought for His people's abode in this western world." The chronicler was particularly satisfied that the plague had swept away "chiefly young men and children, the very seeds of increase."[7]

The next social contract in United States agriculture, called agrarianism, was epitomized by Thomas Jefferson's views. In the narrow sense, agrarianism can be described as the belief that farming is the best way of life and the most important economic endeavor.[8] Newer forms of agrarianism take a broader view and include important concepts of community and justice in both rural and urban settings.[9] Jefferson wrote with hyperbole that "those who labor in the earth are the chosen people of God, if he had a chosen people," and "cultivators of the earth are the most valuable citizens. They are the most vigorous, the most independent, the most virtuous, and they are tied to their country and wedded to its liberty and interests by the most lasting bonds."[10]

The agrarian populism concept has guided (and still guides) United States agriculture. Two contemporaries of Jefferson, Alexander Hamilton and James Madison advocated that the United States would best be served by investing power in an elite, educated class of gentlemen whose financial interests would be tied to large landed estates. They felt that common citizens would shirk their responsibility for public good and press only for personal interests. In one sense, the Civil War was a war over whose philosophy, Jefferson's or Hamilton's, would be the guiding principle for United States agriculture.

The last two social contracts for United State agriculture, both products of the twentieth century, often conflict with each other. The first is the industrialization of agriculture, which started with World War I and continues in some sectors today. The concept here is to produce food and fiber with the least number of people possible. Early on, this freed up people to help in war efforts; later, it freed them to pursue a "better life." Labor, under this system of thought, is a cost that should be avoided when possible, and education is the ticket to the "better life."

A social contract often in conflict with this industrial one involves society's expectations that farmers maintain open space, clean air, and clean water while engaging in agriculture. This conflict has created confusion for many people involved in agriculture who, when faced with decisions about which direction to follow, find themselves pulled by conflicting economic forces, policies, and worldviews. This ambivalence leads us to the present situation described at the beginning of this chapter. To better understand this present situation, we must examine different types of agriculture.

Traditional Agriculture

Traditional agriculture is that which has been practiced for a long time, whether a hundred years or thousands of years. For example, in some parts of China agriculture has been practiced with little change for over four thousand years. In addition, terraces built on steep hillsides have been around for thousands of years. Practices that have enhanced such long-term agriculture include composting, using animal manure, using human night soil, conserving water judiciously, reforesting, selecting region-appropriate crops, rotating crops, intercropping, using beneficial insects, and implementing intense methods to increase the soil's organic matter.

In tropical areas, a method of slash-and-burn agriculture was used. Forests were cut and burned in small areas, releasing nutrients from the forest canopy to the soil. This practice gave an immediate but short-term increase in soil nutrients. After a few years, when soil nutrients were depleted, people would move to another region and repeat the process. With low human population levels and only localized forest burning, this system was sustainable. By the time humans returned to the original burned locality, the forest had regenerated itself.

In North America, variations of the slash-and-burn technique were also used in forested areas. In the large Midwestern prairie areas, fire was used to control unwanted tree growth so that prairie grasses remained available as food for large grazing animals like bison. In addition, many different root crops and other plants were used for food and medicinal purposes. After

320

the invention of the steel moldboard plow, the prairie soil was turned over and planted with other crops. These crops in some cases mimicked the prairie system by including a wide variety of legumes and cereal grains. In other cases, marginal ground was planted to monocultures that were dissimilar to the prairie that it replaced.

Another term used to describe traditional agriculture is subsistence agriculture. One question raised regarding subsistence agriculture is whether this method can feed the world's present population. Many people answer no, arguing instead that we must rely on pesticides, commercial fertilizers, other chemically based inputs, and high-energy use in land-intensive crop production systems. This argument claims that subsistence agriculture involves low yields per acre, resulting in the need to expand production onto marginal lands or face an additional world food crisis. As will be pointed out later, sustainable agriculture may be a solution to this impasse.

Practitioners of traditional agriculture recognized that humans were finite beings limited in what food they could grow. They were limited by their location: the nutrients in the soil and the rainfall they received. They also recognized the symbiosis between plants and animals. In summary, traditional agriculture was sustainable in the context that it was practiced. Today, however, few people would consider it sustainable because of the large human population that must be fed. In this type of agriculture, creation was recognized as fruitful and humans were a part of creation but subject to its laws. This type of agriculture had little negative impact on creation compared with the present system.

Conventional Agriculture

Conventional agriculture is the predominant method practiced today in industrialized countries. Moreover, it is widely considered the success story that should be imitated globally. Relying heavily on large amounts of synthetic fertilizers and energy to grow and transport food, conventional agriculture is inefficient. However, it relies on fewer people to grow the food than traditional agriculture, and in this sense it can be considered more efficient. This efficiency also leads to arrogant claims that the North American farmer feeds himself and 170 other people (with the number changing annually), when in reality the farmer may not make enough money to buy food to feed his own family. The driving force behind conventional agriculture is economics instead of culture—economics in the narrow sense. Social and environmental costs are considered externalities and are thus ignored in calculations of production costs.

While conventional agriculture has certain benefits, such as the production of large amounts of food in certain locations, this system encourages exploitation of people and the land. Instead of owners being operators of agricultural enterprises, as was almost always the case in traditional agriculture, owners may be large corporations that have their headquarters hundreds or thousands of miles away from the operations. The number of corporations that control food production, from growing to the grocer, is becoming fewer as competition squeezes out independent producers.[11] Commodities are taken from one region and brought to another in order to benefit the corporate stockholders who may live far from where the commodity is produced.

Moreover, employees in these operations are not educated in the liberal arts but are narrowly trained to do the work that the current system requires, work that often pays substandard wages. Bright people living in rural communities often move to cities in order to escape this injustice. This predicament goes largely unnoticed in urban areas because city dwellers have little concern for what happens in rural areas as long as goods keep flowing. In fact, some economists make statements like, "This situation frees up people to pursue better jobs in urban areas." Few people question whether that "freeing" is what displaced people want or whether this system is just. In many countries, urban areas are overflowing with poor people displaced by this agricultural system.

In the last decade, the term *bio-piracy* has emerged. Bio-piracy involves a person or company taking or patenting genetic material and traditional knowledge without proper informed consent and fair terms. Because of the economics that drive conventional agriculture, multinational corporations in Western nations (using intellectual property rights) often facilitate piracy of the indigenous knowledge and biodiversity of developing nations. Some people in the developing nations charge that bio-piracy robs these countries of their biological and intellectual heritage just as in the colonial era European countries robbed non-European countries of their land and gold.[12]

A related result of conventional agriculture is globalization, a shift from local control to global control. Such globalization weakens local and national governments and strengthens transnational corporations. Because of a desire to maximize profits, these corporations scour the world for the cheapest place to grow their crops or produce their products. A product may be grown in Chile one year and in Zambia the next year. This practice severely disrupts the social fabric of societies that may be encouraged to grow a specific crop only to be dumped when this crop can be grown cheaper elsewhere. The practice may also harm the environment because crop monocultures may replace the region's native plant diversity. While these corporations are interested in their own long-term existence, they have little concern for the long-term existence of the people and the economy of the individual countries where they grow the crops.

At its root, conventional agriculture promotes disconnection between farming as husbandry and food as a cultural activity. The only thing that industrial agriculture notes is that food costs must continue to be lowered.

It is based on the faulty belief that consumers will always choose the lowest price. Since consumers do not always do so, industrial agriculture finds it necessary to "educate the consumer" that industrially grown food is good. As consumers demand to know how their food is raised and whether it is wholesome, industrial agriculture will discover that cheap food also cheapens food as a cultural feature.

Ironically, industrialized agriculture in the developed world is heavily subsidized by government payments. For example, European countries, Japan, and the United States heavily subsidize their agriculture, supporting this practice with rhetoric claiming that subsidies save family farms and rural communities, when in fact subsidies encourage more industrialization, usually at the expense of family farms and rural communities. If other forms of agriculture were to receive the same subsidies as conventional agriculture does, they would flourish and the creation would not suffer as much.

One could document in extensive detail the current state of conventional agriculture, a state usually ignored by people with a full stomach of cheap food. We are surrounded by the results of such agriculture. The purpose of simply listing a few details is to show that certain issues in conventional agriculture must be addressed. Under conventional agriculture, creation is groaning, subjugated to human whims. Money and human wishes are the driving forces in conventional agriculture, while the creation waits for Christians to promote justice for both the human and nonhuman creation (see Romans 8:18–27).

Organic Agriculture

Organic agriculture has emerged largely as a reaction to the industrialization characteristic of modern conventional agriculture. In the past, subsistence or traditional agriculture was de facto organic because synthetic products were unavailable, as was wealth to purchase off-farm inputs. In the wealthy, developed countries of Europe, organic agriculture has become widely accepted; in fact, many European Union countries have set a target for organic farming adoption on 10–20 percent of agricultural land area by 2010.[13] In the United States, organic agriculture is growing at a double-digit rate annually. However, in 2001 less than 1 percent of U.S. cropland and pasture was in organic production.[14] The December 2003 identification of a single animal in Washington State that tested positive for the prion that causes Mad Cow Disease will probably increase consumer demand for more organic products in the United States.

By employing third-party certification, present-day organic agriculture assures consumers that products measure up to the standards set by the USDA and others. A representative of an organic organization evaluates producers, processors, and handlers to determine if they conform to an established set of operating guidelines called organic standards. Those who conform are certified by the agent and are allowed to use a logo, product statement, or certificate to document that their product has been certified organic. In other words, the certifier vouches for the producers and assures buyers of the organic product's integrity.[15]

Organic agriculture is an environmentally responsible approach to producing high quality food and fiber. Personal health, environmental concerns, and economic benefits are the usual motivating factors for those who choose to farm organically. Personal health and environmental concerns are usually the reasons consumers purchase organic food, which is usually more expensive than nonorganic food.

Organic production involves farming practices that conserve and build the soil resource, cause little pollution, and encourage the development of healthy and diverse agroecosystems that support natural pest management. Techniques that accomplish these goals include diverse crop rotations, as well as the use of green manure, cover crops, livestock manure, and composting. These techniques are some of the same ones used in China for 4,000 years, as described previously.

To maintain organic integrity, producers must prevent contamination of organic production by prohibited materials and avoid commingling organic and conventional products. One method is to avoid the use of prohibited synthetic fertilizers and pesticides. Another method involves precautions against pesticide drift from other farms. Equipment used to grow organic products must be dedicated only to this purpose or be thoroughly cleaned between conventional and organic use. The same principles apply to storing and transporting organic products. Considerable documentation is required to ensure organic integrity, which adds to the cost of organic production.

In organic agriculture, strict adherence to rules ensures that organic practices are followed, with the result that the creation is cared for. However, in order to meet these rules, sometimes nonsustainable practices need to be followed. For example, organic fertilizers may need to be shipped thousands of miles. While organic agriculture is an improvement over industrial agriculture, I believe that there is room for more appropriate types of agriculture.

Community Supported Agriculture (CSA)

Within the last decade, a new type of agriculture has emerged around the world. With Community Supported Agriculture (CSA), consumers know how and where their food is raised. Subscriptions or shares in the CSAs are sold to customers. The subscription allows them to receive weekly portions of food from a local grower during the growing season. As part of their subscription service, some CSAs include the sale of animals that are humanely raised.

The purchaser and the grower both share in the risk of crop failure since the money is usually paid at the beginning of the growing season. Often, the holder of the subscription is required to spend some time working in the CSA as part of purchasing the subscription. This interaction results in trust between the grower and the consumer. While presently CSAs are small in scale compared with conventional agriculture, this movement is rapidly growing around the world.

Sustainable Agriculture

While industrial agriculture remains prominent today, sustainable agriculture is gaining acceptance around the world. Two websites supported by the federal government have existed for several years: the Sustainable Agriculture Information Center (www.attra.ncat.org) and Sustainable Agriculture Research and Education (www.sare.org). Sustainable agriculture is economically viable, resource efficient, and environmentally sound. It also promotes justice to both the human and nonhuman creation and builds community while providing food and fiber for humans for long periods of time.[16] Because no single method offers a panacea, sustainable agriculture involves diverse practices tailored to the local soils, topography, growing season, livestock, and rainfall. Diversity and adaptation to local conditions are key. Lands and soil cannot be managed by mass-produced mono-technologies.

The sustainable model of agriculture must mimic the creational model of the ecosystem because agricultural systems are, in fact, highly modified ecosystems. Ecosystems are made up of biotic communities that have the following features:

1.   The communities use solar energy (income), which flows through to reproduce and regenerate the living components and to recycle the raw materials (mineral elements) locally.
2.   Raw materials are accumulated and/or held in place by the biotic parts of the system (roots, soils, biomass).
3.   The communities depend on high species diversity to accomplish total function.
4.   The communities do not displace resources over long distances.
5.   If changes and displacements occur, they do so at a rate and on a scale compatible with maintaining internal integrity.

With this description of ecosystems in mind, we can see that sustainable agriculture will be characterized by agroecosystems that

a.   are less dependent on external energy, material, and nutrient inputs and are more dependent on on-farm renewable resources.
b.   have less or no adverse impact on ground water, downstream watersheds, and local wetlands.

c. depend on local cultural wisdom and decision making.
d. move towards polycultural and biogenetic diversity.
e. have green space and room for creatures other than humans and their domestic plants and animals.
f. depend more on biological and ecological methods of pest control.
g. are site- or region-specific with respect to plants and animals grown, matching biological adaptations to local climate and soils.
h. are less centralized in terms of markets and processing centers, reducing fossil-fuel use for transportation and refrigeration.[17]

Implementing sustainable agriculture will require more local knowledge, wisdom, and care; such a system will therefore require and support greater community. While this method offers a holistic approach to land, creatures, water, and people, sustainable agriculture cannot be accomplished without the political and social support of those living in urban areas. City dwellers will need to demand that politicians adopt policies in line with sustainable practices.

Sustainable Agriculture and Worldview

Sustainable agriculture, I am arguing, is most consistent with a theocentric worldview and the theme of creation stewardship; therefore, Christians especially should promote and practice it. Some of my ideas on this topic are in an article by Roger W. Elmore, which appeared in the *Journal of Production Agriculture* in 1996.[18] The very fact that his article appeared in a scientific publication at all may be the result of the Cyrus principle, where God uses unbelievers to accomplish his will.[19]

People's relationship with the ecosystem does affect their perception of sustainable agriculture. As we all live according to our worldview, either God (theocentric), the rest of creation (biocentric), humans (anthropocentric), or something else is exalted. We are not passive observers of the ecosystem. Humans are directly involved in the ecosystem and, like the rest of creation, are created by God. We derive food, water, and air from the ecosystem; we add wastes to it. How we interact with the rest of creation is largely a spiritual matter. We must ask if our own individual philosophy, when extended to its logical conclusion, leads to sustainability.

A biocentric person elevates the ecosystem over humans. Humans are often seen as a pathogen threatening the planet's health. While exalting the rest of the creation may appear unselfish, people who take this position tend to either worship creation or remove themselves from it in order to conserve ecosystem resources. It is pointless to discuss the sustainability of this worldview if people are removed from the world, however good this might be for environmental quality. If humans are allowed to exist under a biocentric worldview, their food and fiber needs as well as the economic

326

viability of agricultural producers would have little, if any, priority. Most people reject this view as being outlandish.

Conversely, the anthropocentric worldview exalts humans, placing people above the rest of creation and assuming that people are accountable to no higher authority for their treatment of it. Everything created is made for humans; nothing has intrinsic or God-given value. Things gain value only if humans decide they are valuable. Land has worth based only on the income it will produce for its owner. Therefore, the best use of land is what brings in the most income. Similarly, an anthropocentric worldview assumes that forests and prairies have value only when humans can use them. Thus, these parts of the creation should be preserved because they can provide us with a plentiful supply of oxygen or because some plant species could serve as future sources of medicine. The anthropocentric view puts the economic value of forests and prairies above their intrinsic or God-given value. An anthropocentrist will often speak against short-term greed and selfishness while advocating long-term greed and selfishness. Since creation exists solely for human benefit, according to this worldview, all technology is good technology because it hastens the human exploitation of creation for human good.

Fallen humans, including many Christians, often embrace this worldview, largely because of the misinterpretation of Genesis 1:28. Christians who recognize that humans are created in God's image often believe that they can use their power to do as they please rather than practicing the servant leader model as exemplified in Jesus Christ. Our selfish human nature is exhibited most in this worldview. Biologist G. Hardin illustrated this concept already in 1968 using animal grazing as an example.[20] A grazing area is a public area where each villager can graze his animals during the day. In a common grazing area open to all herders, all will work together for their mutual benefit until the carrying capacity of the land is reached. At that point, each herder may consider the cost and benefit of adding one more animal to his herd. This person may soon discover that his benefit is an additional animal but that the cost of adding one more animal is divided among all herders. As each individual herder seeks to add more animals, the commons is ruined and tragedy ultimately results. Hardin concludes, "Ruin is the destination toward which all men rush, each pursuing his own interest in a society that believes in the freedom of the commons. Freedom in a commons brings ruin to all."[21]

An anthropocentric view does not promote sustainable agriculture. Under this view, some people but not all will have food and a reasonable quality of life; some but not all agricultural producers will be economically viable. This outcome is considered a normal economic process because a "survival of the fittest" mentality drives this worldview. Except for what humans decide to be just, this worldview has no place for justice. The first herders to take advantage of creation get the most economic gain before the commons area collapses. Destruction of creation is driven by human selfishness.

By contrast, theocentrists believe that God is in charge, every part of creation belongs to him, and people were created in part to be faithful stewards of the ecosystem. Theocentrists acknowledge that there is a separation between God, the Creator, and his creation, and thus the creation is not equal to God. While people like Berkeley historian Lynn White often blame Christians for the environmental crisis and the exploitation of creation, it is a misinterpretation of the biblical message that is more likely the cause.[22] Evidence of severe environmental problems in the former Soviet Union indicates that huge problems do exist in all types of societies.

However, some Christians have added to the environmental crisis by emphasizing the "upper story" (saving the soul and getting to heaven). They see no value in the rest of creation beyond consuming it or using it to prove the existence of God. They believe that God's Word has something to say about one's spiritual life or how many wives one should have, but little or nothing about how to practice agriculture. These views result from a failure to understand Scripture's teachings about agriculture and the delight that God takes in his creation.[23] Humans must use special discernment to understand which agricultural practices to promote.

Creation, Fall, Redemption

Even though God created everything good, sin through the disobedience of humans has destroyed the perfect relationship that existed among humans, between God and humans, and between humans and the rest of creation. However, because he loved the world (John 3:16) that he had made, God in the person of Jesus Christ came into this world to pay the penalty for all sin. Through his suffering, death, resurrection, and ascension, Christ has redeemed his people and all of creation. In gratitude, with the help of the Holy Spirit and by the use of Scripture, we are called to spread this good news and seek to reform human activities to be in accord with the original mandate. As Chuck Colson writes in his book *How Now Shall We Live?*, "Salvation does not consist simply of freedom from sin; salvation also means being restored to the task that we were given in the beginning, the job of creating culture. . . . Christians are saved not only from something (sin) but to something (Christ's lordship over all life)."[24]

Because of the Fall, all creation developed enmity toward God. Yet God established a covenant with humans and the rest of creation (Genesis 9:8–11, 22) that he would never destroy the world again with a flood. This covenant makes obvious that God delights in all parts of his creation, not just humans. This delight starkly contrasts the utilitarian view that the creation's value is determined solely by how it can benefit humans. The covenantal view makes Christians responsible for their interaction with creation. For while the natural world obeys God's laws without any choice in the matter, in culture and society God rules indirectly, entrusting to humans the tasks that need to be done. For example, all of creation is subject to God's law of gravity and will suffer immediate consequences by ignoring it. However, humans can often and do rebel against God's created order and moral law, assuming that they can escape the consequences.

The covenant that was fulfilled in Christ's death and resurrection has personal consequences for believing Christians as well as cosmic consequences for creation. As Fred Van Dyke states in *Redeeming Creation,* "God's saving grace through Christ not only pays the price for people, but redeems an oppressed cosmos. This does not demean the work of Christ, but rather amplifies it. Just as the sin of Adam affected all creation, so the sacrifice of Christ begins the redemption of it."[25] That this redemption is not just for humans but for all of God's creation is shown in Romans 8:21: "the creation itself will be liberated from the bondage of decay." This claim is echoed powerfully in Colossians 1:15–20, where we learn that everything was made for and by Christ; everything holds together in Christ; and everything will be reconciled by Christ. Redemption at the end of time is not an end to the creation, but the beginning of a new heaven and a new earth (Revelation 21:5).

God enjoys the great diversity that he has made (Genesis 1; Psalm 104; Job 38–41). This fact has great implications for how we practice agriculture. For example, weeds are not evil plants cultivated by the devil, but simply plants growing where humans wish they were not growing. This plant still functions as God intended by preventing soil erosion, producing carbohydrates through photosynthesis, and serving as food and protection for other creatures. Similarly, domestic animals are not objects to be used by humans. Animals are part of God's creation and their diversity apparently gives him great pleasure. An animal gives praise to God by being the animal that God intended it to be. Humans must remember this fact as we raise our animals for food and fiber. Christians especially need to remember that they are dealing with something that is not theirs but a gift from the Creator himself. This fact should instill awe and respect in Christians.

In summary, theocentrists exalt God over creation, including humans. Following the example of Christ as servant leader, theocentrists can put others above self and see humans as caretakers of creation accountable to God. This view is consistent with sustainable agriculture and promotes good environmental stewardship and sufficient food production. This approach results in a reasonable quality of life and thus the long-term sustainability of the creation.

However, all of this begs a question. If sustainable agriculture is most consistent with a theocentric worldview, why are not more Christians practicing it? Two powerful forces prevent Christians from embracing it: inertia and pragmatism.

It takes a visionary person to farm in a way that is counter to what is considered normal. It is analogous to a person getting a routine physical being told that he has cancer even though he feels well. His first reaction might be, "How is that possible? I feel normal." Only with more testing can he be convinced that he is ill and needs to address the disease. The same inertia applies to practicing agriculture that feels normal.

Sometimes tradition or theology gets in the way of recognizing the problem. A humorous illustration can be found in Stan Wiersma's "Calvinist Farming."[26] The Calvinists defend farming up and down the hill and reject contour farming because they believe that God is a God of rigid order. As a result, the hilltops on the Calvinists' farms turn clay-brown from erosion while those non-Calvinists who use contour farming have hilltops still black with fertility. While Scripture does not change, a more correct interpretation of it may allow us to see what God would have us do.

A second force that opposes the adoption of sustainable agriculture is pragmatism. In a nutshell, this is the argument: If it works, it must be all right. This thinking is extended one step further: If so many Christians are doing something, it must be correct. When Christians unthinkingly follow the status quo, and do so in large numbers, they add to the belief that the practice being followed is appropriate. This thinking adds to the inertia mentioned earlier.

The practice of slavery is a good analogy for such pragmatism. Human slavery is condemned by Christians today based on Scripture. However, many past Christians practiced slavery extensively. They did so because it was considered normal, so many Christians were doing it, and it worked. Since it worked, it must be all right. Scripture did not change, but as Scripture was studied more carefully, humans discovered that Scripture did not condone slavery, and it was abandoned. This same process may need to occur to conventional agriculture before sustainable agriculture gains wider acceptance.

Usufruct

The concept of "usufruct" should be a principle guiding how we practice agriculture. Usufruct, a word rarely used now in our modern economic climate, literally means to "use the fruits of." Specifically, it is the right to use and enjoy the profits and advantages of something belonging to another so long as the property is not damaged or altered in any way. With usufruct in mind, Wendell Berry argued already in 1986 that "[t]o receive the gift of creation and then to hasten directly to practical ways of exploiting that gift for maximum production without regard to long term impacts is at best ingratitude and at worse blasphemy (the act of claiming for one's self the attributes and rights of God)."[27] May God guide us as we seek to do his will in terms of how we practice usufruct in our agriculture.

Notes

1. F. H. King, *Farmers of Forty Centuries—Permanent Agriculture in China, Korea, and Japan* (New York: St. Martin's Press, 1911).

2. While estimates vary, *Justpeace News* 2, no. 1 (January 2004) used the figure of 34,000 under the age of five, and others, including the United Nations Food and Agriculture Organization, have used numbers as high as 54,000.

3. Associated Press, "BBB Rejects Egg Industry Ads," *Sioux City Journal,* May 11, 2004. This Associated Press article was carried in hundreds of newspapers throughout May 2004.

4. "The Means by Which We Know God," Belgic Confession Article 2, in *Psalter Hymnal,* ed. Emily R. Brink (Grand Rapids: CRC Publications, 1987), 818. See also Article 12, "The Creation of All Things," and Articles 9, 10, and 13 of Our World Belongs to God: A Contemporary Testimony, in *Psalter Hymnal,* 1022–23.

5. See also Jeremiah 7:1–8, 12–15; Isaiah 56:7; Matthew 21:13; Mark 11:17; and Luke 19:46.

6. Tom Sine, *Mustard Seed versus McWorld* (Grand Rapids, MI: Baker, 2000), 195.

7. Alvin M. Josephy, Jr., ed., *The American Heritage Book of Indians* (New York: Simon and Schuster, 1961), 179.

8. R. Douglas Hurt, *American Agriculture—A Brief History* (West Lafayette, IN: Purdue University Press, 2002), 71.

9. See Eric R. Freyfogle, *The New Agrarianism—Land, Culture, and the Community of Life* (Washington, DC: Island Press, 2001).

10. Merrill D. Petersen, ed., *Writings—Thomas Jefferson* (New York: Literary Classics of the United States, 1984), 8–12.

11. See Mary Hendrickson and William Heffernan, *Concentration of Agricultural Markets* (Columbia, MO: Department of Rural Sociology–University of Missouri, February 2002).

12. Vandana Shiva, "North-South Conflicts in Intellectual Property Rights," *Peace Review* 12, no. 4 (2000): 501.

13. George Kuepper, "Organic Farm Certification and the National Organic Program," National Sustainable Agriculture Information Service (Appropriate Technology Transfer for Rural Areas, October 2002). Available at http://attra.ncat.org.

14. Nicolas Lampkin, "Development of Policies for Organic Agriculture" (proceedings of the COR Conference, UK Organics Research, University of Wales in Aberystwyth, Wales, UK, March 2002). Available at http://www.organic.aber.ac.uk/conference/ proceedings.shtml.

15. Catherine Green and Amy Kremen, "US Organic Farming in 2000–2001: Adoption of Certified Systems," *Agriculture Information Bulletin* no. 780 (USDA, 2002). Available at http://ers.usda.gov/publications/aib780/aib780.pdf.

16. See Ron Vos and Del Vander Zee, "Trends in Agriculture: Sustainability," *Pro Rege* 18 (March 1990): 19–28.

17. Del Vander Zee and Ron Vos, "Sustainable Agriculture," in *Signposts of God's Liberating Kingdom* (Potchefstroome, South Africa: Potchefstroome University Press, 1998).

18. Roger. W. Elmore, "Our Relationship with the Ecosystem and Its Impact on Sustainable Agriculture," *Journal of Production Agriculture* 9, no. 1 (1996).

19. See 2 Chronicles 36:22, 23 and Ezra 1:1–4 for the details.

20. G. Hardin, "The Tragedy of the Commons," *Science* 162 (1968): 1243–48.

21. Ibid.

22. Lynn White, Jr., "The Historical Roots of Our Ecological Crisis," *Science* 155 (1967): 1203–7.

23. See Genesis 1 and Job 38–42, for example.

24. Charles Colson and Nancy Pearcey, *How Now Shall We Live?* (Wheaton, IL: Tyndale House Publishers, 1999), 296.

25. Fred Van Dyke et al., *Redeeming Creation* (Downers Grove, IL: InterVarsity, 1996), 86.

26. Stan Wiersma, "Calvinist Farming," in *Purpaleanie and Other Permutations* (Orange City, IA: Middleburg Press, 1982).

27. Wendell Berry, quoted by Wes Jackson (in a presentation given at the Theology of Land Conference, St. John's University, Collegeville, MN, 1986).

Ecological Literacy in Christian Higher Education:
Status and Prospects

Delmar Vander Zee[*]
....

Introduction

After three plus decades of "celebrating" Earth Day,[1] after mainline and most smaller denominations have made declarations regarding environmental "issues,"[2] after national laws and international conventions were enacted to conserve ecosystem and planetary processes,[3] why does the phenomenon and challenge of earthkeeping seem to remain the agenda of special interest groups? Students raise the same question when they become aware of their ecological place and sense their connections to Earth's processes and see ramifications for their lives and callings. Uneasy with cognitive and confessional dissonance, they too ask, why?

---

[*] Dr. Vander Zee is a Dordt graduate (1966) and Professor of Biology and Environmental Studies. His Ph.D. is from Washington State University. He spent twenty-one summers at the Au Sable Institute of Environmental Studies in Michigan and Washington.

During these same decades Christian colleges in North America have experienced something of a renaissance. Enrollments have increased and campuses have been modernized. What were once somewhat sleepy Bible colleges are now considered first-class regional liberal arts centers for higher education.[4] The mission statements of these schools increasingly call for integrating faith and learning, all the while quality contributions by Christian scholars have been increasingly recognized by secular academics.[5] Many things have changed, often for the better. However, one thing that has not increased on many Christian college campuses is the perceived need for ecological literacy.

The purpose of this essay is to reflect on what has happened during the last three-plus decades regarding the place of environmental stewardship in the minds and practices of Christian colleges, including Dordt College. I will use the term *ecological literacy* (EL) to refer to specific knowledge about how the world works, awareness of the environment and care for it (or lack thereof) as a cultural function, and commitment to making earthkeeping a focal concern[6] at Christian colleges that typically identify the creation as a foundational tenet of their mission. In what follows I highlight changes that have occurred regarding the place of EL in Christian higher education, suggest some reasons for EL remaining in the margins, and then propose ways for faithful earthkeeping or EL in Christian higher education.

Ecological Literacy: The Concept Enlarged

The term *ecological literacy* comes from David Orr and is commonplace in environmental education literature.[7] Orr unpacks this concept as a way of thinking called "ecological design intelligence," which

> . . . is the capacity to understand the ecological context in which humans live, to rec-
> ognize limits, and to get the scale of things right. It is the ability to celebrate human
> purposes and natural constraints and do so with grace and economy. Ecological de-
> sign intelligence is not just about things like technologies; it also has to do with the
> shape and dimensions of our ideas and philosophies relative to the earth. At its heart
> . . . it is motivated by an ethical view of the world and our obligations to it. . . . The
> surest signs of . . . [its] achievements: healthy, durable, resilient, just, and prosperous
> communities.[8]

Although not overtly Christian or informed by Scripture, Orr's definition nevertheless speaks eloquently to a worldview that is unquestionably holistic and inclusive of humankind's rightful place. This definition resonates well with a Christian view that sees humankind as part of the creation, with a stewarding and accountable role. It also counters, as would a Christian view, the Modernist, Enlightenment, technicist view that humankind is the measure of all things and rightful recipient of the earth's resources.

So, for the Christian in higher education, ecological literacy is knowing how the world works, what is right, and what should be done.[9] How the world works ecologically is indeed very complex, the details and ramifications of which are continually being worked out by environmental scientists in fields from climatology to oceanography. But specialized knowledge is probably not as important as a keen and caring awareness of how humankind fits into the ecological flow of energy and materials on the finite green and blue planet called Earth, aware of limits, dependencies, and responsibilities.

Reaching consensus on what is right regarding the ecological footprint of humankind on planet Earth is a difficult challenge. That important discussion has begun but will not be included in this brief essay.[10] The point to be made here is that ecologically sustainable living is itself a critical question confronting Christian higher education today. It is crucial both on theoretical academic grounds as regards the ethical place of humankind on Earth and on practical grounds given the continuing critical nature of the decline in life-support systems. In other words, doing God's will on Earth is not contingent on whether there are signs of planetary distress, but must be based on foundational principles.[11]

For the Christian the obligation for service (what should be done) is not only directed to the world or Earth. As *imago dei*, "con-serving" is stewardship for the Master, the Creator Jahweh.[12] Ecological literacy is obviously missing from Christian theology and academic reflection in the past—including the last thirty-five years of environmental awareness. Christian higher education has humankind, society, and culture in mind, not Earth in mind. Earth is assumed to be the stage for the human drama; its props, we presume, can be moved around or used at will to satisfy the needs we perceive or the wants to which we are committed. Before ecological literacy can emerge, Christian higher education will have to change its anthropocentric focus and turn from culture to the creation. With Earth in mind, human culture is not discarded, but properly grounded in the creation. We can then acknowledge that civilizations are built on six inches of topsoil, that what we do culturally does affect the physical and biotic parts of creation, but also that topography, geology, plants, animals, microbes, and climate affect cultures.

A keen sense of ecological place must ground all that education includes so that all students develop a proper sense of place, wherever they are from or wherever they intend to go on Earth. A practical example of this is the ignorant damage many missionaries have done historically because they tried to move North American culture and technology to places where they did not fit. They were culturally literate and knew the requisite languages, but too often they were ecologically illiterate.[13]

Changes in Christian Higher Education

After the first Earth Day in 1970, many Christian colleges began to resonate with popular culture and the environmental awakening. This movement is reflected in an increase in scholarly responses to Lynn White's

1967 argument that the roots of our ecologic crisis lay in Christianity.[14] Publications regarding environmental issues and related theological foundations increased dramatically, from less than five per year in the 1950s and 1960s, to peaks of sixty to eighty per year in the early 1970s and again in the 1980s.[15] A second response was the addition of courses in the curriculum that were designed to address ecological and environmental crisis issues. These courses had various names, from "Environmental Biology" to "Environment and Man."[16] Even though the root of environmental problems was not biological but more broadly cultural and economic, these courses were usually spawned from biology departments. (I suspect that too few in the humanities and social sciences saw their subject matter in jeopardy; the loss of integrity of soils, atmospheres, biodiversity, and aquatics was assumed to be something for the natural sciences.) These courses were inherently integrative and interdisciplinary; as such they provided bridges and fruitful dialog between many disciplines.

As experience and conviction grew regarding ecological literacy, many colleges introduced programs beyond a single course, organized as minors, emphases, or complete majors. The majors were either named environmental studies or environmental science depending on the kinds of courses included and interdisciplinary requirements. To be sure, these developments ran parallel to similar curricular changes in secular higher education and the plethora of new textbooks published for that market.[17]

Meanwhile there was also a greening of Protestant theology, viewed by Fowler as initially marching "in tandem with the broader movement" and applying religious language and metaphor in support of the cause. Christian green theology did distinguish itself, however, from the broader secular movement in being more optimistic (a theology of hope), rooting its arguments in a theocentric view vs. an ecocentric view of the earth, and calling for stewardly healing by way of communitarian policy changes and eco-justice in the broader world.[18] Many evangelical churches also found reason to enact position statements regarding the theology of nature and earth-keeping.

A unique contribution to Christian higher education came from the Au Sable Institute of Environmental Studies. Begun in 1980, Au Sable Institute is devoted to "bringing the Christian community and the general public to a better understanding of the Creator and the stewardship of God's Creation."[19] This institute has been an effective leader and formative influence for advancing EL among Christian colleges throughout the world. It has done this by making resources available to students and faculty from more than fifty participating colleges via summer collegiate programs of study and by convening forum conferences among international Christian environmental scholars, thereby influencing faculty and curriculum development.[20]

Ecological Literacy at the Margins in Christian Higher Education

However, in spite of excellent advances made at many Christian colleges, EL remains at the margins of Christian higher education and in some
cases is simply not on the radar screens of its leaders and planners. Whether
one evaluates this marginal place as positive, negative, or neutral depends,
of course, on how one views the relationship between creation care (earthkeeping) and the task of Christian higher education.

A sense of "crisis" regarding the environment did not germinate in the
Christian church or the Christian college; rather it grew out of concerns
generated by many scientists and naturalists who were observing the loss of
integrity of the planet's life-support systems. An articulated concern for the
environment can be traced back at least 100 years to John Muir and Gifford
Penchot.[21] But as several environmental disintegrations became critical or
chronic,[22] and the average urbanite was experiencing smog and dying
beaches, and historians blamed Christianity, the Christian public began to
listen and respond. The environment, however, was not the only "issue"
coming to the attention of Christian higher education in the 1970s and
1980s. There were also many other social issues clamoring for attention.
When these issues were granted a place at the academic table, it was often at
the fringe because of the time and resources required by the time-honored
disciplines in the curriculum. Furthermore, new programs usually had to be
justified by bringing in more students (and revenue).

What do I take as evidence of the marginal place of EL? To assess the
presence of "earth-in-mind" and the place of environment in Christian
higher education, I reviewed several authors, some very current, some a bit
dated, but all within the time span of the last thirty-five years. What follows
is not a comprehensive review, but a representational sampling. Given the
titles and the stated intention of the texts I studied, one would expect them
to articulate the ideals and goals that the respective constituencies consider
the foundation and substance Christian higher education. I read with an eye
to determining the focal concerns of Christian higher education. What do
its leaders have in mind? How is the theology/philosophy of creation
treated? What is the role and place of culture? What is the role and place of
humankind? How is "faith and learning" treated? Is environmental or
ecological literacy clearly evident, nascent, or absent?

Arthur Holmes is probably best known for his belief that all truth is God's
truth. In his *Idea of a Christian College,* Holmes describes a Christian college as
having a "constructive task, far more than a defensive one," and a general call
to excellence and integration of faith and learning.[23] The presence of sin in
creation is seen when "we misuse" created things because of "not valuing as
we should the resources God has made."[24] The liberal arts are presented as the
best way to open the student to culture and to prepare for one's career. Of
society's sins, all are personal or social. The only explicit mention of environ-

ment comes with ethical issues that arise "in what we do or not do to our environment and with nonrenewable resources, in genetic research and over nuclear wastes."[25] Earth is in mind with theological grounding, as valued resource, and for which there must be accountability, but it is not central and foundational.

In presenting a *Rationale for a Christian College,* Theodore Plantinga observes that a curriculum has to be selective, but besides extra courses in Bible and theology, it must also include an emphasis on perspective. The main themes of the curriculum include: 1) the biblical teachings of creation, redemption, covenant, an historical incarnation, and the Kingdom of God, 2) Western civilization and coming to grips with secularization, 3) a philosophical understanding of humankind and the meaning of science, and 4) human autonomy and role of technology. Under the last theme he mentions briefly the impact of industrial technology on "problems of pollution and environmental death," but also that technology might come up with helpful answers. The natural sciences help one "see what the problems are in such a field as environmental studies. It looks more and more as though man will make life impossible for himself on this planet."[26] Environment is apparently important, even life-threatening, but something to study selectively at a distance with proper perspective.

The theological interpretations presented in *Shaping a Christian Worldview* are anthropocentric relative to salvation and distinctly dominionistic relative to the place of humankind in creation. "As a result of sin, the image of God ... is severely tarnished and marred. The role of exercising dominion ... has been drastically limited by the effects of sin on humans and the course of nature."[27] The chapter treating worldview in the sciences sees knowledge as power (Bacon), where "research ... has a religious end, dominion," and affirms the Miltonian-Baconian view that "the end of learning [is] to repair the ruins of our first parents." Environmental thinking is disparaged, because "[i]f we are to exercise dominion over the earth, then we need technology and therefore science." (Apparently prescientific Adam did not exercise dominion!) Regarding extant natural areas, a truly ambiguous worldview emerges: "The rainforest is inhospitable, as close to hell as you get on earth. But the tropical rainforest is one of the most beautiful of all ecosystems, and its importance in the global scheme of things cannot be overestimated." However, regarding cutting rainforests, "sooner or later we have to be careful. Destruction is not real dominion either."[28] Social, cultural, and political issues are to be covered by the curriculum; natural resources, ecological footprints, and life-support systems are not listed. Earth is partly in mind, but not very clearly, and not shaped by caring obedience.

Models for Christian Higher Education, a volume edited by Richard Hughes and William Adrian, surveys via institutions and historical biography the broad-scope issues and contributions of seven Christian faith traditions.[29]

Faith and learning, the role of scholarship and teaching, the need to link learning with activism and outreach, engaging culture, college-church relationship, and maintaining identity are some of the topics addressed. Earth is not centrally in mind, only with occasional reference or example.

In a collection of his essays titled *Education for Shalom,* Nicholas Wolterstorff provides a thoughtful overview of Christian higher education from his vantage point as a Christian philosopher.[30] He insightfully identifies four models of Christian higher education (to which I return in the next section of this essay) and analyzes changes in its primary goals over the past century. The educational philosophy that grounds Wolterstorff's observations and suggestions has room for ecological literacy, but Earth is referenced only indirectly. Likewise his call for a change toward *shalom* seems to be limited to educating for shalom in social and cultural aspects of human life; humanity's impact on Earth and the groaning creation are in the margins of his thinking and application.

Religion, Scholarship, and Higher Education summarizes a three-year-long Lilly-supported interinstitutional seminar that addressed a variety of broad issues, including religion and scholarship, pluralism, engaged fallibilism, behaviorism in social sciences, student formation, and warranted assertibility.[31] For reasons not given, the seminar only included people from the humanities and social sciences; the fine arts and natural sciences—one place where environment is usually considered—were unfortunately not represented. The quality of this discussion notwithstanding, if Earth was in the minds of these scholar-leaders, it was not explicit or central.

In *Faithful Learning and the Christian Scholarly Vocation,* educators from several faith traditions address topics and themes dear to Christian higher education. These include faith and the life of the mind, calling, church relations, mission and scholarship, spirituality, and the opening of the Christian mind. Even though these topics do not overtly deal with earth-keeping, this group of essays, more than the others, moves from example or reference to more directly dealing with earthkeeping. One highlights the reality of shalom, of "that day when our world will enjoy the full reign of justice, peace, and plenty, when *all of nature* and society will be restored to right relationships."[32] Another emphasizes that "the Judeo-Christian worldview accords inherent purpose and worth to all creation, . . . [which] undergirds the history of redemption, . . . grounds both the scientific and artistic enterprises, . . . [and provides] an environmental ethic. . . ."[33] From the curriculum the Christian student "would learn the lessons of ecologists, and guide the Christian community to live responsibly in relationship to the environment."[34] However, the closing essay, which places Christian higher education in the context of civilization, does not have Earth in mind.

When I say that EL has a marginal position (or less) in Christian higher education, I am being more generous than some authors who have written extensively about this subject. Whether marginal or not, David Orr suggests the problem is not in education but a problem of education.[35] He identifies several myths in contemporary education, namely: that ignorance is a solvable problem; that with enough knowledge and technology we can manage the planet; that knowledge, and by implication human goodness, is increasing; that education will enable us to restore what we have dismantled or lost; that education's goal is to give students the means for upward mobility and success; and that today's culture represents the highest of human achievement.[36] For Orr, the question is not about marginality or centrality, but rather about foundational presuppositions and goals and, hence, the very agenda of education.

Perhaps we are educating for the wrong thing; perhaps our education has foundational problems that disables rather than enables its students to be better stewards. My sense after reviewing many models and views of Christian higher education is that its agenda is commonly stymied or limited by an anthropocentric view of education. Or to use Orr's words, there is too often little or no "earth in mind."

Faithful Earthkeeping, or EL in Christian Higher Education

There is a dramatic difference in the goals and foundation statements of Christian colleges reviewed for this essay and David Orr's challenge for higher education.

> If the environment and the human prospect that depends on it are to be rescued . . . those now being educated will have to do what the present generation has been unable or unwilling to do: stabilize world population, reduce the emission of greenhouse gases, . . . protect biological diversity, reverse the destruction of forests everywhere, and conserve soils. They must learn how to use energy and materials with great efficiency. They must learn how to run civilization on sunlight. They must rebuild economies in order to eliminate waste and pollution. They must learn how to manage renewable resources for the long term. They must begin the great work of repairing, as much as possible, the damage done the Earth in the past 150 years of industrialization. And they must do all this while they reduce worsening social, ethnic, and racial inequities. No generation has ever faced a more daunting agenda.[37]

The challenge is given to higher education because presumably education matters and is formative. Even if Orr is guilty of hyperbole, this challenge cannot be ignored or left at the margins.

I believe the best critique of the history and goals of Christian higher education and a possible next step comes from Nick Wolterstorff, who identifies four types or models:

1. the Christian service model where students are trained for special Kingdom service,

2. the Christian humanist model which inducts the student into the great cultural heritage of humanity from a Christian perspective,

3.   the Christian academic discipline model which, again via Christian perspective, introduces students to the academic disciplines, and

4.   a Christian vocation model (actually a variation of the Christian service model) where students are trained to enter a variety of callings—professional and occupational roles, wherein they conduct themselves Christianly.[38]

In a sense these models parallel the development of thinking among Christian colleges regarding overall goals, with the Christian service model being the oldest. The oft-used label, Christian liberal arts, finds a comfortable fit with models 2, 3, and 4. However, notes Wolterstorff, none of these models adequately addresses the "wounds of humanity" nor seeks to dispose students to act justly. Hence, he argues for another model or emphasis, not one to replace the valuable goals of cultural heritage, academic excellence, and professional preparation, but to enlarge the academic table and overarching goal to include pursuing justice and struggling against injustice. This model he calls "educating for shalom." In this model, teaching for justice serves as the ground floor for shalom, where human flourishing is the expected outcome.

This is an exciting and promising new insight for Christian higher education. However, as in the many other foundational studies and papers, this model also lacks the proper recognition and place of the nonhuman creation. Wolterstorff repeatedly talks about the wounds of humanity and the need for justice and flourishing of humanity; he is seldom explicit regarding the wounds and suffering of the nonhuman creation—the environment is marginalized. How can there be shalom for humankind if there is not shalom for other kinds? The creation blessing ("be fruitful") was given first to other kinds (Genesis 1:22) before it was given to humankind (Genesis 1:28), coupled with the command to care and keep (Genesis 2:15).[39]

The shalom model is clearly heading in the right direction with its biblical resonance with both the Old and New Testaments' recognition of where the heart of God is—with the poor and socially marginalized. But, ironically, with this new focus, we may now marginalize the nonhuman creation, which also suffers because of sin's dis-integrating effects. Just as Wolterstorff recognizes social analysis as indispensable for the shalom model for addressing human woundedness, likewise ecological analysis (and literacy) would be indispensable for addressing the woundedness found in the nonhuman creation and its processes.

Wolterstorff further critiques the Christian humanist model, noting that when we introduce "students to high culture, we inculcate in them habits and tendencies relevant to engaging high culture; there is no evidence that we also, coincidentally, shape what they tend to do in life and society."[40] Furthermore, I would suggest, if students are exposed to high culture but are ecologically illiterate, how will they act in society other than to the signals from popular culture? For students to become earthkeepers they need to be ecologically literate with an Earth-in-mind-formed conscience.

The mission of the Christian college has changed in the last century according to Wolterstorff.[41] He designates as "stage one" the retreat of many evangelical colleges in response to Darwinism in natural science and higher criticism in theology in the first half of the twentieth century. They went "underground," he says, emphasizing personal piety, foreign evangelism, and selected exposure to cultural accomplishments. After World War II a "second stage" began to emerge. Being less defensive, the evangelical college grasped the liberal arts and sought to merge and integrate faith with learning the best of culture and science. A renewed emphasis on competence and academic excellence was prominent. But, another stage seems to be nascent, argues Wolterstorff. In the pursuit of excellence and integration with faith, it is becoming apparent that learning must be for something other than engaging high culture with excellence and piety. Learning must be for service and must be in response to the suffering of humanity and the suffering in the natural world. This is stressed even more emphatically in his essay "Teaching for Shalom" where he suggests, "We are touching here not on issues of taste or judgment but on issues of right teaching, orthodoxy. We are touching on our understanding of the nature of God."[42]

Dordt College's educational philosophy is itself poised to enter the next stage of educating for shalom. When it was faced with justifying more education for the professions, the concept "serviceable insight" was developed to bridge the more traditional liberal arts and scientific disciplines with professional application.[43] Furthermore, in its more recent document *Educational Framework of Dordt College*, three of the four parameters of curricular organization—creational structure, creational development, and contemporary response—use language that identifies stewardship and human accountability for all creatures.[44] However, the language used and examples given clearly are oriented to culture and society; language with regard to earthkeeping is much less explicit.

Is an educational culture of liberal arts and career preparation with a lived anthropocentric worldview capable of developing a curriculum that really holds "earth in mind" rather than self or humankind in mind? Can a Christian college that has made *bona fide* attempts to bring all things *soli deo gloria* meet the challenge? Will Christian colleges that claim a theology of creation, but that have not seriously grappled with what the book of creation really means, dare to nurture the academy to have and to hold Earth in mind?

Given where we are culturally and planetarily, this grappling has to mean more than seeing creation as a set of complex objects for study in the specialized sciences (chemistry, physics, climatology, geology, and so on). It has to mean more than seeing creation as a set of natural resources for consumption and refinement, to be acculturated and unfolded for humankind's enjoyment. Creation is more than a temporary home waiting for the eschaton; it is more than the world and its beauty and the recreation it affords us. What is this "more than?"

Grappling with what the book of creation means begins with an attitude of humility and respect for the Creator and the creation and its pronounced goodness. Assuming that creation must be unfolded by our culture-making activities too easily leads to hubris. Our cultural activities may unfold creation, but our artifacts pale into insignificance when compared to the intricate and complex structures and processes spoken into existence by the Word "in the beginning." Moreover, most of the works of our hands are not forming so much as they are deforming, reforming, or conforming to what is already there.

Building on an attitude of humility and respect, we need to learn to walk carefully and caringly in the light of the creation blessings (Genesis 1:22, 28), heeding the call to serve (Genesis 2:15).[45] This attitude and practice of "serving worship" sees dominion as stewardship, to use Douglas Hall's words,[46] and in today's discultural world confesses and admits the need to restore as well—which connects to the biblical themes of salvation and restoration. In spite of much written opposition to Lynn White and others, the overriding conclusion by environmental writers is that the West has had its view vis-à-vis the earth shaped by the "command to have dominion." To get beyond this claimed judgment, Christians and their academies must draw out and educate a different kind of disciple—people who walk the talk.

These people will need to respectfully (not worshipfully) come to understand that the limits of the planet's biogeochemical cycles and energy exchange mechanisms must be taken as seriously as God's moral laws (limits) revealed in the "first" great book, Scripture. They will acknowledge that the extent of moral obligation (duty) has to include otherkind as well as humankind and that justice and shalom will not be found unless the land with its sojourners and wildlife (Leviticus 25) also be allowed a place to participate in and benefit from Sabbath.

Graduates from Christian colleges with such creation awareness will not plan on competing for a place in the global economy. They will sooner see their vocation as designing and maintaining cultural artifacts (agriculture, machines, buildings, transportation systems, and institutions) that fit into a created order "of microbes, plants, animals, and entropy."[47] These colleges will also model this Earth-in-mind mentality on campus, in operations, purchasing, investment, grounds, and campus architecture.[48]

Herein lies the challenge for the academic and curricular agenda for the Christian college of the twenty-first century. The intent will be to rediscover and reclaim humankind's rightful, joyful, and fruitful place as bearing the image of the Creator in his garden, so that in the New Kingdom the leaves of the trees along the river of life can be for the healing of the nations. This

343

Christian Earth-in-mind worldview (strange construct, I know, but sadly too often worldview does not include the Earth!) does not limit human-kind's culturing work; rather it focuses it and directs it outward and gives temporal and eternal meaning to humankind's biblical calling.

Beyond Stewardship: Toward Virtue and Creative Restoration

Two recent publications, *For the Beauty of the Earth,* by Steven Bouma-Prediger, and "Partnership with Nature: Beyond the Theology of Steward-ship" by H. Paul Santmire, bring refreshing insights and challenges to the Christian community by offering wise direction to guide Christian colleges as they seek to develop EL.[49] Moving beyond historical blame for the ecologic crisis, in pastoral, convincing language, Bouma-Prediger draws a compelling apologetic for a theology for creation care that focuses not on what should we do, but rather, how we should *be,* i.e., what kind of people should Christians *be* relative to Earth? In answering Orr's question, "Is it possible to live sustainably, within the boundaries of Earth, without being a people of virtue?"[50] Bouma-Prediger presents an ecological ethics and virtue theory as a helpful and hopeful avenue for *being* earthkeepers. This contri-bution fits in very well with my opening description of ecological literacy. EL includes knowledge but also requires a disposition to *be* and do right toward a future of shalom for humankind and otherkind. Appealing to virtue helps take the sometimes strident edge off arguments on both sides, for and against creation care.

> The good work of earthkeeping is impossible without respect, receptivity, self-restraint, frugality, humility, honesty, wisdom, hope, patience, serenity, benevolence, love, justice, and courage. To do the work God calls us to do, these fundamental traits of character are necessary. *Character is central to the care of the earth.*[51]

He quickly notes, however, that although necessary, character alone is not sufficient to silence the "groaning of the earth."

Although Santmire has contributed much to the discussion of biblical the-ology of creation care, what I find especially helpful for this discussion is his critique of the concept of stewardship. He unfolds another view, namely, human partnership with the Creator in nature. In an effort to be distinctive from secular uses of the term *stewardship* (widely employed by both the corpo-rate world and NGOs such as The Nature Conservancy) Christian writers frequently have used "earthkeeping" and "creation care" as alternative words for environmental stewardship. These words give nuance to a meaning that is perceived to be deeper and richer than (merely) stewarding for a master, although that is certainly an element. Santmire also finds it increasingly diffi-cult to use a word meaningfully that in Christendom is often limited to the wise use of time, talents, and treasure and in the corporate world is used to define wise managerial and efficient exploitation of resources. In both cases the intended biblical meaning of creation care is lost.[52] Hence his search for a deeper and more comprehensive biblical idea led to the theology of partnership. The following captures the essence of this theology:

> We have before us . . . [a] complex and rich biblical theology of partnership between God and humans, between God and all creatures, and between humans and every other creature. That God has a partnership *with us humans,* and we *with one another,* is a thought that most students of the Bible . . . will take for granted. That God has a partnership *with nature,* and humans *with nature* likewise, are thoughts that may well need to be introduced to our churches . . . preachers and teachers. . . . God has a history with nature and values nature in itself, independent of his relationship with the human creature. God creates a grand and beautiful world of nature for His own purposes. It is harmonious. It is very good. But at its edges, it is also mysterious and even threatening to us. But that is God's business, His infinite joy (cf. Psalm 104:31), not ours. God does fashion us and invite us, however, to be in partnership—a limited partnership—not only with Him and with one another, but also with the beautiful and harmonious world of nature and to encounter its deep mysteries and its occasionally horrendous ambiguities. More particularly, God calls us to be in partnership with nature in three major ways. . . .[53]

Resonating with Ecclesiastes, this three-way partnership sees a time to build (creative intervention with nature), a time to care (sensitive caring for nature), and a time to contemplate (awestruck contemplation of nature).

I find Santmire's refreshing view meshing very well with Wolterstorff's call for Christian higher education to intentionally move into a third stage of education for shalom. To do so we would have to rethink our theology of creation and our theology of man in order to develop the educational implications of partnership on Earth for shalom for all Earthlings.

Implementing Ecological Literacy in Light of Partnership for Shalom

If Christian college curricula are essentially in Wolterstorff's stage two with elements or characteristics of models 2, 3, and 4, it is not surprising that cultural-social issues will find a central place in the curriculum before Earth issues do. If EL is to become a substantial part or a pervasive theme in higher education, the basic mission and self-conscious purpose of an institution will have to change or develop accordingly. It is probably the case that most Christian colleges would not be averse to creation stewardship. But how that is to be developed and the extent to which it is taught will require heuristic practice.

Indeed, there are some aspects about EL that when practiced will lend themselves to fitting in and solving other educational issues. For example, because it connects to so many aspects of the traditional disciplines, EL by its very nature is interdisciplinary and provides a tremendous opportunity for integrative teaching and learning. However it is approached, EL will build bridges spanning the specialization and fragmentation that is so often cited as a weakness in higher education. This kind of necessary integration would not only prepare graduates to be agents of shalom but would first of all bring a kind of shalom or wellness to the curriculum itself, inasmuch as it would undo some of the fragmentation.

Second, with the subject matter for integration within EL coming from creation and/or its groanings, the educational aspects of relevancy and application are immediately addressed.

Third, EL fits squarely onto the biblical foundations of a Christian college as well is its commitment to foster a sense of calling that includes all kinds of service in God's Kingdom. By contrast, in a secular setting enlightened self-interest is about all that can be ultimately claimed for EL. For the Christian college EL is completely at home in the overarching biblical story of creation–fall–redemption/restoration–consummation. Furthermore, EL can provide the academic context for learning the virtues that image bearers need to bring sensitive care, creative intervention, and restoration to a groaning creation.

Fourthly, moving EL to a more central place in the curriculum will give opportunity for the necessary reevaluation of the role of humankind and culture. This may well be the most difficult in terms of educational and institutional philosophy. Dominion theology and the cultural mandate will have to be reexamined with Earth in mind. But this redirection is also a wonderful avenue for connecting the biblical idea of fruitfulness and Sabbath with planetary sustainability and with the New Testament call for contentment. It also provides a renewed way of seeing technology in the mode of genuine healing rather than finding and providing efficiency.

Regarding the actual nuts and bolts needed to make EL more central and foundational, I can only offer introductory ideas here, and I offer them as opening suggestions and questions rather than as a final or definitive list.[54]

Idea one (infusion model): All departments, programs, curricula, and courses be infused with EL ideas, themes, contexts, applications—something like (but not the same as) what is now intended when we say all courses and curricula are taught with a biblical perspective. Would it be possible to have all things taught from a perspective that nurtures ecological literacy?

Idea two (opportunity model): For each discipline or discipline area, particular aspects of EL would be packaged into a course. This could be an elective opportunity or a requirement. Examples already exist in many colleges: environmental literature, environmental history, environmental chemistry. Would this be sufficiently comprehensive? Would this reduce fragmentation?

Idea three (core model): EL would be included in the requirements for general education (the so-called liberal arts). This would require rethinking and revising general education—is there "room" for more at the table? Should general education be representational? An introduction to the disciplines? Foundational skills for academic and later life, including EL? A survey of the best of human culture? Could life and off-campus experience count, as is sometimes done with cross-cultural requirements?

Idea four (capstone model): Each department or academic area would offer a capstone senior seminar in "partnership for shalom." The scope would be more interdisciplinary than, for example, a discipline course in environmental history. It would also differ from present senior "capstone" courses that deal with calling and culture and in which an environmental theme or issue is one among many. Such a course could be designed so that the peculiar insights of a discipline area would be applied to a particular problem or issue that begs for EL—in that sense be amalgamated with a service-learning flavor.

There are no doubt many more ideas and models that could be imagined and discovered through experience.

Finally, moving toward EL will necessarily include comprehensive changes in the culture and climate of the whole college. First of all, there should be a place for and a spirit of creation celebration before one ventures into concerns for justice and restoration.[55] EL should be visible on campus in its grounds and architecture as well as in each course or curricular component. It will involve faculty and staff development; it will include the kinds of service projects undertaken; it will include a change in the spiritual ethos on campus; and more. If done with integrity and thoroughness, it may well attract many generations of new image-bearing disciples for whom the creation waits with neck outstretched (Romans 8:19).

Changes of this magnitude and importance are both scary and exciting. However EL is accomplished, the participants must be open to new ways of thinking, doing, and *being*. The Christian college is a wonderful setting for this venture.

Notes

1. Earth Day was first celebrated on April 22, 1970, at the call of U.S. Senator William Proxmire, marking the emerging awareness of humankind's impact on environmental deterioration.

2. For some examples see: http://www.webofcreation.org/education/policystatements/index.html; http://environment.harvard.edu/religion/religion/christianity/statements/index.html; and http://www.creationcare.org/resources/signatores.php.

3. Early key legislation included: the Wilderness Act of 1964, the National Environmental Policy Act of 1969, the Clean Air and Water Acts of 1970 and 1972, the Endangered Species Act of 1973, and the "Superfund" Act of 1980.

4. One example, chosen for contrast, is Messiah College, founded in 1909. With fewer than 250 students in 1964, Messiah enrolled 2400 students by 1994 (Jacobson, in *Models for Christian Higher Education*, ed. Richard T. Hughes and William B. Adrian (Grand Rapids, MI: Eerdmans, 1997), 327. By comparison Dordt College, founded in 1955 with 35 students, grew from 448 students in 1964 to 1153 students in 1994.

5. Alan Wolfe, "The Opening of the Evangelical Mind," *Atlantic Monthly* 286, no. 4 (October 2000): 55–76.

6. The term *earthkeeping* comes from the book *Earthkeeping in the Nineties,* ed. Loren Wilkinson (Grand Rapids: Eerdmans, 1991), and popularized by the Au Sable Institute of Environmental Studies. In many ways this term is equivalent to "environmental stewardship" and "creation care."

7. See David W. Orr, *Ecological Literacy: Education and the Transition to a Postmodern World* (Albany: SUNY Press, 1992) and his *Earth in Mind: On Education, Environment and the Human Prospect* (Washington DC: Island Press, 1994). See also C.A. Bowers, *Education, Cultural Myths, and the Ecological Crisis* (Albany: SUNY Press, 1993). See also my earlier overview, "The Environmental Pulse in Academia," *Pro Rege* 22, no. 3 (1994): 24–30.

8. Orr, *Earth in Mind,* 2.

9. This trilogy of basic questions is used often by Calvin B. De Witt. They appear with elaborations in his *The Just Stewardship of Land and Creation: A Report of the Reformed Ecumenical Council* (Grand Rapids, MI: REC, 1996). Another way De Witt formulates this is science, ethics, and praxis.

10. In addition to other works cited in this essay, consult: Wesley Granberg-Michaelson, ed., *Tending the Garden: Essays on the Gospel and the Earth* (Grand Rapids, MI: Eerdmans, 1987); Scott Hoezee, *Remember Creation: God's World of Wonder and Delight* (Grand Rapids, MI: Eerdmans, 1998); and Fred Van Dyke, David C. Mahan, Joseph K. Sheldon, and Raymond H. Brand, *Redeeming Creation: The Biblical Basis for Environmental Stewardship* (Downers Grove, IL: Intervarsity, 1996).

11. For elaboration of this key point, see Kenneth L. Petersen's essay, "The Educational Imperative of Creation Care," *Christian Scholars Review* 32, no. 4 (2003): 433–54.

12. A book-length rationale for stewardship *imago dei* is found in Douglas J. Hall, *Imaging God: Dominion as Stewardship* (Grand Rapids: Eerdmans, 1986).

13. Calvin B. De Witt and G. T. Prance, eds., *Missionary Earthkeeping: Glimpses of the Past, Visions of the Future* (Macon, GA.: Mercer University Press, 1992).

14. Lynn White, "The Historical Roots of Our Ecologic Crisis," *Science* 155 (March 10, 1967): 1203–7.

15. Joseph K. Sheldon, "Twenty-One Years After 'The Historic Roots of Our Ecologic Crisis'—How Has the Church Responded?" *Perspectives on Science and the Christian Faith* 41 (Sept. 1989): 152–58 (Formerly the *Journal of American Scientific Affiliation*). See also Joe Sheldon in *Rediscovery of Creation: A Bibliographical Study of the Church's Response to the Environmental Crisis* ATLA Bibliography Series, No. 29 (Metuchen, NJ/London: Scarecrow Press/American Theological Library Association, 1992).

16. Dordt introduced its first course in 1970, called Environmental Biology, using several paperbacks and articles as reading resources. A major in Environmental Studies was introduced at Dordt College in 1983.

17. An ongoing analysis of ES programs is conducted and reported at Macalester College, available online at http://www.macalester.edu/environmentalstudies/MacEnvReview/equalarticle2003.htm.

18. For a review, see Robert Booth Fowler, *The Greening of Protestant Thought* (Chapel Hill: University of North Carolina Press, 1995), 3.

19. From Au Sable Institute 2004 Bulletin. Also available online at http://www.ausable.org/au.ourmission.cfm.

20. The design of courses offered by Au Sable Institute (ASI) has changed over the years; as cooperating colleges developed similar courses, the institute would drop such a course, desiring not to be competitive. It has also developed courses at the interfaces of traditional disciplines, thereby fostering integration. (Personal experience based on twenty-one summers of work at ASI.)

21. See Fred Van Dyke in *Conservation Biology* (New York: McGraw Hill, 2003), especially 6–12, for review of historical roots of the conservation movement in the United States.

22. For an example, see Rachel Carson, *Silent Spring* (Boston: Houghton Mifflin, 1962).

23. Arthur Holmes, *The Idea of a Christian College* (Grand Rapids, MI: Eerdmans, 1987), 7.

24. Ibid., 14.

25. Ibid., 50.

26. Theodore Plantinga, *Rationale for a Christian College* (St. Catharines, ON: Paideia Press, 1980), 68.

27. David S. Dockery and Gregory A. Thornbury, eds., *Shaping a Christian Worldview: The Foundations of Christian Higher Education* (Nashville: Broadman and Holman, 2002), 6.

28. Ibid., 183–86.

29. Richard T. Hughes and William B. Adrian, eds., *Models for Christian Higher Education: Strategies for Success in the Twenty-First Century* (Grand Rapids, MI: Eerdmans, 1997).

30. Nicholas Wolterstorff, *Educating for Shalom: Essays on Christian Higher Education*, ed. Clarence W. Joldersma and Gloria G. Stronks (Grand Rapids, MI: Eerdmans, 2004).

31. Andrea Sterk, ed., *Religion, Scholarship, and Higher Education: Perspectives, Models, and Future Prospects* (Notre Dame, IN: University of Notre Dame, 2002).

32. Douglas V. Henry and Bob R. Agee, eds., *Faithful Learning and the Christian Scholarly Vocation* (Grand Rapids, MI: Eerdmans, 2003). This is a compilation of lectures from a series sponsored by the Association of Southern Baptist Colleges, 67 (italics added).

33. Ibid., 105.

34. Ibid., 153.

35. Orr, *Earth in Mind*, 5.

36. Ibid., chapter 1.

37. David W. Orr, "Educating for the Environment: Higher Education's Challenge of the Next Century," *Journal of Environmental Education* 27, no. 3 (Spring 1996): 7-10.

38. From "The World for Which We Educate," in Wolterstorff, *Educating for Shalom: Essays on Christian Higher Education*, 87–99.

39. The Hebrew *shamar* in Genesis 2:15 is the same as in the Aaronic blessing of Numbers 6:22ff., "The Lord bless you and keep (*shamar*) you." Adam's task was to image God by keeping the garden as God kept his people—to flourish and be fruitful in a state of shalom.

40. From "The World for Which We Educate," in Wolterstorff, *Educating for Shalom: Essays on Christian Higher Education*, 99.

41. From "The Mission of the Christian College," in Wolterstorff, *Educating for Shalom: Essays on Christian Higher Education*, 27–35.

42. From "Teaching for Shalom," in Wolterstorff, *Educating for Shalom: Essays on Christian Higher Education*, 10–26.

43. "Serviceable insight" is described in "The Educational Task of Dordt College." See pages 9–11 and 13–14 above.

44. "The Educational Framework of Dordt College" is included earlier in this volume. See pages 17–24.

45. These rich Old Testament foundational teachings are mirrored in the New Testament. The children of God are coheirs in Christ (Romans 8:17), in whom all things hold together (Colossians 1:15ff.), and called to follow the second Adam (1 Corinthians 15:20ff.), who came to accomplish what the first Adam could/did not do.

46. Douglas J. Hall, *Imaging God: Dominion as Stewardship* (Grand Rapids, MI: Eerdmans, 1986).

47. David W. Orr, "Education for Environment," *Journal of Environmental Education* 27, no. 3 (Spring 1996): 7–10.

48. It should be noted that Dordt College has made substantial retrofits to save energy in its older buildings and in lighting replacements. When the chapel-music complex was built in 1978, its energy needs were matched by energy savings elsewhere on campus, obviating the need to expand central heating plant at the time. At this writing preliminary planning for "green certification" for a new/remodeled natural sciences building is seriously being considered.

49. Steven Bouma-Prediger, *For the Beauty of the Earth: A Christian View of Creation Care* (Grand Rapids, MI: Baker, 2001), especially the introduction and the last four chapters; H. Paul Santmire, "Partnership with Nature According to the Scriptures: Beyond the Theology of Stewardship," *Christian Scholars Review* 32, no. 4 (Summer 2003): 381–412.

50. Orr, *Earth in Mind: On Education, Environment and the Human Prospect,* 62.

51. Bouma-Prediger, *For the Beauty of the Earth: A Christian View of Creation Care,* 160.

52. Santmire, "Partnership with Nature According to the Scriptures: Beyond the Theology of Stewardship," 381–412 (see his extended footnote on page 383).

53. Ibid., 411–12.

54. There are sources of curricular components available: Jonathan Collett and Stephen Karakashian, eds., *Greening of the College Curriculum* (Washington, DC: Island Press, 1996) has examples of syllabi with bibliographies from across the typical college curriculum; and in Orr, *Ecological Literacy: Education and the Transition to a Postmodern World,* chapter VII is a syllabus/bibliography for ecological literacy.

55. Durkee strongly suggests that celebration of biodiversity, for example, should come before considering the challenges regarding biodiversity loss and conservation, in Collett and Karakashian, *Greening of the College Curriculum,* 53.

About Dordt College

Dordt College is a Christian liberal arts college in Sioux Center, Iowa. It believes the Bible is the infallible and inspired Word of God and bases the education it provides upon the Bible as it is explained in the Reformed creeds. Hence, the college confesses that our world from creation to consummation belongs to God, that Jesus Christ is the only way of salvation, and that true comfort and reliable strength can be had only from his Holy Spirit.

Dordt College was established in 1955 in rural Iowa to prepare teachers for area Christian day-schools. Over the years the college diversified into a B.A.-General institution with several specialized professional programs such as agriculture, engineering, nursing, and social work. We currently enroll approximately 1300 undergraduate and 60 graduate education students from 37 states, six Canadian provinces, and 15 other countries.

Dordt owes its continuing existence to a community of believers that is committed to supporting Christian schools from kindergarten through college. Believing in the *Creator* demands obedience to his principles in all of life: certainly in education, but also in everything from art to zoology.

The Dordt College community believes in the *Word* of God. God's revelation in word and deed finds its root in Jesus Christ, who is both Savior from our sin and Lord over the heavens and the earth. The Bible reveals the way of salvation in Christ Jesus and requires faithful thanksgiving to him as the Lord of life, also when exploring, coming to understand, and unfolding the diversity of creation.

Dordt College in its many departments and programs celebrates that diversity and challenges students not merely to confess Christ with their mouth, but to serve him with their lives. Empowered by the strength of his *Spirit*, Dordt College stands ready to meet the challenge of providing and developing serviceable insight for the people of God.

Printed in the United States
22043LVS00002B/43-219

9 780932 914569